T0205748

Lecture Notes in Computer Science 12850

More information about this subseries at http://www.springer.com/series/7409

Hans Jochen Scholl · J. Ramon Gil-Garcia ·
Marijn Janssen · Evangelos Kalampokis ·
Ida Lindgren ·
Manuel Pedro Rodríguez Bolívar (Eds.)

Electronic Government

20th IFIP WG 8.5 International Conference, EGOV 2021
Granada, Spain, September 7–9, 2021
Proceedings

 Springer

Editors
Hans Jochen Scholl ⓘ
University of Washington
Seattle, WA, USA

Marijn Janssen ⓘ
Delft University of Technology
Delft, The Netherlands

Ida Lindgren ⓘ
Linköping University
Linköping, Sweden

J. Ramon Gil-Garcia ⓘ
Center for Technology in Government
University at Albany, State University
of New York
Albany, NY, USA

Evangelos Kalampokis ⓘ
University of Macedonia
Thessaloniki, Greece

Centre for Research and Technology Hellas
(CERTH)
Thessaloniki, Greece

Manuel Pedro Rodríguez Bolívar ⓘ
Department of Accounting and Finance
University of Granada
Granada, Spain

ISSN 0302-9743   ISSN 1611-3349 (electronic)
Lecture Notes in Computer Science
ISBN 978-3-030-84788-3   ISBN 978-3-030-84789-0 (eBook)
https://doi.org/10.1007/978-3-030-84789-0

LNCS Sublibrary: SL3 – Information Systems and Applications, incl. Internet/Web, and HCI

This Springer imprint is published by the registered company Springer Nature Switzerland AG
The registered company address is: Gewerbestrasse 11, 6330 Cham, Switzerland

Preface

The EGOV-CeDEM-ePart conference is now in the fourth year of its existence after the successful merger of three formerly independent conferences, that is, the IFIP WG 8.5 Electronic Government (EGOV) conference, the Conference for E-Democracy and Open Government (CeDEM), and the IFIP WG 8.5 IFIP Electronic Participation (ePart) conference. This larger, united conference is dedicated to a broad area of digital or electronic government, open government, smart governance, e-democracy, policy informatics, and electronic participation. Scholars from around the world have found this conference to be a premier academic forum with a long tradition along its various branches, which has given the EGOV-CeDEM-ePart conference its reputation of one of the leading conferences worldwide in the research domains of digital/electronic, open, and smart government as well as electronic participation.

Unfortunately, due to the ongoing COVID-19 pandemic, this year's conference, held during September 7–9, 2021, at the University of Granada, Andalusia, Spain, was provided in a hybrid format of on-site and online attendances. All presentations and discussions, workshops keynotes, and panels were provided in this hybrid format. Despite this adjustment and a lower-than-normal on-site attendance, the conference was a great success.

The call for papers attracted completed research papers, work-in-progress papers on ongoing research (including doctoral papers), and project and case descriptions, as well as workshop and panel proposals. The submissions were assessed through a double-blind peer-review process, with at least three reviewers per submission, and the acceptance rate was 38%.

The conference tracks of the 2021 edition presented advances in the digital and socio-technological domain of the public sphere, demonstrating cutting-edge concepts, methods, and styles of investigation by multiple disciplines. The papers were distributed over the following tracks:

- General E-Government and E-Governance
- General E-Democracy and E-Participation
- AI, Data Analytics, and Automated Decision Making
- Digital and Social Media
- Digital Society
- Emerging Issues and Innovations
- Social Innovation
- Legal Informatics
- Open Data: Social and Technical Aspects
- Smart and Digital Cities (Government, Communities, and Regions)

Among the full research paper submissions, 23 papers (empirical and conceptual) were accepted for this year's Springer LNCS EGOV proceedings (vol. 12850) from the General E-Government track as well as from the tracks on Smart Cities, AI, and

Open Data. Another 16 completed research papers from the General E-Democracy and E-Participation track as well as from the tracks on Digital and Social Media, Legal Informatics, Digital Society, Social Innovation, and the Emerging Topics and Innovation went into this LNCS ePart proceedings (vol. 12849).

The papers included in this volume have been clustered under the following headings:

- Digital Transformation
- Digital Services and Open Government
- Digital Open Data: Social and Technical Perspectives
- Smart Cities
- Data Analytics, Decision Making, and Artificial Intelligence

As in the previous years and per the recommendation of the Paper Awards Committee under the leadership of Noella Edelmann (Danube University Krems, Austria) and Evangelos Kalampokis (University of Macedonia, Greece), the IFIP EGOV-CeDEM-ePart 2021 Conference Organizing Committee granted outstanding paper awards in three distinct categories:

- The most interdisciplinary and innovative research contribution
- The most compelling critical research reflection
- The most promising practical concept

The winners in each category were announced during the obligatory awards ceremony at the conference.

Many people behind the scenes make large events like this conference happen. We would like to thank the members of the Program Committee and the reviewers for their great efforts in reviewing the submitted papers. We would also like to express our deep gratitude to Manuel Pedro Rodríguez Bolívar, Laura Alcaide Muñoz, and their local team at the University of Granada (UGR) for hosting the conference.

Voted the best institution of higher education in Spain by international students in 2014, the public UGR does not only reside on very famous historical premises, for example, the former Royal Hospital of Granada (1511-1526) and its unique Renaissance Courtyard, but it also was founded in historical times (1531) some forty years after the last Muslim rulers were forced to leave the Iberian Peninsula. Today, the university, with about 60,000 students, is the fourth largest in Spain with a large contingent of international students seeking and receiving their higher-education degrees at this extraordinary institution. UGR provides a wide range of studies organized in 5 schools, 22 faculties, and 116 departments.

The attendees who were able to make it to the conference in person were greatly reimbursed for their traveling efforts by finding themselves for a few days in a stunning environment of natural and architectural beauty, the latter of which spans many centuries with world-famous complexes such as the Alhambra, the famous palace city of the Muslim rulers, and the Cathedral, among other examples of outstanding architectural skill, taste, and ingenuity. Today, the quarter-million population City of Granada has remained a bustling Andalusian center of diverse culture, exquisite gastronomy, modern and traditional commerce, and great Mediterranean outdoor life surrounded by the august scenery of the Sierra Nevada and its snow-topped peaks. Granada and the UGR were unforgettable hosts of the 2021 conference.

September 2021

Hans Jochen Scholl
J. Ramon Gil-Garcia
Marijn Janssen
Evangelos Kalampokis
Ida Lindgren
Manuel Pedro Rodríguez Bolívar

Organization

Conference Chairs

Noella Edelmann	Danube University Krems, Austria
Marijn Janssen	Delft University of Technology, The Netherlands
Ida Lindgren	Linköping University, Sweden
Laura Alcaide Muñoz	University of Granada, Spain
Peter Parycek	Fraunhofer Fokus, Germany/Danube University Krems, Austria
Gabriela Viale Pereira	Danube University Krems, Austria
Manuel Pedro Rodríguez Bolívar	University of Granada, Spain
Hans Jochen Scholl	University of Washington, USA
Gerhard Schwabe	University of Zürich, Switzerland
Efthimios Tambouris	University of Macedonia, Greece
Shefali Virkar	Danube University Krems, Austria

Program Committee Chairs

Karin Axelsson	Linköping University, Sweden
Csaba Csaki	Corvinus University of Budapest, Hungary
Noella Edelmann	Danube University Krems, Austria
J. Ramon Gil-Garcia	University at Albany, SUNY, USA
Sara Hofmann	University of Agder, Norway
Marijn Janssen	Delft University of Technology, The Netherlands
Evangelos Kalampokis	University of Macedonia, Greece
Robert Krimmer	University of Tartu, Estonia
Thomas Lampoltshammer	Danube University Krems, Austria
Habin Lee	Brunel University London, UK
Katarina Lindblad-Gidlund	Mid Sweden University, Sweden
Ida Lindgren	Linköping University, Sweden
Nuno Lopes	DTx - Digital Transformation CoLab, Portugal
Euripidis Loukis	University of the Aegean, Greece
Gianluca Misuraca	European Commission, Spain
Francesco Mureddu	Lisbon Council, Belgium
Anna-Sophie Novak	Danube University Krems, Austria
Panos Panagiotopoulos	Queen Mary University of London, UK
Peter Parycek	Danube University Krems, Austria
Manuel Pedro Rodríguez Bolívar	University of Granada, Spain
Marius Rohde Johannessen	University of South-Eastern Norway, Norway
Hans J. Scholl	University of Washington, USA
Efthimios Tambouris	University of Macedonia, Greece
Gabriela Viale Pereira	Danube University Krems, Austria
Shefali Virkar	Danube University Krems, Austria
Anneke Zuiderwijk	Delft University of Technology, The Netherlands

Outstanding Papers Awards Chairs

Noella Edelmann	Danube University Krems, Austria
Evangelos Kalampokis	University of Macedonia, Greece

PhD Colloquium Chairs

Gabriela Viale Pereira	Danube University Krems, Austria
J. Ramon Gil-Garcia	University at Albany, SUNY, USA
Ida Lindgren	Linköping University, Sweden

Web master

Sergei Zhilin	Delft University of Technology, The Netherlands

Program Committee

Karin Ahlin	Mid Sweden University, Sweden
Suha Alawadhi	Kuwait University, Kuwait
Valerie Albrecht	Danube University Krems, Austria
Laura Alcaide-Muñoz	University of Granada, Spain
Leonidas Anthopoulos	University of Thessaly, Greece
Wagner Araujo	UNU-EGOV, Portugal
Oscar Avila	University of the Andes, Columbia
Karin Axelsson	Linköping University, Sweden
Dian Balta	fortiss GmbH, Germany
Peter Bellström	Karlstad University, Sweden
Flavia Bernardini	Universidade Federal Fluminense, Brazil
Nitesh Bharosa	Delft University of Technology, The Netherlands
Radomir Bolgov	Saint Petersburg State University, Russia
Alessio Maria Braccini	University of Liechtenstein, Liechtenstein
Paul Brous	Delft University of Technology, The Netherlands
Matthias Buchinger	fortiss GmbH, Germany
Kelvin Bwalya	University of Johannesburg, South Africa
Edna Dias Canedo	Universidade de Brasília, Brazil
Jesus Cano	UNED, Spain
João Carvalho	University of Minho, Portugal
Youngseok Choi	University of Southampton, UK
Soon Chun	City University of New York, USA
Wichian Chutimaskul	King Mongkut's University of Technology Thonburi, Thailand
Vincenzo Ciancia	Istituto di Scienza e Tecnologia dell'Informazione "Alessandro Faedo", Consiglio Nazionale delle Ricerche, Italy

Verena Huber	Danube University Krems, Austria
Roumiana Ilieva	Technical University of Sofia, Bulgaria
Tomasz Janowski	UNU-EGOV, Portugal
Marijn Janssen	Delft University of Technology, The Netherlands
Marius Rohde Johannessen	University of South-Eastern Norway, Norway
Björn Johansson	Linköping University, Sweden
Luiz Antonio Joia Luiz	Getulio Vargas Foundation, Brazil
Gustaf Juell-Skielse	Stockholm University, Sweden
Yury Kabanov	National Research University Higher School of Economics, Russia
Natalia Kadenko	Delft University of Technology, The Netherlands
Muneo Kaigo	University of Tsukuba, Japan
Evangelos Kalampokis	University of Macedonia, Greece
Eleni Kanellou	National Technical University of Athens, Greece
Evika Karamagioli	Université Paris 8, France
Areti Karamanou	University of Macedonia, Greece
Naci Karkin	Pamukkale University, Turkey
Rao Karna	Centre for Electronic Governance and Open Democracy, Australia
Ilka Kawashita	University of Phoenix, USA
Jong Woo Kim	Hanyang University, South Korea
Fabian Kirstein	Fraunhofer FOKUS, Germany
Jens Klessmann	Fraunhofer FOKUS, Germany
Bozidar Klicek	University of Zagreb, Croatia
Ralf Klischewski	German University in Cairo, Egypt
Michael Koddebusch	European Research Center for Information Systems, Germany
Robert Krimmer	University of Tartu, Estonia
Peter Kuhn	fortiss GmbH, Germany
Maximilian Kupi	Hertie School, Germany
Zoi Lachana	University of the Aegean, Greece
Mariana Lameiras	UNU-EGOV, Portugal
Thomas Lampoltshammer	Danube University Krems, Austria
Habin Lee	Brunel University London, UK
Hong Joo Lee	The Catholic University of Korea, South Korea
Azi Lev-On	Ariel University Center, Israel
Matthias Lichtenthaler	Bundesrechenzentrum GmbH, Austria
Katarina Lindblad-Gidlund	Mid Sweden University
Ida Lindgren	Linköping University, Sweden
Johan Linåker	Lund University, Sweden
Nuno Lopes	DTx - Digital Transformation CoLab, Portugal
Euripidis Loukis	University of the Aegean, Greece
Rui Pedro Lourenço	INESC Coimbra/FEUC, Portugal
Nikolaos Loutas	European Commission, Belgium
Edimara Luciano	Pontifical Catholic University of Rio Grande do Sul, Brazil

Luis F. Luna-Reyes	University at Albany, SUNY, USA
Bjorn Lundell	University of Skövde, Sweden
Ahmad Luthfi	Delft University of Technology, The Netherlands
Johan Magnusson	University of Gothenburg, Sweden
Michael Marti	Berner Fachhochschule, Switzerland
Flavia Marzano	Link Campus University, Italy
Ricardo Matheus	Delft University of Technology, The Netherlands
John McNutt	University of Delaware, USA
Keegan Mcbride	Hertie School, Germany
Fritz Meiners	Fraunhofer FOKUS, Germany
Ana Melro	University of Aveiro, Portugal
Tobias Mettler	University of Lausanne, Switzerland
Morten Meyerhoff Nielsen	UNU-EGOV, Portugal
Yuri Misnikov	University of Leeds, UK
Gianluca Misuraca	European Commission, Spain
Solange Mukamurenzi	University of Rwanda, Rwanda
Francesco Mureddu	Lisbon Council, Belgium
Galia Novakova Nedeltcheva	Sofia University, Bulgaria
Alessia Caterina Neuroni	Bern University of Applied Sciences, Switzerland
Mille Nielsen	IT University of Copenhagen, Denmark
Marco Niemann	European Research Center for Information Systems, Germany
Anna-Sophie Novak	Danube University Krems, Austria
Hannu Nurmi	University of Turku, Finland
Ann O'Brien	NUI Galway, Ireland
Monica Palmirani	CIRSFID, Italy
Panos Panagiotopoulos	Queen Mary University of London, UK
Peter Parycek	Danube University Krems, Austria
Samuli Pekkola	Tampere University, Finland
Sergio Picazo-Vela	Universidad de las Americas Puebla, Mexico
Luiz Pereira Pinheiro Junior	Universidade Positivo, Brazil
Athanasios Priftis	Ynternet.org, France
Luis Felipe M. Ramos	University of Minho, Portugal
Barbara Re	University of Camerino, Italy
Nicolau Reinhard	University of São Paulo, Brazil
Aya Rizk	Luleå University of Technology, Sweden
Manuel Pedro Rodríguez Bolívar	University of Granada, Spain
Alexander Ronzhyn	University of Koblenz-Landau, Germany
Athanasia Routzouni	University of the Aegean, Greece
Boriana Rukanova	Delft University of Technology, The Netherlands
Per Runeson	Lund University, Sweden
Saquib Saeed	Imam Abdulrahman Bin Faisal University, Saudi Arabia
Rodrigo Sandoval-Almazan	Universidad Autónoma del Estado de Mexico, Mexico
Hans J. Scholl	University of Washington, USA

Hendrik Scholta	Universität Münster, Germany
Harrie Scholtens	European Institute of Public Administration/ PRIMO Europe, The Netherlands
Johannes Scholz	Graz University of Technology, Austria
Judith Schossböck	Danube University Krems, Austria
Luiza Schuch de Azambuja	Tallinn University of Technology, Estonia
Johanna Sefyrin	Linköping University, Sweden
Uwe Serdült	Ritsumeikan University
Masoud Shahmanzari	Brunel University London, UK
Kerley Silva	University of Porto, Portugal
Anthony Simonofski	Katholieke Universiteit Leuven, Belgium
Søren Skaarup	IT University of Copenhagen, Denmark
Ralf-Martin Soe	Tallinn University of Technology, Estonia
Karin Steiner	Danube University Krems, Austria
Leif Sundberg	Mid Sweden University, Sweden
Proscovia Svärd	Mid Sweden University, Sweden
Øystein Sæbø	University of Agder, Norway
Efthimios Tambouris	University of Macedonia, Greece
Ioanna Tamouridou	University of Macedonia, Greece
Luca Tangi	Politecnico di Milano, Italy
Lörinc Thurnay	Danube University Krems, Austria
Jean-Philippe Trabichet	HEG Genève, Switzerland
Andrea Trentini	University of Milano, Italy
Jolien Ubacht	Delft University of Technology, The Netherlands
Afe Vanveenstra	TNO, The Netherlands
Marco Velicogna	IRSiG-CNR, Italy
Gabriela Viale Pereira	Danube University Krems, Austria
Shefali Virkar	Danube University Krems, Austria
Gianluigi Viscusi	Imperial College London, UK
Felipe Vogas	Federal University of Rio de Janeiro, Brazil
Frederika Welle Donker	Knowledge Centre Open Data, The Netherlands
Guilherme Wiedenhöft	Federal University of Rio Grande, Brazil
Elin Wihlborg	Linköping University, Sweden
Peter Winstanley	Semantechs Consulting, UK
Stijn Wouters	Katholieke Universiteit Leuven, Belgium
Anja C. Wüst	Bern University of Applied Sciences, Switzerland
Maija Ylinen	Tampere University of Technology, Finland
Chien-Chih Yu	National Chengchi University, Taiwan
Mete Yıldız	Hacettepe Üniversitesi, Turkey
Qinfeng Zhu	University of Groningen, The Netherlands
Saleem Zoughbi	International Adviser
Anneke Zuiderwijk	Delft University of Technology, The Netherlands
Adelson de Araújo	University of Twente, The Netherlands
Ana Paula dos Santos Tavares	FGV EBAPE, Brazil
Sélinde van Engelenburg	Delft University of Technology, The Netherlands
Colin van Noordt	Tallinn University of Technology, Estonia
Jörn von Lucke	Zeppelin Universität, Germany
Anastasija Ņikiforova	University of Latvia, Latvia

Additional Reviewers

Nina Rizun	Gdansk University of Technology, Poland
Annika Hasselblad Hasseblad	Mid Sweden University, Sweden
Carsten Schmidtt	Tallinn University of Technology, Estonia
Dimitris Zeninis	Centre for Research Technology Hellas (CERTH), Greece
Vera Spitzer	University of Koblenz, Germany
Christina Deutsch	Technische Universität München, Germany
Marissa Hoekstra	TNO, The Netherlands

Contents

Digital Transformation

Data Science or Process Science? How to Promote the Next Digital Transformation in the Public Sector

Ralf Klischewski[✉]

German International University, Am Borsigturm 162, 13507 Berlin, Germany
ralf.klischewski@guc.edu.eg

Abstract. As citizen orientation and public value creation are more in the focus, how do we set priorities for the upcoming digital transformation in the public sector? Distinguishing data science and process science as paradigms that promote different directions for the transformation, this research seeks to improve the transparency of how IT-related decisions are directing projects and resources and thus promoting directions of public value production and delivery. Digital government research along this line may help constituents, IT experts and other stakeholders to engage in the needed discourse about the (not) wanted future of government performance and related technology usage.

Keywords: Data science · Process science · Digital transformation · Public sector · Public value · Digital government research · Paradigm

1 Introduction

Since the 1970s public administrations around the world are in a continuous process of adopting and adapting computer-based information and communication technology, leading to many organizational changes and re-shaping the government-citizen relationship. Nowadays CIOs, also in the public sector, are increasingly confronted with a plethora of data-driven innovations and applications, promising to open the door to the next level of computer-based organizational operation. Developments labeled under the paradigm of 'data science' certainly have a lot to offer for public administrations, especially for decision support. Hence, should public sector CIOs direct their strategic vision, their IT infrastructure, and their human and financial resources to focus on this paradigm? And similarly digital government research? Or does it still hold that electronic government is "a special case of ICT-enabled business process change" [28]? Which would imply that rather 'process science' should be (or remain) the leading paradigm to guide public sector IT developments, with data-driven innovations and applications just supporting the efforts to primarily improve the process performance.

Contrasting the choice between data science and process science and discussing the implications for research and practice follows the much debated paradigm construct as it was introduced by Kuhn to explain fundamental changes in the basic concepts and

© IFIP International Federation for Information Processing 2021
Published by Springer Nature Switzerland AG 2021
H. J. Scholl et al. (Eds.): EGOV 2021, LNCS 12850, pp. 3–15, 2021.
https://doi.org/10.1007/978-3-030-84789-0_1

practices of a scientific discipline. The term embraces several dimensions, and here we confine to the meaning of a 'disciplinary matrix' as "the entire constellation of beliefs, values, techniques, and so on shared by the members of a given community" ([15], p. 175), which has a "concrete problem solving ability" (p. 169), thus relating to society needs. The Kuhnian paradigm has been subjected to an extensive and longstanding debate also in Information Systems research. Here we adopt the stance of Hassan & Mingers [12] that the "received view of the paradigm concept in IS needs to be revisited, and the paradigms' other more potent components reintroduced, in order for a transformative understanding to be realized." Accordingly, the key terms are connoted as follows:

- A paradigm is considered as "a shared exemplar for scientific practice, which communities of scientists and researchers agree in part or completely, that provide models from which coherent scientific traditions may emerge." [12] This implies emphasizing the more practical and problem-solving nature of scientific practice rather than focusing on the epistemological aspects of producing and transmitting knowledge.
- Scientific practice embraces not only the research methodologies but also the science-driven approaches to solving real-life problems. This implies the "community of scientists" to include also practitioners as far as they adopt and advance scientific techniques and methods.

Digital government research as a scientific community – as individuals, research groups, institutional research programs and funding – always makes choices about how to contribute to the digitally enabled transformation in the practice of administration. Contrasting data science and process science therefore aims to reflect about the choices in agenda setting, in educating graduates and in directing resources for the research of the years to come. And it may equally impact the practice of ICT application in the public sector through perspective building, research-practice alignment, projects and funding, artifact innovation and dissemination, training etc.

Asking for the path to take in digital government research is not meant to sideline any research effort in any corner. Presuming that digital government research always strives for relevance to practice, this discussion contributes to the reflection about why certain paradigms might be most appropriate to guide strategy building, IT resource allocation and usage as well as digital transformation processes in the public sector.

The structure of the paper reflects the flow of the argument: How do actors related to the public sector approach digital transformation nowadays? What do data science and process science entail as candidate 'paradigms'? Given the expanding scope of digital transformation, how do we set priorities? The final section distinguishes the two paradigms along a set of characteristics and aligns them to impacts and outcomes, this way seeking to improve transparency, which helps constituents, IT experts and other stakeholders to engage in the needed discourse about the (not) wanted future of government performance.

2 Transformation of the Public Sector

A 2015 survey, conducted among more than 1,200 public sector officials around the globe, revealed that 76% of the respondents perceive digital technologies as disrupting the public sector, while at the same time nearly 70% said their organization's digital capabilities lag behind the private sector [7]. The study found that the degree of maturity in mastering the disruption scales with the clearness and coherence of a "digital strategy" and the degree of including organizational aspects beyond the technicalities. On the basis of more than 140 interviews the authors also identified five factors shaping digital transformation: strategy, leadership, workforce skills, digital culture, and user focus. As developments in each of these factors highly depend on the mindset of the actors involved, it is even more important to clarify the perceptions and expectations related to 'digital transformation', also for the public sector.

2.1 From Digitization to Digital Transformation

The basic step of the digital disruption – often called digitization – is the conversion of information representation from a physical format to a digital one to be used by computers feeding information systems and automating processes. Digitization is an operational necessity, and sometimes the term is even used embracing business process standardization in order to make a difference to digitalization or digital transformation: "Digitization is an important enabler of digital, but all the digitization in the world won't, on its own, make a business a digital company." [26] Ross adds that a digital transformation involves rethinking the company's value proposition and that a digital company innovates to deliver enhanced products, services, and customer engagement. Notably, she refrains from the term digitalization, which usually denotes the efforts towards creating a digital business. While often used synonymously, digital transformation emphasizes more the strategic approach to the needed transformational process.

Vom Brocke et al. [35] trace the research on IT-enabled organizational transformation back to the 1990s. They found it dominated by behavioral research approaches, but often not substantiated with theory. The vast majority of the examined studies (158 of 201) focused on higher levels of transformations, namely business process redesign, business network redesign and business scope redefinition.

Highlighting digital transformation as a fresh conceptualization, Wessel et al. [36] are keen to maintain the difference to IT-enabled organizational transformation. Both streams of activities are driven by technological change and based on a transformation agenda that leverages and iteratively refines the use of digital technologies. However, the conceptual difference relates to the value propositions: whereas for digital transformation, digital technology (re)defines the value proposition, in IT-enabled organizational transformation the digital technology supports the pre-existing value proposition. Accordingly, the digital transformation leads to a new organizational identity, while IT-enabled organizational transformation reinforces the existing organizational identity.

As digital transformation has gained momentum, the technical and organizational perspective is not sufficient to reflect the encompassing societal effects, opportunities and needs to shape and frame the ongoing changes. In view of unprecedented challenges to societal values related to digital transformation, Rowe [27] argues for a more philosophy-based embedded discourse "if we want IS scholarship to be relevant and critical."

However, it remains questionable whether IS research on that level will really make a difference in the transformation practice. The language of the IT industry and the consultants is different as they are addressing directly the actors and drivers who decide about bringing the IT into the organization. For example:

- "Making time available to become an 'evangelist' on digital is crucial. [...] CIOs are in a perfect position to make the difference between being a victim of disruption and a digital leader." [14]
- "The three waves of digitalization in the CFO function are: 1) Operational efficiency, 2) Business partnering and 3) Business transformation. Each wave outlines what digitalization means for the CFO function in terms of both actions and, more importantly, how the overall role of the CFO changes." [2]
- "A recent published Gartner's annual global survey of CIOs showed that the CIO role is transitioning from delivery executive to business executive, from controlling cost and engineering processes, to driving revenue and exploiting data." [8]

At the beginning of this millennium Dennis [5] had conceded that "much IS research is irrelevant to practice" due to its focus on knowledge for exploration while hardly focusing on exploitation (which is the practitioner's view). 20 years later not much has changed, and the debate how to improve the relevance of information systems research is still on (cf. e.g. [16]). For example, the MISQ editorial "Designing for digital transformation" [19] advises "IS researchers interested in societal or business change" to define the ICT artifact and to examine related affordances and constraints as well as the artifact's unintended consequences. These researchers should "couple research findings with public policy and regulation recommendations where relevant", but this does not reach out to the transformation logic of the practitioners.

2.2 Digital Transformation in Government

Selling IT to governments and administrations is an ever growing business. Major consultancy firms also engage in this sector, coining the government's digital transformation e.g. as the "digital technology's ability to fundamentally transform the way the public sector operates and delivers services to customers" [4]. The consultancy often relies on roadmaps, pointing to building blocks such as continuous budgetary support, coordination and governance, open data and technology platforms, and human capabilities as key enablers for the digitalization of government services [6]. Other efforts seek to understand and categorize their public customers: for example, Eggers & Bellman [7] conducted a survey based on a "digital maturity estimation framework" and found that most government organizations still lack the strategy to achieve digital transformation, the lack of digital workforce skills represents a major obstacle to transformation, and most agencies lack key elements of a "digital mindset".

Meanwhile, the scope of selling IT to governments has been extended much beyond administrative process automation, emphasizing that a "successful digitalization approach should be viewed from the citizens' experience perspective" ([6], p. 3). This is in line with government agencies pointing mainly to citizen demands as well as cost and budget pressures as the key drivers of digital transformation [7].

While some years ago it was conceded that digital transformation is still "to a large extent a promise yet to be realized for many government organizations" [38], digital government research is nowadays keen to gather empirical evidence. For example, Mergel et al. [21] seek to go beyond consultancy reports and provide systematic insight into how public administrators themselves define digital transformation in their own practices, how they are approaching digital transformation projects, and what they expect as outcomes. Their expert interviews revealed that the drivers for change mainly come from the external environment (similarly confirmed by [29]), the main objects of transformation are processes and services, "using new technology" seems to be the leading idea of transformation processes, and the main result to be achieved are rather related to long-term impacts than to measurable, concrete outputs.

Since the focus of digital transformation has shifted more towards servicing the citizens, the citizen-government relationship and the digitalization of public services have climbed up on the agenda of digital government research. Focusing on the interaction between citizens and public officials, Lindgren et al. [17] identify problem areas and research gaps arising from digitalizing the "public encounter", including the "double nature" (benefits vs. risks) of digital public services, the changing place of citizen-government interaction, the "casting and roles" of the actors involved, and the unexplored lateral dimensions of the services and related technologies. As the "public encounter" seems to shift from man to machine, the authors raise questions and ethical concerns regarding accountability and reskilling of both citizens and public officials.

Digitalization is moving in "waves", each combining new technologies plus new application potentials plus new products and/or services along with supporting cognitive perspectives and a stimulating hype. As the far-reaching consequences gain more attention, Mergel et al. [22] assert that digital transformation "describes the departure from digitization efforts to a full stack revision of the policies, processes and services in order to create simpler user experiences for citizens and frontline workers." In contrast to previous waves of digitization aiming to increase efficiency and effectiveness of government services, government services are now redesigned and reengineered "from the ground up to fulfill changing user needs."

The need for a digitalization strategy is undisputed as administrations need visions and (scientific?) guidance for their digital transformation. Yet, so far very few publications seek to support the actual transformation process. Notable exceptions include Ylinen & Pekkola [37], who propose a process model for public sector IT departments to adjust their operations as a response to digitization efforts, and Gong et al. [10], who seek to assists practitioners in anticipating what adaptations may arise while enacting digital technologies to create infrastructures and process flexibility. As the strategy development itself is left to the stakeholders on the ground, it seems that digital government research concerned with digital transformation faces the same dilemma as IS research in general, i.e. struggling to integrate critical reflection and relevance to practice.

As we witness the citizen-government relation undergoing substantial changes, we are certainly well advised to avoid any premature closure and to apply multiple perspectives to guiding the digital-driven transformation processes. For example, could "citizen orientation" be the leading idea to guide the next digital transformation in administration? For reflecting about which paradigm might be most appropriate to guide the strategy building and digital transformation processes in the public sector, the next section investigates two candidates that center on critical objects of transformation.

3 Data Science Versus Process Science

Data and processes are at the core of all IS-related efforts, also in the public sector. Both types of objects in the center of the digital transformation gave rise to distinct communities of scientists, each sharing practices along with constellation of beliefs, values, techniques, and each with a concrete problem solving ability. However, these communities do not seem to be on an equal footing: Searching for "data science" in the title, Scopus returns 1,742 articles since 2016, for "process science" the corresponding list includes only 6 articles (in January 2021). Yet, both communities, with only little communality, build on decades of influential scientific practice in each of their related fields and strive to make a distinct real-world impact.

3.1 Data Science

The first appearance of 'data science' in the scientific community (proposed as an alternative name for computer science) is attributed to Peter Naur in 1974 [3]. And the Data Science Journal as well as the Journal of Data Science were already launched in the early 2000s. However, the term data science has gained popularity only in 2010 to denote what "data scientists" do: a new type of IT professionals who started to organize themselves online just a year before [25].

Data science embraces different subdisciplines and numerous practical approaches (see also Fig. 1) that serve four categories of aims: reporting (what happened?), diagnosis (why did it happen?), prediction (what will happen?), and recommendation (what is the best that can happen?) [31] While defining data science, Cao [3] denotes the "ultimate data products of value [as] knowledge, intelligence, wisdom, and decision."

Data science qualifies as a 'paradigm' (as introduced above) because we find a scientific practice shared by the data scientists to solve concrete and relevant problems. The techniques mainly relate to analytics, including statistics, mining algorithms and computerized tools. The community shares the belief that data-driven discovery delivers value for business and society, assuming that data analysis will provide relevant answers, even if we do not know the (exact) question. From the epistemological perspective Jim Gray even imagined "data-intensive science" as a fourth paradigm of science (in addition to, or integrating, empirical, theoretical, and computational science) [18].

3.2 Process Science

Van der Aalst & Damiani [33] have coined the term process science as "the broader discipline that combines knowledge from information technology and knowledge from management sciences to improve and run operational processes", referring to the work of Frederick Taylor as the starting point of scientifically managing processes.

Embracing scientific branches such as Operations Research or Workflow Management, most of the "process scientists" nowadays flock to the area of Business Process Management (BPM). The "concrete problem solving ability" is enormous because all organizations seek to computerize the automatable parts of their business processes and to control the whole process life cycle through modeling, implementation, enactment, monitoring, analysis and redesign. The token-based semantics adopted from Petri nets is the mostly cited theoretical basis for such endeavors, followed by queueing theory and Markov analysis. While the BPM community itself is vivid and well established, the expansion towards a larger community of "process scientists" still seems to be underway. For example, Mendling [20] discusses "how BPM research can be further developed towards a true process science" in order to provide insights for practitioners on "how to apply scientific process management".

The website process-science.net claims: "So far, processes have been investigated from the lens of single disciplines [...]. We cannot rely on a single discipline if we want to obtain a full picture of processes. We need to bundle and synthesize contributions, theories and methods from multiple disciplines."

On the basis of this, Vom Brocke [34] answers the question "what does a Process Scientist do?" as discovering and implementing new ways to do things, in particular analyzing and automating processes as well as designing effective interventions, while applying distinct strategies (evidence-based, multi-sourced, context-sensitive, impact-oriented). From that perspective, process science points to shared scientific practice to solve concrete and relevant problems, based on the belief that process management is the key to deliver business value and/or public value. In principle, process science may qualify as a 'paradigm' (as introduced above). However, it seems that the term has been purposely constructed to contrast data science, yet it (still) lacks the comparable popularity among proponents to identify themselves as "process scientists".

3.3 Maintaining Disjunctive Identities

After contrasting data science and process science, Van der Aalst & Damiani [33] continue advocating that process mining shall bridge the gap between these two (Fig. 1). Process mining makes use of event logs and mainly aims for process discovery, conformance checking, and performance analysis [32]. It could even reach beyond the mere process view and, for example, support theorizing about organizational change [11].

Fig. 1. Process mining as the bridge between process science and data science [33]

Process mining originated in the BPM community and flourished first in a world of rather small data [9]. Only throughout the last decade huge data pools representing process events emerged, and their exploitation now requires data science approaches and techniques, while the objective of using these and the subsequent calibration and control remain related to process science. For succeeding in process mining projects it usually needs collaboration of experts from both fields [9]. In that sense it is an interdisciplinary endeavor indicating that distinct ingredients from two different paradigms are essential, and there is no sign of disciplinary merge and community building beyond the establishment as a subset of both fields.

4   Creating Public Value Through Managing Process Portfolios

Since the focus of digital transformation in the public sector has shifted from improving efficiency more towards servicing the citizens, the basic question is even more in the focus: what are governments and administrations doing (or should be doing) to create public value? The impact reaches far beyond saving resources through efficiency gains, and the role of technology is subject to debate in the digital government community. Accordingly, any debate about which path to take in digital government research and practice must take into account the changing expectations regarding what digital government should deliver.

Twizeyimana & Andersson [30] identify improved public services, improved administration, and improved social value as the three overarching (and also overlapping) dimensions of the public value of e-government. For them, achieving public value in e-government should be understood as "the ability of e-government systems to provide improved efficiency in government, improved services to citizens, and social values such as inclusion, democracy, transparency, and participation."

Ability refers to capability, and here Pang et al. [24] were the first to theorize the relationship between IT resources, organizational capabilities, and organizational performance in the public sector. They found that IT resources contribute to creating public value through five organizational capabilities in government agencies: the capabilities for public service delivery, public engagement, co-production, resource-building, and public-sector innovation. Notably, governments and administrations strive to fulfill a variety, often even competing values concurrently, which do not combine into one single value as a target (e.g. sales or profits). Therefore, the authors introduce the construct of the "public-value frontier", which they define as "the set of maximum multiple public values that is achievable given available resources and the constraints among certain values." In conclusion, they see the role of IT in supporting the public sector organizations in advancing their frontier to a higher level.

Panagiotopoulos et al. [23] argue in the same line: "Public value creation can be considered the outcome of a production process of different public services pursued by public agencies to fulfil the collective goals that citizens define in the democratic process [...]." Additionally they emphasize that "citizens do not value services per se but rather value what services deliver when consumed," i.e. it needs an integrated view of public value creation that perceives value creation from the citizen perspective. To support this public value production process, it needs organizational capabilities as dynamic capabilities (i.e. the ability to integrate, build, and reconfigure resources and competences to adapt to changes), which are distinct from operational capabilities referring to the systematic use of resources to perform core tasks and execute business processes.

In order to make this process, or rather, processes of public value production manageable, Alford & Yates [1] proposed modeling these processes starting from the core activities (by public sector and others) to produce a particular value and enhancing business-process-like models with outcomes, (potential) actors, influencing factors and various relationship types between the model elements. Such "public value process maps" are designed for policy analysts and public managers in order to clarify valuable outcomes as well as to identify and prioritize the actors and activities (or sub-processes) involved. Taking the practitioner's perspective, Kirchmer et al. [13] also identify "the transfer of the strategy of an organization into the appropriate portfolio of process improvement initiatives" as a key digitalization gap.

Summarizing the perspective of public value production, it is all about creating organizational and operational capabilities on the basis of which public managers manage a portfolio of value creation processes aiming to improve the balanced perception of values on the side of the constituencies.

5   Choices in the Driving Seat

In practice, choices have to be made for hiring, resource allocation, strategic alignment, project management etc. We assume that building and maintaining identities of the IT experts involved will make a difference in the outcome of the digital transformation. Given the expanding scope of digital transformation, also in the public sector, how do we set appropriate priorities? Distinguishing the two paradigms along a set of dimensions, we aim to contribute to the basis for making informed choices in digital government research and practice.

Table 1. Paradigm characteristics

Data science	Characteristic	Process science
Analytic	Perspective	Functional
Statistics, data mining	Core community	Business process management
Data-driven discovery creates business value/public value	Essential belief	Processes & process management create business value/public value
Reporting, diagnosis, prediction, recommendation	Activities & aims	Discovering and implementing new ways to do things
Advanced analytics (statistics, mining, machine learning etc.)	Techniques	Process modeling, implementation, enactment, monitoring, analysis, redesign
Support and automation of decision making	Main use case	Analyzing and automating processes, designing effective interventions
Knowledge, intelligence wisdom, and decision	Products of value	Process improvements

The two paradigms in focus can be distinguished along their characteristics regarding main perspective, core community, essential belief, activities and aims, techniques, use cases, and products of value (see Sect. 3 and Table 1). Both paradigms and communities coexist in guiding distinct efforts of research and development. However, IT managers in public administration do not go by paradigms, but make their choices according to a number of factors such as a given digital transformation strategy, service demands and requirements, investment frame, legacy systems and infrastructure, available know-how etc. (cf. [13]). Therefore, choices in terms of input such as research, development and resource allocation (if linked to one of the paradigms) should be related to the impacts and outcomes, i.e. the direct effects and the long-term results (see Table 2).

In the process of digital transformation, data science focusses on data-driven decision making, whereas process science targets the concatenation of functionality in administrative service production. While citizens relating to government and administration will always experience a combination of various transformation efforts, changes driven by data science intensify encounters of algorithmic decisions, while those driven by process science rather intensify encounters of automated services.

Table 2. Paradigm-related impacts and outcomes in public administration

Impact/outcome	Data science	Process science
Transformation focus	Data-driven decision making in government and administration	Processes enabling administrative service production
Citizen experience	Encounter of algorithmic decisions	Encounter of automated services
Public value production	Analyze outcome	Improve processes
Capabilities for public value	Public engagement, public-sector innovation, public service delivery	Public service delivery, co-production, public engagement

If we seek to link digital government research and development to public value production, we find that the two paradigms point to different directions. Based on their characteristics, data science may rather guide analyzing outcomes of public value production, while process science may help leading process improvements. And focusing on the IT resources feeding into the organizational capabilities needed to push the public value "frontier" to a higher level (according to the theoretical model of [24], see Sect. 4), both digitized processes and data analytics can make their contributions. Yet, we can assume that process science sets the focus on processes supporting public service delivery, co-production, and public engagement, while data science relates rather to public engagement, public-sector innovation and only secondarily to public service delivery.

Notably, the conceptualization of paradigm used here emphasizes the more practical and problem-solving nature of scientific practice rather than focusing on the epistemological aspects of producing and transmitting knowledge. Accordingly, scientific practice embraces not only research methodologies but also science-driven approaches to solving real-life problems, thus including also practitioners as far as they adopt and advance scientific techniques and methods. This may be a contribution to reducing the gap between IS research and practice (also in the area of digital government), but at the same time it is a limitation because this conceptualization is not fully compatible with most of the extant discourse on paradigms in IS research.

Contrasting the paradigms of data science and process science is just one possible starting point, and the shortened paradigm analysis is certainly another limitations of this research. However, it seems that currently we can only speculate how IT-related decisions driven by certain paradigms are directing projects and resources and thus impacting the public value production and delivery. As public agencies seek to fulfil the collective goals defined, the value production process and the IT resource allocation and usage should be as transparent as possible. Future digital government research should therefore seek to understand this relation in much more detail. This would help the constituents, the IT experts and other stakeholders to engage in the needed discourse about the (not) wanted future of government performance and related technology usage.

References

1. Alford, J., Yates, S.: Mapping public value processes. Int. J. Public Sector Manage. **27**(4), 334–352 (2014)
2. BearingPoint: The three waves of digitalization. https://www.bearingpoint.com/en-fi/blog/three-waves-of-digitalization. Accessed 05 Mar 2021
3. Cao, L.: Data science: a comprehensive overview. ACM Comput. Surv. (CSUR) **50**(3), 1–42 (2017)
4. Deloitte: Digital Government Transformation. https://www2.deloitte.com/global/en/pages/public-sector/articles/digital-government-transformation.html. Accessed 05 Mar 2021
5. Dennis, A.R.: Relevance in information systems research. Commun. Assoc. Inf. Syst. **6**, Article 10 (2001)
6. Duneja, R., Lasku, A., Pichai, H., Kilefors, P.: Digitalization of government services (2018). https://www.adlittle.com/en/Government_Digitalization. Accessed 21 Feb 2021
7. Eggers, W., Bellman, J.: The Journey to Government's Digital Transformation. Deloitte University Press, UK (2015)
8. Express Computer: Digitalization wave to transform CIOs role completely: Gartner. https://www.expresscomputer.in/news/digitalization-wave-to-transform-cios-role-completely-gartner/22478/. Accessed 21 Feb 2021
9. Gal, A., Senderovich, A.: Process minding: closing the big data gap. In: Fahland, D., Ghidini, C., Becker, J., Dumas, M. (eds.) BPM 2020. LNCS, vol. 12168, pp. 3–16. Springer, Cham (2020). https://doi.org/10.1007/978-3-030-58666-9_1
10. Gong, Y., Yang, J., Shi, X.: Towards a comprehensive understanding of digital transformation in government: analysis of flexibility and enterprise architecture. Gov. Inf. Q. **37**(3), 101487 (2020)
11. Grisold, T., Wurm, B., Mendling, J., Vom Brocke, J.: Using process mining to support theorizing about change in organizations. In: Proceedings 53rd HICSS. IEEE (2020)
12. Hassan, N.R., Mingers, J.: Reinterpreting the Kuhnian paradigm in information systems. J. Assoc. Inf. Syst. **19**(7), 568–599 (2018)
13. Kirchmer, M., Franz, P., Gusain, R.: From strategy to process improvement portfolios and value realization. In: Shishkov, B. (ed.) BMSD 2018. LNBIP, vol. 319, pp. 32–55. Springer, Cham (2018). https://doi.org/10.1007/978-3-319-94214-8_3

14. KPMG: Enabling the Digital Enterprise: A CIO Checklist for Digital Transformation. https://assets.kpmg/content/dam/kpmg/pdf/2016/04/digital-enterprise-cio-checklist.pdf. Accessed 21 Feb 2021
15. Kuhn, T.: The Structure of Scientific Revolutions, 2nd edn. University of Chicago Press, Chicago (1970)
16. Lee, J.K., Park, J., Gregor, Sh., Yoon, V.: Axiomatic theories and improving the relevance of information systems research. Inf. Syst. Res. (2021, published online in Articles in Advance 01 Feb 2021).
17. Lindgren, I., Madsen, C.Ø., Hofmann, S., Melin, U.: Close encounters of the digital kind: a research agenda for the digitalization of public services. Gov. Inf. Q. **36**(3), 427–436 (2019)
18. Lynch, C.: Jim Gray's fourth paradigm and the construction of the scientific record. In: Hey, T., Tansley, S., Tolle, K. (eds.) The Fourth Paradigm: Data-intensive Scientific Discovery, pp. 177–184. Microsoft Research, Redmond (2009)
19. Majchrzak, A., Markus, M.L., Wareham, J.: Designing for digital transformation: lessons for information systems research from the study of ICT and societal challenges. Manage. Inf. Syst. Q. **40**(2), 267–277 (2016)
20. Mendling, J.: From scientific process management to process science: towards an empirical research agenda for business process management. In: Hochreiner, Ch., Schulte, S. (eds.) Proceedings 8th ZEUS Workshop, Vienna, Austria, pp. 1–4 (2016)
21. Mergel, I., Edelmann, N., Haug, N.: Defining digital transformation: results from expert interviews. Gov. Inf. Q. **36**(4), 101385 (2019)
22. Mergel, I., Kattel, R., Lember, V., McBride, K.: Citizen-oriented digital transformation in the public sector. In: Proceedings of the 19th Annual International Conference on Digital Government Research: Governance in the Data Age, pp. 1–3 (2018)
23. Panagiotopoulos, P., Klievink, B., Cordella, A.: Public value creation in digital government. Gov. Inf. Q. **36**(4), 101421 (2019)
24. Pang, M.-S., Lee, G., DeLone, W.H.: IT resources, organizational capabilities, and value creation in public-sector organizations: a public-value management perspective. J. Inf. Technol. **29**(3), 187–205 (2014)
25. Press, G.: A Very Short History of Data Science. Forbes Technology (2013). http://www.forbes.com/sites/gilpress/2013/05/28/a-very-short-history-of-data-science/. Accessed 11 Feb 2021
26. Ross, J.W.: Don't confuse digital with digitization. MIT Sloan Manage. Rev. (2017). https://sloanreview.mit.edu/article/dont-confuse-digital-with-digitization/
27. Rowe, F.: Being critical is good, but better with philosophy! From digital transformation and values to the future of IS research. Eur. J. Inf. Syst. **27**(3), 380–393 (2018)
28. Scholl, H.J.: E-government: a special case of ICT-enabled business process change. In: Proceedings 36th Hawaii International Conference on System Sciences. IEEE (2003)
29. Tangi, L., Janssen, M., Benedetti, M., Noci, G.: Barriers and drivers of digital transformation in public organizations: results from a survey in the Netherlands. In: VialePereira, G., et al. (eds.) EGOV 2020. LNCS, vol. 12219, pp. 42–56. Springer, Cham (2020). https://doi.org/10.1007/978-3-030-57599-1_4
30. Twizeyimana, J.D., Andersson, A.: The public value of E-Government–a literature review. Gov. Inf. Q. **36**(2), 167–178 (2019)
31. Aalst, W.M.P.: Data scientist: the engineer of the future. In: Mertins, K., Bénaben, F., Poler, R., Bourrières, J.-P. (eds.) Enterprise Interoperability VI. PIC, vol. 7, pp. 13–26. Springer, Cham (2014). https://doi.org/10.1007/978-3-319-04948-9_2
32. Van der Aalst, W.: Process Mining: Data Science in Action, 2nd edn. Springer, Berlin (2016)
33. Van der Aalst, W., Damiani, E.: Processes meet big data: connecting data science with process science. IEEE Trans. Serv. Comput. **8**(6), 810–819 (2015)

34. Fahland, D., Ghidini, C., Becker, J., Dumas, M. (eds.): BPM 2020. LNCS, vol. 12168. Springer, Cham (2020). https://doi.org/10.1007/978-3-030-58666-9

35. Vom Brocke, J., Schmid, A. M., Simons, A., Safrudin, N.: IT-enabled organizational transformation: a structured literature review. Bus. Process Manage. J. (2020, ahead-of-print). https://doi.org/10.1108/BPMJ-10-2019-0423

36. Wessel, L., Baiyere, A., Ologeanu-Taddei, R., Cha, J., Blegind Jensen, T.: Unpacking the difference between digital transformation and IT-enabled organizational transformation. J. Assoc. Inf. Syst. **22**(1), Article 6 (2021)

37. Ylinen, M., Pekkola, S.: A process model for public sector IT management to answer the needs of digital transformation. In: Proceedings of the 52nd HICSS. IEEE (2019)

38. Zhang, J., Luna-Reyes, L.F., Mellouli, S.: Transformational digital government. Gov. Inf. Q. **4**(31), 503–505 (2014)

Digital Transformation Initiatives in Public Administration During the Covid-19 Pandemic in Brazil: Unveiling Challenges and Opportunities

Ana Paula Tavares[1]([✉]) [iD], Luiz Antonio Joia[1]([✉]) [iD], and Marcelo Fornazin[2]([✉]) [iD]

[1] Getulio Vargas Foundation, R. Jorn. Orlando Dantas, 30, Botafogo, RJ, Brazil
`luiz.joia@fgv.br`
[2] Fluminense Federal University, Av. Gal. Milton Tavares de Souza, São Domingos, RJ, Brazil

Abstract. The development of ICT is an important factor in boosting the economies of developing countries. Despite the multiplicity of technological novelties and recipes for their successful implementation, these initiatives are taking much longer and facing more difficulties than it has been expected. During the outbreak of the Covid-19 pandemic and with the implementation of social distancing, digital transformation has become a major issue. The world has encountered several challenges as the adoption and use of technologies became mandatory. In public administration, the development of an environment capable of keeping up with this pace of change was paramount. Hence, this study aims to understand the role of digital transformation during the Covid-19 pandemic, by analyzing several mini-cases in Brazil. Therefore, adopting a qualitative approach based on multiple longitudinal mini-case studies grounded on a critical interpretive approach, one analyzed the positive, negative, and unforeseen outcomes accrued from digital transformation initiatives in Brazil, thereby unveiling potential challenges and opportunities for technology in a post-Covid-19 reality.

Keywords: Digital transformation · Information and communication technology · Covid-19 · Pandemic · Digital government

1 Introduction

The uncertainties triggered by the Covid-19 pandemic revealed dangerous and complex problems of society, and its management and mitigation by the government are challenging [1, 2]. The implementation of digital transformation initiatives worldwide accelerated drastically [3], and Information and Communication Technology (ICT) has had a central role to play [4]. Some studies have examined the relationship between Covid-19 and ICT risk management and continuity [4], leadership [5], consumer behavior patterns [6], supply chain decisions [7], digital privacy [8], and ICT-mediated classroom [9]. Hence, although it was not the first pandemic of this century, the Covid-19 pandemic has had unprecedented impacts on society.

© IFIP International Federation for Information Processing 2021
Published by Springer Nature Switzerland AG 2021
H. J. Scholl et al. (Eds.): EGOV 2021, LNCS 12850, pp. 16–28, 2021.
https://doi.org/10.1007/978-3-030-84789-0_2

Brazil is an emerging market and so offers a unique opportunity to explore ICT-based social and business innovations at a societal level of analysis [10]. Indeed, its significant participation in social networks, the impressive growth rate of e-commerce and adoption of technology innovations such as online banking and electronic voting, indicate the country's insertion in the digital economy and presents a noteworthy occasion to explore the Brazilian context.

Thus, this article addresses the following research question: how were digital technologies used to deal with emergency issues during the Covid-19 pandemic in a developing country like Brazil? Therefore, this study aims to understand the positive, negative, and unforeseen effects of digital transformation initiatives implemented in Brazil to respond to the challenges of the Covid-19 pandemic.

2 Literature Review

The development of ICT is an important factor in boosting the economies of developing countries [11], and it has been the focus of studies in emerging markets [12–14]. In Brazil, ICT, encompassing products and services, produces 4% of Brazilian GDP, and the number is increasing primarily due to public authorities' active IT usages such as the e-voting system and electronic reporting to the police [11]. Since 2010, Internet access by the low-income population has increased remarkably with more than 200 million phone subscriptions in the country [14]. In short, Brazil has become an important laboratory of ICT-mediated social, and business innovations. Important areas using innovative technology are government and public administration [15], banking technology [16], digital inclusion [17], and e-democracy [18] to name a few.

Applications such as electronic voting and online income tax declarations have attracted international attention since the 1990s [14]. Indeed, the electronic voting system of Brazil is seen as a trustworthy mechanism of producing election results that accurately represent the choices of the electorate [12]. In addition, the rapid growth of Brazilian participation in social networks [19] places the country in the third world position in hours/day spent on social networks, and in second in hours/day spent on the internet [20]. Moreover, Brazil has an impressive growth rate in e-commerce, accounting for almost 66 million online shoppers and more than 150 million Internet users, with a penetration rate of 71% among the population [21]. These figures highlight the country's insertion in the digital economy and an exceptional opportunity to be explored by researchers.

Despite the development of infrastructure for the digital economy, the country faces important challenges related to digitization. In fact, 23% of the adult population, in 2018, had never used the Internet [22]. In addition, the low qualification of Brazilians, with more than 50% of adults without high school education, prevents many citizens from using technology effectively, benefiting from them. ICTs are potentially capable of contributing to the improvement of various aspects of life, from reducing poverty to strengthening democratic policies [23]. However, the application of ICT has not always been successful in developing countries [24]. In this sense, the Covid-19 pandemic revealed a complex scenario in Brazil, with successful experiences of large-scale adoption of technologies (for example, the banking sector), living with a digital divide in the health and education sectors.

2.1 Theoretical Framework

Digital technologies are transforming the socio-economic and political arenas, having provided groundbreaking beneficial innovations to the world [25]. So far, most research has focused on the development and implementation of digital technologies. The present study intends to contribute to the field reflecting on and understanding the influence of actors, technologies, and discourses and how they are integrated.

Bringing together the theories on contextualist ICT innovation [23, 26], the social shaping of technology [27, 28], and the structuralism view of technology [29, 30], one presents below an empirical framework combining three central concepts: social groups, technologies, and discourses.

Contextualism, Social Shaping of Technology, and Structuration Theory. The social constructivist approach allows the understanding of the acceleration of digital transformation in the pandemic addressing conceptual relationships such as technology/society, agency/structure, and technical reasoning/institutional dynamics [23]. That way technology could be considered as part of a broader social context raising questions concerning the way specific categories of technologies and social actors' clusters are formed and shaped, leading to specific socioeconomic outcomes. Actors, discourses, and technologies elements derive from the social shaping of technology line of research by which two broad categories emerge: socio-economic shaping of technology and social construction of technology (SCOT). Pozzebon and Diniz [14] argue that the actor's interpretations of technology presented by the social shaping view strengthen the opportunities for decision making regarding technology management. Another theoretical influence on the present study is the structuration view of technology or the Giddens' structuration theory, which has been developed by some researchers [29–31]. The concept of technology-in-practice, derived from the structuration theory, explains how social groups, negotiating meanings and applications of a given ICT, adapt them locally and what are the consequences. According to the theory, different cultures will be involved differently with local adaptations or appropriations. In addition, the concept of improvisation that emerges from emergency or crisis situations [32], in response to unexpected opportunities or unexpected actions sown in intuition to solve a problem [33], opens space for research in the Brazilian context. In fact, improvisation is frequent in developing regions due to the less stable political and economic environment [33].

Framework Dimensions. Table 1 presents the main dimensions of the Multilevel and Pluralistic Conceptual Framework developed by Pozzebon and Diniz [14], considering the three theoretical perspectives abovementioned: contextualism, social shaping of technology, and structuration view of technology.

'Actors' refer to the social setting where the ICT artifact is being implemented and used. It helps define the boundaries of the investigation and includes the identification of different relevant social groups. Social groups refer to a group of people who share a common geographical space, a common social class, a common professional occupation, to name a few. It also includes the identification of interpretive frames for each social group, allowing the recognition of shared and conflicting perceptions, expectations, and interests that characterize the community context.

'Technologies' refer to the socio-technical characteristics of the ICT artifact being implemented, as used by specific actors at a given level of analysis (individual, social groups, society). The technologies-in-practice resulting from the process of negotiation is both intended and unintended, and their choice emerges from the literature on digital transformation in addition to the analysis of the mini-cases.

'Discourses' refer to the understanding of "how social groups influence the negotiation process taking place around the implementation and use of a given ICT artifact. The implementation of ICT in a community or region can be seen as an opportunity to change information flow, resource allocation, and responsibility attributions" [14].

Table 1. Framework components.

	Dimensions	Concepts
Actors	Context	Social groups
Technologies	Content	Technology-in-practice
Discourses	Process	Mechanisms of negotiation

In sum, the present study focuses on the categories of negotiation that consider the different interests, commitments, plans, perspectives, and positions of the network of social groups interacting with the technology, and how they will influence the process and outcomes of technologies-in-practice and the emergent social structures.

3   Research Method

The present study intends to analyze four mini-cases in the Brazilian context vis-à-vis the aforementioned theoretical framework. The adopted criterion for selecting each mini case was based on three main components: relevance, reliability, and impact on society. Such criterion provides a unique research opportunity to understand an important phenomenon through the lens of real-life cases which, according to Kardos and Smith [34] usually ends with issues and points for discussion. In fact, the mini-cases are not as deep as traditional case studies however, the mini-cases chosen presented a favorable occasion for data collection, being extremely relevant in the Brazilian pandemic context. Also, each mini-case brings a different and complementary perspective, which allows abstraction and generalization of the findings through the discourses presented.

The research method was developed considering the following steps. First, the mini-cases were analyzed through data collection. The data collection comprised a logbook of events recorded during the outbreak of the Covid-19 pandemic. The procedure conducted sought consistent and trustworthy data, and information collected through several methods like observation [47] and document analysis [48]. The Table 2 presents the synthesis of the data collection. In science in action studies all the material within reach should be gathered in a logbook, thus comprising recording notes of events and interviews during the outbreak of the Covid-19 pandemic [48]. Second, the theoretical framework was applied to each mini-case in order to understand the meaning or knowledge constructed by people and the way people make sense of their world and their experiences in this world [35].

The theoretical perspectives were then articulated through a primary coding of actors and technologies. It was followed by the analysis of discourses in a dialogue between the theory and the field. Finally, specific outcomes were presented from the analysis of the selected mini-cases. The criterion to define the outcomes considered the results of each case at the societal level, and how the technologies, actors, and discourses impacted such results.

Table 2. Summary of data collection.

Data sources	Description	Period	Role
Public documents	Articles in the media, annual reports, books, podcasts, websites	October 2020 to March 2021	Important for establishing the chronology of main events and for understanding different viewpoints
Observation	Field notes from participation in public conferences/events	October 2020 to March 2021	Important for understanding the dynamics of interactions among the social groups and the discourses that emerged
Cetic.br Survey	Studies on the use of ICTs in Brazil during the Pandemic	January 2021 to March 2021	Important for monitoring and evaluating the socioeconomic impact of ICTs for development

4   Brazilian Mini-Cases

4.1   Emergency Aid as a Measure of Social Protection

The Emergency Aid, instituted by Law 13.982, of 2020, is one of the biggest initiatives of the Brazilian Federal Government to minimize the economic effects of the Covid-19 pandemic [36]. This aid is directed at the most vulnerable population, among them, the beneficiaries of the conditional cash transfer program 'Bolsa Família' and those enrolled in the single registry for social protection 'Cadastro Único para Programas Sociais do Governo Federal'. The benefit also covers informal employees, self-employed and individual microentrepreneurs. This new aid covers a gap in the social protection of so-called informal workers as long as they meet the conditions stipulated by the law.

The 'Cadastro Único' currently contains data on more than 74 million citizens [37], and is used by various federal programs, with the largest user program being the 'Bolsa

Família'. More than ten years ago, the 'Cadastro Único' was defined as a tool that could be widely used due to its three essential characteristics: broad census information (for the poor population), registry data (with identification and address data), and for its broad identification of information about the conditions of these families' lives [38]. According to the Caixa Econômica Federal, the operating agent of the 'Cadastro Único' and the 'Bolsa Familia' (2020), approximately half of the Emergency Aid target was unknown to the Ministry of Citizenship, as they were neither 'Bolsa Família' beneficiaries nor registered in the 'Cadastro Único', which generated additional complexity for the policy's successful implementation.

4.2   Health System: Monitoring the Number of Covid-19 Cases and Deaths

Before the first Covid-19 cases were reported in the country, a variety of measures have been implemented including the adjustment of a legal framework to carry out isolation and quarantine [39]. The first case of coronavirus in Brazil and in South America was registered on February 26th, 2020 in São Paulo. On March 13th, the Ministry of Health announced recommendations to prevent the spread of the disease and recognized that community transmission was occurring across the country, as a strategic measure to ensure a collective effort by all Brazilians in order to reduce virus transmission.

"The Brazilian government's response to the Covid-19 pandemic, under the presidency of Jair Bolsonaro, has caused a political crisis resulting from a divide on how to handle the spread of the disease" [40]. In March 2020, Brazil's Ministry of Health declared that each state should devise guidelines to fight the virus and strongly recommended social distancing and self-isolation. Meanwhile, the president dismissed the severity of the pandemic, and encouraged people to "go back to normality". In June 2020, after sacking two ministers, the Ministry of Health has reduced the quantity and quality of the data available about the pandemic, which urged the creation of a partnership between the media groups to collect Covid-19 statistics directly from the state health departments. The main goal was to draw public attention guaranteeing transparency and accountability in regard to the disclosure of data related to the pandemic.

4.3   The Impact of Covid-19 in Education

According to the United Nations children's agency Unicef [41], in Latin America and the Caribbean, 97% of children are not having face-to-face classes. That is around 137 million students. Covid-19 pandemic imposed an unseen situation on the Brazilian educational system: the need to adapt to remote learning. Unequal access to digital tools, connectivity, and lack of training has imposed challenges for governments, schools, and teachers to engage students in long-distance education. Such abrupt change affects all actors in the education systems, however low socioeconomic students faced it more critically. The Brazilian National Council of Education argues that Brazil is facing an unprecedented situation in an area that traditionally does not have a culture of digital, remote work, or distance education. That is new and complex for those who are working with basic education in public and private schools. Indeed, Brazil is one of the most unequal regions in the world, and Covid-19 has brought out those inequalities when it comes to education. As stated by Unicef [41], schools also provide important services beyond education, such as school feeding programs and health programs. That way, the impacts go beyond education, having a long-lasting effect that surpasses the learning process. As per higher education, the Covid-19 pandemic has revealed weaknesses and difficulties that threaten students' access and retention. The instability of the labor market, loss of jobs, and latent uncertainties about the future of the labor market weaken the ability of students to remain in higher education. Altogether, the Covid-19 crisis has rendered more visible and urgent the need to improve the access of socially disadvantaged students to education.

4.4 Fake News and Data Protection

The acceleration in digitalization has brought an inevitable acceleration in cyberattacks and fake news, forcing companies to invest more in cybersecurity and data protection. Besides fighting the pandemic, the society faced the spread of speculations and fake news about the disease [42]. The main issue regarding the fake news is that misinformation makes people confused and unsure as to what sources can be trusted. In addition, the spread of misguided news about the Brazilian Unified Health System and Ministry of Health spread rumors that have eventually challenged the very legitimacy of these organizations. Considering Brazil's political and economic context, such media repercussions have a strong impact on the population's decisions [40].

Nine in every 10 Brazilians have been exposed to fake news about the pandemic, which is typically shared via WhatsApp groups [43]. Seven in 10 say they believed in the information they received. The risks of fake news have gained new urgency because of the seriousness of the health issue. In order to fight fake news, the Ministry of Health created a channel called "Health without fake news" to analyze viral news and determine whether it is true or false. To manage the Covid-19 situation more carefully, the former ministry created a specific channel for information related to the pandemic. Also, Brazil's Congress is pushing for legislation to stop this flood of disinformation. The bill, however, has raised fears about freedom of speech and government surveillance. Despite the discussion around information transparency, fake news is rampant, and one can affirm that the spread of the same has contributed to discrediting science and global public health institutions, thereby weakening people's adherence to the necessary preventive care [42].

5   Results

In this section, one presents and consolidates the main outcomes of each mini-case by applying the proposed framework.

5.1 Emergency Aid as a Measure of Social Protection

The introduction of the Emergency Aid and the expansion of Bolsa Família represented an increase in the income of the poorest by 40%. For instance, the average 'Bolsa Família' family received less than USD 37 per month and with the Emergency Aid, they received USD 110 to USD 222 monthly. According to Caixa Econômica Federal,

58 million Brazilians received at least one installment of emergency aid through digital accounts. Positive innovative factors have been developed such as the remote request solutions, collaborating with social distancing measures. The package of assistance made a difference in how families coped with the pandemic.

5.2   Health System: Monitoring the Number of Covid-19 Cases and Deaths

When the World Health Organization declared the novel coronavirus a pandemic on March 11th, 2020, Brazil was still a week away from reporting its first death due to Covid-19. Nevertheless, the country soon claimed global attention, as the number of Covid-19 cases and deaths in the country grew exponentially, reaching the third and second highest figures worldwide, respectively, only behind the U.S. and India. In January 2021, Brazil surpassed the threshold of seven million cases and 200,000 deaths. Brazilian government's response to the Covid-19 pandemic, under the presidency of Jair Bolsonaro, has caused a political crisis resulting from a divide on how to handle the spread of the disease [40]. The absence of reliable information on the pandemic affected potential countermeasures at local and national levels.

5.3   The Impact of Covid-19 in Education

More than 180,000 schools were closed in 2020 and 47 million students tried to adapt to a new routine of distance education in Brazil [44]. A concern shared by the government and schools is how to prevent dropouts and provide additional support to students with fewer opportunities for virtual learning. Most public schools lack adequate technological infrastructure to support teachers in conducting online courses. In addition, teachers in Brazil feel unprepared to deal with technological resources, digital platforms, and virtual classrooms [45].

5.4   Fake News and Data Protection

The Ministry of Health created the channel "Health without fake news" to analyze viral news and determine whether they were true or false. Also, Brazil's Congress is pushing for legislation to stop the flood of disinformation. Platforms that do not comply would be subject to fines as large as 10% of their group revenues in Brazil the previous year. In 2020, the most-viewed YouTube channels concerning Covid-19 were the ones spreading fake news [42].

After analyzing the mini-cases and surveying the scientific literature, four main discourses related to digital transformation were drawn, namely: (1) Economic Development; (2) Sustainability; (3) Data Privacy & Citizenship; (4) Transparency & Participation. Digital technologies have the potential to impact Economic Development by increasing productive capacity, reducing social inequalities, redesigning government, or delivering public services. The mini-cases such as the Emergency Aid, provides evidence of such influence. Sustainability encompasses prosperity, social inclusion, environmentally oriented policies, inclusive good governance, and peace. While the positive cases showed how action provides sustainable outcomes, others such as the Health System monitoring, the education system, and fake news exacerbate the inequalities and the challenges to achieve human capacity through improvements in education and health care. Data Privacy and Citizenship aims to make the digital environment a safe and reliable place, conducive to services and consumption and in which citizens' rights are respected. The pandemic made visible the growing volume of commercial and financial online transactions and the provision of public services virtually, reducing the boundaries between online and offline. There have been important legislative improvements, however the rise of fake health news during the pandemic contributed to discrediting science and public health institutions. Finally, Transparency & Participation involve expanding channels for citizen collaboration in public policymaking to achieve online transparency, accountability, inclusion, and participation. The mini-cases showed how digital platforms should converge to enable the application of such principles effectively.

In sum, such categories are relevant as they offer a comprehensive diagnosis of the challenges to be faced, a vision of the future, and a set of strategic actions to monitor progress in achieving the social and economic goals. Table 3 reports the summary of the analyses performed.

Table 3. Summary of the mini-cases.

Mini-Cases	Actors	Technologies	Discourses	Outcomes
Emergency aid as a measure of social protection	Government Citizens	Mobile, Big Data Analytics, Artificial Intelligence, Cloud Computing	Economic Development, Transparency & Participation	Positive
Health system: monitoring the number of covid-19 cases and deaths	Government Media groups Civil society Citizens	Big Data Analytics, Artificial Intelligence, Cloud Computing, Smart Cities	Sustainability, Data Privacy & Citizenship, Transparency & Participation	Negative
The impact of covid-19 on education	Government Civil society Families Citizens	Mobile, Big Data Analytics, Cloud Computing, Smart Cities	Economic Development, Sustainability	Negative
Fake news and data protection	Government Private companies Media groups Citizens	Cloud Computing, Big Data Analytics, Mobile, Social Media	Sustainability, Data Privacy & Citizenship, Transparency & Participation	Unforeseen

6   Discussion and Conclusions

The Covid-19 pandemic has provoked unprecedented changes in society, health systems, economies, and governments worldwide. Social groups combined with technologies and discourses associated with each scenario provide a viewpoint in which such categories can be articulated to establish a theoretical relationship between the success and failure of each case. While the case of Emergency Aid showed how the technological measures adopted by the main social groups via important discourses impacted positively the lives of millions of Brazilians, the lack of articulation between government, media groups, and citizens, in the case of the Health System Monitoring, not only caused a political crisis but also resulted in a divide on how to manage and mitigate the pandemics. The same was observed in the case of the education system, where the lack of adequate technological infrastructure to support the professors, schools, and families in delivering courses online not only increased the extant digital divide but also will generate a long-lasting effect that surpasses the learning process and will have implications for the future of an entire generation. Besides, unforeseen outcomes were also identified such as fake news and data protection which show how digital platforms, transparency, and participation are fundamental in the aggregation and convergence of common interests from government, private companies, media groups, and citizens.

The contribution of this study is twofold. First, it contributes to academic research as no study investigated and categorized the impact of the digital transformation acceleration by analyzing mini-cases in the context of a global pandemic in order to unveil the role of actors, technologies, and discourses in the Brazilian context in the midst of a crisis. Second, from a public policy perspective, this study presents a set of reflections that can help policy makers to identify the positive, negative, and unforeseen consequences of a pandemic, which is a learning opportunity for them to be better prepared for future outbreaks. The study also presents some limitations which point toward avenues for future research. Firstly, the researchers draw reflexivity processes while conducting the data collection, and interpretation of the results. Thus, the study focused on the socially constructed reality of the subjects [48]. Such criteria imply the authors' reflections revealing their personal role and selection of the mini-cases and the actors represented in the study. Secondly, the study does not seek to find objective truth, but rather to understand which speeches about digital transformation emerged during the pandemic, and how the actors mobilized these speeches and technologies to socio-technical proportions and potential consequences at a society level. Finally, the study analyzed four mini-cases based on the extensive material produced during the research [47]. Future research could re-examine the assumptions that underlie the work, which can be handled through the selection of multiple longitudinal case studies providing an in-depth and unique research opportunity to understand an important phenomenon through the lens of real-life cases [48] in the context of a pandemic.

Venkatesh [46] argues that one of the virtues of theories and by association empirical work is often considered to be generalizability. However, Covid-19 reveals that some contexts can be unique to the point where generalizability becomes irrelevant. In this sense, the present study aimed to understand the impact of digital transformation during the Covid-19 pandemic to unveil potential challenges and opportunities in a post-Covid-19 world.

References

1. Castillo-Chavez, C., et al.: Beyond Ebola: lessons to mitigate future pandemics. Lancet Global Health **3**(7), e354–e355 (2015)
2. Rodrigues, F.K., Carpes, M.M., Raffagnato, G.C.: Preparação e resposta a desastres do Brasil na pandemia da COVID-19. Revista de Administração Pública. Rio de Janeiro **54**(4), 614–634 (2020)
3. Soto-Acosta, P.: COVID-19 pandemic: shifting digital transformation to a high-speed gear. Inf. Syst. Manage. **37**(4), 260–266 (2020)
4. Papagiannidis, S., Harris, J., Morton, D.: WHO led the digital transformation of your company? A reflection of IT related challenges during the pandemic. Int. J. Inf. Manage. **55**, 102166 (2020)
5. Sobral, F., Lagowska, U., Furtado, L.: Leadership under crisis: a research agenda for the post-COVID-19 era. Braz. Adm. Rev. **17**(2), e200062 (2020)
6. Kirk, C.P., Rifkin, L.S.: I'll trade you diamonds for toilet paper: consumer reacting, coping and adapting behaviors in the COVID-19 pandemic. J. Bus. Res. **117**, 124–131 (2020)
7. Sharma, A., Adhikary, A., Borah, S.B.: Covid-19's impact on supply chain decisions: strategic insights from NASDAQ 100 firms using Twitter data. J. Bus. Res. **117**, 443–449 (2020)
8. Fahey, R.A., Hino, A.: COVID-19, digital privacy, and the social limits on data-focused public health responses. Int. J. Inf. Manage. **55**, 102181 (2020)
9. Joia, L.A., Lorenzo, M.F.: Zoom in, zoom out: the impact of the covid-19 pandemic in the classroom. Sustainability **13**(5), 2531 (2021)
10. Avgerou, C.: Information systems in developing countries: a critical research review. J. Inf. Technol. **23**(3), 133–146 (2008)
11. Biryukova, O.V., Matiukhina, A.I.: ICT services trade in the BRICS countries: special and common features. J. Knowl. Econ. **10**(3), 1080–1097 (2018). https://doi.org/10.1007/s13132-017-0517-6
12. Avgerou, C., Ganzaroli, A., Poulymenakou, A., Reinhard, N.: Interpreting the trustworthiness of government mediated by information and communication technology: lessons from electronic voting in Brazil. Inf. Technol. Dev. **15**(2), 133–148 (2009)
13. Heeks, R.: Do information and communication technologies (ICTs) contribute to development? J. Int. Dev. **22**(5), 625–640 (2010)
14. Pozzebon, M., Diniz, E.H.: Theorizing ICT and society in the Brazilian context: a multilevel, pluralistic and remixable framework. Braz. Adm. Rev. **9**(3), 287–307 (2012)
15. Joia, L.A.: Developing Government-to-Government enterprises in Brazil: a heuristic model drawn from multiple case studies. Int. J. Inf. Manage. **24**, 147–166 (2004)
16. Diniz, E.H., Barbosa, A.F., Junqueira, A.R.B., Prado, O.: O governo eletrônico no Brasil: perspectiva histórica a partir de um modelo estruturado de análise. Revista De Administração Pública **43**(1), 23–48 (2009)
17. Joia, L.A., Teles, A.: Assessment of digital inclusion via the actor-network theory: the case of the Brazilian municipality of Piraí. Telematics Inform. **28**, 191–203 (2010)
18. Cunha, M.A., Pozzebon, M.: O uso das tecnologias da informação e comunicação para melhoria da participação na tomada de decisão pública. In: Proceedings of the Encontro Nacional da Associação Nacional de Pós-Graduação e Pesquisa em Administração, SP, Brasil, p. 33 (2009)
19. Ahmad, A.: Rising of social network websites in India. Int. J. Comput. Sci. Netw. Secur. **11**(2), 155–158 (2011)
20. We are Social. Digital 2020. https://datareportal.com/reports/digital-2020-brazil. Accessed Jan 2021

21. Webshoppers: Relatório de pesquisa da Câmara Brasileira de Comércio Eletrônico. https://drive.google.com/file/d/1GARLXu6gyuDJJ8vfBU2D73ubGZIYde8N/view. Accessed Jan 2021
22. OECD: Going Digital in Brazil. OECD Reviews of Digital Transformation, Paris (2020)
23. Avgerou, C.: Discourses on ICT and development. Inf. Technol. Int. Dev. **6**(3), 1–18 (2010). ISSN 1544-7529
24. Avgerou, C., Walsham, G. (eds.): Information Technology in Context: Studies from the Perspective of Developing Countries. Ashgate, London (2000)
25. Viale Pereira, G., et al.: South American expert roundtable: increasing adaptive governance capacity for coping with unintended side effects of DT. Sustainability **12**(2), 718 (2020)
26. Pettigrew, A.M.: Longitudinal field research on change: theory and practice. Organ. Sci. **1**(3), 267–292 (1990)
27. MacKenzie, D., Wajckman, J.: The Social Shaping of Technology. Open University Press, Philadelphia (1999)
28. Bijker, W.E., Law, J.: Shaping Technology/Building Society: Studies in Socio-Technical Change. MICT Press, Cambridge (1992)
29. Walsham, G.: Cross-cultural software production and use: a structurational analysis. MIS Q. **26**(4), 359–380 (2002)
30. Barrett, M., Walsham, G.: Electronic trading and work transformation in the London insurance market. Inf. Syst. Res. **10**(1), 1–21 (1999)
31. Orlikowski, W.J., Hofman, J.D.: An improvisational model for change management: the case of groupware technologies. Sloan Manag. Rev. **33**(2), 11–21 (1997)
32. Weick, K.: The collapse of sensemaking in organizations: the Mann Gulch disaster. Adm. Sci. Q. **38**(4), 268–282 (1993)
33. Silva, L.: Outsourcing as an improvisation: a case study in Latin America. Inf. Soc. **18**(2), 129–138 (2002)
34. Kardos, G., Smith, C.O.: On writing engineering cases. In: Proceedings of ASEE National Conference on Engineering Case Studies (1979)
35. Yazan, B.: Three approaches to case study methods in education: Yin, Merriam, and Stake. Qual. Rep. **20**(2), 134–152 (2015)
36. Cardoso, B.B.: The Implementation of Emergency Aid as an exceptional measure of social protection. Braz. J. Public Adm. **54**(4), 1052–1063 (2020)
37. CECAD: Consulta, Seleção e Extração de Informações do CadÚnico. https://aplicacoes.mds.gov.br/sagi/cecad20/painel03.php. Accessed Jan 2021
38. Barros, R.P., Carvalho, M., Mendonça, R.: Sobre as utilidades do Cadastro Único. Ipea, Rio de Janeiro (2009)
39. Croda, J., et al.: COVID-19 in Brazil: Advantages of a Socialized Unified Health System and Preparation to Contain Cases (2020)
40. Joia, L.A., Michelotto, F.: Universalists or utilitarianists? The social representation of COVID-19 pandemic in Brazil. Sustainability **12**(24), 10434 (2020)
41. UNICEF: Government digital services and children: pathways to digital transformation. Office of Global Insight and Policy United Nations University (2020)
42. Galhardi, C.P., Freire, N.P., Minayo, M.C.S., Fagundes, M.C.M.: Fact or Fake? An analysis of disinformation regarding the Covid-19 pandemic in Brazil. Ciênc. saúde coletiva **25**(suppl.2), 4201–4210 (2020). Cited 25 Feb 2021
43. Financial Times: Spread of fake news adds to Brazil's pandemic crisis. https://www.ft.com/content/ea62950e-89c0-4b8b-b458-05c90a55b81f. Accessed Jan 2021
44. World Bank: Social Protection Measures to overcome Covid-19. https://www.worldbank.org/en/news/opinion/2020/07/10/social-protection-measures-can-help-brazilian-families-overcome-Covid-19-economic-crisis. Accessed Jan 2021

45. Pinto, F.R.M.: COVID-19: A new crisis that reinforces inequality in higher education in Brazil. SciELO - Scientific Electronic Library Online (2020)
46. Venkatesh, V.: Impacts of COVID-19: a research agenda to support people in their fight. Int. J. Inf. Manage. **55,** 102197 (2021)
47. Myers, M.D.: Qualitative Research in Business & Management. Sage, London (2013)
48. Walsham, G.: Interpretive case studies in IS research: nature and method. Eur. J. Inf. Syst. **4**(2), 74–81 (1995)

How to Redesign Government Processes for Proactive Public Services?

Peter Kuhn[✉] , Matthias Buchinger, and Dian Balta

Fortiss GmbH, Research Institute of the Free State of Bavaria for Software-Intensive Systems,
Munich, Germany
pkuhn@fortiss.org

Abstract. Proactive government is a promising approach to user-friendly public services. By acting proactively instead of reacting, governments reduce the interaction effort of a public service for the user and, in doing so, increase its user-friendliness. However, implementing such proactive services in practice is challenging and requires the redesign of the according processes. For example, the data that currently is provided by the user, now has to be collected by someone else. The goal of this paper is to identify reoccurring challenges in the redesign of processes for proactive public services and to develop strategies to overcome them. We analyse business processes from nine public services and conduct ten expert interviews with practitioners. We synthesis the reoccurring challenges into three implementation dimensions and present three implementation strategies. The implementation dimensions inform the feasibility of proactive services in practice and the strategies can be used by practitioners to streamline their efforts to provide user-friendly public services.

Keywords: Proactive government · Proactive public services · Business processes

1 Introduction

In the course of digital transformation, governments aim at providing user-friendly services, i.e. public services that are not only digital but also have a high service quality [1]. To this end, concepts like "once-only", the "single digital gateway" and the "one-stop-shop" are pursued in various countries (e.g. [2]).

One approach to user-friendliness is proactive government. The approach aims at eliminating any effort for the user whatsoever, resulting in a "no-stop-shop" [3, 4]. In particular, a service from such a government is provided proactively to the user [5] and without any application or user-government interaction [6]. The approach has been implemented in practice, e.g. for child benefits in Austria [7], and declared a strategic goal of countries like estonia [4]. While the exact relation of non-interaction and service quality is yet to be understood in detail [8], proactive public services are arguably the next step for governments towards user-friendliness [9].

© IFIP International Federation for Information Processing 2021
Published by Springer Nature Switzerland AG 2021
H. J. Scholl et al. (Eds.): EGOV 2021, LNCS 12850, pp. 29–40, 2021.
https://doi.org/10.1007/978-3-030-84789-0_3

Although promising from a conceptional point of view and despite the successful examples from practice, the implementation of proactive services remains challenging [10]. Current public services often rely on the user's activity, e.g. to provide necessary data. When attempting to minimize those user efforts, the data that currently is provided by the user, has now to be collected by other entities. Consequently, scholars argue that proactive government requires a fundamental shift in the way government works [5] and a redesign of government processes [3].

Literature on proactive services has investigated the differences between reactive and proactive public services [5, 6, 9], and conceptualized the integration of data collection and storage in proactive governments [3]. However, according to our review of literature, there exist no guidelines on how to redesign government processes for proactive services in practice.

We address this gap by identifying the dimensions of reoccurring challenges in the redesign of processes for proactive public services and develop strategies to overcome them. To this end, we analyse process models of nine public services and conduct ten expert interviews. We synthesis three dimensions of those reoccurring challenges in the redesign of government processes for proactive public services. Namely, the service trigger, the data collection, and the process control. Based on that, we develop three strategies - internalize user activities, leverage other parties, and enable the user to outsource - to overcome these challenges. The strategies are applied to an exemplary public service to demonstrate their applicability.

The findings of this paper show that there are fundamentally different strategies to the implementation of proactive public services. We contribute to theory by informing the feasibility of proactive services in practice and provide practical guidance for organizations that want to offer proactive services.

The paper is organized as follows. After this introduction the existing literature on proactive government and business process redesign is summarized in Sect. 2. We then explain the methodology of the conducted research in Sect. 3 before we present the results in Sect. 4. The paper is concluded by a discussion of the results (Sect. 5) and final conclusions as well as an outlook (Sect. 6).

2   Theoretical Background

2.1   Proactive Government

The notion of proactivity in government is a current topic of research and is discussed from different perspectives and for different aspects [3, 5, 6, 9]. The proactive service provision by governments can be defined as delivering "a service to a citizen when a life event occurs, without the citizen having to request the service" [3]. A government that delivers proactive services is considered user-friendly and improving service quality, since it supplies a service to the user (user-centric) instead of just approving it (government-centric) [3]. Consequently, proactive services can be distinguished from non-proactive services.

In a continuous interpretation, proactivity of a service can be seen as inversely proportional to the interaction effort the has user to get the service [6]. In the spirit of this interpretation, truly proactive services are therefore non-interactive, i.e. do not require user-government interaction from user to government whatsoever [8]. In this context, a distinction between two-way and one-way interactions can be made [9]. Whereas a two-way interaction requires an effort from the user, a one-way interaction from the government to the user, e.g. the transfer of money, causes no effort for the user and, thus, can occur even in a strictly proactive service.

The implementation of proactive services has been studied from a conceptual perspective and on a government level. Numerous authors ([3, 5, 8, 11, 12]) describe general challenges and requirements from technical and organizational perspectives. For instance, in the stage model of Scholta et al. [3] proactive service delivery affects the storage and use of data inside government. Yet, examples from practice like in Estonia show, that data integration not automatically results in proactive services [11]. While legal regulations can hinder the implementation [13], process management and use of technology enables it [3, 5, 9].

2.2 Business Processes and Business Process Redesign

Business processes and the redesign of business process are a studied field in information systems and e-government literature (e.g. [14–16]). Business processes have a clearly defined starting and end point, in between which an input is transformed by the process into an output. The transformation can be split up into process steps [17].

Literature on the redesign of Business Processes includes Business Process Change (BPC), which has its origins in Business Process Reengineering and Total Quality Management [18] and can be defined as a fundamental rethinking and radical redesign of business processes [19]. The goal of BPC is an improvement in performance and is dependent on capabilities such as project management, change management, and IT to be successful [18].

Like in the private sector, in the public sector the modelling of processes supports the comprehension of structures and dependencies and, thus, can help to understand and analyse organisational challenges (e.g. [14, 20]).While there are many similarities to the private sector, research has identified unique characteristics of BPC implementation in the public sector [16]. Examples are strategic volatility and resource forecasting. However, also in the private sector, the redesign of processes can provide benefits [21].

3   Methodology

The paper follows the methodology of design science research [22] and analyses data from a literature review, nine public service process models and ten expert interviews. In order to determine the research gap, we conducted a literature review [23] and studied the theoretical foundations on proactive government and redesign of business processes in the public sector. For the literature on proactive services we used the work of Scholta et al. [3] as a starting point; for literature on the redesign of business processes the paper by Jurisch et al. [18]. We used the results to guide the analysis of the process models and structure the expert interviews.

According to our literature review there are no clear guidelines on how to redesign government processes for proactive services in practice yet. Based on this research gap, the goal of this paper is to design such guidelines. In order to achieve that goal we collected qualitative data from the analysis of process models from nine public services. Table 1 lists the analysed services, including their service category.

Table 1. Analyzed services.

Process ID	Public service	Service category
Process 1	Sponsorship for community services	Leisure activities
Process 2	Application for "yellow" gun ownership license	Leisure activities
Process 3	Application for "green" gun ownership license	Leisure activities
Process 4	Petition for a referendum	Leisure activities
Process 5	Visitor's tax (Tourism)	Business activities
Process 6	Proceedings of administrative fines	Law and order
Process 7	Federal grant for university studies	Education
Process 8	Formal obligation	Immigration
Process 9	Residence for work	Immigration

The process models are official modellings from the database FIM and were obtained from the so-called "FIMportal" website. The database is a project of the German government to standardize service descriptions, data schemas and process models [24]. The process models are notated in BPMN and conform to the legal regulations of the respective service. Following [8] we considered the processes through the lens of user-government interactions. I.e., we identified the interactions of each public service by selecting the BPMN arrows that cross the swim lane boundaries of the user and clustered them into interaction types. This analysis of the process models revealed 29 user-government interactions that distinguish the service from a proactive one. Based on the interaction types and by modelling proactive versions of the services, we identified three implementation dimensions for proactive services.

Based on the identified dimensions, we developed three strategies for the implementation of proactive public services with the help of 10 semi-structured expert interviews. The interviewed experts were selected for their knowledge in process and services design. Their selection also considered the different stakeholders in the implementation of new (digital) public services, i.e. IT service providers and consulting experts. We conducted the interviews from 26th June 2020 until 04th August 2020 and they lasted between 31 and 49 min. The interviews were recorded, transcribed and coded. Before coding the transcriptions were send to the expert for approval. Table 2 gives an overview over the interviewed experts and their positions.

Table 2. Conducted interviews.

Interviewee	Organisation	Position
Interviewee 1	Large municipality 1	Organization expert
Interviewee 2	Large municipality 1	Process expert
Interviewee 3	State owned IT service provider	Process expert
Interviewee 4	IT service provider	Digitalization expert
Interviewee 5	State ministry	Innovation and technology expert
Interviewee 6	Large municipality 2	Digitalization expert
Interviewee 7	State owned IT service provider	IT Systems expert
Interviewee 8	Large municipality 1	IT Systems expert
Interviewee 9	Medium municipality 1	Process expert
Interviewee 10	In-house consulting municipality 1	Strategy expert

4 Results

4.1 Reoccurring Implementation Challenges and Their Dimensions

A major user-government interaction in many public services is the application. For that reason, we describe the consequences of making a reactive public service application-free in order to illustrate the challenges in the implementation of proactive public services. In a reactive version the service, the provision is initiated by an application of the user. The application serves the purpose of triggering the service as well as providing data. This raises the question, how the service can be implemented such that the trigger and the data is not coming from the user. An example is the federal grant for university studies (Process 7) which currently requires the student to collect data about the parent's income but also about the current enrolment status and previous grants. Thus, the student has to orchestrate multiple public and private agencies to get the necessary data. Then, by applying, the student also triggers the service. In a proactive version of this service, government or another entity has to trigger the service and also organise the data collection. Given that the income data is sensitive, this extents to the question whether a central government entity should have access to all the data necessary.

Our analysis of nine process models from non-proactive services revealed 29 user-government interactions that have to be eliminated for a proactive version. Attempting to eliminate these interactions towards a proactive service creates various challenges including but not limited to the elimination of the application. While the challenges vary, the possible solutions to overcome them have similar properties. We synthesized those properties into three dimensions that reflect the central questions that have to be answered when implementing proactive service. The dimensions and their manifestations are summarized in Table 3.

Service Trigger. All nine investigated services include an application by the user. I.e., a user-government interaction to trigger the process. In a completely proactive version of the service, this trigger has to happen without the user. In the example of the federal grant

Table 3. Implementation dimensions.

Dimension	Central question	Manifestations
Service trigger	By whom is the service triggered?	User, other
Data collection	How is the data collected?	concentrated, distributed
Process control	Who is controlling the process across the involved entities?	User, other

for university, the service trigger could be triggered by the university which informs the responsible entity about new students. However, this depends on the knowledge of the university that the student is in need of a grant. The implementation of proactive public services, thus, has to consider which non-user entity has the necessary information to trigger the service.

Data Collection. In all investigated services data is supplied to the government by the user. I.e., the user serves a central data hub where the data collection is concentrated. Some data comes from the user directly, other data is collected by the user from other parties. In a proactive version of the service, this data has to be obtained without the user. In the case of the federal grant for university the data of the university can be requested by a government agency or be sent by the university automatically. The two options differ in the mode in which the data is collected: Either by a central player, e.g. the responsible government agency, in a concentrated effort. Or in a distributed way by decental entities. The former constitutes mostly two-way, the latter one-way interactions.

Process Control. Finally, in all but one investigated services the user is in contact with more than one party in order to get the service. The orchestration of these parties is a central user effort that goes beyond the collection of data. Not only needs the data be collected but also the order of these steps needs be in the right order. In a proactive version this control of the process is not exercised by the user anymore. In the example of federal grant for university, this role can be fulfilled by the responsible government entity but also by a third party like the university or a hired company. The implementation of proactive public services, thus, has to consider which entity controls the process.

4.2 Implementation Strategies

Based on the identified dimensions, we synthesised three strategies for the implementation of proactive public services in ten expert interviews. The strategies can be seen as distinct approaches for an agency to achieve user-friendliness via proactive public services and can be used as guidelines to redesign the respective processes. They are described from the perspective of the service providing agency. In order to contrast the differences, we proceeded the descriptions of the different strategies by a description of a reactive process.

The strategies can be visualized using the three dimensions presented in the previous section (Fig. 1). A strategy constitutes the movement in the three dimensional space of the cube into a certain sub-cube. While there is a potential fourth strategy in the back top right, this strategy was excluded by the experts for impracticability.

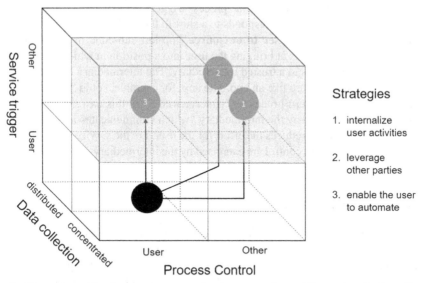

Fig. 1. Illustration of implementation strategies from proactive public services in three dimensional space using the dimensions presented above.

In reactive processes (bottom-left sub-cube in the front) the users serves as the trigger of the service, collects the data in a concentrated manner and controls the overall process. An exemplary user journey starts with the need for a service, which prompts the user to gather data, i.e. certificates from a third party. In this collection the user has to consider which data needs to be organized first and what are the dependencies between the parties that provide the data. The data is then forwarded by the user in form of an application to the responsible agency. Based on the application the service is finally provided by the service providing entity.

Strategy 1: Internalize user activities (top-right sub-cube in the front). Following this strategy the service providing entity aims at taking over all activities from the user and handles them itself. In this case the activities of the user are fulfilled by the government and, thus, reducing the effort for the user. "This has to happen within the public entity itself" (Interviewee 1), e.g. "initialized by some kind of event or data condition" (Interviewee 8). I.e,, the service is triggered, the data is collected and the process is controlled by the providing entity. In the visualisation this strategy corresponds to a shift to the right and up.

Strategy 2. Leverage other parties (top-right sub-cube in the back). The service providing entity aims at leveraging third parties in taking over activities from the user. A third party can be another public entity or a trusted organisation. In this case, the activities of the user will be taken over by the third party and, thus, reduce the effort for the user. The third party triggers a service by notifying the providing entity based on an event or an information state, initiating a "whole chain of data exchange" (Interviewee

2). Also the providing entity can organize third parties to provide data that is necessary for the service provision. Finally, a third party can also orchestrate different parts of the service, e.g. initiating the provision of certificates, potentially leading to "a process network [...] which makes sure that one process triggers another" (Interviewee 10). In the visualisation this strategy corresponds to a shift to the back-right and up.

Strategy 3: Enable the user to outsource (top-left sub-cube in the front). The service providing entity aims at bringing the user into a position in which he or she can outsource certain activities to a trusted intermediary. The intermediary can be a person, an organization or a software like an app. The app, for example, could "manage several applications [...] and govern processes" (Interviewee 7) In this case, the activities of the user will be taken over by the intermediary "which communicates in all directions" (Interviewee 7) and, thus, reduces the effort for the user. I.e. the service trigger, the data collection, and the process control are exercised by the intermediary. In the visualisation this strategy corresponds to a shift up.

4.3 Exemplary Application

In order to demonstrate the applicability of the presented strategies we applied them to a simplified version of the service "federal grant for university". In this version the income of the parents is not required. Consequently, only the service providing entity and the university are involved. For each strategy we modelled a resulting process model. For the sake of limited space, Table 4 provides simple schematic visualizations of the resulting processes, emphasising the major interactions of the process with arrows.

Table 4. Schematic visualizations of the implementation strategies for an exemplary service.

Currently, in the simplified, reactive version there are two two-way user-government interactions. The user first requests a enrolment certificate from university and then uses that certificate to apply for the grant from the agency. In both cases the user triggers the interactions and controls the process. The data is also collected by the user in a concentrated manner.

Pursuing strategy 1, the service providing agency redesigns the service such that all activities of the user are now conducted by itself. I.e. the agency has a two-way interaction with university to obtain the certificate. It then uses the certificate and provides the service to the user in a one-way interaction. Following this strategy, the service is triggered and the process is controlled by the agency. In addition, the agency also collects the data in a concentrated manner.

Pursuing strategy 2, the service providing agency redesigns the service such that the university can trigger the service by providing the enrolment certificate to the agency in a one-way interaction. The agency then uses the certificate in order to provide the service to the user in a one-way interaction. Following this strategy, the service trigger and the process control lies with lies with the university. The data collection is organized in a distributed manner, indicated by the one-way arrow.

Pursuing strategy 3, both, the service providing agency and the university, allow an intermediary to take over the activities of the user. This changes the data collection such that the intermediary instead of the user obtains the enrolment certificate in a two way interaction with the university. It then uses the certificate to apply for the grant from the agency – again in a two-way interaction. Finally, after receiving the service, the intermediary provides the service to the user in a one-way interaction. Following this strategy, the service trigger and the process control lie with the intermediary which is controlled by the user. Also, the data is collected by the intermediary in a concentrated manner.

5   Discussion

The findings of this paper show that there are fundamentally different strategies to the implementation of proactive public services. The responsible agency can take over activities from the user, but also leverage third parties or enable the user to outsource activities. Based on this insight, three remarks can be made.

First, the diversity of potential implementation strategies for proactive services is not yet reflected in theoretical conceptualizations. For example, in their investigation of differences in the conceptualization of reactive and the proactive "No-Stop" government, Scholta und Lindgren [9] stress that for the latter internet-based technology is "necessary for the government, not for the citizen" (page 6). However, outsourcing activities to an intermediary, as suggested by strategy 3, could be automated in a software-based user assistant. Thus, this approach to proactivity would use internet-technology. This is relevant for practice, since proactive government can, for instance, enable proactive services by providing application programmable interfaces (APIs), while taking over as an agency requires know how on internal process automation.

Second, proactive government does not necessarily mean a fundamental change in how government works. In the case of user outsourcing but also when leveraging third parties, the two-way interactions between the service providing agency and other parties remain the same in principle. There is only a change in the parties that the agency interacts with. Taken together this suggests that proactive services not necessarily require a proactive government. The shift from pull to push, as observed by Linders et al. [5], thus, represent only one option, and proactivity not necessarily requires a pull. This has also implications for the redesign of business processes in practice which might not need a fundamental redesign.

Third, proactive government does not necessarily mean data integration within government or government process control. Scholta et al. argue that for proactive services government departments need to "have access to their own data and the data of all other government departments" [3]. However, when leveraging third parties or letting the user outsource, the data collection can also be decentralized or lie with the user. A practical implication of this is, that privacy concerns may be avoided. Similarly, even for proactive services, the trigger of a service can be still under the control of the user. That adds another option to the government-based trigger that literature suggests [3].

6   Conclusion and Outlook

In this paper we present strategies for the implementation of proactive public services. The strategies are based on reoccurring challenges extracted from process models and are developed in expert interviews. The strategies address the challenges from different angles and provide guidelines for practice. We contribute to theory by informing the requirements of proactive services for implementation and provide practical guidance for organizations that want to offer proactive services.

The findings of this paper have limitations that restrain their general applicability and should be met with further research. The number of analysed processes and the interviewed experts are limited in their number and originate from one country only. The findings should be evaluated in other contexts and from more experts to validate their transferability. Also, the strategies are not necessarily equally suitable and advisable for usage in practice. For example, the potentially different effects on service quality have not been studied. Potentially the trust in a service is higher when the process control lies with the user. This should be considered when applying. Finally, the strategies remain abstract and do not specify concrete implementation steps. Further research should aim at operationalizing the strategies with methods and tools for practice.

Although limitations exist, we believe that our research is valuable to both theory and practice. In particular, we hope that the presented strategies support the implementation of proactive public services and increase user-friendliness in the public sector.

References

1. Jansen, A., Ølnes, S.: The nature of public e-services and their quality dimensions. Gov. Inf. Q. **33**, 647–657 (2016). https://doi.org/10.1016/j.giq.2016.08.005
2. European Council: Tallinn Ministerial Declaration on eGovernment. https://ec.europa.eu/cef digital/wiki/cefdigital/wiki/display/CEFDIGITAL/2017/10/12/Tallinn+Ministerial+Declar ation+on+eGovernment
3. Scholta, H., Mertens, W., Kowalkiewicz, M., Becker, J.: From one-stop shop to no-stop shop: an e-government stage model. Gov. Inf. Q. **36**, 11–26 (2019). https://doi.org/10.1016/j.giq. 2018.11.010
4. e-Estonia Briefing Centre: All Estonian public e-services to function "invisibly". https://e-est onia.com/all-estonian-public-e-services-to-function-invisibly/. Accessed 16 Mar 2020

5. Linders, D., Liao, C.Z.-P., Wang, C.-M.: Proactive e-Governance: flipping the service delivery model from pull to push in Taiwan. Gov. Inf. Q. **35**, 68–76 (2018). https://doi.org/10.1016/j. giq.2015.08.004
6. Brüggemeier, M.: Auf dem Weg zur No-Stop-Verwaltung. Verwaltung Manage. **16**, 93–101 (2010). https://doi.org/10.5771/0947-9856-2010-2-93
7. Bundeskanzleramt Österreich: Antragslose Familienbeihilfe bei Geburt eines Kindes: Frauen, Familien und Jugend im Bundeskanzleramt. https://www.frauen-familien-jugend. bka.gv.at/familie/finanzielle-unterstuetzungen/familienbeihilfe0/antrag-familienbeihilfe. html. Accessed 16 Feb 2021
8. Kuhn, P., Balta, D.: Service quality through government proactivity: the concept of non-interaction. In: Viale Pereira, G., et al. (eds.) EGOV 2020. LNCS, vol. 12219, pp. 82–95. Springer, Cham (2020). https://doi.org/10.1007/978-3-030-57599-1_7
9. Scholta, H., Lindgren, I.: The long and winding road of digital public services—one next step: proactivity. In: ICIS 2019 Proceedings (2019)
10. Kuhn, P., Balta, D., Krcmar, H.: Was sind Herausforderungen proaktiver Verwaltungsleistungen in Deutschland? In: Wirtschaftsinformatik 2020 Proceedings (2020)
11. Sirendi, R., Taveter, K.: Bringing service design thinking into the public sector to create proactive and user-friendly public services. In: Nah, F.-H.-H., Tan, C.-H. (eds.) HCIBGO 2016. LNCS, vol. 9752, pp. 221–230. Springer, Cham (2016). https://doi.org/10.1007/978-3-319-39399-5_21
12. Schuppan, T., Koehl, S.: One stop government: stalled vision or a matter of design? – empirical findings from social services in Germany. In: Hawaii International Conference on System Sciences 2017 (HICSS-50) (2017)
13. Vestues, K., Mikalsen, M., Monteiro, E.: Using digital platforms to promote a service-oriented logic in public sector organizations: a case study. Presented at the Hawaii International Conference on System Sciences (2021). https://doi.org/10.24251/HICSS.2021.269
14. Hughes, M.: Business Process Redesign in Implementing E-Governement in Ireland. Presented at the January 1 (2006). https://doi.org/10.4018/9781591407898.ch022
15. Niehaves, B., Plattfaut, R., Becker, J.: Business process management capabilities in local governments: a multi-method study. Gov. Inf. Q. **30**, 217–225 (2013). https://doi.org/10. 1016/j.giq.2013.03.002
16. Jurisch, M.C., Ikas, C., Wolf, P., Krcmar, H.: Key differences of private and public sector business process change. e-Service J. **9**, 3–27 (2013). https://doi.org/10.2979/eservicej.9.1.3
17. Krcmar, H. (ed.) Informationsmanagement, pp. 85–111. Springer, Heidelberg (2015). https:// doi.org/10.1007/978-3-662-45863-1_4
18. Christin Jurisch, M., Palka, W., Wolf, P., Krcmar, H.: Which capabilities matter for successful business process change? Bus. Process Manage. J. **20**, 47–67 (2014). https://doi.org/10.1108/ BPMJ-11-2012-0125
19. Hammer, M., Champy, J.: Reengineering the Corporation: A Manifesto for Business Revolution. HarperBusiness, New York (1993)
20. Olbrich, S., Simon, C.: Process Modelling towards e-Government–Visualisation and Semantic Modelling of Legal Regulations as Executable Process Sets (2008)
21. Kasemsap, K.: The roles of business process modeling and business process reengineering in E-government. In: Handbook of Research on Innovations in Information Retrieval, Analysis, and Management, pp. 401–430. IGI Global (2015). https://doi.org/10.4018/978-1-4666-8833-9.ch015
22. Hevner, A.R., March, S.T., Park, J., Ram, S.: Design science in information systems research. Manage. Inf. Syst. Q. **28**, 75 (2004)

23. Boell, S., Cecez-Kecmanovic, D.: A hermeneutic approach for conducting literature reviews and literature searches. Commun. Assoc. Inf. Syst. **34** (2014). https://doi.org/10.17705/1CAIS.03412

24. FITKO (Föderale IT-Kooperation): Föderales Informationsmanagement (FIM). https://fimportal.de/. Accessed 25 May 2021

Digital Services and Open Government

Understanding Actor Roles in Inter-organizational Digital Public Services

Stijn Wouters[1]([⊠]) [iD], Marijn Janssen[2] [iD], and Joep Crompvoets[1] [iD]

[1] KU Leuven, Leuven, Belgium
{Stijn.Wouters,Joep.Crompvoets}@kuleuven.be
[2] Delft University of Technology, Delft, The Netherlands
M.F.W.H.A.Janssen@tudelft.nl

Abstract. Different actor roles in inter-organizational digital public services are often neither understood nor acknowledged. This can result in challenges regarding the proper design and result in a lack of adoption of these services. In the literature, there exist various taxonomies outlining roles such as users, consumers or co-creators, although their value is limited. We define roles as the expectations regarding the actors and their responsibilities in the governance of a digital public service. The aim of this research is to better understand the various roles in inter-organizational digital service provisioning. This objective is achieved by examining existing classifications and using them to analyze the roles in three inter-organizational cases in Belgium. The multiple-case study reveals natural persons and legal entities often combine several roles. Public administrations have to collaborate to establish inter-organizational digital public services, but might be confronted with different perspectives regarding the end-user or other roles. This might lead to tensions and could have consequences regarding adoption. The results show that intermediary roles performed by non-public sector parties, such as mandate holders or private service providers, are lacking in existing classifications. A novel classification is proposed together with suggestions for the concept of roles, taking a comprehensive view on actor roles in the entire service delivery chain.

Keywords: Public service delivery · Actor roles · Inter-organizational services · E-government

1 Introduction

To foster digital government success, comprehending the roles that actors such as public legal entities and natural person assume in inter-organizational digital public services is key. An actor role (or role) can be defined as a "the responsibility for performing specific behavior, to which an actor can be assigned, or the part an actor plays in a particular action or event" [40, p. 60]. One actor typically can play multiple roles and roles can change over time. Through ICT's, traditional actor roles are changing [5, 22, 23, 42]. This evolution creates a challenge for governance. Clarity of roles – and the

© IFIP International Federation for Information Processing 2021
Published by Springer Nature Switzerland AG 2021
H. J. Scholl et al. (Eds.): EGOV 2021, LNCS 12850, pp. 43–58, 2021.
https://doi.org/10.1007/978-3-030-84789-0_4

underlying responsibilities – among collaborating public organizations has in this regard been put forward as an important characteristic for digital government succes [14, 28, 36]. Defining and assigning actor roles can contribute to alleviating governance challenges created by interdependencies between involved actors [18, 45]. This is especially the case for inter-organizational digital public services, that require a multitude of actors to collaborate in order to link building blocks that form integrated service chains through which various services can be delivered [45].

A research gap presents itself regarding the understanding of the roles actors assume in the initiation, design, implementation and evaluation of digital public services and the larger societal context [23, p. 433; 1, p. 254, 257, 265]. If there is no mutual understanding of each other's perception regarding the roles they assume, then this can impact the effectiveness of collaboration [14]. It also potentially leads to resistance among involved actors in its governance [1]. Unclarity about roles can further adversely affect the design of a service and impact a service's adoption and its eventual use [9, 20].

Concepts such as users, citizens and consumers are used interchangeably and are often given different meanings. As Garcia [13, p. 335] points out, predefining an actor as a citizen already gives them certain rights and responsibilities, while a user is a more neutral term that is also applicable to non-citizen service users. At the same time, research has noted the different roles actors assume in the context of digital public service provision [e.g. 34]. Examples include roles such as a customer when comparing utility providers on a public website or applying for subsidies, or as client when obtaining e-health services. Differences in actor roles influence how public services are developed and what part actors are expected to play or themselves expect to take part in in the design and delivery processes [23, 35].

Prior research has investigated roles in specific settings (e.g. web service orchestration [16], open-source software (OSS) using agile methods [31] or Open Government Data [12]). A general examination and classification or taxonomy of roles in inter-organizational digital public services remains lacking. This research aims to understand the different roles actors can assume in the context of inter-organizational digital public service delivery. Our research question is the following: *what are different actor roles in inter-organizational digital public service delivery?*

We achieve our research aim through an exploratory multiple-case study involving three cases that entail inter-organizational digital services with respect to natural persons, private legal entities and public legal entities in the region of Flanders, Belgium. These cases show an intricate and complex landscape of actor roles, with three distinct but interacting types of actor roles.

The structure of the paper comprises 6 parts. Following the introduction, Sect. 2 looks at the research background on actor roles, including classifications. Section 3 details the multiple-case study approach. Section 4 provides a description of the cases and their characteristics. Section 5 presents the analysis of actor roles in the three cases. Section 6 contains the conclusion.

2   Research Background

To get an extensive overview on actors roles, in this section we review actor roles and classifications in the e-Government, Information Systems (IS) and Public Administration literature.

2.1   Actor Roles in the e-Government Literature

In the e-Government literature, various taxonomies, typologies and categorizations have been developed or proposed for end-user roles [e.g., 9, 34, 37, 43]. Based on a systematic review of stakeholder roles in the e-Government literature and building on Mintzberg [27], Rowley [34], distinguishes between 4 different roles that natural persons can adopt: customer, client, subject (of the state) (or legal subject) and citizen (which includes the role of voter and participator in the political process). For each of those roles, the auhor describes the nature of the roles, which can be viewed as the perspective that public administrations take towards them.

Stakeholder theory is often used to describe and analyze users and their roles [e.g., 2, 34, 35]. However, where stakeholder theory looks at power relations between stakeholders [35], the scope in this paper is limited to identifying the different actor roles.

In their apprehension of citizens in the context of digital public services, Distel and Lindgren [9, p. 126] (1) delineate how a natural person is conceptualized, i.e. what perspective is taken towards them, (2) posit natural persons' interaction in the policy, design and service process, and (3) examine the general position of natural persons in service governance. The authors [9, p. 125] found that in the literature there are often neither clear definitions of actor roles, nor explicit perceptions public service providers have with respect to the roles of an actor. They argue that the e-Government literature often treats users of digital public services as homogenous and public administrations only view them from a single perspective or role at the same time. In an era that considers user-centric digital public services a principal requirement of service delivery [8], understanding the expectations and perspective of users by public service providers becomes crucial in the design phase [20].

While most authors look at external end-users, Ashaye and Irani [1] examine the role of public servant. The authors also point to changing roles actors have during the phases of a digital public service's life cycle. They note how these roles have to be critically understood to ensure proper coordination in the different phases and that execution capacity can be undermined by excluding actors.

Furthermore, the e-Government literature mainly focusses on natural persons, while private legal entities (e.g., businesses, companies, self-employed workers or associations) have been studied to a much lesser extent [21, 34]. In addition to the roles of consumer [21], subject [3], or co-producer [33], private legal entities can also assume the role as (co-)producers of goods and services [45].

Besides the role of and perspective on (end-)users, the e-Government literature also has looked at the role of intermediaries in the service chain [17, 24, 38, 39]. An intermediary can be "any public or private organization facilitating the coordination between public service providers and their users" [17, p. 38]. The role of intermediary has been closely examined in multichannel management (MCM) public service delivery [17]. In this context intermediaries can serve as an additional service delivery channel and provide value to end-users, by for example aggregating various digital public services and delivering them based on the specific requirements of user groups. Bharosa et al. [3, p. 153, 394] found that intermediaries can perform various functions and take advantage of economies of scale and specialization. Millard [25, pp. 53–54] stresses the existence of actors who use digital public services on behalf of others. The author's research points to one out of four users of digital public services acting on behalf of someone else (not including accessing digital public services as part of someone's job).

In addition to perspective roles and service chain roles, coordination roles have also often brought forward to alleviate dependencies and potential governance challenges between the involved actors [8]. Roles in this respect include (inter alia) these of initiator, enabler, developer and facilitator [16].

2.2 Actor Roles in the IS Literature

In the IS literature, roles are well established with respect to more technical roles of IS or IS managers, such as process engineer or enterprise architect [7], but less regarding inter-organizational digital services. In the context of processes Earl [10] conceptualizes actors as "people who perform a certain task based on a role" [10 in 3, p. 149]. In an enterprise architecture approach, roles comprise the responsibilities undertaken in different process steps and a role model describing the roles in a service can be seen as complementary to a service's process and data models [7]. Poniszewska-Marańda [30] highlights the complexity of identifying and organizing roles, especially in settings where roles are not very formalized, such as within organizations. Regarding access control models, the author represents roles as a set of functions, i.e., actions actors can undertake to achieve the responsibilities they are assigned to. Roles can be shared among various actors and actors can take up multiples roles simultaneously or over time, for example over the different phases of a service's design, development and implementation. Millerand and Baker [26] have shown how the traditional distinction between developer and user gets fuzzy as collaboration practices transform traditional interaction patterns.

2.3 Actor Roles in the Public Administration Literature

In the public administration literature, actor roles can be viewed from the three main governance paradigms. In the Classical Public Bureaucracy [42], which is centered around the hierarchy-type, the role of natural persons is one as a passive subject or client [29]. Under the role of subject, actors have a duty to the State, such as paying taxes, or, as client, they receive a professional service such as education or healthcare [27]. By contrast, under New Public Management (NPM), which is dominated by the market-type, natural persons came to be seen as customers [29]. This perspective added the importance of user satisfaction to the development and delivery of public services, but not necessarily through active involvement. It changed the characterization of public administrations to that of a service provider, rather than a legal authority [42].

Partly reacting to NPM, New Public Governance (NPG) is grounded in the network-type perspective and provides another narrative on actors' roles. This narrative is based around public service provision through inter-organizational networks [33]. (Groups of) Natural persons (and private legal entities) can be seen as co-creators of public services (or as partners [22]). They actively collaborate in multiple or all phases of a service's life cycle as an equal partner to public administrations [5, 42]. We follow Torfing, Sørensen and Røiseland [42], who perceive a co-producer as natural persons or private legal entities who jointly produce and deliver a public service. Consequently, co-producer is a type of intermediary role and part of the service chain that delivers a public service to an end-user. A role as co-producer can also be combined with that of a user.

A number of authors in Public Administration have also presented typologies of actors roles. For example, Mintzberg [27] distinguishes between customers, clients, subjects, and citizens, each with differing views on what external actors and public administrations expect from each other regarding public service delivery. Whereas, Thomas [41] differentiates customers, citizens and partners.

Leadership roles are often emphasized as a key enabler in inter-organizational policy-making and networks [19]. For example, Emerson and Nabatchi [11] distinguish between several leadership roles that coordinators or participants can assume, such as initiator, champion, convener, facilitator, mediator, expert and public decision-maker.

While the importance of roles is often emphasized in the e-Government, IS and Public Administration literature and individual actor roles are frequently put forward as a key enabler to realize inter-organizational digital public services, existing typologies or conceptualizations are rather limited. They mostly focus on either the conceptualization of natural persons as end-users, or accentuate coordination and leadership from the side of public administrations. Moreover, the literature largely concentrates on digital public services for natural persons, rather than private legal entities or public legal entities. These gaps make it relevant to add to the literature on actor roles, more particularly by shedding more light on actor roles in inter-organizational digital public services.

From the classifications we found in the different literature domains, three dimensions seem to be apparent with respect to actor roles: (1) roles that consist of the perspective through which public service providers view service recipients, such as citizens, co-creators or consumers (2) roles with respect to the delivery of a service, and (3) roles with respect to the steering of public services across its phases. We will use these three groups of actor roles as a basis to look at the actor roles in practice. Based on both literature and practice we will generate a taxonomy for actor roles that also explores the interaction between different roles.

3   Research Approach

To understand actor roles in inter-organizational digital public services, we take on an interpretive and pragmatic epistemology [15]. Thus, our own understanding of actor roles in inter-organizational digital public services is based on the meanings of the involved actors [44]. The interpretivist approach is instrumental to the pragmatic approach. This means that we aim to understand the phenomenon to improve the governance of inter-organizational digital public services in practice. In line with the research question ("what" question) and the scarcity of empirical work, we opted for a qualitative exploratory case study design. Qualitative research is suited to look into the patterns of behavior and explore a research problem, rather than making predictions or providing explanations [4]. A case study approach allows investigating phenomena in their real-life context [32, 46]. We intend to gather a more comprehensive view on possible roles and their interactions through a multiple-case study design than a single case study could provide [46]. Three cases have been selected: Digital Invoicing, eBox and My Citizen Profile. All three are cases deal with digital public service users in the region of Flanders, Belgium and include public administrations on the federal, Flemish (regional) level and/or local level. These cases were selected based on 3 criteria. (1) The cases had to entail various public administrations, preferably over several levels of government. (2) Those public administrations had to collaborate to achieve inter-organizational public service provisioning. (3) The end-users across the cases needed to be diverse (i.e., including natural persons, private and/or public legal entities).

We rely on an iteration between deductive and inductive research approaches to develop the taxonomy, alternating between insights from literature and the cases. A taxonomy can be viewed as a "collection of controlled dictionary definitions that are organized into a hierarchical structure" [3, p. 106]. Following Rowley [34, p. 55], deriving this taxonomy relied on an iterative process, where we compared roles in the cases to those in the literature and grouped similar roles in the literature.

The data collection focused on documents and semi-structured in-depth interviews as data sources. For each case, we first held interviews with the main actors in each case to apprehend the situation. These interviews provided us with (internal) policy documents, white papers and technical specifications; gave access to collaboration spaces, and (partly) provided contacts for the interviews (based on the purposive sampling strategy). These documents, together with laws, regulations, and publicly available policy documents allowed us to inquire into the involved actors and the formal roles.

The interviews relied on a purposive sampling strategy intended to examine the roles of the public sector administrations/organizations involved in the coordination. Interviews were conducted with product, project and program managers, civil servants at the operational level, management level and legal experts. We followed a broad interview guide through which we inquired into the context of the service, the service chain(s), several governance aspects and the involved actors and roles. We asked (1) who the actors were, (2) what roles they assumed, (3) who the users were, (4) if they had an approach towards their end-users, (5) how they were involved in the service delivery chain, and (6) how they were involved in the steering of the case. For each organization, we also inquired how they viewed their own role(s). Through the interviews, we could clarify roles found in the documents, identify additional roles and inquire into the shifting (of) roles as the service chain evolved over multiple phases over time. In total, 63 interviews (respectively 22, 19 and 27, whereas five interviews covered 2 cases) of 60–120 min took place. The interviews were either face-to-face or through video-conference tools (for the interviews in 2020). We opted for a broad sampling to gather many perspectives from the involved actors. The time horizon is cross-sectional and data collection took place in two rounds. First from January 2017 to January 2019 for the first round of Digital Invoicing (8 interviews with the lead government organizations that cover the context, coordination, governance and general actors roles). Based on the results, we opted for an additional round of data collection that more clearly focused on actor roles. From April to October 2020 we undertook the second round of Digital Invoicing (with the lead government organizations and other public service providers), including the data collection for the other two cases.

4 Cases

In this section, we describe the background of each of the cases (Digital Invoicing, eBox and My Citizen Profile). Table 1 provides the characteristics of the cases, following the taxonomy presented in the next section. Each of the cases are in their expansion phase, following their initiation, piloting and operationalization [45].

Digital Invoicing relates to the realization of a common digital public service to send invoices and related business documents from private legal entities to procuring federal, Flemish and local public legal entities [45]. Private legal entities either send invoice-related documents through (1) a central portal, or (2) through an interoperable network infrastructure where Belgian public legal entities, natural persons and private legal entities can be reached through invoice/procurement services providers (i.e., Access Points). The financial systems of public legal entities (either their own or the one of a Shared Service Centre) integrate through their service integrator (who manages a central data exchange infrastructure).

The **eBox** is an ecosystem of secure digital mailboxes. Natural persons can access all messages from public legal entities through public human interface providers or combine the stream of public correspondence with private messages (such as from banks or utility companies) through private interfaces offered by private human interface providers. Private legal entities either have access through a single public portal that interfaces with different public websites, a direct Machine-to-Machine (M2M) integration, or an indirect M2M integration through a private data service provider that offers mail processing services. Public legal entities deliver messages to a document provider that stores and exposes the messages. Delivery to document providers is direct or indirect. The latter is through a document service provider (who can also send messages through mail) and/or service integrator of the respective administrative level.

My Citizen Profile is a digital communication channel that can be integrated into the headers of regional and local portals and websites in the region of Flanders. It (1) allows a single sign-on for portals, websites and services and implements the no-wrong-door principle, (2) contains profile information that can be used when initiating digital public services, (3) shows information public administrations have regarding natural persons, and (4) as a horizontal digital counter consists of a collection of common portal functionalities regarding (inter alia) notifications and status updates. Public legal entities directly integrate to the different components from their business processes or do this indirectly through the central Flemish data exchange platform depending on the information flow and component.

Table 1. Case characteristics

Roles	Actors	Digital Invoicing	eBox	My Citizen Profile
Perspective roles	Natural persons	/	Citizen, Client, Customer, Subject	Citizen, Client, Customer, Subject
	Private legal entities	Customer, Producer	Customer, Client Subject, Producer	/
	Public legal entities	Co-creator Client Leader	Co-creator Client Leader	Client Co-creator → Client Participant Leader
Service chain roles: Users	Natural persons	No	Yes	Yes
	Private legal entities	Yes (incl. legal representatives)	Yes (incl. legal representatives)	No
	Public legal entities	Yes (federal, Flemish, local)	Yes (federal, Flemish, local)	No
Service chain roles: Intermediaries	Natural persons	/	Mandate holders	Mandate holders
	Private legal entities	Access Points Accountants	Private service intermediaries	/
	Public legal entities	Digital invoicing provider Service integrator Shared Service Center	Service integrators Document provider Document service provider	Regional service integrator
Coordination roles	Natural persons	/	Passive user feedback	Passive user feedback
	Private legal entities	Passive/active user feedback	Passive user feedback	/
	Public legal entities	Lead organizations Public service providers	Lead organizations Public service intermediaries	Lead organization Public service providers

5 Analysis

This section presents the taxonomy of actor roles in inter-organizational digital public service delivery that we could ascertain from the literature and the cases. Moreover, the cases explicate the types of roles and their interaction. For the **actor roles** (Fig. 1) we follow the three groups of roles we identified in the literature: (1) perspective roles, (2) service chain roles, and (3) coordination roles. The specialization type of relationship (white arrow) shows how a role can be specialized into more concrete roles. Several roles in the taxonomy with regard to natural person roles also have the association type of relationship (simple black lign). A role as co-creator can for example be closely related to the one of citizen when it entails natural persons, but a role of co-creator can also apply to legal entities. Roles can also serve other roles (black arrow).

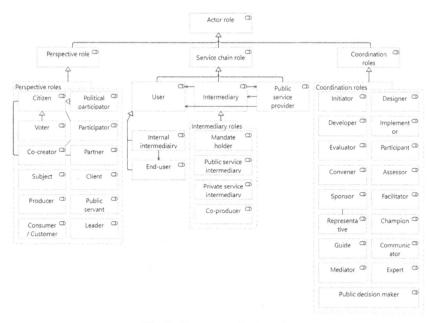

Fig. 1. Taxonomy of actor roles

Perspective roles entail the viewpoint that coordinators take towards the actors involved in the digital public service, but also how those actors view their own role in the delivery and steering of the service provisioning. In line with [34, 37], we found multiple combinations of perspective roles within each case. Building on the classifications in the literature [9, 34], these roles cannot just be associated with actors who are external end-users, but with all actors who take on service chain roles and/or coordination roles. The existing classifications seem to be too limited for the variation we observed. In the Digital Invoicing Case, private legal entities who send invoices for procured goods and service they delivered are not just viewed as a customer of the offered inter-organizational digital public services. At the same time, they are also viewed as producers who deliver goods and services for private and public legal entities alike.

"A company should be able to submit its bid digitally. It has to be much more streamlined, and European. This philosophy, namely e-procurement is a part of the government, but is just as much a part of the business world. Both aspects must be treated equally." Project manager, Digital Invoicing Case.

This much broader perspective was one of the reasons not to just develop a government website to send invoices to public legal entities, but also to integrate the inter-organizational digital public invoicing service within a broader platform.

The cases affirm how perspective roles can change over the service's life cycle [1, 5, 30, 42]. In the case of My Citizen Profile the roles shifted as the phases of the service progressed from piloting to operationalization/expansion and as new public service providers (who integrate particular services or deliver particular citizen data to the application) became involved. The perspective roles associated with public service providers changed from both clients of the central intermediary and co-creators to a more passive role as participant. According to some of the interviewees, this seems to be related to on the one hand the growing number of public service providers, increasing from ten to almost a hundred.

> "I think, with 100 people, can you decide something by consensus? No. I think we can all agree on that. [...] A partner council with 100 clients, that makes little sense. A feedback group with a number of people who are interested in contributing makes sense. It is correct, the bigger you become, the more important that account management and client management will become." Director ICT Division, My Citizen Profile Case.

On the other hand, there are constraints to deliver a shared infrastructure that is flexible to include legacies and can cope with the capabilities of the involved public service providers [45]. At the same time, some participants involved in the initiation and development saw a much narrower role for themselves, rather as pure clients for who the application was merely an extra communication channel or who were only interested in one or some of the building blocks of My Citizen Profile. Hence, role perspectives also might be dependent on the perspective actors have of themselves.

> "Actually, we mainly cooperated on the status updates. [...] We have also attended quite a number of meetings, steering groups and so on. But we mainly focused on how we can exchange status updates as efficiently as possible." Product manager, My Citizen Profile Case.

Service chain roles refer to the responsibilities and expected actions of all actors within the service delivery network [3]. Building on the literature [17], we identified three main roles: (i) the user, (ii) the intermediary, and (iii) the public service provider. In an inter-organizational digital public service setting, multiple public service providers and one or more intermediaries can link up various service chains to deliver (a) common type(s) of service(s) to users. A clear relationship exists between these three roles, i.e. a service provider creates value, which is carried to the intermediary, who adds value by integrating multiple service chains to give the user full access through one channel of their choice [3]. In the My Citizen Profile Case, there is no associated portal or website that directly delivers the information and services to users. Rather, the public service intermediary who manages the building block integrates the services in the portals and websites of the public service providers.

While individual users themselves are often portrayed as homogenous, we could differentiate between two types of users: end-users and internal intermediaries. For the G2B eBox services this pertained to the legal representative of a private legal entity who manages the eBox for the entire entity and who routes the individual messages to the actual individual end-user. The same holds true for public legal entities regarding the B2G and C2G eBox services, where messages have to be routed to case handlers.

From the three cases, we found that multiple combinations between these three roles are likely. The eBox ecosystem serves natural persons, private legal entities, as well as public legal entities. Perceived as clients by the intermediaries/coordinators, public legal entities can take both the public service provider and user roles. As the former, they use one of the many central services offered by the intermediaries. As the latter, they use the same interface as the private legal entities to get access to replies from natural persons and private legal entities. Multiple public legal entities, who are public service intermediaries for other public entities, also take on a public service provider role.

The cases also demonstrate the variety of intermediaries [39] and key position they have, both inside and outside public administrations. Public service intermediaries not only developed the main building blocks, but also aligned and standardized processes and data in our cases. Other public service intermediaries managed other building blocks, such as data exchange platforms, that were already part of the larger digital government infrastructures, so public services could be integrated. As the integrated public services progressed through their life cycles, the roles of intermediaries often changed, reflecting the needs and challenges within the larger internal and external service context. For example, in the Digital Invoicing case, private service intermediaries were only actively engaged in the development of the service chain infrastructure after the perspective regarding the users had changed (supra). As the eBox case proceeded from the operationalization to the expansion phase, the central public service intermediary at the regional level opted to combine two intermediary roles to deal with dependencies further down the chain.

A final intermediary role that we observed is that of mandate holder. In the My Citizen Profile Case, this refers to natural persons such as parents, guardians or custodians, who need access to information and public services on behalf of someone else. According to Millard [25, p. 53], a quarter of e-government usage is by somedoby acting on behalf of someone else. Developing an infrastructure supporting mandate holders and internal intermediaries is an important requirement for success. With different systems, different semantics and mandates often service-specific, this proved a significant challenge for governance.

"The part about roles and mandate management, we notice that's a very difficult story. You actually have because they include that generically. A mandate or a particular role can be very diverse for different applications. And the more generic that they build it, the less fine-grained it sometimes is for your own application, because you notice that the need is still slightly different. So on that front we are waiting to see how that the vision of mandates, certain roles, its management can be further developed and that we can build on that." Project leader, My Citizen Profile Case.

Coordination roles, as a third group of actors roles, comprise responsibilities about the steering of the inter-organizational digital public service's design and accomplish the strategic and operational goals set up by policy-makers. In line with earlier research, coordination roles were crucial towards establishing and maintaining adequate service levels, promoting the service to new groups of users and public service providers, and interacting with the political level [e.g., 11]. Differences in the perspective roles public service providers have regarding their own role and others have of their own role can lead to the identification of tensions on how the inter-organizational digital public service should operate [14]. This was prevalent in the eBox Case, where some public legal entities only halfheartedly integrated with the service and joined in the coordination.

"The battle has been won by eBox you might say, because we only send notifications via eBox." Project manager, eBox Case.

Our findings affirm [9] that roles in inter-organizational service provisioning are more diverse than previous studies that focus on specific aspects of digital public services, such as the interaction with the external users. Users can exist on both ends of a service chain. In the eBox Case, public legal entities are end-users of the inter-organizational service when receiving reply messages, while natural persons and private legal entities are end-users when they get messages from public legal entities.

Roles can be composed of different roles, be part of other roles and can be allocated to or performed by multiple partners [16]. In the three cases, the coordination roles were linked to the public service intermediaries. Though, this is possibly due to the selection of the cases and is a limitation with respect to the research findings. For all three groups of actor roles, role definitions, role combinations and role relationships changed or shifted as the inter-organizational services changed from one phase to another and reacted with the internal and external service context.

6   Conclusion

In digital public services, natural persons, private legal entities and public legal entities interact with each other based on various roles. These roles can be interrelated and change over time. Understanding roles is a critical element in the design and adoption of public services. Based on a multiple-case study approach, a taxonomy of roles was presented. Building on the types of roles in the literature, the cases show that actor roles are quite diverse and interact with one another. We identified three types of roles: (1) perspective roles that describe how public administrations view the recipients and delineate how those actors view themselves (10 roles were found). (2) Service delivery chain roles relate to the activities of actors that take part in the actual delivery of the digital public service from public service providers (over intermediaries) to users (3 main roles). (3) Coordination roles pertain to the responsibilities regarding the overall governance of the inter-organizational digital public service over its life cycle from initiation, development, operationalization, expansion, adaptation and evaluation (17 roles). While many roles were present in each case, not all roles occurred at the same time. This especially pertains to the perspective roles. We recommend to use the role taxonomy for understanding interorganizational services delivery and also use the taxonomy as the basis for designing and stakeholder analyses.

Our research results into several suggestions for the concept of roles. First, we recommend to distinguish between actors and their expected behavior. Second, classifications are often limited to natural persons instead of private legal entities and public legal entities. This can help to understand their adoption of digital public services and point to whether enablers and barriers of e-government adoption are shared between different actor groups. Third, users themselves are not a homogenous group. From the cases, we could differentiate between internal intermediaries and end-users. Fourth, the research shows that private service intermediaries can play an important role in delivering digital public services to the intended external end-users. The role of mandate holders seems vital to expand service adoption to a large number of groups in society who are not typical digital public service users. Fifth, actor roles come in multiple forms and often several roles are shared or combined. This combination can also change over time. Hence, it is not possible to have a hierarchical relationship between the three groups of actor roles, with the exception of the perspective role of leader.

The research presented in this exploratory study has limitations that affect its generalizability. First, its results are limited to the Flemish/Belgian e-government context, the type of inter-organizational digital public service delivery, the specific roles (not) encountered in the cases, and the governance that is characterized by central digital public organizations who act as the main coordinators. Second, to map the roles of external users, we relied on the document and questions asked to actors within public administrations. Third, exploratory research has a broad scope and cannot fully apprehend all different actor roles in inter-organizational digital public service delivery.

The research presented in this paper could thus be relevant for similar inter-organizational digital public services to incrementally add roles and examine the relationships between the perspective roles, service chain roles and decision making roles. Future research could look into inter-organizational digital public services that involve coproduction and co-creation in the service delivery and decision making processes, and examine possible role conflicts for users who as recipients and potential decision makers are conceptualized by public service providers from different perspectives.

Implications for practice include a further understanding of the governance challenges with respect to the approach to the user that collaborating public administrations delineate. Viewing users from different perspectives can help to identify tensions in the development and the operationalization of an inter-organizational digital public service. In line with earlier research [14, 18, 28, 36], our cases confirm that a clear division of roles and responsibilities seems a principal enabler for inter-organizational collaboration and integrated digital public service delivery. Understanding the perspective through which users, intermediaries and public service providers view each other might also contribute to better deal with governance challenges related to stakeholder and expectations management. Giving more attention to the role of mandate holders might be taken into consideration as a potential strategy to advance goals with respect to inclusion.

Acknowledgements. This research was made possible through funding of the Policy Research Centre on Governance Innovation in Flanders, Belgium. The authors would like to thank Maxim Chantillon (KU Leuven) for providing valuable feedback and suggestions.

References

1. Ashaye, O.R., Irani, Z.: The role of stakeholders in the effective use of e-government resources in public services. Int. J. Inf. Manag. **49**, 253–270 (2019)
2. Axelsson, K., Melin, U., Lindgren, I.: Public e-services for agency efficiency and citizen benefit – findings from a stakeholder centered analysis. Gov. Inf. Q. **30**(1), 10–22 (2013). https://doi.org/10.1016/j.giq.2012.08.002
3. Bharosa, N., van Wijk, R., de Winne, N., Janssen, M. (eds.) Challenging the Chain: Governing the Automated Exchange and Processing of Business Information. IOS Press, Delft (2015). https://doi.org/10.3233/978-1-61499-497-8-i
4. Bhattacherjee, A.: Social Science Research: Principles, Methods, and Practices. Global Text Project, Tampa (2012)
5. Bovaird, T.: Beyond engagement and participation: user and community coproduction of public services. Public Adm. Rev. **67**(5), 846–860 (2007). https://doi.org/10.1111/j.1540-6210.2007.00773.x
6. Brandsen, T., Honingh, M.: Definitions of co-production and co-creation. In: Brandsen, T., et al. (eds.) Co-Production and Co-creation: Engaging Citizens in Public Service, pp. 9–17. Routledge, New York (2018)
7. Birkmeier, D., et al.: The role of services in governmental enterprise architectures: the case of the german federal government. In: Saha, P. (ed.) Enterprise Architecture for Connected E-Government: Practices and Innovations, pp. 262–287. IGI Global, Hersey (2012). https://doi.org/10.4018/978-1-4666-1824-4.ch011
8. Chen, Y.-C., Hu, L.-T., Tseng, K.-C., Juang, W.-J., Chang, C.-K.: Cross-boundary e-government systems: determinants of performance. Gov. Inf. Q. **36**(3), 449–459 (2019). https://doi.org/10.1016/j.giq.2019.02.001
9. Distel, B., Lindgren, I.: Who are the users of digital public services? In: Panagiotopoulos, P., et al. (eds.) ePart 2019. LNCS, vol. 11686, pp. 117–129. Springer, Cham (2019). https://doi.org/10.1007/978-3-030-27397-2_10
10. Earl, M.J.: The new and old of business process redesign. J. Strat. Inf. Syst. **3**(1), 5–22 (1994). https://doi.org/10.1016/0963-8687(94)90003-5
11. Emerson, K., Nabatchi, T.: Collaborative Governance Regimes. Georgetown University Press, Washington, DC (2015)
12. Ferretti, G., et al.: Orchestrated co-creation of high-quality open data within large groups. In: Lindgren, I., et al. (eds.) EGOV 2019. LNCS, vol. 11685, pp. 168–179. Springer, Cham (2019). https://doi.org/10.1007/978-3-030-27325-5_13
13. Garcia, L.M.: User centric E-government: the modernization of national migration institute in the Southern Mexican border. In: Scholl, H.J., et al. (eds.) EGOV 2016. LNCS, vol. 9820, pp. 328–335. Springer, Cham (2016). https://doi.org/10.3233/978-1-61499-670-5-328
14. Gil-Garcia, J.R., Guler, A., Pardo, T.A., Burke, G.B.: Characterizing the importance of clarity of roles and responsibilities in government inter-organizational collaboration and information sharing initiatives. Gov. Inf. Q. **36**(4), 101393 (2019). https://doi.org/10.1016/j.giq.2019.101393
15. Goldkuhl, G.: Pragmatism vs interpretivism in qualitative information systems research. Eur. J. Inf. Syst. **21**(2), 135–146 (2012). https://doi.org/10.1057/ejis.2011.54
16. Janssen, M., Gortmaker, J., Wagenaar, R.W.: Web service orchestration in public administration: challenges, roles, and growth stages. Inf. Syst. Manag. **23**(2), 44–55 (2006). https://doi.org/10.1201/1078.10580530/45925.23.2.20060301/92673.6
17. Janssen, M., Klievink, B.: The role of intermediaries in multi-channel service delivery strategies. Int J. Electr. Gov. Res. **5**(3), 36–46 (2009). https://doi.org/10.4018/jegr.2009070103

18. Klievink, B., Janssen, M.: Coordinating e-government service delivery. In: Chun, S.A., et al. (eds.) Proceedings of the 11th Annual International Conference on Digital Government Research, pp. 209–216. Digital Government Society, Puebla (2010)
19. Klijn, E.-H.: Networks and inter-organizational management: challenging, steering, evaluation and the role of public actors in public management. In: Ferlie, E., et al. (eds.) The Oxford Handbook of Public Management, pp. 257–282. Oxford University Press, Oxford (2005)
20. Kotamraju, N.P., van der Geest, T.M.: The tension between user-centred design and e-government services. Behav. Inf. Tech. **31**(3), 261–273 (2012). https://doi.org/10.1080/014 4929X.2011.563797
21. Lee, J., Kim, H.J., Ahn, M.J.: The willingness of e-Government service adoption by business users: the role of offline service quality and trust in technology. Gov. Inf. Q. **28**(2), 222–230 (2011). https://doi.org/10.1016/j.giq.2010.07.007
22. Linders, D.: From e-government to we-government: defining a typology for citizen coproduction in the age of social media. Gov. Inf. Q. **29**(4), 446–454 (2012). https://doi.org/10.1016/j.giq.2012.06.003
23. Lindgren, I., Madsen, C.Ø., Hofmann, S., Melin, U.: Close encounters of the digital kind: a research agenda for the digitalization of public services. Gov. Inf. Q. **36**(3), 427–436 (2019). https://doi.org/10.1016/j.giq.2019.03.002
24. Löbel, S., Paulowitsch, B., Schuppan, B.: Intermediaries in the public sector and the role of information technology. Inf. Polity **21**(4), 335–346 (2016). https://doi.org/10.3233/IP-160387
25. Millard, J.: User attitudes to E-government citizen services in Europe. Int. J. of Elec. Gov. Res. **2**(2), 49–58 (2006)
26. Millerand, F., Baker, K.S.: Who are the users? Who are the developers? Webs of users and developers in the development process of a technical standard. Inf. Syst. J. **20**(2), 137–161 (2010). https://doi.org/10.1111/j.1365-2575.2009.00338.x
27. Mintzberg, H.: Managing government, governing management. Harvard Bus. Rev. **74**(3), 75–83 (1996)
28. Pardo, T.A., Burke, B., Gil-Garcia, J.R., Guler, A.: Clarity of roles and responsibilities in government cross-boundary information sharing initiatives: identifying the determinants. In: Lavin, L. (ed.) Proceedings of 5th International Conference on e-Government, pp. 148–155. Curran Associates, Redhook (2009)
29. Pestoff, V.: Co-production and third sector social services in Europe: some concepts and evidence. Int. J. Vol. Nonprofit Org. **23**(4), 1102–1118 (2012). https://doi.org/10.1007/s11 266-012-9308-7
30. Poniszewska-Marańda, A.: Modeling and design of role engineering in development of access control for dynamic information systems. Bull. Pol. Acad. Sci. Tech. Sci. **61**(3), 569–579 (2013). https://doi.org/10.2478/bpasts-2013-0058
31. Robles, G., Gamalielsson, J., Lundell, B.: Setting up government 3.0 solutions based on open source software: the case of X-road. In: Lindgren, I., et al. (eds.) EGOV 2019. LNCS, vol. 11685, pp. 69–81. Springer, Cham (2019). https://doi.org/10.1007/978-3-030-27325-5_6
32. Robson, C.: Real World Research. Blackwell, Oxford (2002)
33. Rodriguez Müller, A.P., Steen, T.: Behind the scenes of coproduction of smart mobility: evidence from a public values' perspective. In: Lindgren, I., et al. (eds.) EGOV 2019. LNCS, vol. 11685, pp. 338–352. Springer, Cham (2019). https://doi.org/10.1007/978-3-030-27325-5_26
34. Rowley, J.: e-government stakeholders - who are they and what do they want? Int. J. Inf. Manag. **31**(1), 53–62 (2011)
35. Sæbø, Ø., Flak, F.K., Sein, M.J.: Understanding the dynamics in e-Participation initiatives: looking through the genre and stakeholder lenses. Gov. Inf. Q. **28**(3), 416–425 (2011). https://doi.org/10.1016/j.giq.2010.10.005

36. Sayogo, D.S., Gil-Garcia, J.R., Cronemberger, F.: Determinants of clarity of roles and responsibilities in interagency information integration and sharing (IIS). In: Scholl, H.J., et al. (eds.) EGOV 2016. LNCS, vol. 9820, pp. 126–134. Springer, Cham (2016). https://doi.org/10.1007/978-3-319-44421-5_10
37. Scott, M., DeLone, W.H., Golden, W.: Measuring eGovernment success: a public value approach. Eur. J. Inf. Syst. 25(3), 187–208 (2016). https://doi.org/10.1057/ejis.2015.11
38. Sharma, R., Mishra, R.: Investigating the role of intermediaries in adoption of public access outlets for delivery of e-government services in developing countries: an empirical study. Gov. Inf. Q. 34(4), 658–679 (2017). https://doi.org/10.1016/j.giq.2017.10.001
39. Sorrentino, M., Niehaves, B.: Intermediaries in E-inclusion: a literature review. In: Sprague, R.H., Jr., (ed.) Proceedings of the 46th Hawaii International Conference on System Sciences (HICSS), pp. 1–10. IEEE, Honolulu (2010). https://doi.org/10.1109/HICSS.2010.239
40. The Open Group: ArchiMate 3.1 Specification. Van Haren Publishing, Zaltbommel (2019)
41. Thomas, J.C.: Citizen, customer, partner. Rethinking the place of the public in public management. Public Adm. Rev. 73(6), 786–796 (2013)
42. Torfing; J., Sørensen, E., Røiseland, A.: Transforming the public sector into an arena for co-creation: barriers, drivers, benefits, and ways forward. Admin. Soc. 51(5) 795–825 (2019). https://doi.org/10.1177/0095399716680057
43. van Duivenboden, H.: Citizen participation in public administration: the impact of citizen oriented public services on government and citizens. In: Khosrowpour, M. (ed.) Practicing E-government A Global Perspective, pp. 415–445. Idea Group, Hershey (2005). https://doi.org/10.4018/978-1-59140-637-2
44. Walsham, G.: Interpretive case studies in IS research: nature and method. Eur. J. Inf. Syst. 4(2), 74–81 (1995). https://doi.org/10.1057/ejis.1995.9
45. Wouters, S., Janssen, M., Crompvoets, J.: Governance challenges of inter-organizational digital public services provisioning: a case study on digital invoicing services in Belgium. In: Viale Pereira, G., et al. (eds.) EGOV 2020. LNCS, vol. 12219, pp. 223–235. Springer, Cham (2020). https://doi.org/10.1007/978-3-030-57599-1_17
46. Yin, R.K.: Case Study Research: Design and Methods. Sage, Thousand Oaks (2018)

Perceived and Actual Lock-in Effects Amongst Swedish Public Sector Organisations When Using a SaaS Solution

Björn Lundell[1]([✉]), Jonas Gamalielsson[1], Andrew Katz[1,2], and Mathias Lindroth[3]

[1] University of Skövde, Skövde, Sweden
{bjorn.lundell,jonas.gamalielsson}@his.se
[2] Moorcrofts LLP, Marlow, UK
andrew.katz@moorcrofts.com
[3] ACF Legal Intl. AB, Malmö, Sweden
mathias.lindroth@acflegal.org

Abstract. When a public sector organisation (PSO) uses a software as a service (SaaS) solution from a global provider this imposes risks for different types of lock-in effects. In turn, use of such solutions by PSOs may prevent full control of digital assets that need to be created, processed, maintained, and archived for use and reuse over long life-cycles. This paper addresses perceived and actual lock-in effects related to use of SaaS solutions in the public sector. We review perceptions of lock-in amongst government agencies and investigate how 46 PSOs have addressed challenges related to obtaining licences and an effective exit plan related to use of the Microsoft Office 365 SaaS solution. Through a review of responses to a survey conducted by the Swedish Government Offices we find significant misconceptions concerning lock-in effects. We find that every one of the 46 PSOs investigated neither obtained necessary licences nor established an effective exit strategy to allow the PSO to independently access, process and maintain digital assets processed by the SaaS solution after decommissioning. We present recommendations for any PSO considering use of a SaaS solution.

1 Introduction

On 26 September 2019 the Swedish Government issued a directive which commissioned an investigation relating to secure and cost-effective IT operations for the Swedish public sector [32]. On 15 January 2021 the Swedish Government Offices presented a report from that investigation which "focus[es] on the conditions for the outsourcing of IT operations by government agencies, municipalities and regions" [37]. The report shows extensive use of SaaS (Software as a Service) solutions amongst governmental agencies and reports that 95% of the agencies "use some form of Software as a Service" [37]. The overarching goal of this study is to investigate and explain critical aspects of how perceived and actual lock-in effects in the Swedish public sector impact on a public sector organisation's ability to conduct lawful and cost-effective IT operations through use of a SaaS solution from a global provider.

© The Author(s) 2021
H. J. Scholl et al. (Eds.): EGOV 2021, LNCS 12850, pp. 59–72, 2021.
https://doi.org/10.1007/978-3-030-84789-0_5

The European Commission has highlighted the importance to the EU of "technological sovereignty" [8] and there are initiatives for addressing digital and data sovereignty [14]. Many individuals, organisations, and member states in the EU are concerned over exposure and an increasing dependency on global providers of cloud-based SaaS solutions [8, 12, 14, 22, 23, 28, 30, 37]. For example, as stated by Hon et al. [17]: *"A major lock-in concern is risk of dependence (or over-dependence) on one provider's, often proprietary, service. If the service is terminated for whatever reason, users wanted to recover all their data and metadata in formats that are easily accessible, readable, and importable into other applications, whether running internally or in another provider's cloud."* Further, a study of a widely deployed SaaS solution from a global provider: Microsoft (Office 365, the Microsoft Office 365-solution, hereinafter referred to as 'O365') shows that the customer is required to acquire patent licences for the ITU-T H.265 standard and findings show that the 33 investigated public sector organisations (PSOs) have failed to obtain all necessary patent licences *"which would allow for use of the adopted SaaS solution"* [22].

Extensive investigations of a large number of projects undertaken by many different PSOs recognise that adoption and use of SaaS solutions provided by global providers typically involves dealing with complex and incomplete contracts which expose organisations to a range of different lock-in effects [21–23]. For example, a study which investigated 33 PSOs that have adopted and use O365 found that "none of the organisations had investigated whether digital assets created and maintained in the SaaS solution can be exported in open file formats and open standards to allow use and reuse after exit" [22]. Further, the same study found that no PSO "has obtained all licences from third parties as detailed in the contract terms for" the specific SaaS solution [22]. In addition, findings also show that none of the investigated PSOs "have presented any analysis which addresses how to obtain all licences they require when, and after, the adopted SaaS solution is used" [22]. It should be noted that such an exit-strategy requires the use of software and its associated licences as well as (potentially) licences covering file formats used when exporting files.

This study investigates the *following research questions*:

RQ1: How do public sector organisations that use commercial SaaS solutions perceive lock-in effects?
RQ2: How are public sector organisations that use commercial SaaS solutions actually locked-in?

The paper presents three principal contributions. First, we identify perceptions of lock-in amongst the Swedish Government, the Swedish Government Offices, and Swedish PSOs through a review of a directive [32] and a report which investigated IT operations for the Swedish public sector [37]. Specifically, we identify perceptions of lock-in amongst governmental agencies through a critical review of survey results in order to report on how the investigation has addressed its directive related to analysis of lock-in effects (Sect. 4). Second, for addressing the second research question we investigate use of a widely deployed SaaS solution (O365) amongst 46 PSOs with a focus on licences and the risks of lock-in effects, and report on actions taken by organisations before use with a review of availability of licenses for lawful use and strategies that would allow for a sustainable exit (Sect. 5). Hence, the present investigation of actual lock-in related to use of O365 extends previous research which also investigated use of O365 amongst 33 other PSOs [22]. Third, we present five key questions which any organisation needs to analyse and answer in the affirmative before (and during the entire life-cycle for when) a SaaS solution from a global provider is used (Sect. 6).

2   On Lock-in Effects and SaaS Solutions

Interoperability amongst heterogeneous ICT solutions is essential for long-term maintenance of digital assets and the success of effective eGovernment solutions. Faithful implementations of open ICT standards and open file formats promote software interoperability and avoid lock-in effects, which are essential prerequisites for cost-effective eGovernment solutions. Research shows that lock-in effects can impose many different types of technical, legal, economic and societal challenges for PSOs [1–3, 5–7, 9, 10, 15, 18, 19, 23, 25]. For example, challenges related to use of cloud and SaaS solutions from global providers have been elaborated as follows [14]: *"**Lock-in effects** emerge between customers and providers of cloud services if the switchover to an alternative provider of solutions or services is made more difficult, or indeed impossible, by switchover costs and barriers. The barriers to a switchover can be of a technical-functional kind (dependence on the specific features of certain providers); they can arise from contractual agreements (e.g. license models and penalty costs), but also result from a high, customer-specific degree of personalisation, from familiarisation effects, or from the sheer data volume that is to be migrated."*

The public sector has seen significant deployment of SaaS solutions over the past few years. For example, in August 2019 it was reported that, in Sweden, all large municipalities and about half of all municipalities of any size used O365 [30]. Further, recent research indicates that use of O365 amongst all 290 Swedish municipalities may be even more widespread, in light of the observation that 97% (29 of 30) of the municipalities that were randomly selected for a study used the solution [22].

For several decades, PSOs have considered standardisation and utilisation of standards as a strategy for avoiding problematic lock-in effects [16] and studies have recognised the importance of open source software projects for implementation of standards [2]. However, research shows that it may be impossible to clarify conditions and obtain all patent licences for standard essential patents (and all necessary rights) for use of the O365 solution [21]. In fact, use of specific formal standards that are provided on FRAND-terms may inhibit implementation in software projects [20, 21]. Such conditions may significantly inhibit an effective exit-strategy for a PSO that wishes to abandon use of a specific SaaS solution.

The importance of an exit strategy has been stressed by various policy recommendations [11, 23, 38]. For example, the UK Government has stated that exit costs from an IT solution used by a government authority must be associated with the initial investment: *"As part of examining the total cost of ownership of a government IT solution, the costs of exit for a component should be estimated at the start of implementation. As unlocking costs are identified, these must be associated with the incumbent supplier/system and not be associated with cost of new IT projects."* [38] Further, to promote software interoperability and avoid lock-in effects, the UK Government highlights the importance of open standards when formulating an exit strategy: *"In preparation for any technical refresh projects, or in exceptional circumstances, where extensions to IT contracts or to legacy solutions have been agreed, government bodies must formulate a pragmatic exit management strategy. These must describe publicly the existing standards used together with the transition to open standards and compulsory open standards."* [38].

Policy initiatives in several countries have recognised the importance of open standards and open file formats in order to avoid lock-in effects into specific platforms and solutions [20, 26, 27, 31, 38]. To avoid lock-in effects, it is important that an adopted SaaS solution is able to export digital assets in open standards and open file formats [21, 27].

3 Research Approach

We investigated *perceived lock-in effects* amongst PSOs as follows (RQ1). First, through a review of how lock-in effects have been considered by the Swedish Government as presented in its directive for an investigation of secure and cost-effective IT operations for the Swedish public sector [32], we establish a contemporary national policy goal for public administration related to lock-in effects. Second, through a critical review of the report [37], we establish how the investigation undertaken by the Swedish Government Offices has fulfilled their task (as detailed in the directive [32]). Third, through a review of responses from Swedish PSOs (in this case, governmental agencies) to a questionnaire and an analysis of how the report presents perceived lock-in effects, we consider the extent to which the report [37] reflects responses to the questionnaire by PSOs and considers fulfilment of the directive related to policy goals concerning planned investigation of how PSOs are able to address lock-in effects as presented in the directive [32].

We investigated *actual lock-in effects* amongst PSOs (RQ2) by drawing from a previously conducted literature review which identified four essential factors that impact on a PSO's ability to lawfully use a SaaS solution from a global provider [22]. This study considers two of those four factors, namely *availability of all necessary licences* and *availability of an effective exit strategy*, that impact on a PSO's ability to lawfully use the O365 solution whilst maintaining control of their digital assets, both during and after use of O365. First, we selected 46 PSOs that use O365 (based on indications of use presented in public sources) for investigation of the two factors. The selected PSOs comprised 13 PSOs under the government, 8 regional PSOs, and 25 local authorities (municipalities). None of these 46 PSOs were investigated in the previous study [22] covering O365-using PSOs. Second, we reviewed the *availability of all necessary licences* based on documentation we requested from each PSO. We analysed the contract terms and licences provided as part of that documentation with a view to considering whether each PSO had obtained all licences necessary for using O365 (as detailed in the applicable O365 contract terms) and also whether manipulation, import and export of digital assets was possible independently of the O365 solution. Third, we reviewed the *availability of an effective exit strategy* based on an analysis of the documentation we requested from each PSO. In particular, we considered whether the exit strategy included provision for continued maintenance and re-use of digital assets should the PSO cease to use the O365 solution.

4   Observations on Perceived Lock-In Amongst Public Sector Organisations

The importance of obtaining all necessary licences for lawful and effective data processing of digital assets has been recognised in different contexts [21, 22, 38]. Related to a national eGovernance initiative, the Swedish Government has stressed the importance of open standards for avoiding dependence on specific platforms and solutions [31]. We find that the first report from the national eGov initiative recognised the importance of using open standards for avoiding lock-in [36]. Further, on 31 October 2018 we find that eSam (a subsequent Swedish national initiative) presented a checklist for PSOs related to use of cloud and SaaS solutions which stresses the importance of availability of a plan for exit [11].

The recent Swedish government directive recognises lock-in effects as an important factor which needs to be considered when analysing cost-effective IT operations and emphasises that a task for the investigation is to review the ability amongst PSOs to identify risks for lock-in effects [32]. Specifically, the directive states that the investigator shall survey PSOs' ability to identify risks for lock-in effects [32].

The survey is based on a questionnaire to *"government agencies, case studies of five agencies and a workshop attended by representatives of 16 agencies"* [37]. On 17 March 2020 the Swedish Government Offices sent the questionnaire (containing 31 questions) to 180 Swedish government agencies[1] (see Appendix 3 [37]) with a request for responses to the questionnaire no later than 31 March 2020. Amongst the respondents, 158 government agencies in total responded to (at least some) questions in the questionnaire [37].

The report includes results from the survey conducted amongst governmental agencies which show that "lock-in effects" are major obstacles preventing "cost effective IT operation" [37]. Specifically, the report presents findings from the survey as follows [37]: *"The greatest obstacles to secure IT operations are deficient information classification and a lack of expertise in IT and security, as well as of procurement expertise. Lack of expertise is seen as a risk factor for secure IT operations among both small and large agencies. The greatest obstacles to cost-effective IT operations are high security requirements and various types of lock-in effects, as well as shortages of expertise."*

We find that 52 government agencies provided a response to the questionnaire with comments related to *vendor lock-in or other lock-in effects* which is included as one (of a total of six) potential factors (in question 27 of the questionnaire) that may prevent cost-effective IT operations. Further, we find that 83 government agencies provided a response with comments related to *other* as another potential factor (in question 27) and that several of these comments also indicate perceived lock-in effects amongst respondents. In addition, we find that 88 government agencies provided additional comments (of which some government agencies highlighted challenges related to lock-in) in their response to a question about *other* issues that a respondent wanted to add or clarify as part of their response (question 31 of the questionnaire).

---

[1] The report states that the survey is based on a questionnaire to 200 government agencies [37]. However, on 24 March 2020 it was clarified (by a representative from the Swedish Government Offices) that the survey was sent to 180 government agencies.

Further, we note that amongst government agencies which provided a response to *other* (in question 31), several of these agencies did not provide a response related to the factor *vendor lock-in or other lock-in effects*. This, in turn, shows that any thorough analysis of perceived lock-in effects amongst respondents needs to consider, at least, all responses and comments related to *vendor lock-in or other lock-in effects* and *other* issues (related to question 27) and also other issues (related to question 31). However, we find that the report fails to present such a thorough analysis, and several critical aspects of lock-in which have been raised and highlighted by respondents in responses to the questionnaire have been ignored by the investigation.

The report [37] states (in Figure 4.4) that 21% of the government agencies express that *vendor lock-in or other lock-in effects* prevent cost-effective IT operations. However, from analysis of responses to the questionnaire we find that this is misleading. In fact, we find that the proportion of government agencies which in their responses have expressed that *vendor lock-in or other lock-in effects* prevent their cost-effective IT operations is much higher.

Based on a dialogue with representatives for the investigation we have received information[2] which stresses that 33% of the government agencies express that *vendor lock-in or other lock-in effects* prevent cost-effective IT operations. However, from analysis of responses we find that this number is also misleading (since responses related to lock-in effects have been reported under others and also that this proportion is based on the total number of government agencies (i.e. 158) which responded to some questions). Hence, since only 52 government agencies responded (and of which more than 80% report lock-in effects) we find the report is misleading concerning the proportion of agencies that have experienced lock-in effects.

Many government agencies state in their respective response to the questionnaire that they experience different types of lock-in effects which prevent cost-effective IT operations for their own agency. Several respondents experience vendor lock-in and express concern over dependence of specific global suppliers that prevent cost-effective IT operations. For example, amongst responses we observe government agencies which express dependence on a global supplier of a SaaS solution (e.g. responses mention dependence on Microsoft for O365) and others which express dependence on Swedish suppliers (e.g. Statens Servicecenter, Ladok, and Försäkringskassan). We also observe concern over problematic dependencies between software and hardware which imply problematic dependencies on specific suppliers. Further, some respondents express concern over *contract lock-in* and yet other over *competence lock-in* related to use of external suppliers (cloud and SaaS solutions). Some respondents raise legacy issues with already procured licences as inhibitors which cause lock-in. In addition, *format lock-in* is also mentioned amongst respondents as a concern which prevents cost effective IT operations, and mention that they try to use open standards to mitigate such lock-in. One governmental agency also highlights legal issues related to format lock-in as a serious risk which prevents longevity of digital assets. This, in turn, inhibits cost-effective IT operations.

---

[2] For example, on 3 February 2021 a representative for the investigation explained that analysis of responses to the questionnaire (which reports 21%) is based on consideration of all six factors under question 27 which includes several factors that are unrelated to lock-in.

Amongst responses we observe government agencies which express positive experiences from their use of SaaS solutions from global suppliers (e.g. several mention Microsoft 365). Further, one respondent raises concern over risks that government agencies become dependent on solutions from three specific global providers (Amazon, Google, and Microsoft), whilst at the same time highlighting that it may be unrealistic for organisations to develop alternatives without international collaboration.

Respondents express different views concerning whether SaaS solutions are cost-effective. For example, as expressed by one respondent: *"We currently have cost-effective IT operations which fulfil the needs for our organisation. To only use SaaS solutions or to outsource IT operations in a traditional sense cannot be motivated from a cost nor a functionality perspective."* On the contrary, another respondent (representing a small governmental agency) expresses that the internal policy is to avoid using a SaaS solution from a global provider for legal reasons, even though such solutions may be more cost-effective.

Several respondents express concern related to legal issues and we find that the report only addresses a few of these legal issues which may impact on IT operations. Further, responses to the questionnaire, observations from case studies of the five selected government agencies, and the workshop (attended by representatives of 16 agencies) highlight challenges under different jurisdictions for any PSO that uses (or plans to use) cloud and SaaS solutions from global providers. For example, we find that the report does not address several critical technical and legal issues related to lock-in and use of a widely deployed SaaS solution (specifically, O365): copyright, patents, archiving, laws related to governance of digital assets, and national laws (in Sweden and other countries) which may impact on data processing when PSOs use O365 (e.g. the Swedish Säkerhetsskyddslagen and the Chinese NIL [24]). Reports from the questionnaire and the case studies [37] show that O365 is used in a number of government agencies. However, critical licensing issues, lock-in challenges, and several legal challenges identified in responses to the questionnaire and the five case studies are not addressed in the report [37]. In addition, we find that the report lacks a comprehensive coverage of several other legal issues and regulations which impact on widely used SaaS solutions from global providers, especially in light of the observation that many SaaS solutions use subprocessors for data processing in several different countries [22].

Further, the directive highlights that public procurement impacts on lock-in effects [22]. However, we find that the report from the investigation fails to analyse important strategies for addressing lock-in effects, including experiences from other countries (despite that a goal for the investigation is to review experiences from the UK). This includes published strategies for addressing exit costs which have been presented by eSam [11], adopted in the UK [38] and recommended in a report from commissioned research published by the Swedish competition authority [23].

5 Observations on Actual Lock-in Amongst Public Sector Organisations

Concerning availability of all licences necessary for the use of digital assets created and processed by O365 we find that no PSO has obtained all third party licences as detailed in the contract terms for the O365 solution. Specifically, the contract terms state: *"Customer must obtain its own patent license(s) from any third party H.265/HEVC patent pools or rights holders before using Azure Media Services to encode or decode H.265/HEVC media."* [29] Hence, since the O365 licence explicitly does not provide such licences, the customer must obtain its own licences from any third party rights holders related to the ITU-T H.265 standard.

Based on the information that has been provided during the study, we find that it is unclear if it will be possible to obtain all necessary rights from all third party rights holders for the ITU-T H.265 standard which the PSOs are bound by when using the O365 solution. Further, this standard is normatively referenced (via other standards) in the ISO/IEC 29500 standard (OfficeOpen XML). Observations from the study showed no indication to suggest that any of the 46 PSOs have obtained (or even considered the need to obtain) such licences. Consequently, under the assumption that the ISO/IEC 29500 standard is faithfully implemented by the O365 solution it follows that digital assets exported from the O365 solution (and stored locally as '.docx' files) may impinge on patents that have been declared as standard essential for the ISO/IEC 29500 standard (and including all its normative references) in the ISO and ITU-T patent databases (and also on patents which may be standard essential patents (SEPs) even if those have not been declared in any of these patent databases).

Concerning availability of an exit strategy which allows for reuse of digital assets we find that no PSO has access to an effective exit strategy that can be implemented after exit from the O365 solution at short notice. We find that any effective exit strategy must cover a PSO's continuing ability to make it possible to read and write files exported from the O365 solution. This will require software and associated licences which cover those formats. It is clear that no PSO has sought to obtain licences for SEPs potentially impinging on the file format referenced in the Online Services Terms for the O365 solution. Hence, it follows that no PSO has considered all costs (i.e. costs including potential fees covering all applicable licences) related to their ability to create and maintain their digital assets during (and after) use of the O365 solution.

Further, we find that all PSOs have been unable to export files in the PDF/A-1 format from the O365 solution. The PDF/A-1 format is an open file format [27] which is suitable for long-term maintenance of digital assets and required by Riksarkivet for archiving [34, 35]. Hence, it follows that all PSOs that use the O365 solution fail to fulfil requirements for archiving expressed by Riksarkivet. In addition, any effective exit strategy needs to consider how to address exit costs at time for the initial investment, for example, as detailed in the UK policy [38]. However, we note that none of the 46 respondents have adopted a strategy for how to address exit costs as part of the initial investment (i.e. at the time for when the PSO procured the O365 solution). Hence, hidden costs (at time for the initial investment) are ignored by all respondents. Finally, in response to requests during data collection we find that some PSOs are able to provide files in the closed file format standard PDF/A-3 and other PSOs in other closed file formats (e.g. PDF 1.5) which are not even recognised as international standards. In general, we find significant unawareness amongst PSOs of the need to obtain licences that would prevent format lock-in.

6 Analysis

Our study shows that the Swedish Government, the Swedish Government Offices, and Swedish Government Authorities each have significantly diverging views on the importance of analysing and addressing lock-in challenges related to the investigation of cost-effective IT operations for the Swedish public sector.

Concerning *perceived lock-in effects*, our analysis shows a number of misconceptions related to importance of addressing technical, legal, and societal implications of different types of lock-in effects amongst key stakeholders which, in turn, have significant impact on prerequisites for cost-effective IT operations. We specifically elaborate three critical misconceptions.

First, in acknowledging that the directive [32] states that the investigation shall analyse risks related to lock-in effects, we find that the directive indicates problematic misconceptions concerning the opportunities provided by effective public procurement (with reference to the national procurement strategy, see [33]). Specifically, we find that underlying assumptions in the directive convey problematic misconceptions concerning regulations and current practice for public procurement in the IT domain. For example, we find problematic misconceptions concerning the relationship between opportunities for use of international standards and how such standards may impact on lock-in effects [21, 23]. We note that the directive does not refer to previously published studies from commissioned research, studies which are published by several Swedish government authorities, including the Swedish competition authority [23], the Swedish national agency responsible for all framework agreements for public procurement which are to be used by all Swedish government agencies [27], and an independent analysis of a strategy presented by the Swedish Agency for Digital Government [4] that addresses licensing of software recommended for PSOs. In addition, we note that the directive [32] also lacks recognition of the importance of open standards. The Swedish Government, it should be noted, stressed the importance of open standards for addressing lock-in in its directive for the Swedish e-Government initiative [31] and by Swedish PSOs in the first report from that initiative [36].

Second, we find that the report [37] lacks a thorough analysis of lock-in effects and related challenges which impact on cost-effective IT operations through use of cloud and SaaS solutions. Further, the report fails to recognise significant technical and legal obstacles related to use of such solutions. We find that lock-in effects prevent lawful creation, processing, maintenance, and archiving of digital assets through use of SaaS solutions from global providers that currently are widely deployed amongst Swedish PSOs. Further, we lack analysis related to patent laws that would address identified challenges related to format lock-in [20, 21]. We also lack a comprehensive analysis of laws and regulations (potentially with proposals for revised laws and regulations) related to archiving [34, 35] and long-term maintenance of digital assets [13], which considers the potential for lawful use of SaaS solutions (such as O365) from global providers.

Third, we find that the report [37] ignores important policy recommendations presented by a national policy in the UK [38] which emphasise the importance of using open standards for promoting software interoperability and avoiding lock-in effects (to avoid hidden costs caused by unsuitable procurement practices) by stressing the importance of exit strategies.

Concerning *actual lock-in* amongst PSOs, we find significant confusion amongst PSOs related to critical prerequisites which would ensure that an organisation, technically and lawfully, can create, process, maintain, and archive digital assets during and after use of a SaaS solution. Specifically, results from the study show that amongst 46 investigated PSOs that use the O365 solution there is significant confusion related to the need for obtaining licences and an effective exit-strategy that, technically and legally, would allow for use and reuse of digital assets created by a PSO during and after use of the specific SaaS solution. Hence, given that none of the 46 organisations has obtained all necessary licences for the SaaS solution it follows that any analysis of actual costs for use of the solution will be misleading. Consequently, any analysis of cost-effective IT operations for use and reuse of digital assets created, processed, maintained, and archived by PSOs will be based on misleading and incorrect underlying assumptions.

Further, despite the fact that the investigation undertaken by the Swedish Government Offices has received details concerning challenges related to format lock-in and research results concerning the need for obtaining licences related to SEPs for a commonly used SaaS solution, we note that the investigation has chosen to ignore those issues in the report [37]. Hence, since research shows that patent issues and format lock-in cause significant costs it follows that any assessment of cost-effectiveness neglecting those costs becomes speculative.

In summary, since none of the 46 PSOs that use O365 has obtained all necessary licences and all lack an effective exit strategy (which considers costs for exit) we find that their actual lock-in may be significantly worse than their (self-assessed) perceived lock-in. Unavailability of all necessary licences which would allow for data processing and maintenance of a PSOs own digital assets also implies significant other risks, beyond risks related to cost issues.

Finally, based on our analysis of results from the present study and results from previous research [22], we recommend that any PSO undertakes an analysis which includes consideration of the following five questions, each requiring a clear "yes" both prior to adoption and throughout the entire life-cycle of deployment and use of a SaaS solution from a global provider:

(1) Is the text of all applicable contract terms for the SaaS solution available and maintained by the PSO?;
(2) Has the PSO obtained all applicable licences for the SaaS solution that provide the PSO all technical abilities and all necessary rights that allow for creation, processing, maintenance, and archiving of digital assets during use of the SaaS solution?;
(3) Has the PSO obtained all applicable licences for the SaaS solution that provide the PSO all technical abilities and all necessary rights that allow for creation, processing, maintenance, and archiving of digital assets with available software (provided under open source software licences) after the PSO has ceased to use the SaaS solution (i.e. after exit)?;
(4) Is the PSO only exposed to Swedish law for data processing and maintenance of digital assets when the SaaS solution is used?;
(5) Has the PSO control over which foreign laws, regulations, and jurisdictions may impact on data processing and maintenance of the PSO's digital assets when the SaaS solution is used?

We find that none of the 46 PSOs in the present study and none of the other 33 PSOs in a previous study [22] fulfils all these five recommendations (i.e. none of 79 PSOs in total).

7 Conclusions

Fundamental to IT operations for any public sector organisation is the ability to create, process, maintain, and archive digital assets that are relevant for individuals, organisations and society at large. When an organisation creates, processes, maintains, and archives digital assets through use of IT solutions it is critical that the organisation has autonomy and full control of all its digital assets over the full life-cycle of those assets. Further, for society at large it is critical to maintain digital and data sovereignty which allows for cost effective, technically suitable, and lawful IT operations of digital assets that allow for use and reuse of those assets amongst all public sector organisations. In particular, for a public sector organisation which uses cloud and SaaS solutions from global providers there are a number of additional challenges that impact on the organisation's ability to maintain autonomy and full control of its digital assets. In conclusion, we find that the investigation undertaken by the Swedish Government Offices has failed to address several critical factors in its report [37] in order for it to successfully address the goals detailed in the directive [32].

Any analysis of cost-effective IT operations needs to be grounded in some sort of realistic perception of actual costs. We find that the investigation by the Swedish Government Offices fails to address critical aspects which impact on actual costs for use of commonly used SaaS solutions. Critical aspects, such as exit costs and hidden costs for IT-operations, are omitted despite the fact that responses to the questionnaire have highlighted the importance of such aspects. Specifically, the report lacks coverage of how to address exit costs at time for procurement of an IT solution to be used by a public sector organisation.

The study shows stark unawareness of critical technical, legal, and societal challenges which impact on digital and data sovereignty that impact on cost effective IT operations for public sector organisations. For example, the review of the UK presented in the Swedish report [37] fails to address effective exit strategies, despite the fact that the directive from the Government explicitly mentions that experiences from the UK should be reviewed. We find that exit strategies have been elaborated and recommended in the UK as a critical factor which needs to be analysed as it often represents a 'hidden cost' for IT operations [38].

Findings show that none of the 46 investigated public sector organisations have successfully addressed critical issues that need to be considered before adoption and use of a specific SaaS solution (Microsoft Office 365) from a global provider. Amongst the 46 public sector organisations the study shows that no organisation has acquired all licences which are needed for IT operations of this SaaS solution. Further, the same 46 organisations have also failed successfully to obtain all necessary licences which allow for continued use of all digital assets exported from the SaaS solution in a potential future scenario if the organisation will cease to use the SaaS solution.

Related to *perceived lock-in* amongst public sector organisations, we find that the vast majority of organisations in the Swedish public sector express significant concern related to use of SaaS solutions from global providers. Further, based on our analysis of the directive provided by the Swedish government and the report provided by the Swedish Government Offices, the study shows stark unawareness of critical factors that impact on previously investigated lock-in effects, and consequently fail to recognise important prerequisites for any analysis of cost effectiveness of IT operations.

Related to *actual lock-in* amongst public sector organisations, we find no single example of any public sector organisation that has obtained all necessary licences that allow for use of a commonly deployed SaaS solution, and no single example of any organisation which has access to an effective exit strategy that allows for continued use and reuse of an organisation's own digital assets after exit from the specific SaaS solution currently used. Hence, it follows that no public sector organisation that has adopted a commonly deployed SaaS solution (Microsoft Office 365) has any idea about the actual cost for IT operations related to creation, processing, maintenance, and archiving of the organisation's own digital assets during and after use of the SaaS solution. As many public sector organisations lack access to the text of all applicable contract terms for the specific SaaS solution used (and instead rely on the supplier for maintenance of its own contracts) we find widespread lack of autonomy and control amongst public sector organisations. Further, we find that the Swedish Government Offices has failed to recognise critical factors, such as the need for obtaining licences and calculation of exit costs, which impact on cost effective IT-operations.

Acknowledgement. This research has been financially supported by the Swedish Knowledge Foundation (KK-stiftelsen) and participating partner organisations in the SUDO project. The authors are grateful for the stimulating collaboration and support from colleagues and partner organisations.

References

1. Bekkers, R., Updegrove, A.: IPR Policies and Practices of a Representative Group of Standards-Setting Organizations Worldwide. Commissioned by the Committee on Intellectual Property Management in Standard-Setting Processes, National Research Council, Washington, May 2013
2. Blind, K., Böhm, M.: The relationship between open source software and standard setting. In: Thumm, N. (ed.) EUR 29867 EN, JRC (Joint Research Centre) Science for Policy Report, Publications Office of the European Union, Luxembourg (2019). ISBN 978-92-76-11593-9
3. Contreras, J.L.: A brief history of FRAND: analyzing current debates in standard setting and antitrust through a historical lens. Antitrust Law J. **80**(1), 39–120 (2015)
4. DIGG: Analys av DIGG:s policy för utveckling av programvara. Agency for Digital Government, 3 June 2020. https://www.digg.se/om-oss/nyheter/2020/analys-av-diggs-policy-for-utv eckling-av-programvara
5. EC: Communication from the Commission to the European Parliament, the Council, the European Economic and Social Committee and the Committee of the Regions: Unleashing the Potential of Cloud Computing in Europe, SWD (2012). 271 final, European Commission
6. EC: Patents and Standards: A modern framework for IPR-based standardization. Final report, A study prepared for the European Commission Directorate-General for Enterprise and Industry, 25 March 2014. ISBN 978-92-79-35991-0

7. EC: Standard-essential patents. European Commission, Competition policy brief, Issue 8 June 2014. ISBN 978-92-79-35553-0

8. EC: Shaping Europe's Digital Future, Communication from the Commission to the European Parliament, the Council, the European Economic and Social Committee and the Committee of the Regions, European Commission, Communication, COM(2020) 67 final, 19 February 2020

9. Egyedi, T.: Standard-compliant, but incompatible?! Comput. Stand. Interf. **29**(6), 605–613 (2007)

10. Egyedi, T.M., Hudson, J.: A standard's integrity: can it be safeguarded? IEEE Commun. Mag. **43**(2), 151–155 (2005)

11. eSam: Checklista inför beslut om molntjänster i offentlig sektor. eSam, 31 October 2018. www.esamverka.se

12. Försäkringskassan: Cloud Services in Sustaining Societal Functions–Risks, Appropriateness and the Way Forward, Swedish Social Insurance Agency, Dnr. 013428-2019, Version 1.0, 18 November 2019

13. Furberg, P., Westberg, M.: Måste myndigheter följa lagarna? Om utkontraktering och legalitet i digital miljö. Juridisk tidskrift **2**, 406–417 (2020)

14. GAIA: Project GAIA-X: A Federated Data Infrastructure as the Cradle of a Vibrant European Ecosystem. Federal Ministry for Economic Affairs and Energy (BMWi), Berlin, October 2019

15. Ghosh, R.A.: Open Standards and Interoperability Report: An Economic Basis for Open Standards. Deliverable D4, MERIT, University of Maastricht, December 2005

16. Guijarro, L.: Interoperability frameworks and enterprise architectures in e-government initiatives in Europe and the United States. Gov. Inf. Q. **24**(1), 89–101 (2007)

17. Hon, W.K., Millard, C., Walden, I.: Negotiating cloud contracts: looking at clouds from both sides now. Stanford Technol. Law Rev. **16**(1), 79–129 (2012)

18. Katz, A.: Google, APIs and the law. Use, reuse and lock-in. In: Lopez-Tarruella, A. (ed.) Google and the Law: Empirical Approaches to Legal Aspects of Knowledge-Economy Business Models, pp. 287–301. T.M.C. Asser Press, The Hague (2012). ISBN 978-90-6704-845-3

19. Kritikos, K., et al.: Multi-cloud provisioning of business processes. J. Cloud Comput. **8**(1), 1–29 (2019). https://doi.org/10.1186/s13677-019-0143-x

20. Lundell, B., Gamalielsson, J., Katz, A.: On implementation of open standards in software: to what extent can ISO standards be implemented in open source software? Int. J. Standard. Res. **13**(1), 47–73 (2015)

21. Lundell, B., Gamalielsson, J., Katz, A.: Implementing IT standards in software: challenges and recommendations for organisations planning software development covering IT standards. Eur. J. Law Technol. **10**(2) (2019)

22. Lundell, B., Gamalielsson, J., Katz, A.: Addressing lock-in effects in the public sector: how can organisations deploy a SaaS solution while maintaining control of their digital assets?. In: Virkar, S., et al. (eds.) CEUR Workshop Proceedings: EGOV-CeDEM-ePart 2020, vol. 2797, pp. 289–296 (2020). ISSN 1613-0073

23. Lundell, B., Gamalielsson, J., Tengblad, S.: IT-standarder, inlåsning och konkurrens: En analys av policy och praktik inom svensk förvaltning, Uppdragsforskningsrapport 2016:2, Konkurrensverket (the Swedish Competition Authority) (2016). ISSN: 1652-8089

24. Mannheimer Swartling: Applicability of Chinese National Intelligence Law to Chinese and non-Chinese Entities, Mannheimer Swartling AB, Stockholm, January

25. Mowbray, M.: The fog over the Grimpen Mire: cloud computing and the law. SCRIPTed **6**(1), 132–146 (2009)

26. NOC: The Netherlands in Open Connection: An action plan for the use of Open Standards and Open Source Software in the public and semi-public sector. The Ministry of Economic Affairs, The Hague, November (2007)

27. NPS: Open IT-standards. National Procurement Services, Kammarkollegiet, Stockholm, 7 March 2016. Dnr 96-38-2014

28. NPS: Förstudierapport Webbaserat kontorsstöd. National Procurement Services, Kammarkollegiet, Stockholm, 22 February 2019. Dnr 23.2-6283-18

29. Online Services Terms: Microsoft Volume Licensing Online Services Terms (Worldwide English, February 2021), Microsoft, February 2021

30. Radar: Moln över kommunerna: hot eller möjlighet?. Radar Ecosytem Specialists, Stockholm. radareco.se (2019)

31. Regeringen: Delegation för e-förvaltning. Dir. 2009:19, Swedish Government, 26 March 2009

32. Regeringen: Säker och kostnadseffektiv it-drift för den offentliga förvaltningen. Kommittédirektiv, Dir. 2019:64, Infrastrukturdepartementet, Regeringen, 26 September 2019

33. Regeringskansliet: Nationella upphandlingsstrategin, Finansdepartementet, Stockholm (2016)

34. Riksarkivet: Riksarkivets föreskrifter och allmänna råd om elektroniska handlingar (upptagningar för automatiserad behandling). Riksarkivets författningssamling, RA-FS 2009:1, Riksarkivet (2009). ISSN 0283-2941

35. Riksarkivet: Riksarkivets föreskrifter och allmänna råd om tekniska krav för elektroniska handlingar (upptagningar för automatiserad behandling). Riksarkivets författningssamling, RA-FS 2009:2, Riksarkivet (2009). ISSN 0283-2941

36. SOU: Strategi för myndigheternas arbete med e-förvaltning. Statens Offentliga Utredningar: SOU 2009:86. e-Delegationen, Finansdepartementet, Regeringskansliet, Stockholm, 19 October 2009

37. SOU: Säker och kostnadseffektiv it-drift – rättsliga förutsättningar för utkontraktering. Statens Offentliga Utredningar, SOU 2021:1, Delbetänkande från IT-driftsutredningen, Stockholm (2021). ISBN 978-91-525-0001-9

38. UK: Open Standards Principles: For software interoperability, data and document formats in government IT specifications. HM Government, 7 September 2012

The Importance of ICT in Local Governments: Results from a Survey on the Characterization of the ICT Function in Portugal

Luis Felipe M. Ramos[1]([envelope]) [ID], Mariana Lameiras[2] [ID], Delfina Soares[2] [ID], and Luis Amaral[3] [ID]

[1] JusGov/University of Minho, Braga, Portugal
id8856@alunos.uminho.pt
[2] UNU-EGOV, Guimarães, Portugal
lameiras@unu.edu, soares@unu.edu
[3] University of Minho, Guimarães, Portugal
amaral@dsi.uminho.pt

Abstract. This work presents the results of a project developed to characterize the role of ICTs in Portuguese municipalities, providing a picture of the efforts and successes reached using ICTs to improve their internal functioning and their interaction with the residents. Results here presented refer to some of the technical aspects surveyed among all 308 Portuguese municipalities. The findings encompass a comprehensive description of the ICT function in terms of seven dimensions, covering the characterization of the municipality, financial resources allocated to the ICT function, ICT infrastructure, organization and governance of the ICT function, digital applications and services, and regulations and guidelines. Globally, data show how vital the ICT function is for the Portuguese cities, but also reveal how much it can improve, with many aspects to enhance and promote.

Keywords: e-Government · Portugal · Municipalities · ICT characterization

This paper is a result of the project "SmartEGOV: Harnessing EGOV for Smart Governance (Foundations, methods, Tools)/NORTE-01-0145-FEDER-000037", supported by Norte Portugal Regional Operational Programme (NORTE 2020), under the PORTUGAL 2020 Partnership Agreement, through the European Regional Development Fund (EFDR). This work was also supported by the Portuguese Foundation for Science and Technology (FCT), through the individual research grant 2020.04726.BD.

H. J. Scholl et al. (Eds.): EGOV 2021, LNCS 12850, pp. 73–85, 2021.
https://doi.org/10.1007/978-3-030-84789-0_6

1   Introduction and Background

The digital government trend has gained ground in the last two decades. World-wide efforts put in place strategies and measures under this umbrella with many purposes, namely to reduce the administrative burden, ease the relationship with stakeholders, encourage e-participation and foster transparency in information sharing, to name a few. These are vehicles to improve trust in government and public institutions and increase confidence in their policies and actions [20].

Tolbert and Mossberger [17] sustain a positive link between e-government and political trust, showing that readily accessible information available on government websites facilitates citizen access, promotes greater transparency of local government and empowers citizens to monitor government performance more closely. Pina, Torres and Royo [9] suggest that frequent and timely disclosure of information online increases the transparency of local government and empowers citizens to monitor government performance more closely. Others highlight the role of Information and Communication Technologies (ICTs) in helping governments restore confidence in public institutions, create greater involvement, and foster greater interaction and political participation [3,6,20]. Although there is extant literature addressing the positive effects of transparency and data availability by governments, the same enthusiasm is not found in these reflections around local e-government.

The local level is of utmost importance. It entails basic service delivery with direct impact in citizens' everyday life, not only providing information and services that are essential for different stages of a person's lifetime cycle, but also in terms of problem's resolution. In a nutshell, it is the most direct interface of citizens with government. Its importance is grounded on the local government's closeness to citizens and on a related sense of belonging [15,16].

ICTs are core for the digital government advances. They have been playing a pivotal role in organizations as a determining factor in the development and transformation of the economy and societies, while contributing to the achievement of the Sustainable Development Goals proposed by the UN [18]. As they can provide deep integration, interoperability, and effective information sharing, many countries worldwide have been resorting to them [12]. The public sector in general and municipalities in particular, are no exceptions to this phenomenon. Indeed, citizens' increasing expectations of public services have required constant administrative modernization to streamline processes, reduce costs, provide information and services in a friendlier and more agile way [5,10]. Aware of this reality, and although at different rates and following different strategies, local governments have been using ICT to improve their performance, both regarding internal processes and in their relationship and interaction with citizens and stakeholders [7,19].

The work presented in this paper draws on the data collected and analysed within the umbrella of a series of biennial studies about the internet presence of Portuguese municipalities, published since 1999. These studies and the most recent data are available online and show how information technologies in general, and web technologies in particular, are used by local governments to inform citizens and make publicly available information regarding the municipality and its management, to facilitate navigation and interaction with the website, to make available online services as well as to foster e-participation and launch initiatives that can engage citizens in decision-making processes and municipal public policymaking [14]. In this case, understanding the ICT function in local governments is crucial for the overall study aiming at knowing and understanding their web presence maturity. Indeed, ICT adoption and usage to promote digital government is a good indicator of a closer and more citizen-aware government [11].

Web presence is, however, one facet of the use of ICTs by local governments. Indeed, ICTs have a much broader existence and application comprising a set of systems, applications, infrastructures, and resources that support all municipality operations. Understanding the size and organization of these infrastructures, systems, applications and resources is therefore considered a crucial aspect when looking for a holistic picture of the state of development of e-government at the local level [2,4].

This work presents the results of a research to characterize the role of ICTs in Portuguese local governments, providing a complete and integrated picture of the efforts and achievements deployed regarding the use of ICTs to improve their internal functioning and their interaction with citizens and stakeholders. Results here presented refer to some of the technical aspects surveyed, trying to answer to the question: *"Which technical aspects are limiting the ICT function at the local government level?"*. The main objective is to understand how the technical components of the ICT function are described and considered by municipalities within the realm of local e-government objectives.

This paper is organized as follows: the survey methodology is described in Sect. 2; quantitative results and comparisons are presented in Sect. 3; conclusion remarks and initial recommendations are summarized in Sect. 4.

2 Methodology

Data was gathered through a survey addressed to all 308 municipalities in Portugal. The questionnaire was developed based on literature review and similar instruments (questionnaires and other, as scientific and technical guidelines) to help in the identification of the dimensions and the specific questions to cover. It was sent to the Mayor', Mayors' offices or to the general e-mail addresses found in the respective websites. It included 93 questions, most of them closed and mandatory, organized in nine main dimensions: characterization of the municipality, characterization of the respondent, characterization of the responsible for the ICT function, human resources allocated to the ICT function, financial resources allocated to the ICT function, ICT infrastructure, organization and governance of the ICT function, digital applications and services, and regulations and guidelines.

This paper presents the results of 63 questions and excludes the characterization of human resources, which have been analyzed in a separated work.

Thus, it covers the following aspects: characterization of the municipality, financial resources allocated to the ICT function, ICT infrastructure, organization and governance of the ICT function, digital applications and services, and regulations and guidelines.

Regarding the first dimension - Characterization of the Municipality - as it is related to information publicly available on trusted repositories, the answers were previously filled, so the respondents should only indicate if they agreed with the presented values and, if not, inform the correct data.

The questionnaire was made available to municipalities through the *LimeSurvey* platform for five months. The data collected were exported and submitted to a careful "cleaning" process, aiming to detect information that could indicate invalid answers, and for that reason, should be excluded from the analysis. Two such cases were identified and after some phone contacts with the respective municipalities to clarify the doubts, they were excluded. Thus, from the 141 submitted questionnaires, 139 were considered valid and used for the final analysis.

There are a few questions for which the number of valid answers is lower than 139. It happens for one of two reasons: (i) some municipalities did not provide an answer to that specific question, or (ii) the provided answer presented an incoherent and dissonant value with the question and the answers provided to some of the remaining questions; as such, it was considered that it resulted from an inaccurate interpretation from the respondent of what was asked. In these cases, only the specific answer was removed, and not the full municipality reply.

During the analysis, some data were aggregated, to better visualize the obtained results.

3   Findings

The findings reported in this paper include a brief characterization of respondent municipalities, the results related to financial resources, ICT infrasctructure, organization and governance of the ICT function, digital applications and services, and regulations and guidelines. As previously indicated, the results of the dimension on human resources shall be published separately.

3.1   Characterization of the Municipality

Of the total 308 municipalities targeted, which represent all municipalities in the country, 139 (45%) successfully submitted questionnaire. Table 1 presents the data analysis of the municipalities by populational dimension (large, medium, small)[1]. Among these respondents, more than half (53%) are of small dimension, with 20.000 inhabitants or less. However, this number represents only 40% of

---

[1] For the purpose of this study, a small municipality is the one with a population inferior or equal to 20.000 people. In contrast, a medium municipality is the one with a population superior to 20.000 people and inferior or equal to 100.000 people, and a large municipality is the one with a population superior to 100.000 people.

the total number of small municipalities in the country, while 71% of the large municipalities replayed to the questionnaire.

Table 1. Dimension of municipalities (n = 139).

Dimension category	# of Municipalities in the country	Answers		
		# of answers	% of answers	% in the category
Large municipality	24	17	12%	71%
Medium municipality	98	48	35%	49%
Small municipality	186	74	53%	40%

Most of the Portuguese municipalities (138 out of 308) are located in the interior of the country, while 41% are in the coastline and the remaining in the islands. Accordingly, most of the answers came from municipalities placed in the interior of the country (52%), while those in the islands registered the lowest response rate (9 municipalities out of 30).

According to another territorial classification[2], 55% of the municipalities located in the North region of the country replied to the questionnaire, while in other regions (namely Alentejo, Center and Lisbon), approximately 50% of the municipalities in each region submitted valid answers.

3.2   Financial Resources Allocated to the ICT Function

The analysis of the financial resources allocated to the ICT function focused on the amount of the budget set aside for the ICT function, presented as a percentage of the global budget of the 135 municipalities that provided this information, as well as an analysis of the segmentation of the overall ICT budget by specific headings.

As Fig. 1 shows, in 65% of the municipalities, the budget allocated to the ICT function is less than 2% of the municipality global budget, and in 21% of the cases, it is less than 1%. Only in 9% of the cases, the budget exceeds 5% of the municipality global budget. It is worth noting that in one municipality, located in the continental coastline of the region Center, and of small size, the budget allocated was reported as being 11.9% of the municipality global budget.

Also, it was possible to notice the distribution of the ICT budget by headings, considering the 129 municipalities that provided that information. On average, the percentage of the budget allocated to "acquisition of goods (equipment and software)" is 24%, followed by expenses with human resources (17%). "Employee training" is the heading with the least weight in the allocated budget (2%).

---

[2] NUTS - Nomenclature of Territorial Units for Statistics, established by Regulation (EC) N° 1059/2003 of the European Parliament and of the Council of 26 May 2003.

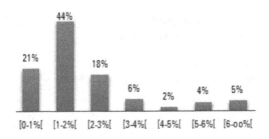

Fig. 1. Percentage of global budget allocated to the ICT function (n = 135).

3.3   ICT Infrastructure

This section aims to characterize the ICT infrastructure available and the tools used by the surveyed Portuguese municipalities.

The most frequent types of equipments available in the municipalities are desktop computers (85% on average) and the least frequent are tablets (2% on average). Two municipalities reported having just desktops (100% of the available equipment), while two others stated not having notebooks, and 48 not having tablets. Regarding the network structure, all 139 municipalities reported having wired internet connections, although 23 of them do not have wireless connections.

Microsoft Windows is the predominant operating system, running on more than 75% of the computers of 136 municipalities (95%). Apple macOS has a residual usage in 59 cities (43%). Regarding open-source operating systems, Linux has a residual usage in 57% of the municipalities, while Unix is residually used by 37% of the cities. Eight municipalities reported also using other operating systems, like Android, iOS, BSD, DOS, and Synology DSM 6.3.

As to the most used programming languages to perform development, maintenance, and operational activities, SQL and PHP represent more than 50% of the programming effort in 22% and 12% of the municipalities, respectively. Considering that these programming languages can be used to manage databases and develop websites, this data may indicate the concern of those cities to develop and provide online services to the citizens.

Server virtualization technologies are very used by the Portuguese municipalities, as 106 (76%) of them make intensive use of it, and 23 (17%) make reasonable use. Only 2% of the cities reported not using this technology. A different situation can be seen in the use of cloud computing, which is used by only 45 municipalities (32%), with 20 of them recurring to private external solutions, while only 12 store their files in an internal cloud server. Regarding the most used services on the cloud[3], Fig. 2 shows that Infrastructure as a Service (IaaS), Platform as a Service (PaaS), and Software as a Service (SaaS) are the main ones.

---

[3] IaaS: Infrastructure as a Service; PaaS: Platform as a Service; DaaS: Desktop as a Service; SaaS: Software as a Service; CaaS: Communication as a Service; XaaS: Everything as a Service; DBaaS: Data Base as a Service; SECasS: Security as a Service; FaaS: Function as a Service; MBaaS: Mobile "Backend" as a Service.

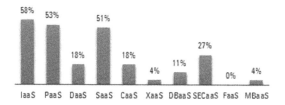

Fig. 2. Services used on the cloud (n = 45).

3.4   Organization and Governance of the ICT Function

Concerning the decision to perform some of the main ICT functions in-house or to outsource them, it was presented a list with 15 different functions and asked where they were performed. 40% of the municipalities indicated to fully perform them in-house, while in 13% of the cases, more than 50% of the ICT function was outsourced. Systems development is the most outsourced activity, followed by auditing, compliance, and risk management. On the other hand, outsourcing management, IT operations, service management, and planning are the activities most cities (on average, 59%) perform entirely in-house.

Regarding the adoption of ICT frameworks and methodologies, 113 municipalities (81%) reported not applying any of the 13 presented[4], nor any other than those. The alleged reason, in 69% of the cases, was the lack of knowledge of their existence. However, of the municipalities that do adopt some framework and methodology, Fig. 3 shows that 22 use ITIL, five use Agile Scrum, and four use COBIT5. A similar result was observed regarding the adoption of standards. Most municipalities (60%) reported not applying any of the six presented[5]. In 41% of the cases, it was because they were unaware of the existence of those standards. ISO 9001:2000 is the most adopted standard, used by 39 cities. The other five cities reported to use ISO 9001:2015, and one to use ISO 9001:2008. Figure 4 summarizes the results.

3.5   Digital Applications and Services

This section aims to describe a set of elements that allow characterizing how ICT is being used to offer public services by the municipalities. Providing online services to citizens is one of the significant goals that municipalities have been pursuing, with more encouraging results in some cases and less in others.

From the data gathered, it can be concluded that, on average, the percentage of services that the municipalities provide exclusively online[6] is about 12% of their total services. Further analysis of the answers also show that 99 of the 136

---

[4] COBIT5, Six Sigma, CBPP, Prince2, CMMI, CISM, TOGAF, Edison, SNABOK, Agile Scrum, HFI, ISTQB, and ITIL.

[5] ISO 20000, ISO 27000, ISO 27001, ISO 9001:2000, ISO 10303, ISO 37120:2017.

[6] For this study, a service is provided exclusively online if there is no equivalent service offered in person.

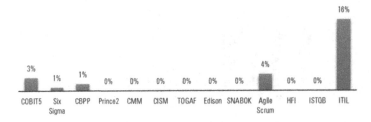

Fig. 3. Percentage of municipalities that adopt ICT frameworks and methodologies (n = 139).

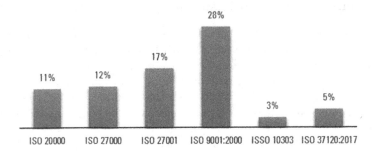

Fig. 4. Percentage of municipalities that adopt ICT standards (n = 139).

municipalities that validly answered this question (73%) provide less than 10% of their total services exclusively online, with a very substantial part of them (72) not providing any services this way. Only 11 municipalities (8%) indicated doing so in more than 50% of their services.

Regarding the availability of services simultaneously online and in person, the data showed that, on average, the percentage of services offered simultaneously by these two channels is 37% of the total services of the municipalities. Moreover, in this case, there are still municipalities (16%) that claim not to have any services offered to citizens simultaneously in both directions, as shown in Fig. 5.

Among municipalities providing services to citizens simultaneously online and in person, the data collected showed that, on average, 34% of them are fully available online[7], and the others only partially available, *i.e.*, require some form of presential interaction and eventual use of paper.

The previous data may have some influence on the percentage of online requests of services made by citizens. The analysis of the 121 municipalities that stated to have online services available shows that, on average, only 11% of all requests received throughout 2018 were made online, and 13 municipalities had less than 1% of requests made online.

As regards to the mechanisms available to citizens who wish to make online requests of services, 51% of the municipalities declared to request a previous

---

[7] For the purpose of this study, a service is fully available online when it does not require any face-to-face interaction and without the use of paper.

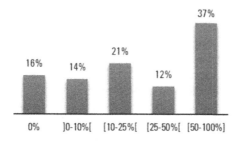

Fig. 5. Percentage of municipalities with simultaneous online and in person services (n = 139).

registration, based on personal data provided by the citizens. The authentication using "Digital Mobile Key" (Chave Móvel Digital - CMD)[8] is not accepted by most municipalities, with 126 (90%) alleging not to accept this method without previous registration, and 130 (93%) declaring not to accept it even combined with the provision of additional data by the citizens.

Concerning the forms of payment available for services requested online, the most used is face-to-face payment, accessible in 121 municipalities, followed by the ATM system[9], used by 56% of the municipalities, and other online payment services, like credit card and PayPal, used by only 11 municipalities.

A little more than half of the municipalities keep their websites mobile-friendly (57%) and send SMS messages to residents (55%). None use applications like WhatsApp or Telegram to communicate with citizens. And regarding access channels available to citizens to interact with the municipalities, data shows that, on average, 60% of the calls are made by personal assistance. The telephone is the chosen channel, on average, in 12% of the cases, while traditional mail (letters) are sent in 8% of times, on average. Electronic access channels, like web portals and social networks, are used only in 6% of the calls.

The low use of social networks as an access channel for citizens to interact with the municipalities is surprising, given the high attention all Portuguese cities give to these platforms, with more than 85% of them having a Facebook account and more than 50% having a YouTube account, as observed by [13].

Another intriguing remark from data analysis is related to the acceptance of qualified electronic signatures by the municipalities, as 65% of them alleged to accept documents with qualified electronic signatures in all circumstances in which the citizen wishes to do so, and the law permits. However, four municipalities reported not accepting documents with qualified electronic signatures in any circumstance.

---

[8] The Digital Mobile Key (CMD) is an alternative method of authentication of citizens in Portuguese Public Administration Internet portals and sites using the mobile phone, where, after a previous registration, the citizen can authenticate using the telephone number, a personal PIN, and a security code received via SMS.

[9] Portugal's Multibanco System is a fully integrated interbank network that offers a wide range of services, including online payment.

3.6   Regulations and Guidelines

This section aims to characterize how the Portuguese municipalities (i) observe and act under a set of laws, regulations, standards and good practices that have been published in the country, and (ii) adopt a set of tools that have been developed in Portugal in the field of e-governance.

Concerning the adoption of good practices proposed in the usability guide developed by the Portuguese Agency for Administrative Modernization (AMA)[10], only 9% of the municipalities reported fully adopting the practices set out in the guide, while most cities (41%) alleged to adopt it partially. The lack of adoption of good practices by 27% of the cities is because they are unaware of its existence. A similar situation occurs with the adoption of accessibility recommendations issued by law[11]. Most cities (64%) reported to partially adopt it, while 13% not adopting it for being unaware of its existence.

The adoption of standards presented in the procedure manual about the application of the "once only" principle aims to ensure the procedural right of citizens to ask to be released from delivering information already held by the Public Administration bodies. Regarding that, only 2% of the cities alleged to fully apply this principle according to the manual, while 44% of the municipalities stated not adopting it for being unaware of its existence.

Regarding open data publication, only 31 cities (22%) stated to publishing datasets in the Portuguese Public Administration's open data portal (*dados.gov.pt*).

About the application of the EU General Data Protection Regulation, 47% of the municipalities reported being in an early stage and without a designated Data Protection Officer (DPO). All other cities alleged to have a designated DPO, although they are still on different implementation levels of the regulation.

4   Discussion and Conclusions

Globally, the results from the survey show how vital the ICT function is for the Portuguese municipalities, but also reveal how much it can improve, with many aspects to enhance and promote.

Adequate level of financial resources for training IT officers allows a higher level of knowledge and skills in technical activities, *e.g.*, system development and maintenance [8]. However, the budget allocation in the Portuguese cities is still low, with 65% of them applying, on average, less than 2% of the total budget for ICT-related activities, and only 2% of that amount is allocated for staff training.

The data presented in this paper shows that of the available ICT budget, $\frac{1}{4}$ of the total is focused on acquiring goods (equipment and software). However, without adequate training, these goods may not be used in their full potential. It

---

[10] Within the objectives of the *usabilidade.gov.pt* initiative.

[11] Stated in Decree-Law n° 83/2018 of October 19, that implemented Directive (EU) 2016/2102, on the accessibility of the websites and mobile applications of public sector bodies.

would be interesting to follow up the level of allocated financial resources and its distribution within the surveyed headings, to see if an increase in the investment in this sector by the Portuguese municipalities, reflecting the importance of these functions to better provide digital services to the citizens.

A better trained ICT personnel may impact the municipality's online presence and digital performance, as well as facilitate the adoption of ICT frameworks and methodologies, which represents a considerable gap identified in the survey. It may also contribute to the availability of new digital services offering.

Mobile communications in Portugal are in constant growth in the last years, where the number of mobile lines effectively used in 2019 reached 120 per 100 inhabitants, and about 76% of the population use mobile Internet [1]. However, the adoption by the municipalities of services through mobile devices is shallow, as described in Sect. 3.5. There is here an excellent opportunity to develop new ways for the municipalities to interact with citizens.

An increased availability of online services may represent a reduction of operational costs, administrative burden, and bureaucracy, eliminating the need of personal interactions and paper-based procedures. As the Portuguese national government incentivizes the use of the Digital Mobile Kye (CMD) for personal authentication on various online services, both public and private, and for signing digital documents, it should be adopted by a growing number of municipalities, in order to ease the interaction of its citizens with the services they offer.

In the last years, Portugal has developed a regulatory framework to assist the adoption of user-friendly tools by the municipalities, but as identified in this work, most cities still are not aware of them. Further efforts must be made, not only to disclose these regulations but also to encourage their adoption.

The municipalities can use this work as an opportunity for improvement and as an evidence-based tool for internal decision-making. It allows performance assessment and peer comparison. This comparison, in conjunction with their general strategic priorities, can lead the way in informing the process of defining a digital transformation policy.

For national policymakers and governance structures, this work contributes for a clear perspective on the *status quo* of local ICT use and to think of national strategies and recommendations for e-Government globally, and targeted to the needs and interests of entities at all levels of government, so that conditions are created for the gradual and convergent development of digital governance in the country.

Also, this work is equally important both for academics and researchers in the field of digital governance, for showing how ICTs can be used to transform country governance mechanisms, as well as for ICT companies and service providers, particularly those with management as one of the main sectors of activity.

References

1. ANACOM: Serviços móveis - 1° semestre de 2019. Technical report (2019). https://bit.ly/2ThOcfU
2. Cegarra-Navarro, J.G., Pachón, J.R.C., Cegarra, J.L.M.: E-government and citizen's engagement with local affairs through e-websites: the case of Spanish municipalities. Int. J. Inf. Manage. **32**(5), 469–478 (2012)
3. Cuillier, D., Piotrowski, S.J.: Internet information-seeking and its relation to support for access to government records. Gov. Inf. Q. **26**(3), 441–449 (2009)
4. Janssen, M., Wagenaar, R., Beerens, J.: Towards a flexible ICT-architecture for multi-channel e-government service provisioning. In: Proceedings of the 36th Annual Hawaii International Conference on System Sciences, pp. 10-pp. IEEE (2003)
5. Mawela, T., Ochara, N.M., Twinomurinzi, H.: E-government implementation: a reflection on South African municipalities. South Afr. Comput. J. **29**(1), 147–171 (2017)
6. Moon, M.J.: The evolution of e-government among municipalities: rhetoric or reality? Public Adm. Rev. **62**(4), 424–433 (2002)
7. Nasi, G., Frosini, F., Cristofoli, D.: Online service provision: are municipalities really innovative? The case of larger municipalities in Italy. Public Admin. **89**(3), 821–839 (2011)
8. Omar, A., Bass, J.M., Lowit, P.: Exploring the factors that influence the success of insourced government ICT projects. Electron. J. Inf. Syst. Dev. Ctries. **77**(1), 1–21 (2016)
9. Pina, V., Torres, L., Royo, S.: Are ICTs improving transparency and accountability in the EU regional and local governments? An empirical study. Public Admin. **85**(2), 449–472 (2007)
10. Rohman, I.K., Veiga, L.: Against the shadow: the role of e-government. In: Proceedings of the 18th Annual International Conference on Digital Government Research, pp. 319–328. ACM (2017). https://doi.org/10.1145/3085228.3085321
11. Scott, J.K.: Assessing the quality of municipal government web sites. State Local Gov. Rev. **37**(2), 151–165 (2005). https://doi.org/10.1177/0160323X0503700206
12. Silva, J.M.C., Ramos, L.F.M., Fonte, V.: Qualification offer in EGOV competencies in PALOP-TL. In: Proceedings of the 11th International Conference on Theory and Practice of Electronic Governance, ICEGOV 2018, pp. 308–311. ACM, New York (2018). https://doi.org/10.1145/3209415.3209514
13. Silva, T., Tavares, A., Lameiras, M.: 'Trendy' cities: exploring the adoption of different types of social media by Portuguese municipalities. In: Panagiotopoulos, P., et al. (eds.) ePart 2019. LNCS, vol. 11686, pp. 26–34. Springer, Cham (2019). https://doi.org/10.1007/978-3-030-27397-2_3
14. Soares, D., Amaral, L., Ferreira, L.M., Lameiras, M.: Presença na internet das câmaras municipais portuguesas em 2019: Estudo sobre local e-government em Portugal (2019)
15. United Nations E-government Survey: Gearing e-government to support transformation towards sustainable and resilient societies (2018)
16. United Nations E-government Survey: Digital government in the decade of action for sustainable development (2020)
17. Tolbert, C.J., Mossberger, K.: The effects of e-government on trust and confidence in government. Public Adm. Rev. **66**(3), 354–369 (2006)

18. United Nations General Assembly: Transforming our world: the 2030 agenda for sustainable development. Technical report, A/RES/70/1, 21 October 2015
19. Wang, S., Feeney, M.K.: Determinants of information and communication technology adoption in municipalities. Am. Rev. Public Admin. **46**(3), 292–313 (2016). https://doi.org/10.1177/0275074014553462
20. Welch, E.W., Hinnant, C.C., Moon, M.J.: Linking citizen satisfaction with e-government and trust in government. J. Public Admin. Res. Theory **15**(3), 371–391 (2005)

Beyond Substantive Goals – A Framework for Understanding Citizens Need and Goals in Bureaucratic Encounters

Søren Skaarup[✉]

IT University of Copenhagen, Copenhagen, Denmark
skaa@itu.dk

Abstract. This paper contributes to e-government research by presenting a conceptual framework of citizens' needs and goals for bureaucratic encounters. The framework is developed through a qualitative hermeneutic approach involving several different literatures. The framework goes beyond the prevalent focus on substantive needs. It identifies four needs related to the BE process: process-security, relational security, discretion and efficiency and effectiveness; and three outcome-goals: substantive outcome, identity-related outcome, and justice- and fairness outcome. These interrelated needs and goals may guide citizens' approaches to the bureaucratic encounter and their choice of channel(s) for the encounter. The degree to which these needs and goals are met may have consequences for the efficiency of the service delivery seen from the authorities' perspective as well as for the citizens' satisfaction and sense of a fair and just application of authority. The framework can be a useful tool for analysing citizens' strategies concerning the bureaucratic encounters and their use of self-service systems and the effects thereof for both citizens and authorities. In addition, the framework can be used by researchers and practitioners alike to analyse self-service-systems and multi-channel strategies and service designs to identify how they take the different needs into account.

Keywords: Citizen-government interaction · Digitalization · Theory-building · Digital services · Needs and goals

1 Introduction and Background

As more of citizens' interactions with government occur online [1], it becomes important to understand what citizens seek from these encounters. Citizens' needs and goals may affect their approaches to the different mediations of the encounters and have implications for the design of systems and services.

Citizens encounter government in a wide range of situations and for a wide range of reasons. In this paper, the focus is on what Goodsell calls "bureaucratic encounters" (BE) [2, 3]. This is where most people have direct experience with government authorities. Goodsell's work focuses on face-to-face encounters. As Nass and Moon

© IFIP International Federation for Information Processing 2021
Published by Springer Nature Switzerland AG 2021
H. J. Scholl et al. (Eds.): EGOV 2021, LNCS 12850, pp. 86–102, 2021.
https://doi.org/10.1007/978-3-030-84789-0_7

have shown [4, 5], people unwittingly apply social and human attributes to interactive systems such as self-service systems. Thus, interactions with self-service systems may qualify as encounters with proxies for humans and the organizations they represent. In this paper, "Encounters" covers all types of "bureaucratic" interactions between citizens and authorities, no matter what channels are used.

What citizens want and expect from BEs (their needs and goals) has, in the e-government literature, primarily been studied from a channel-choice (CC) perspective [6–9]. In the CC literature, goals and needs are often treated as independent variables for channel choice. However, a gap exists when it comes to examining needs and goals as the focus of the analysis and analysis from a situated, citizen perspective where the citizen and not channels are the unit of analysis [10, 11].

The need for citizen-centred research has been stated repeatedly in the literature [9, 12–14], and not understanding the citizen perspective may have consequences for the authorities as well as for citizens. As Kolsakker and Lee-Kelly [15]:73 puts it, "if the needs of the citizens are not understood, provision will be designed around the needs of the state", which often implies the dominance of an economic/administrative rational [16, 17].

The present study contributes to the e-government literature by presenting a conceptual framework of the needs and goals that are important for citizens and their actions and strategies regarding bureaucratic encounters. Thus, the study answers the repeated call for native theory development within e-government studies [9, 18]. Scholars can use this framework to investigate the effects for citizens of applying different technologies in the BE. Practitioners can use the framework in the design of self-service systems, the organizational designs of BE service delivery, and in the design of multichannel strategies.

The paper is structured as follows: Sect. 2 outlines the research approach. Section 3 describes the framework that has been derived from this review. Section 4 provides a discussion of the framework's implications for different mediations and outlines an agenda for future research.

2 Method

The framework presented here is an artefact developed through a "hermeneutic literature review" [19], based on the principles of the hermeneutic circle [20], synthesising theory and findings from previous research. Following Rose et al. [21], I examine literature five different literatures which can shed light on citizens needs and goals for their BEs: 1) the public administration literature, 2) the E-government literature, 3) the private sector service encounter literature, 4) literature from the legal field on justice and fairness in citizens encounters with authorities, 5) Literature on the sociology of encounters. Each field of research contributed with perspectives on goals and needs which could be relevant for the framework.

The selection and search of these literatures is based on a set of initial assumptions. These assumptions are founded both in previous literature readings and on my career as a civil servant with extensive experience serving citizens at the frontlines (Table 1).

Table 1. Initial assumptions

	Assumption	Inspired by
1	The trigger for initiating a bureaucratic encounter/set of encounters will typically be because the citizens have some substantive need (benefit, permit, service) or must fulfil some obligation	Godsell 2018 [3], Lindgreen et al. 2019 [9]
2	The BE is a highly asymmetrical encounter, where the citizen typically has less power, information, and resources than the authority. The assumption is that citizens will have needs related to handling this asymmetry, maintain a sense of control and project and protect a positive identity), and feel that they are treated fairly by those in authority	Godsell 2018 [3], Lenk 2002 [22]
3	Much of the process in and around a BE may be complex and opaque for citizens resulting in uncertainty and ambiguity. The assumption is that citizens will have needs related to handling this uncertainty and ambiguity, to feel secure in their understanding and actions, and in the functioning of those elements of the process that takes place in back-offices or are inscribed in IT systems	Pieterson 2009 [6], Jarvis 2014 [23]
4	In BEs, citizens will often find themselves in unfamiliar situations with insufficient domain skills. The assumption is that citizens will have needs related to establishing a sufficient understanding of what they can and should do and what is going on	Skaarup 2020 [24], Madsen and Christensen 2019 [25], Grönlund, Hatakka, and Ask 2007 [26]

The process included the steps outlined by [19]: 1) reading, 2) identifying ideas and concepts of relevance for the research objective and placing them into the emerging conceptual framework, 3) critically assessing the literature, 4) developing and revising the framework as new concepts and ideas were identified 5) Identifying areas for further study and possible applications of the framework, 6) searching based on references and new perspectives found in the literature consulted so far. These steps were applied iteratively and not necessarily in the order presented here. Searching, reading, analysing, and framework development were closely interconnected.

During this iterative process of searching, reading, and analysis, I synthesise the framework through a series of revisions and elaborations. The process stopped when saturation was reached, and no further dimensions for the framework were identified [19].

3   Conceptual Framework

The result of the literature review is a conceptual framework intended to serve as a foundation and reference point for further investigation [27]. The framework identifies relevant citizens' needs and goals for the BE. Table 2 presents this framework. Note that the distinctions here are analytical. While the table format indicates a certain order and linearity, a specific BE may not include all the needs and goals in equal measure or follow this order.

The citizen's needs and goals presented in Table 2 covers two phenomena. (1) the process-internal aspects of the encounter (needs): process-security, relational security, discretion, and efficiency and effectiveness. (2) the outcome goals, i.e., what the citizen hopes to achieve through the encounter: substantive goals, identity-related goals, and justice- and fairness goals. Each need and goal can be achieved through one or more aspects of the encounter.

The needs and goals in the framework are not mutually exclusive. While they are sufficiently distinct to constitute separate elements in the framework, they still overlap and may sometimes, in concrete cases, be contradictory to some extent.

Table 2. Framework of needs and goals

Need	Achieved through	Description	References
Process-related needs			
Process-security	A) A sense of understanding	Framing the problem or task in a way the fits the bureaucratic conceptualization and organization of information and services in order to search for information, plot a course, find the right authority(ies), etc., and reducing ambiguity to a level that allows the citizen to proceed with a sufficient level of security	[28–32]
	B) A sense of SLB competence	Gauging whether the street-level bureaucrat (SLB) or the authority appears competent in what they do - to bolster the sense of security further	[33–38]
	C) A sense of closure	Need for clarity about what the citizen has done and what is going to happen next	[6, 8, 39–41]

(*continued*)

Table 2. (*continued*)

Need	Achieved through	Description	References
Relational security	A) A sense of respect and recognition	Being allowed to project the identity you wish to project (typically a situationally relevant, positive identity) and being recognized as a competent individual and member of society	[3, 33, 35, 42–53]
	B) A sense of positive intentions	Establishing a rapport and gauging attitudes and intentions of SLBs involved increasing the sense that your case is in the hands of someone with a positive attitude towards you and your needs	[28, 42]
	C) A sense of justice and fairness	Feeling that one is being treated justly and fairly in the process	[54–63]
Discretion	Flexibility in the process, in interaction and the interpretation of rules	A process that to some extent can be adapted to you and your situation, allowances for interaction that goes beyond the strict needs of the authority for data, and some flexibility in the interpretation of rules where grey areas exist or can be construed	[50, 64–68]
Efficiency and effectiveness	A sense of time and resources well spent	Procedures and systems that fit the citizens' preferences and skills, investing what the citizen considers a reasonable effort. Providing a sense of self-efficacy, including ease of use and a sense of convenience	[6, 43, 45, 69–74]
Outcome goals			
Substantive outcome	Process-security and discretion	Achieving the substantive goals for the BE	See process security and discretion above
Identity-related outcome	Relational security	Feeling respected and recognized as a valued member of society and preserving a positive sense of situationally relevant identity	See relational security above
Justice and fairness outcome	Relational security and discretion	Feeling treated justly and fairly by the authority, regardless of the substantive outcome	See relational security and discretion above

These needs and goals are fundamentally technology-neutral, but fulfilling them may require different strategies and skills and be provided different affordances in different channels used for the encounter.

Needs and goals may not be fulfilled and reached through one encounter. It may, in some cases, take several encounters with the same authority or several different authorities using different mediations. Also, all of the needs and goals are not necessarily important for a specific encounter and a specific citizen. In many encounters, only a few of the needs and goals may be important, while in some encounters, most of them could come into play. What goals and needs are important would presumably depend on the individual and the circumstances of the situation.

3.1 Process-Security Needs

Process-security needs focus on the course of the BE process as a means for achieving a sufficient level of certainty or security that everything necessary has been done, and done correctly, and to optimize the chances of achieving the desired outcomes, with an effort that feels manageable and appropriate for the task.

Research by Pieterson, Ebbers, and others [6, 8, 39, 40] indicate that the course of the BE process may involve its own needs. Process needs are related to the encounter experience and to the way outcomes are achieved. Three such needs stand out in the e-government literature: "sense of closure", "ease of use", and "efficiency", in other words: the process has to be easy, efficient, effective, and provide a sense of security that the task is done, and everything is OK. Similar process needs are described in the private sector service-encounter literature. This literature also has a focus on what Dasu and Chase [75] call the "soft side of customer service": emotions, perceived control, and trust, and it has a focus on the perceived competence of the service personnel as a source of assurance and security.

A. A sense of understanding – through frame-alignment and disambiguation
Establishing a sense that you understand where you have to go, what information you need, understanding the information you find or receive, and what you have to do, is important for fulfilling a need for security in the process. In BEs, citizen will often find themselves in situations that are unfamiliar to them, with insufficient domain skills [24] to assists them in plotting a course, searching for, understanding, and evaluating information, and translating their problems and needs into something that fits the relevant bureaucratic framing [30], and to "overcome different frames of reference or clarify ambiguous issues and change understanding in a timely manner" [29]:560.

A "frame" is "a perceptual matrix that systematises experience and helps one define a situation and make it understandable and to some extent predictable" [31]:150. Frames usually only become visible when non-alignment is discovered and acknowledged [28]:39. Frame alignment is necessary when two different ways of understanding or structuring the issues exist and have to be reconciled, giving rise to disambiguity and uncertainty. If agreement on framing is not reached, we may get (potential) conflict (if disagreement is acknowledged) or misunderstandings (if unacknowledged).

Highly ambiguous messages are open to interpretation, and a shared definition must be constructed through some form of interactive communication [32]:1546.

B. A sense of authority competence
In order to feel secure in the process, it may be important for the citizen to have a sense that the people he or she interacts with (directly or indirectly) are competent and know what they are doing. Service encounters in general and BEs, in particular, are asymmetrical encounters where one party possesses skills and knowledge the other typically does not [35]. In the BE, there is also a clear underlying asymmetry of power. Credibility and a sense of competence, therefore, become important [33]. This can be achieved through a projection of competence by the SLB: understanding customers' (citizens) needs, knowing the rules, procedures, and services involved and performing effectively in the service process [45]. As the citizen usually does not have the knowledge necessary to evaluate this competence directly, it may have to be assessed through surface- or "proxy"-indicators [36, 37], often connected to immediately ascertainable behaviour [38] such as the assuredness with which the SLB performs and cues in body language, facial expressions, and tone of voice.

C. A sense of closure
Having a sense that you have done things correctly and that your application is in the right hands and will be taken care of within a reasonable timeframe may be important for fulfilling a need for security in the process. Pieterson and van Dijk [39] and Pieterson [6]:188ff talks about how citizens may need "uncertainty reduction", "a sense of closure," or "a need for clarity" and how this may influence their strategies for the encounter. Ebbers et al. [8] describe how this need may be particularly salient in situations characterized by a high degree of uncertainty for the citizen. The "need for closure" is also recognized in the private sector service literature [41].

Vermeir (ibid.) highlights the informational aspects of achieving a sense of closure when he defines it as "an individual's desire for clear, definite, or unambiguous knowledge that will guide perception and action, as opposed to the undesirable alternative of ambiguity and confusion." (ibid.:xvi).

3.2 Efficiency, Effectiveness, Ease of Use and Convenience

Feeling that you have spent your time and resources efficiently and effectively in a way that suited your skills and preferences could be considered a need in its own right. Efficiency – conducting the process with minimum use of time, cost and effort, and effectiveness – the process achieving its goals are important process needs in both the e-government and service-encounter literatures [6, 43, 45, 72, 73]. However, efficiency may not so much be a matter of the objective amount of time and resources spent, as a subjective feeling of being efficient often connected with a feeling of being able to act [69], and of being capable and competent to act – a sense of self-efficacy [71]. This is also related to the need for respect and recognition (see below).

Perceived Ease of use is a key factor in the often-cited Technology Acceptance Model, defined as "the degree to which the user expects the system to be free of effort" [70]. For the purpose of this study, I would argue that this is an aspect of the encounter experience that contributes to the feeling of being efficient and the sense of competence on the part of the authority. This also applies to the concept of convenience - receiving the service where, how, and when desired [74].

3.3   Relational Security Needs and Goals

While process-security needs are process-internal, relational security can be seen both as process-internal needs and as "soft" outcome goals.

Relational security has to do with being able to project and protect a positive identity throughout the encounter, feeling recognized as a competent and valued individual, and feeling treated fairly and with respect. As process-needs, they contribute to a sense of security, a sense that the authority is acting fairly, taking all relevant aspects of the individual and his or her situation into account, thus contributing to a fair and just decision on the substantive outcome. As outcome-goals relational security has to do with how the process has affected the citizens' sense of "citizenship" and sense of fairness and justice in the way authority is practiced.

A. Respect and recognition

Needs and goals of respect and recognition are related to the citizen's sense of identity. It has to do with being treated with respect, being able to project and defend a positive identity, and being recognized as a competent member of society [42, 48]. In the private sector service-encounter literature, aspects of the encounter related to respect, courtesy, responsiveness, empathy, helpfulness, and sociability play a significant role in customers' evaluation of encounters [33, 35, 43, 45]. These all have to do with recognizing the customers as worthy individuals.

In the context of the BE, there is, as we have seen, a clear asymmetrical distribution of power which may assign additional importance to the need for recognition. Bureaucratic encounters may, as Goodsell [3] found, besides their instrumental goals (providing benefits and services), also constitute "social exchanges which confirm or alter the status position of clients." BEs may involve the display, negotiation, confirmation, and/or rejection of identities [46, 47, 49, 50].

The identity citizens bring to the encounter and, to some extent, attempts to project and defend is a social self [44]:6–7, a communicated self, created in social interaction it is also, as Goffman argues, a controlled and situated self [51]:156. The conflict that arises between the institutional identities recognized by the authority and the social, moral selves the citizens wish to project and defend is described by Spencer [52] as a conflict between a formal, standardized discourse of rules and resources and a discourse of individuality and morality or, as Hopper puts it, between moral selves and legal selves [76]. The discourse citizens apply in their claim to moral selves often includes information that is irrelevant to the construction of institutional identities [53].

A successful social encounter must allow for "the projected claims to an acceptable self" [42]:105. The individual can only maintain this positive identity and a positive self-relation with the help of the accepting or confirming feedback [48]:85.

B. A sense of positive intentions
Just as competence is often evaluated through proxy indicators, so a sense of respect and recognition may rely on more than the surface of what is said and done. It may depend to an extent on the back channels, which carry the subtle "keyings" [28] that contain information about the modality of what is being said (humour, irony, good-naturedness, etc.) and facilitates a close and nuanced reading of intentions and attitudes [42].

Different mediations of the encounter may allow for "unnecessary" information, confirming feedback and "keying information" to varying degrees.

C. A sense of justice and fairness
Justice and fairness needs have to do with the feeling that the power of the authority is applied in a manner that is just and fair to the individual. In highly asymmetrical encounters, such as BEs, it may be especially important for citizens to feel that they are treated justly and fairly [54–56, 58–60]. The literature on justice and fairness often distinguishes between three types of (perceived) justice [61]: distributive justice: the degree to which the outcome is considered fair, also in relation to what others are assumed/perceived to get; 2) procedural justice: the perceived fairness of practices, policies and procedures; and 3) interactional justice – the enactment of the encounter such as fair treatment, friendliness, objectiveness, honesty, genuine interest, respect, and sensitivity [57].

Tyler and colleagues find that "procedural justice", the way people are treated and their cases are handled in relation to authorities, has an effect independent of any impact on the decisions made and may even be more important for citizens than the substantive outcome (see also [62] and [63] for parallel findings from the private-sector service literature). Blader and Tyler [59] show that how decisions are made in concrete encounters, including the degree of citizen involvement and voice, and the quality of the way citizens are treated (respect, politeness, dignity) is key to the production of a sense of procedural justice (just as it is key to customer satisfaction). While a product of the process, I would argue that justice and fairness is not so much a process-goal as it is another soft-outcome goal, parallel and related to respect and recognition.

3.4   Discretion

Madsen and Kræmmergaard [64] talk about how citizens' wishes to affect the substantive outcome may lead them to choose mediations that allow for some degree of negotiation of the outcome – that is, some degree of discretion.

And indeed, the needs and goals outlined above all, to some extent, imply some degree of flexibility or "discretion" in the process. Discretion has been defined as the power a public officer has "...whenever the effective limits on his power leave him free to choose among possible courses in action or inaction" [77]:166. As Lipsky [65] described, discretion can be a tool for the abuse of power, as it allows SLBs to induce their own prejudices, values, and interpretations of rules and policies into their practice and decision-making. At the same time, many analyses of the "law in practice" suggests that "any policy or rule needs to be modified to fit the circumstances in which it is implemented" [66]:207, and even Lipsky admits that: "Equal treatment may require treating people differently to achieve equal results" [65]:232. Lipsky describes discretion as primarily an aspect of the role of SLBs, but citizens themselves may have an active part in the negotiation of discretion [50]. Dworkin [67] distinguish between "strong" and "weak" discretion. Weak discretion tends to allow for some degree of technical autonomy [68] – focusing on procedural and interactional control, while strong discretion tends to allow also for "ideological" autonomy, with more control of procedures and outcomes. On this basis, I will distinguish between 1) Substantive discretion, which has to do with determining eligibility for benefits and services – the substantive goal of encounters. Here discretion, especially in BEs, may be very limited (weak) due to strict objective criteria for eligibility. 2) Procedural discretion, which allows for flexibility in the process. Procedural discretion in the BE has traditionally been fairly strong but may be circumscribed by the IT systems used for casework and processing. 3) Interactional discretion, which has to do with the way citizens are treated, whether the citizen feels listened to and taken seriously. Citizens may appeal to discretion in order to affect the substantive outcome of the encounter, but as this, in BEs is often highly rule-based, discretion in the other two areas may become important, even when it does not actually affect the substantive outcome. Depending on the citizen's expectations and experiences with authorities, discretion maybe something one seeks to avoid because of the risks it entails, or it may be something one actively seeks out and engage in because of its possibilities.

3.5 Substantive Outcome Goals

The substantive outcome has to do with the original goals for the encounter, that is, the fulfilment of some basic need(s) the citizen has outside of the encounter. This may, for example, be to get a benefit or permit, be afforded access to a service, or fulfil some obligation, like filing taxes. Assuming citizens rarely enter into BEs for the experience, there will arguably always be some substantive goal that triggers the encounter(s). Substantive goals appear so self-evident that they are not the object of much discussion in the literature.

3.6 Summing Up

Based on this review of several literatures, I have identified five interrelated types of needs and goals for the bureaucratic encounter: (1) Process -security: achieving certainty in understanding, in the competence of the SLBs, and of having completed the process correctly; (2) Relational security: achieving a sufficient sense of respect and recognition, of positive intentions of the SLB, and of being treated justly and fairly in the process, (3) Discretion: a sufficient level of flexibility in the process; (4) Efficiency and effectiveness: a feeling of self-efficacy and time well spent; (5) outcome goals: achieving the substantive goal, feeling recognised and accepted and feeling that the substantive outcome has been achieved in a fair and just manner.

The importance of these goals and needs will arguably not be the same for every citizen in every situation. It may depend on how much is at stake for the citizen – substantially or identity-wise. Or it may depend on the citizen's familiarity with the situation/service/authority and his or her domain skills.

4 Discussion and Conclusion

This paper set out to establish a conceptual framework for describing and analysing citizens' needs and goals for bureaucratic encounters, thorough a hermeneutic literature review. The resulting framework shows that several needs and goals besides the substantial goals that usually "trigger" an encounter may be important for the citizens. Most of these needs and goals are "soft," relying mainly on feelings and experiences. All of the needs have some bearing on the perceived chances of achieving the substantial outcome: fulfilment of process-security needs increase the sense of having understood and done things correctly. Relational security needs may be important to the citizen's sense of identity, sense of empowerment, sense of citizenship, and sense of being a valued member of society. The fulfilment of these needs also increases the sense that the SLB has positive intentions and will do what he or she can to help the citizen achieve the substantive goal. Needs for discretion and flexibility may also contribute to a sense of empowerment and citizenship, and of being seen and treated as an individual, at the same time as a sense of discretion – even if "only" interactional or procedural, may contribute to a feeling that the decision reached will be a correct one. These needs are primarily evaluated based on feelings and experience rather than on measurable aspects of the encounter. This may apply even to efficiency and effectiveness needs to the extent that these are not evaluated based on strict measurements of time and resources spent.

I would argue that the framework is, in essence, technology-neutral. All of the needs and goals could arguably be fulfilled to some degree through any mediation, and all mediations could be implemented in a way that did not support any of the needs and goals well. The expectation would, for example, be that face-to-face encounters would be good at supporting most of the "soft" needs, but face-to-face BEs may indeed be practiced in ways that offer limited support to these goals and needs and even in ways that undermine them. Conversely, we might expect BEs conducted through self-service systems to have limited support for the relational and identity-related needs and goals, but that may depend very much on the design of the service.

The framework indicates that the bureaucratic encounter may have purposes beyond the immediate ones identified by Goodsell "to exchange information, provide public service, or control or constrain citizens." They may also have the broader purpose – for citizens and authorities alike – of confirming/strengthening/weakening the citizens' sense of competence, fairness, and reliability of the specific authority involved in the encounter and even of authorities in general. This, in turn, may have implications for the citizens' sense of trust in the authority, for the sense of the legitimacy of their decisions, for compliance with the decisions, and their general support of the authority.

Thus, it is important for e-government researchers to look beyond the immediate goals and effects of digitalization of the BE and take citizens' needs and goals as well as the wider implications of the practices of e-government into account.

4.1 Suggestions for Application and Further Research

The framework provides a valuable tool for e-government researchers to study channel-choice and e-government adoption from a needs- and goals-perspective and for studying the authorities' strategies and choices in designing systems and services. The framework could also serve as a tool for practitioners in designing and evaluating systems, services, and strategies.

The framework contributes to the e-government field in addressing the need for citizen-centred research and understanding the users' needs and resources [13, 14, 17], and in engaging other theoretical fields to advance e-government theory building [18, 78].

To bring the field further forward, I propose a research agenda for the e-government community with the following research questions:

1. How do needs interact with each other and with the outcome goals? Are the process needs, for example, primarily of importance for successfully completing the tasks contained in and around the encounter, or do they have significant implications for how the outcomes are evaluated?
2. What features of systems and user journeys in which they are typically embedded contribute to fulfilling the different needs and goals – or do the opposite?
3. What features of the situation in the citizen's life that gives rise to the encounter contribute to the relative importance of the different needs and goals? Will unfamiliar situations or significant consequences of the outcome, for instance, increase the importance of certain needs?
4. Are some needs and goals more important to some categories of citizens than others, and how can these needs best be met or lowered for these citizens? Are certain needs, for example, more important for citizens with fewer resources or lower skills?
5. What is the effect on the efficiency of service delivery of better addressing citizens' needs and goals? Will an improvement in process security, for example, decrease the need for contact on other channels during or after a self-service encounter?
6. What is the effect of improvements in the way needs and goals are met in delivering a service on compliance and, for cases that require contacts between the citizen and the authority over a longer period of time, on cooperation between the citizen and the authority during that process?

Apart from answering these specific questions, such research could also contribute to further refinement and elaboration of the framework through its application to empirical data. Practitioners could also apply the framework as a tool in the design of services and systems. They could, for example for investigating the importance of the different needs and goals for a given target group/situation before designing a new service/system as input to a multi-channel service design or for evaluating existing systems and services.

4.2 Limitations and Concluding Comments

While I have investigated a wide range of literatures in this paper, my aim has not been an exhaustive investigation of them all, but through an interpretive, hermeneutic approach to identify salient and important perspectives on citizens' needs and goals for the bureaucratic encounter. Through this, I hope to have provided a framework for a more holistic investigation and understanding of citizens" needs and goals.

Dahler-Larsen [79] establishes four criteria for the quality of qualitative research: 1) craftsmanship – applying suitable methods in a proper way, 2) transparency in the way the methods are applied, showing how the data (in this case, the literature) lead to and supports the conclusions (in this case the framework), 3) communicative quality – presenting the work that makes it open and accessible for investigation and discussion with others, and 4) the "heuristic criterium" – that the analysis leads to new insights and perspectives. All four criteria are ultimately subjective as they rely on the reader's assessments.

An interpretive, hermeneutic approach will always and unavoidably rely on the researcher's pre-understanding. As Dey [80]:251 puts it: "There is a difference between an open mind and an empty head." What is important is to make these pre-understandings explicit, as has been done here with the initial assumption.

The initial assumptions have also served to seek alternative perspectives on the encounter that are not usually represented in the e-government literature. At the same time, the selection of literature has been limited by these assumptions. Other literatures, such as the service-design and digital-design literatures, could have provided additional insights. However, the intention of this study has not been to conduct an exhaustive survey of all relevant literatures but, through a limited search of selected literatures, to provide a framework that covers a wider range of citizen's needs and goals for the BE. I hope that the use and applications of this framework by scholars and practitioners will contribute to its improvement and elaboration.

Acknowledgements. An early draft of this paper was presented at the 2021 Scandinavian Workshop on e-Government. I would like to thank my colleagues in the Scandinavian e-Government community for valuable feedback on my work. I am employed and financed by the Research Centre for Government IT, a collaboration between the IT University of Copenhagen and the Danish Ministry for Finance.

References

1. European Commission: Digital Economy and Society Index (DESI) Report on Digital Public Services (2019). https://ec.europa.eu/digital-single-market/en/desi
2. Katz, D., Gutek, B., Kahn, R.L., Barton, E.: Bureaucratic encounters. University of Michigan Survey Reserarch Center, Ann Arbor (1975)
3. Goodsell, C.T.: The New Case for Bureaucracy. SAGE, London (2018)
4. Nass, C., Fogg, B.J., Moon, Y.: Can computers be teammates? Int. J. Hum. Comput. Stud. **45**(6), 669–678 (1996). https://doi.org/10.1006/ijhc.1996.0073
5. Nass, C., Moon, Y.: Machines and mindlessness: social responses to computers. J. Soc. Issues **56**(1), 81–103 (2000). https://doi.org/10.1111/0022-4537.00153
6. Pieterson, W.: Channel choice - citizens' channel behavior and public service channel strategy. University of Twente (2009)
7. Reddick, C.G., Turner, M.: Channel choice and public service delivery in Canada: comparing e-government to traditional service delivery. Gov. Inf. Q. **29**(1), 1–11 (2012). https://doi.org/10.1016/j.giq.2011.03.005

8. Ebbers, W.E., Jansen, M.G.M., van Deursen, A.J.A.M.: Impact of the digital divide on e-government: expanding from channel choice to channel usage. Gov. Inf. Q. **33**(4), 685–692 (2016). https://doi.org/10.1016/j.giq.2016.08.007

9. Lindgren, I., Madsen, C.Ø., Hofmann, S., Melin, U.: Close encounters of the digital kind: a research agenda for the digitalization of public services. Gov. Inf. Q. **36**(3), 427–436 (2019). https://doi.org/10.1016/j.giq.2019.03.002

10. Madsen, C.Ø., Kræmmergaard, P.: Channel choice: a literature review. In: Tambouris, E., et al. (eds.) EGOV 2015. LNCS, vol. 9248, pp. 3–18. Springer, Cham (2015). https://doi.org/10.1007/978-3-319-22479-4_1

11. Madsen, C., Hofmann, S.: Multichannel management in the public sector: a literature review, pp. 20–35 (2019)

12. Reddick, C.G.: Citizen-initiated contacts with government: comparing phones and websites. J. E-Gov. **2**(1), 27–53 (2005). https://doi.org/10.1300/J399v02n01_03

13. Scott, M., DeLone, W.H., Golden, W.: Understanding net benefits: a citizen-based perspective on eGovernment success. In: 30th International Conference on Information Systems (ICIS 2009), pp. 1–11. AIS, Phoenix (2009). Paper 86. http://aisel.aisnet.org/icis2009/86/

14. Meijer, A.J., Bekkers, V.: A metatheory of e-government: creating some order in a fragmented research field. Gov. Inf. Q. **32**(3), 237–245 (2015). https://doi.org/10.1016/j.giq.2015.04.006

15. Kolsaker, A., Lee-Kelley, L.: Citizens' attitudes towards e-government: a UK study. Int. J. Public Sect. Manag. **21**(7), 723–738 (2008)

16. Persson, J., Reinwald, A., Skorve, E., Nielsen, P.: Value positions in e-government strategies: something is (not) changing in the state of Denmark. In: 25th European Conference on Information Systems (ECIS 2017), Guimarães, Portugal, pp. 904–917 (2017)

17. Bertot, J.C., Jaeger, P.T.: The E-Government paradox: better customer service doesn't necessarily cost less. Gov. Inf. Q. **25**(2), 149–154 (2008). https://doi.org/10.1016/j.giq.2007.10.002

18. Bannister, F., Connolly, R.: The great theory hunt: does e-government really have a problem? Gov. Inf. Q. **32**(1), 1–11 (2015). https://doi.org/10.1016/j.giq.2014.10.003

19. Boell, S.K., Cecez-Kecmanovic, D.: A hermeneutic approach for conducting literature reviews and literature searches. Commun. Assoc. Inf. Syst. **34**(1), 257–286 (2014). https://doi.org/10.17705/1cais.03412

20. Gadamer, H.G.: Hermeneutics and social science. Philos. Soc. Crit. **2**(4), 307–316 (1975). https://doi.org/10.1177/019145377500200402

21. Rose, J., Persson, J.S., Heeager, L.T., Irani, Z.: Managing e-Government: value positions and relationships. Inf. Syst. J. **25**(5), 531–571 (2015). https://doi.org/10.1111/isj.12052

22. Lenk, K.: Electronic service delivery-a driver of public sector modernisation. Inf. Polity **7**(2–3), 87–96 (2002). https://doi.org/10.3233/ip-2002-0009

23. Jarvis, M.D.: The black box of bureaucracy: interrogating accountability in the public service. Aust. J. Public Adm. **73**(4), 450–466 (2014). https://doi.org/10.1111/1467-8500.12109

24. Skaarup, S.: The role of domain-skills in bureaucratic service encounters. In: Viale Pereira, G., et al. (eds.) EGOV 2020. LNCS, vol. 12219, pp. 179–196. Springer, Cham (2020). https://doi.org/10.1007/978-3-030-57599-1_14

25. Madsen, C.Ø., Christensen, L.R.: Integrated and seamless ? Single parents' experiences of cross-organizational interaction. Selected Papers of the IRIS, vol. 9, no. 9, pp. 1–18 (2019). https://aisel.aisnet.org/iris2018/5

26. Grönlund, Å., Hatakka, M., Ask, A.: Inclusion in the E-service society – investigating administrative literacy requirements for using E-services. In: Wimmer, M.A., Scholl, J., Grönlund, Å. (eds.) EGOV 2007. LNCS, vol. 4656, pp. 216–227. Springer, Heidelberg (2007). https://doi.org/10.1007/978-3-540-74444-3_19

27. Jabareen, Y.: Building a conceptual framework: philosophy, definitions, and procedure. Int. J. Qual. Methods **8**(4), 49–62 (2009). https://doi.org/10.1177/160940690900800406

28. Goffman, E.: Frame Analysis: An Essay on the Organization of Experience. North Eastern University Press, Boston (1974)
29. Daft, R.L., Lengel, R.H.: Organizational information requirements, media richness and structural design. Manag. Sci. **32**(5), 554–571 (1986). https://doi.org/10.1287/mnsc.32.5.554
30. Gubrium, J.F., Järvinen, M.: Turning Troubles into Problems: Clientization in Human Services. Routledge, London (2013)
31. Jacobsen, M.H., Kristiansen, S.: Erving Goffman: sociologien om det elementære livs sociale former. Reitzel, Copenhagen (2002)
32. Webster, J., Trevino, L.K.: rational and social theories as complementary explanations of communication media choices: two policy-capturing studies. Acad. Manag. J. **38**(6), 1544–1572 (1995). https://doi.org/10.5465/256843
33. Surprenant, C.F., Solomon, M.R.: Predictability and personalization in the service encounter. J. Mark. **51**(2), 86 (1987). https://doi.org/10.2307/1251131
34. Rowley, J.: An analysis of the e-service literature: towards a research agenda. Internet Res. Electron. Netw. Appl. Policy **16**(3), 339–359 (2006)
35. Philip, G., Hazlett, S.A.: The measurement of service quality: a new P-C-P attributes model. Int. J. Qual. Reliab. Manag. **14**(3), 260–286 (1997). https://doi.org/10.1108/02656719710165482
36. Walker, J.L.: Service encounter satisfaction: conceptualized. J. Serv. Mark. **9**(1), 5, 13 (1995).: https://www.emerald.com/insight/content/doi/10.1108/08876049510079844/full/pdf?title=service-encounter-satisfaction-conceptualized
37. Black, S., Briggs, S., Keogh, W.: Service quality performance measurement in public/private sectors. Manag. Audit. J. **16**(7), 400–405 (2001). https://doi.org/10.1108/EUM0000000005715
38. Farrell, A.M., Souchon, A.L., Durden, G.R.: Service encounter conceptualisation: employees' service behaviours and customers' service quality perceptions. J. Mark. Manag. **17**(5–6), 577–593 (2001). https://doi.org/10.1362/026725701323366944
39. Pieterson, W., van Dijk, J.: Channel choice determinants; an exploration of the factors that determine the choice of a service channel in citizen initiated contacts. In: 8th Annual International Conference on Digital Government Research (DG.O 2007), vol. 228, pp. 173–182. Digital Government Research Center, Philadelphia (2007)
40. Madsen, C.Ø., Hofmann, S., Pieterson, W.: Channel choice complications. In: Lindgren, I., et al. (eds.) EGOV 2019. LNCS, vol. 11685, pp. 139–151. Springer, Cham (2019). https://doi.org/10.1007/978-3-030-27325-5_11
41. Vermeir, I.: The influence of need for closure on consumer's choice behaviour. University of Gent (2003)
42. Goffman, E.: Interaction Ritual: Essays on Face-to-Face Behavior. Doubleday, Garden City (1967)
43. Parasuraman, A., Berry, L.L., Zeithaml, V.A.: SERVQUAL: a multiple-item scale for measuring consumer perceptions of service quality. J. Retail. **64**(1), 12–40 (1988)
44. Gubrium, J.F., Holstein, J.A.: The Self We Live by: Narrative Identity in a Postmodern World, vol. 31, no. 3. Oxford University Press, New York (2000)
45. Alotaibi, E.K., Lockwood, P.A.: Interaction quality in service encounter: scale development and validation (2011)
46. Sarangi, S., Slembrouck, S.: Language, Bureaucracy and Social Control. Longman, London (2014)
47. Järvinen, M., Mik-Meyer, N.: At skabe en klient: institutionelle identiteter i socialt arbejde. Reitzel, Copenhagen (2013)
48. Honneth, A.: Behovet for anerkendelse - En tekstsamling. Reitzel, Copenhagen (2003)
49. Mik-meyer, N., Villadsen, K.: Magtens former: Sociologiske perspektiver på statens møde med borgeren. Reitzel, Copenhagen (2007)

50. Lundberg, K.G.: Uforutsigbare relasjoner: Brukererfaringer, Nav-reformen og levd liv. University of Bergen (2012)
51. Goffman, E.: Relations in Public: Microstudies of the Public Order, vol. 51, no. 4. Basic Books, London (1973)
52. William, S.J.: Self-presentation and organizational processing in a human service agency. In: Holstein, J.F., James, A., Gubrium (eds.) Institutional Selves - Troubled Identities in a Postmodern World, pp. 158–176. Oxford University Press, Oxford (2000)
53. Carstens, A.: Aktivering - klientsamtaler og socialpolitik, no. Generic. Reitzel, Copenhagen (1998)
54. Tyler, T.R.: What is procedural Justice? Criteria used by citizens to assess the fairness of legal procedures. Law Soc. Rev. **22**(1), 103–135 (1988). https://doi.org/10.2307/3053563
55. Tyler, T.R.: Why do people rely on others? Social identity and social aspects of trust. In: Trust in Society, pp. 285–306. Russel Sage, New York (2001)
56. Tyler, T.R.: Why People Obey the Law. Princeton University Press, Princeton (2006)
57. Lewicki, R.J., Wiethoff, C., Tomlinson, E.C.: What is the role of trust in organizational justice. In: Bazerman, M.H., Lewicki, R.J., Sheppard, B.H. (eds.) Handbook of Negotiation Research. Research on Negotiation in Organizations, vol. 3. JAI Press, Greenwich (1991)
58. Sunshine, J., Tyler, T.R.: The role of procedural justice and legitimacy in shaping public support for policing. Law Soc. Rev. **37**(3), 513–548 (2003). https://doi.org/10.1111/1540-5893.3703002
59. Blader, S.L., Tyler, T.R.: A four-component model of procedural justice: defining the meaning of a 'fair' process. Pers. Soc. Psychol. Bull. **29**(6), 747–758 (2003). https://doi.org/10.1177/0146167203029006007
60. Tyler, T., Blader, S.L.: Justice and negotiation. In: Gelfand, M.J., Brett, J.M. (eds.) The Handbook of Negotiation and Culture, pp. 295–312. Stanford Business Books, Stanford (2004)
61. Yi, Y., Gong, T.: The effects of customer justice perception and affect on customer citizenship behavior and customer dysfunctional behavior. Ind. Mark. Manag. **37**(7), 767–783 (2008). https://doi.org/10.1016/j.indmarman.2008.01.005
62. Reisig, M.D., Chandek, M.S.: The effects of expectancy disconfirmation on outcome satisfaction in police-citizen encounters. Policing **24**(1), 88–99 (2001). https://doi.org/10.1108/13639510110382278
63. Dolen, V., de Ruyter, W.K., Streukens, S.: The impact of humor in face-to-face and electronic service encounters. In: Advances in Consumer Research, vol. 31, pp. 132–139 (2004)
64. Madsen, C.Ø., Kræmmergaard, P.: The efficiency of freedom: single parents' domestication of mandatory e-government channels. Gov. Inf. Q. **32**(4), 380–388 (2015). https://doi.org/10.1016/j.giq.2015.09.008
65. Lipsky, M.: Street-Level Bureaucracy: The Dilemmas of the Individual in Public Service. Russel Sage, New York
66. Holstein, J.A.: Tenability, troubles, and psychiatric problems in practice. In: Gubrium, J.F., Järvinen, M. (eds.) Turning Troubles into Problems: Clientization in Human Services, pp. 191–210. Routledge, London (2013)
67. Dworkin, R.: Judicial discretion. Rule Law Sep. Powers **60**(21), 157–171 (2017). https://doi.org/10.4324/9781315085302-7
68. Derber, C.: Toward a new theory of professionals as workers: advanced capitalism and postindustrial labor. In: Derber, C. (ed.) Professionals as Workers: Mental Labor in Advanced Capitalism, Boston, pp. 193–208 (1982)
69. Maister, D.H.: The psychology of waiting lines. In: Czepiel, J., Solomon, M.R., Suprenant, C.F. (eds.) The Service Encounter, Lexington, pp. 113–123 (1985)
70. Davis, F.D.: Perceived usefulness, perceived ease of use, and user acceptance of information technology. MIS Q. Manag. Inf. Syst. **13**(3), 319–339 (1989). https://doi.org/10.2307/249008

71. Dimitrova, D.V., Chen, Y.-C.: Profiling the adopters of e-government information and services: the influence of psychological characteristics, civic mindedness, and information channels. Soc. Sci. Comput. Rev. **24**(2), 172–188 (2006)

72. Kolsaker, A., Lee-Kelley, L.: Citizen-centric e-government: a critique of the UK model. Electron. Gov. **3**(2), 127–138 (2006). https://doi.org/10.1504/EG.2006.009214

73. Scott, M., DeLone, W.H., Golden, W.: IT quality and egovernment net benefits: a citizen perspective. In: 19th European Conference on Information Systems (ECIS 2011), Helsinki, Finland, pp. 1–8 (2011). http://aisel.aisnet.org/ecis2011/87

74. Gilbert, D., Balestrini, P., Littleboy, D.: Barriers and benefits in the adoption of e-government. Int. J. Public Sect. Manag. **17**(4/5), 286–301 (2004). http://proquest.umi.com/pqdweb?did=959604501&Fmt=7&clientId=8991&RQT=309&VName=PQD

75. Dasu, S., Chase, R.B.: Designing the soft side of customer service. MIT Sloan Manag. Rev. **52**(1), 33–39 (2010)

76. Hopper, J.: Contested selves in divorce proceedings. In: Institutional Selves: Troubled Selves in a Postmodern World, pp. 127–141 (2001)

77. Davis, M.S.: Discretionary justice. In: The Concise Dictionary of Crime and Justice. Louisiana State University Press, Baton Rouge (2012)

78. Richard, H., Bailur, S.: Analyzing e-government research: perspectives, philosophies, theories, methods, and practice. Gov. Inf. Q. **24**(2), 243–265 (2007)

79. Dahler-Larsen, P.: At fremstille kvalitative data. Odense Universitetsforlag, Odense (2002)

80. Dey, I.: Grounding grounded theory: guidelines for qualitative inquiry. Emerald Publishing Group, Bingely (1999)

eCommerce Platforms Evaluation Framework for Government

Boriana Rukanova[1]($\boxtimes$), Yao-Hua Tan[1], Jolien Ubacht[1], Marcel Molenhuis[2],
Frank Heijmann[2], Han Bosch[2], Zisis Palaskas[3], Hao Chen[4], Toni Männistö[5],
and Ade Ratnasari[6]

[1] Delft University of Technology, Jaffalaan 5, 2628 BX Delft, The Netherlands
{b.d.rukanova,y.tan,J.Ubacht}@tudelft.nl
[2] Customs Administration of The Netherlands, Rotterdam, The Netherlands
[3] Inlecom BV, Brussels, Belgium
zisis.palaskas@inlecomsystems.com
[4] Innovation Exchange, IBM Ireland, Dublin, Ireland
Hao.Chenii@ibm.com
[5] Cross-Border Research Association, Epalinges, Switzerland
toni@cross-border.org
[6] State Islamic University (UIN) Sunan Kalijaga, Yogyakarta, Indonesia
ade.ratnasari@uin-suka.ac.id

Abstract. The international trade flow of e-commerce goods have reached unprecedented volumes. Ensuring undisrupted flow of cross-border eCommerce goods has become one of the top priorities for customs administrations around the world. Customs has a role in safeguarding public values such as safety and security, revenue collection, and stimulation of the economy. Customs administrations are now looking into innovative ways to be able to fulfil their duties for controlling the trade flows while at the same time not hindering trade. But in a broader sense, other government agencies also have responsibilities for safeguarding public values such as product and consumer safety or sustainability and are currently confronted with these eCommerce flows. While eCommerce is a phenomenon that is widely studied in business literature, it is largely unexplored both in research and practice how governments can understand and engage with these eCommerce developments. In this study we focus on the issue revenue collection related to cross-border eCommerce goods. Empirically, our paper builds on insights from the PROFILE EU project, which focuses on the use of data analytics for customs. Theoretically we build on research on control mechanisms in eCommerce platforms and digital trade infrastructures. We present an eCommerce platforms evaluation framework for customs. The evaluation framework consists of two distinct perspectives (i.e. a data analytics and a partnership perspective) that customs can explore when defining their engagement strategies with eCommerce platforms. We limited our study to the interactions of customs with eCommerce platforms and the issue of revenue collection. Further research can study the safeguarding of a wider range of public values by a range of government organisations to account for effects of the vast growth in international flows of goods via eCommerce platforms, such as monitoring product safety and sustainability effects.

© IFIP International Federation for Information Processing 2021
Published by Springer Nature Switzerland AG 2021
H. J. Scholl et al. (Eds.): EGOV 2021, LNCS 12850, pp. 103–116, 2021.
https://doi.org/10.1007/978-3-030-84789-0_8

Keywords: eCommerce · Digital platforms · Customs · Public values · Data analytics · Risk management

1 Introduction

With the emergence of the Internet, we have seen the rise of eCommerce and eCommerce platforms. More than two decades ago researchers have turned attention to understanding the eCommerce phenomenon. Now we live in a world where eCommerce platforms like Amazon, eBay and Alibaba have become dominant players in the global arena. eCommerce has so far been largely business driven and has received limited attention in eGovernment research and practice. Over the last years, however, this has changed. eCommerce is now a key priority for governments across the world due to the unprecedented growth of cross-border eCommerce. In the Netherlands alone, eCommerce has led to an increase from 26 million customs import declarations in 2018, to 61 million in 2019, to 161 million in 2020, and to expected 740 million import declarations of goods below € 150 in 2021. Many governments administrations are confronted with eCommerce; but the eCommerce challenge has become particularly pressing concern for customs, due to their key role in the logistics processes. Operating directly in the logistics flows, customs needs to safeguard public values such as safety and security, and revenue collection, which requires stricter control. At the same time customs also needs to safeguard the economic competitiveness: delays of packages at the border have direct negative economic consequences. eCommerce is regarded as one of the key areas for customs in the newly published Customs Union Action Plan of the EU [4] that outlines the strategic activities of customs in the EU for the coming years. Of particular interest is the value added tax (VAT) collection form eCommerce transactions. This VAT revenue is a substantial source for funding the national budgets of EU Member States. If customs is not able to efficiently and effectively collect the VAT this means loss of revenue for the Member States, which is very needed so that governments can provide citizens and businesses with public services and benefits. For countries with large eCommerce flows this loss can amount to hundreds of millions of euros per year. At the same time, allowing goods for which VAT has not been included in the price on the European market is a disadvantage for businesses operating in the EU. Hence, customs also plays a key role in establishing a level playing field in the eCommerce market.

While customs is currently heavily affected by the eCommerce flows as it acts at the front line when goods cross borders (in our case the EU borders), the effect of eCommerce on government is much broader. Other government agencies are also responsible for safeguarding public values such as consumer and product safety of products sold on the EU market, or public values related to sustainability such as CO_2 footprints, and assurances that no child labor was used in products entering the EU market. While traditionally governments have established mechanisms (or are in a process of establishing such mechanisms) to address these issues in a business-to-business setting, it is an open question how to address these concerns in the eCommerce context. With these enormous flows of small eCommerce packages addressed directly to consumers, it is very hard for governments to assure that the product hidden in the package complies with EU product safety standards, and that no child labor was used in its production. Such eCommerce packages also come with a considerable cost for the environment and increased CO_2 footprint. Therefore, while Customs is the first to experience the eCommerce impact, the consequences for other government inspection agencies is equally far-reaching.

Central to customs in their operations is the availability in advance of data to execute their tasks related to risk analysis in differentiating the trusted from less-reliable trade flows. Researchers in the domain of e-government research advocate that government organizations have the opportunity to create more public value if they go beyond the use of data from governmental organization by also using data provided by business actors and develop collaborative relationships with them [5]. Recent research addresses how business-to-government (B2G) information sharing and collaboration can contribute to the public value creation (see e.g. research on data collaboratives [e.g. 19, 23] and research focusing on the use of business data to create public value [17]). However, so far there is very limited research that explores how government (and in particularly customs) can profit from the large amount of data available in eCommerce platforms.

Therefore, the objective of this paper is to develop an eCommerce platforms evaluation framework for customs. Empirically, this work builds on a case study conducted in the context of the PROFILE project, focusing on the use of data analytics for customs, and specifically the Dutch Living Lab, which focusses on eCommerce. Theoretically we build on research on control mechanisms in eCommerce platforms [15] and digital trade infrastructures [7, 12, 17].

The remaining part of this paper is structured as follows. In Sect. 2 we discuss our theoretical background. In Sect. 3 we present our interpretative case methodology and we describe the iterative process that we followed for developing our eCommerce platforms evaluation framework for customs. We present and demonstrate our framework in Sects. 4 and Sect. 5 respectively. We end the paper with discussion and conclusions.

2 Theoretical Background

2.1 Conceptualizing the eCommerce Business Setting, the Role of Government, and Public Values Safeguarded by Government

In order to understand how government organization can engage with the eCommerce phenomenon, it is important to provide a conceptualization that clarifies the role of business and government in eCommerce transactions. Figure 1 captures the business eCommerce context (marked with (1)), and the government level (marked with (2)), as well as public values that governments pursue (marked with (3)). On a business level, we capture typical actors[1] of a business transaction (i.e. the seller (marked with A), and the buyer (marked with B)), as well as the delivery provider such as express couriers (marked with C), and the payment service providers (marked with D). eCommerce platforms (marked with E) have also emerged as important actors who act as intermediaries between the buyer and the seller. Due to their digital nature, eCommerce platforms now are major hubs containing data about eCommerce transactions. The role of a platform can be a

---

[1] Although in some cases other actors may also play a role (e.g. customs brokers), in view of reducing complexity in this general model we include only the key actors.

reseller (goods owned by other suppliers) or a retailer (own goods). This difference is crucial for the level of data availability, data quality, control mechanisms, etc. In Fig. 1 we also included a vertical line to denote the concept of border crossing (in our case entering the EU). This border crossing aspect is very important, as it triggers involvement and responsibilities of government, related to various public value functions that government performs.

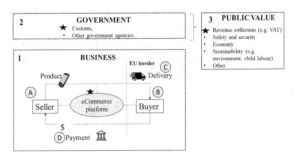

Fig. 1. eCommerce context and the role of government.

Whereas we are interested in the role of customs in this paper, our conceptualization shows that other government organizations can also have an interest in eCommerce flows (see 2 in Fig. 1).

Government organizations have the mandate to perform various tasks to deliver public value (see 3 in Fig. 1). While there are various classifications of public values in the literature [1], for the purpose of our research we are interested in public values that are directly related to international trade flows. These include, but are not limited to: ensuring safety and security (e.g. safety and security checks on goods performed by customs), revenue collection (e.g. collection of VAT and import duties), and facilitation of the economy (e.g. faster goods clearance and trade facilitation arrangements that customs offers to companies). But, as discussed earlier, government organizations have a broader mandate including product safety, values related to sustainability such as ensuring that products involving child labour do not enter in the EU market, or values related to climate goals and CO_2 reduction. While in the eCommerce developments that we see at the moment governments are mainly focussed on revenue collection (mainly VAT), the broader spectrum of responsibilities that governments have in relation to the traditional trade flows is also very relevant to consider in the context of eCommerce.

For the purpose of this paper we will focus on exploring the relationship between customs and eCommerce platforms, and taking the specific focus on fiscal matters (VAT collection). These choices are marked with stars in Fig. 1.

2.2 Customs Interactions with eCommerce Platforms in the Context of VAT Collection

In order to address the issues of eCommerce, the EU develops a diversity of measures and scenarios. Some of these measures refer to legislative changes. For example, for small packages that were previously exempt from VAT (e.g. in the Netherlands: value is max € 22), VAT will be due by July 2021. Next to that, the EU legislation also allows (on a voluntary basis) the use of a new system called Import One Stop Shop (IOSS)[2], which enables eCommerce platforms to collect the VAT for consignments with a value of max € 150, transfer this to a EU tax administration, which will then distribute the VAT to the respective EU Member State where the buyer resides. In this case, the VAT collection is ensured via relationships with eCommerce platforms and in return the sellers on these platforms can receive facilitation in terms of faster import clearances. The participations of platforms in the IOSS is still voluntary. The IOSS procedure allows all eCommerce platforms to participate if they meet certain legal requirements (e.g. having a registered legal representative in the EU). Initial case studies on IOSS developments and challenges have already been reported in literature [14]. Other models of engagement have also been envisaged, where the burden for VAT collection is not put on the intermediaries (the eCommerce platforms) but on the parties that are directly engaged in the eCommerce transaction like the buyer and the seller [8]. Even in such scenarios, it is likely that platforms will play a role in providing services to facilitate payment of VAT between the buyer/seller and customs (possibly in partnership with other payment provider platforms)[3], even though not being the direct responsible party for the VAT payment, such as in the IOSS scenario.

Other countries in the world have developed other approaches. For example, the Australian government has introduced a "Vendor Collection Model" to enhance the country's capacity to collect the Goods and Services Tax on overseas e-commerce imports[4]. In the Australian scheme, foreign vendors of e-commerce goods that sell goods worth more than 75000 AUD a year, must collect the Goods and Services Tax at the point of sale, that is from Australian online shoppers, and pay this tax to Australian authorities eventually. To detect fraudulent overseas e-commerce operators who try to evade the tax collection responsibility, the Australian Tax Office makes use of "data matching, conducts investigations, receives information from industry and the public, and uses import data to monitor compliance"[5]. The media report on other examples of customs-eCommerce cooperation that can someday lead to a direct exchange of data from eCommerce platforms to customs. Alibaba, the Chinese e-commerce giant, is currently building the first European logistics hub in the Belgian city of Liège[6]. The Belgian government and

---

[2] Import One Stop Shop scheme (IOSS) as set out in Title XII, Chapter 6, Section 4 of the VAT Directive as amended by Council Directive (EU) 2017/2455 See also: https://ec.europa.eu/taxation_customs/sites/taxation/files/guidance_on_import_and_export_of_low_value_consignments_final.pdf.

[3] Different scenarios may be considered if platforms are to play a role in facilitating VAT payments of buyers/sellers to Customs, where for the actual VAT payment platforms may also need to develop partnerships with global payment providers, or that some dedicated VAT payment platforms may emerge to which the eCommerce platforms may link to.

[4] https://mag.wcoomd.org/magazine/wco-news-88/australias-vendor-collection-model-explained/.

[5] World Customs Organization (2019). Cross-border e-commerce. Available at: http://www.wcoomd.org/en/topics/facilitation/activities-and-programmes/ecommerce.aspx.

[6] https://www.theguardian.com/business/2021/feb/14/open-sesame-alibabas-push-into-europe-a-mixed-blessing-for-liege.

Alibaba have formed a partnership that will promote digitalisation of customs processes and facilitated clearance of goods, especially for the benefit of small and medium-size companies (AP 2018)[7]. Although these international examples are diverse, they indicate some kind of relationship or partnership between eCommerce platforms and customs.

Alternatively, other custom administrations regard eCommerce platforms as sources of external data. This is a more data analytics-driven approach to eCommerce platforms, where the goal is to use external data (e.g. price data for specific products) available on eCommerce platforms [see e.g. 15, 16, 18]. These data analytics approaches aim to obtain additional external (non-customs) data to help customs cross validate customs declarations and identify possible undervaluation of goods. Despite these practical examples, the eCommerce world is still new to customs and customs has limited knowledge on eCommerce platforms, the data they contain, as well as how to engage with them to handle the enormous increase in eCommerce transactions. In the next section we explore approaches that customs has been developing in the context of the traditional business-to-business trade to deal with the increase in trade volumes.

2.3 Digital Trade Infrastructures and Trusted Traders

Customs administrations have been facing challenges with increased volumes of traditional trade for decades. In order to keep up with these challenges, customs administrations have been looking into innovative technologies and how to deploy them. Heijmann et al. [7, 8] discuss the vision of Dutch customs of how to deal with the large volumes of trade by looking at different innovative technologies such as the use of detection technology, big data analytics, as well as partnership with companies for sharing data. In the enforcement vision of Dutch Customs[8] [2], a differentiation is made among trusted traders, trusted trade lanes, and flows of goods of traders that are less known [7]. The more visibility customs has on the trade flows and the traders, the more facilitation it can provide to these businesses (e.g., faster clearance time and less delays when crossing borders). In the traditional trade flows over the last decades, a series of research projects advocated the idea of the data pipeline [9, 12, 17, 20] as a digital trade infrastructure that allows voluntary information sharing among businesses and government. The data pipeline can be seen as a sort of internet for logistics, which allows supply chain partners to make their business data available to customs (on a voluntary basis), while customs can provide these companies with trade facilitation in return (see e.g. [17]). For those streams of trade that are less known to customs (also referred to as blue streams), customs relies more on physical inspection of the imported goods. In these cases, the use of data analytics and external business data allows customs to gain more information into less-transparent flows.

At the moment, eCommerce flows lack in visibility; customs would need to find other sources to be able to better assess the eCommerce declarations and to cross-validate them. Regarding concepts like trusted traders and trusted trade lanes, which heavily rely on trust relationships between customs and businesses, these have been receiving attention

---

[7] https://apnews.com/press-release/pr-businesswire/01e863a2183244f8bfa03dfb00869243.
[8] See https://youtu.be/iiNKkIBO99k.

in the context of the traditional trade but have been of very little applicability so far in the eCommerce context.

2.4 Trust and Control Mechanisms Applied in e-Marketplaces: Insights from the Literature on eCommerce and Customer

While currently customs is looking at eCommerce transactions from the control perspective from the point of view of undervaluation, in eCommerce research studies have examined the eCommerce transactions from the point of view of customers. In this area already decades ago research examined issues like trust [11] and control mechanisms, such as third party guarantees as mechanisms to mitigate risk and uncertainty [13], as well as customer reviews as a control mechanism on the quality of the goods or services [22]. Building on earlier research on trust and control mechanisms in eCommerce, a recently published study [15] proposes an evaluation framework for assessing eCommerce platforms. This framework was developed in the context of customers buying hand-made products. Both customers as well as customs share an interest in particular types of information, such as knowing the seller and their trustworthiness. When customers buy goods from an eCommerce platform they want to ensure that they can trust the seller and the quality of the product before committing to pay and they want to avoid fraudulent behaviour at all costs. Similarly, customs also wants to prevent fraud in eCommerce. The framework of Ratnasari and de Reuver [15] builds on control mechanisms as discussed by Tiwana [21]. These control mechanisms help platforms to define criteria for parties to join the platform (gatekeeping), as well as other control mechanisms such as process control (related to compliance of participants on the platform), metrics control (relates to the involvement of participants on the platform) and relational control that reflects on shared values and norms that influence the behaviour. In [15] dimensions and control mechanisms of eCommerce platforms are identified. The framework is used to compare and evaluate eight e-marketplaces (local in Asia, as well as international, including Amazon and Alibaba). The framework identifies four dimensions: (1) *Trustworthiness of the platform*: control mechanisms in this dimension include on-line credit card guarantee, escrow services, privacy protection, intermediary protection, third party guarantees and third party trust seals; (2) *Reputation system*: control mechanisms in this dimension include reputation, on-line product reviews, rating, feedback, word-of-mouth, transaction history and reviewer photos. These control mechanisms enable the on-line platform to collect signals from customers and to have a better indicator for the quality of the products, as well as the performance of the sellers operating on the platform; (3) *Product*: control mechanisms in this dimension include product information, product quality information, control quality product, and user generated photos. (4) *Other*: this dimension includes various control mechanisms such as seller identity/profile, legal status of the seller, high quality delivery services, historical sales records, shop and product tagging.

These control mechanisms attributed to eCommerce platforms brings interesting insights in the context of customs in a number of ways. First, the idea to evaluate the trustworthiness of a platform can be interesting for customs, as some platforms may have embedded more control mechanisms than others to ensure a higher degree of trustworthiness. Second, it seems that the platforms have implemented a number of control mechanisms related to the sellers as well as to the products. In risk management of traditional trade flows, knowledge on the true seller and correct information on the product as well as the value of the product is of key importance for customs. Therefore, the platform control mechanisms related to the seller and the product can be also of interest to customs and we will explore this in this paper. In the next section we discuss the empirical context of our investigation and we briefly explain the method used.

3   Method

For the development of our eCommerce platforms evaluation framework for customs we used an interpretative and contextualist case study approach [24], as in our study we were interested in examining how customs approaches eCommerce platforms. In terms of theory types [6], the framework that we developed is aimed at developing theories for: (1) analysis, and (2) explanation. As an empirical context we used the Dutch Living Lab, part of the PROFILE project. The Dutch Living Lab focusses on using data analytics and external data from eCommerce platforms to address the issue of undervaluation in eCommerce declarations. The Living Labs research approach examines innovation in a complex real-world setting [10]. For this study the Dutch Living Lab provided rich access to the empirical setting with regular bi-weekly calls with the key involved parties to follow the progress. For the development of our detailed eCommerce evaluation framework we followed an iterative approach. Using an iterative approach helps to develop theories that are deeply informed by the empirical context [3]. In our study the empirical context guided us in search for relevant theories, which in turn helped us to structure our observations.

The framework development progressed through a number of phases. Phase one was empirically driven, where we engaged with the Living Lab, followed closely the data retrieval and data analytics technical work that was performed by the data analytics experts related to API access to price and product data from the platform and related analytics.

Subsequently in Phase 2 we engaged with existing theories to better understand the role of platforms. We identified a recently published study that took a trust perspective in the context of eCommerce from the perspective of the customer [15]. Based on these insights the scope of the Living Lab was expanded to include the exploration of seller data and trust mechanisms in eCommerce platforms, which provided a bridge to the EU developments and engagements like with platform (i.e. IOSS) and enabled us to make the link to the partnership perspective. Subsequently in Phase 3 this resulted in our final framework, which we present in the next section, and which combines data analytics and partnership perspective.

4   eCommerce Platforms Evaluation Framework for Customs

In Fig. 2 we present our eCommerce platforms evaluation framework for customs. We briefly explain here the components of the framework; the further discussion and elaboration will follow in the next section with case examples.

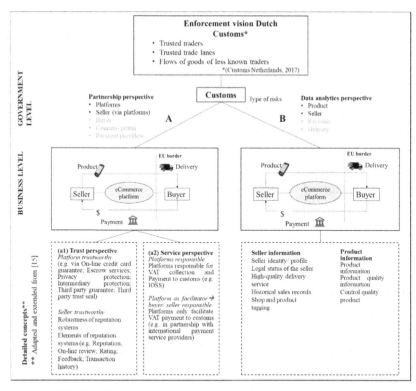

Fig. 2. eCommerce platforms evaluation framework for customs.

On the top of Fig. 2 we capture key elements from the enforcement vision of Dutch Customs. As discussed, key in this vision is the possibility to differentiate among trusted traders and trusted trade lanes and less trusted trade flows. At the moment, for many of the eCommerce shipments little information is known to customs beyond the declaration data that customs receives (i.e. they would fall under the less trusted trade flows in the enforcement vision).

Subsequently, our framework distinguishes two engagement strategies that customs can pursue when engaging with eCommerce platforms, i.e. the *partnership* perspective (indicated with arrow A in Fig. 2) and/or the *data analytics* perspective (arrow B in Fig. 2). In Fig. 2 we repeat two times the basic image of the commercial eCommerce transaction discussed in Sect. 2, as both the data analytics and the partnership approach that Customs may follow refer to the same basic eCommerce transaction. The differences between the partnership and data analytics perspectives (reflected in the bottom part of Fig. 2) is the kind of information customs would need and the approach customs would take.

Under the partnership perspective (A), we distinguish between *trust perspective (a1)* and a *service perspective (a2)*. The *trust perspective* examines control mechanisms related to trust in the platform or trust in the sellers on the platform. The *service perspective* looks at services that the platform implements to facilitate VAT payment.

In the service perspective, we could further differentiate services whether the *platform is responsible* for the VAT payments to customs (as in the case of IOSS). Alternatively, the platform may play a *facilitating role* where the obligation remains with the seller or the buyer, but the platform *facilitates* the VAT payment. Introducing such a facilitation service may also require other partnerships (with global payment providers for example). In the data analytics perspective that customs can take towards platform, the focus of the engagement is data-driven (arrow B). Aspects that are more relevant for a data-driven approach include information on the product (e.g. product information) and information on the seller (e.g. seller identity, legal status of the seller).

5   Demonstration of the Framework

In this section we demonstrate the framework by means of examples. We start with the data analytics perspective and examples from the PROFILE project in Sect. 5.1, and then move to the partnership perspective in Sect. 5.2.

5.1   Data Analytics Perspective

In the PROFILE project a key issue was to address a specific type of risk, namely undervaluation in eCommerce declarations. This type of risk was leading in searching for relevant data on the eCommerce platform. The Dutch Living Lab focussed on one specific eCommerce platform (Platform X). Next to that the immediate data of relevance was for specific key product types (e.g. mobile phones) and the goal was to search for price information. API access and web-data retrieval to search for real-time price information on specific product categories on different national branches of the eCommerce platform yielded average price ranges per product per country. However, in customs declarations goods are not described in such simple terms as the key categories defined for the search assignment (e.g. mobile phones). Customs declarations, but also the product descriptions found on the eCommerce platform, often come with vague text descriptions. Therefore, as a next step, Natural Language Processing (NLP) techniques were used to improve the accuracy of the search result. As a next iteration, also inspired by the eCommerce trust research (see Phase 2 of our framework construction in the method section), the seller information was identified by customs as an important element for the risk analysis. By browsing through the eCommerce platform that was selected for the analysis (Platform X) it was possible to identify that the platform contained (at least for some sellers) rich information on sellers, including information on Seller user name, Seller feedback percentage, Seller feedback score, Seller account type (business), Seller legal info in terms of name and legal contact, its legal address, VAT details and VAT ID, and the issuing country. Furthermore, additional search revealed that at some moment in time, Platform X published a list of top sellers. This entails that customs can potentially tap into a carefully measured and maintained reputation system of eCommerce platforms if the right incentives are in place. This brings us to the second view in our framework, i.e. the partnership view with which customs can approach eCommerce platforms.

5.2   Partnership Perspective

Customs taking a partnership perspective for engaging with eCommerce platforms is different compared to when taking a data perspective. In the data analytics perspective the focus is on the available data on the eCommerce platforms and how customs can use data analytics to create value in terms of better detecting undervaluation fraud. In contrast, in the partnership view the focus is on the relationship between the platform and customs and how it can be of value. Within the partnership view we identified two perspectives, i.e. the *trust perspective* (a1) and the *service perspective* (a2) (see Fig. 2).

When taking a *trust perspective (a1)* customs can evaluate platforms in terms of the trustworthiness of the platforms and in terms of the control mechanisms that the platforms have put in place to control their sellers. Tapping into these control mechanisms may open further opportunities for customs to develop trusted relationships with platforms and a sub-set of their sellers that are trustworthy and turn these eCommerce flows into trusted flows which require limited inspections and allow for trade facilitation. This would mean allowing customs to move some of the unknown eCommerce flows (blue flows) towards trusted eCommerce flows, i.e. yellow or green flows in the enforcement vision.

Platform X that we studied had clear rules for engagement, as well as a system for rating the sellers, based on buyer's feedback on issues like: item description or how accurately the goods were described; communication with the buyers, the shipping time and whether the shipping handling charges were reasonable. Next to that, sellers that score well are offered privileges and the top list of sellers is published, which provides additional publicity for these sellers. Platform X also managed a network of preferred partners related to the delivery services and offers managed payment services. In this way Platform X keeps more control over the complete transaction, knowing the sellers, the delivery partners, and offering payment services. The closer the seller is involved in the managed network of Platform X, the more knowledge the platform has on this seller. In some cases Platform X can even act in approaching sellers in case copyright infringements are identified and request them to solve the infringement. While it is clear that Platform X has a variety of sellers and it will not have the same knowledge about the whole population of sellers, there is a particular sub-set of sellers with high reputation and which are well trusted by the platform. Looking at this sub-set, the situation becomes similar with situations in traditional trade flows, where one party with deep knowledge of a trusted network and embedded control mechanisms in the network is able to play the role of an orchestrator of a trusted trade lane. For example, in an earlier study of traditional business-to-business trade flows on trusted trade lanes [17], a cooperative of growers was in principle able to take up such an orchestration role due to the trusted relationship with their growers, as well as its strong position in facilitating the payment and logistics processes. In that case [see 17], the cooperative of growers was the orchestrator of the trusted trade lane: documents such as invoices and packing lists were made available by the grower to customs via the cooperative of growers. Similarly eCommerce platforms in principle can adopt the role of an orchestrator in a trusted eCommerce flow in a business-to-consumer context.

Alternatively, the partnership between customs and eCommerce platforms can be considered from a *service perspective* (a2) when platforms are willing to implement services to facilitate VAT collection for customs. As discussed earlier, this service perspective is to some extent already inherent in IOSS developments at the EU level. In IOSS, eCommerce platforms can develop extra services (compliant with pre-defined requirements) to collect VAT and to transfer it to the EU to further distribute it to the respective Member States via established mechanisms.

However, as argued by Heijmann [8], other perspectives can be taken, e.g. when customs puts the VAT collection burden on the buyer or the seller. In this case, the platforms can still provide services related to VAT payments but in a more facilitative role (and possibly in partnership with other payment service providers), rather than being direct responsible for the VAT collection.

6   Discussion and Conclusions

eCommerce is a challenge for customs for two reasons. First due to the huge volumes; second due to the lack of visibility for customs on who is behind these streams of packages, what the packages contain, and the value of the goods that are shipped. Customs administrations are now looking for solutions in order to collect the VAT due and to ensure a smooth import process. In this paper we present an eCommerce platforms evaluation framework for customs. Theoretically the framework that we developed is based on literature on control mechanisms of eCommerce platforms, as well as work on digital trade infrastructures in the context of trusted traders and trusted trade lanes. Our eCommerce platforms evaluation framework for customs proposes (A) a *partnership*, and (B) a *data analytics* perspective, which customs can take when defining their strategies of engagement with eCommerce platforms. These two elements are crucial parts in the system-based approach from Dutch Customs. Taking a *data perspective* allows customs administrations to see what kind of data of value can be found on the eCommerce platforms depending on the risk they would like to address. Taking a *partnership perspective*, customs can look at platforms in terms of how to establish relationships with these platforms. The partnership perspective is further refined into (a1) a *trust* (a2) a *services* perspectives.

Further research can proceed in a number of directions. Regarding the data analytics view, follow-up research can conduct a comparative study by examining different eCommerce platforms and providing an overview of which data can be of value for customs risk assessment purposes. Such an overview can lead towards a knowledge base on the eCommerce platform data sources. Second, taking a partnership perspective, a follow-up study can focus on cross-case comparison on how different countries/regions engage in partnerships with platforms or other actors in the eCommerce transaction. This allows to identify different partnership engagement models between customs and eCommerce platforms.

A limitation of our study was that we focussed specifically on examining the link between customs and eCommerce platforms and the focus on fiscal matters. Looking at our broader conceptualization of how government can view the eCommerce phenomena (see Fig. 1) allows to identify additional research opportunities as follows. First, customs can examine in detail other possible scenarios of customs engaging with eCommerce actors. This entails not only looking at the platforms, but also at sellers and buyers, as well as possible partnerships with the delivery and payment providers, or other intermediaries like declaration service providers. Second, further research can go beyond customs to include other government agencies interested in controlling other public values in eCommerce flows. Further research can look at eCommerce from a wider range of public values and wider range of governments to account for effects of the vast growth in international flows of goods via eCommerce platforms, such as monitoring product safety and sustainability effects.

Acknowledgements. This research was partially funded by the PROFILE Project (nr. 786748), which is funded by the European Union's Horizon 2020 research and innovation program. Ideas and opinions expressed by the authors do not necessarily represent those of all partners.

References

1. Bannister, F., Connolly, R.: ICT, public values and transformative government: a framework and programme for research. Gov. Inf. Q. **31**(1), 119–128 (2014)
2. Customs Netherlands: Pushing boundaries: the Customs Administration of The Netherlands' point on the horizon for the enforcement on continuously increasing flows of goods. White paper. Customs Administration of The Netherlands (2017)
3. Eisenhardt, K.M., Graebner, M.E.: Theory building from cases: opportunities and challenges. Acad. Manag. J. **50**(1), 25–32 (2007)
4. European Commission: Taking the Customs Union to the Next Level: a Plan for Action (2020). https://ec.europa.eu/taxation_customs/sites/taxation/files/customs-action-plan-2020_en.pdf
5. Gil-Garcia, J.R.: Towards a smart State? Inter-agency collaboration, information integration, and beyond. Inf. Polity **17**(3, 4), 269–280 (2012)
6. Gregor, S.: The nature of theory in information systems. Manag. Inf. Syst. Q. **30**(3), 611–642 (2006)
7. Heijmann, F.: Supply chain management. In: The EU Customs Union @ 5O Concept to Continuum. European Commission (2018). https://ec.europa.eu/taxation_customs/sites/taxation/files/01_2019_the_eu_customs_union_50th_book_en.pdf
8. Heijmann, F., Tan, Y.H., Rukanova, B., Veenstra, A.: The changing role of customs: customs aligning with supply chain and information management. World Customs J. **14**(2), 131–142 (2020)
9. Hesketh, D.: Weaknesses in the supply chain: who packed the box. World Customs J. **4**(2), 3–20 (2010)
10. Higgins, A., Klein, S.: Introduction to the living lab approach. In: Tan, Y.H., Björn-Andersen, N., Klein, S., Rukanova, B. (eds.) Accelerating Global Supply Chains with IT-Innovation, pp. 31–36. Springer, Heidelberg (2011). https://doi.org/10.1007/978-3-642-15669-4_2
11. Jøsang, A., Ismail, R., Boyd, C.: A survey of trust and reputation systems for online service provision. Decis. Support Syst. **43**(2), 618–644 (2007)
12. Klievink, B., et al.: Enhancing visibility in international supply chains: the data pipeline concept. Int. J. Electron. Gov. Res. **8**(4), 14–33 (2012)
13. Liu, Y., Tang, X.: The effects of online trust-building mechanisms on trust and repurchase intentions. Inf. Technol. People. 666–687 (2018)
14. Liutkevičius, M., Pappel, K.I., Butt, S.A., Pappel, I.: Automatization of cross-border customs declaration: potential and challenges. In: Viale Pereira, G., et al. (eds.) EGOV 2020. LNCS, vol. 12219, pp. 96–109. Springer, Cham (2020). https://doi.org/10.1007/978-3-030-57599-1_8

15. Ratnasari, A., de Reuver, M.: Control mechanisms for assessing the quality of handmade and artistic products in e-marketplace platforms. In: Pucihar, A., Borstnar, M.K., Bons, R., Seitz, J., Cripps, H., Vidmar, D. (eds.) 32nd Bled eConference Humanizing Technology for a Sustainable Society, BLED 2019 - Conference Proceedings, pp. 345–365 (2019)

16. Rukanova, B., et al.: Value of big data analytics for customs supervision in e-commerce. In: Lindgren, I., et al. (eds.) EGOV 2019. LNCS, vol. 11685, pp. 288–300. Springer, Cham (2019). https://doi.org/10.1007/978-3-030-27325-5_22

17. Rukanova, B., Tan, Y.H., Huiden, R., Ravulakollu, A., Grainger, A., Heijmann, F.: A framework for voluntary business-government information sharing. Gov. Inf. Q. **37**(4) (2020). https://doi.org/10.1016/j.giq.2020.101501.

18. Rukanova, B., et al.: Identifying the value of data analytics in the context of government supervision: insights from the customs domain. Gov. Inf. Q. **38**(1), 101496 (2021). https://doi.org/10.1016/j.giq.2020.101496

19. Susha, I., Gil-Garcia, R.J.: A collaborative governance approach to partnerships addressing public problems with private data. In: Proceedings of the 52nd Hawaii International Conference on System Sciences (2019). https://hdl.handle.net/10125/59726

20. Tan, Y.-H., Bjørn-Andersen, N., Klein, S., Rukanova, B.: Accelerating Global Supply Chains with IT-Innovation: ITAIDE Tools and Methods. Springer, Heidelberg (2011). https://doi.org/10.1007/978-3-642-15669-4

21. Tiwana, A.: Platform Ecosystems: Aligning Architecture, Governance, and Strategy, pp. 117–151. Morgan Kaufmann, Burlington (2014). https://doi.org/10.1016/B978-0-12408066-9.00006-0

22. Trenz, M.: The effect of consumer reviews on vendor-related and market-related price sensitivity. ECIS 2013 Research in Progress (2013)

23. Verhulst, S., Sangokoya, D.: Data collaboratives: exchanging data to improve people's lives. Medium (2015)

24. Walsham, G.: Interpreting Information Systems in Organisations. Wiley, New York (1993)

Practitioners' Perceptions of Fitness to Task of a Leading Disaster Response Management Tool

Hans J. Scholl[1]([⊠]) [ID] and Eric E. Holdeman[2]

[1] University of Washington, Seattle, WA, USA
jscholl@uw.edu
[2] Eric Holdeman and Associates, Puyallup, WA, USA
ericholdeman@ericholdeman.com

Abstract. Crisis Information Management Systems (CIMS) have been used in Emergency and Disaster Response Management for decades. However, while these systems have emerged and improved over time, they still appear to provide lower efficacy when incidents become more complex, and, in particular, when used in the context of multijurisdictional responses to large and growing incidents and extreme events. Most CIMS like E Team, Veoci, or WebEOC are commercial off-the-shelf systems (COTS), which allow for and also require from emergency response units the customization of the application to their own specific needs. This survey-informed study took a look at practitioners' experiences with one of the most widely used CIMS, that is, WebEOC. The results were mixed at best and confirm other studies, which pointed at WebEOC's lack of scalability, interoperability, network security, and ease of use. The study concludes that in the face of ever more frequent incidents of greater magnitude the case for developing and deploying securely interoperable and scalable CIMS is compelling and has to be addressed.

Keywords: Disaster response management · Coordination of emergency responses · Information and communication technologies · ICTs · Crisis Information Management Systems · CIMS · WebEOC · National Incident Management System · NIMS · Incident command system · ICS · Commercial off-the-shelf systems · COTS

1 Introduction

Contemporary commercial Crisis Information Management Systems (CIMS), it has been suggested [1, 2], support emergency managers and responders relatively well when used in response to smaller, every-day, and geographically isolated incidents. When, however, multiple jurisdictions and different levels of government agencies need to coordinate their responses, they appear to exhibit limitations and rigidities in terms of interoperability, scalability, reliability, network security, and ease of use. Unfortunately, not only when different vendors' systems have to interact, but rather also when the

© IFIP International Federation for Information Processing 2021
Published by Springer Nature Switzerland AG 2021
H. J. Scholl et al. (Eds.): EGOV 2021, LNCS 12850, pp. 117–133, 2021.
https://doi.org/10.1007/978-3-030-84789-0_9

same system such as WebEOC has to scale up to meet the needs of a more demanding multi-level and multi-jurisdictional context [3], this experience of constraints and lack of scalability seems to be commonplace [4, 5].

As discussed elsewhere, given the wide range of incidents in terms of scale, scope, and duration [6] spanning from local emergencies such as leaks of hazardous materials or a building afire to large-scale, large-scope, and long-duration catastrophes such as the Indian Ocean Earthquake and Tsunami of 2004, the Galveston Hurricane of 1900, or the East Japan Earthquake and Tsunami of 2011, the coordination, integration, and scalability of operations is essential to the effectiveness of the response [7, 8]. In the United States, the National Response Framework (NRF) and the National Incident Management System (NIMS) with its Incident Command Structure (ICS) were designed exactly for the purpose of providing a common terminology and a framework of principles, practices, processes, which would be scalable, flexible, and comprehensive enough to guide responders of any discipline along the whole spectrum of possible disasters (ibid.). While these response frameworks entail a certain degree of organizational standardization, the information management portion of the framework and its supporting information and communication technologies (ICTs), that is, the CIMS would have to carry the burden, as the NIMS/ICS planners anticipated,

> "Communications and information systems should be designed to be flexible, reliable, and scalable in order to function in any type of incident, regardless of cause, size, location, or complexity. They should be suitable for operations within a single jurisdiction or agency, a single jurisdiction with multiagency involvement, or multiple jurisdictions with multiagency involvement. Communications systems should be applicable and acceptable to users, readily adaptable to new technology, and reliable in the context of any incident to which emergency management/response personnel would be expected to respond" [7, p. 24].

By the time, these guidelines were formulated, CIMS such as WebEOC were already in use at all levels of government across the United States, and although WebEOC was still far from having become a kind of de-facto standard, a rather wide variety of non-interoperable CIMS was already in use around the Country. This, however, began to slowly change when in 2012 the US Federal Emergency Management Agency (FEMA) also adopted WebEOC for their internal use [9]. Yet, only a few years into FEMA's use of this particular CIMS, it became evident that for security and performance reasons the WebEOC implementation at FEMA would not interoperate with State, Territory, or Tribal WebEOC sites forcing both FEMA and the respective agencies into tedious, error-prone, and time-consuming double work for necessary data exchanges [10]. It immediately follows that during responses to larger incidents, when the coordination and collaboration between and among agencies, both vertically and horizontally, are badly needed such bottlenecks would be counterproductive and costly. This study's intent was to find out, document, and analyze how practitioners experience their work with WebEOC during a response with the aim of better understanding the efficacy and usefulness of this commercial CIMS along the entire spectrum of emergencies and disasters.

The publication is organized as follows: First, related work on WebEOC in the academic literature is reviewed. Next, research questions and the methodology are detailed. Then, the findings for each research question are presented followed by a discussion of the findings. Finally, concluding remarks and directions for future research are presented.

2 Related Work

While professional response organizations in the United States have chosen from and implemented a wide range of COTS CIMS for the purpose of supporting their respective response operations, WebEOC appears to have become the most proliferated CIMS [4, 11]. Interestingly, in academic research, although CIMS are at the core of modern information management in emergency response, they have not yet systematically been assessed and evaluated in terms of their efficacy over the entire spectrum of incident responses. As a recent study suggested, "the role of information management tools used in <emergency management>... needs further investigation," which according to the authors required to include "studying differences between centralized control and distributed participation; incorporating multiple incident data into a visually informative form for decision makers (e.g., hazardous conditions); and improving designs suitable for updating information in a timely manner" [12, p. 10]. Nevertheless, some research, even with regard to WebEOC, has been conducted while the overall picture has remained spotty. The first well-known quasi-academic comparison of contemporary CIMS was conducted as early as 2002 by the Hart study, which was sponsored by the Department of Justice's National Institute of Justice (NIJ). The study performed a 106 "features" comparison of then contemporary CIMS, among which WebEOC scored highest with 102 desirable "features" identified [13].

A number of WebEOC-related studies went down a similar pathway, when investigating features (such as "boards") and their relative usefulness in incident responses [11, 14–17]. Some studies took a high-level descriptive approach without concerning themselves with any technology or feature details [16, 18]. WebEOC was also found as a unifying connecting link in private-public partnerships between business communities and government agencies [2, 19].

While studies like the former portrayed WebEOC's versatility, others emphasized more critical findings. Around the time that the NIMS/ICS designers detailed their recommendations regarding necessary interoperability, interconnectivity, and scalability requirements for CIMS (as quoted in the introduction), academic research also came to similar conclusions [5, 20]. Along these lines, WebEOC was found incomplete in terms of the availability of needed information [21] also with regard to information sharing between and among different agencies [22]. During a multi-jurisdictional response to a major landslide disaster, WebEOC implementations at Federal level (FEMA) and State levels were found unable to interoperate in most basic ways for security concerns on either side [23]. Similarly, in the simulation of a catastrophic incident, that is, under artificial exercise conditions when no damage of critical infrastructure had actually occurred or was even assumed under the simulated scenario, the interoperation and information sharing between a State-operated WebEOC site and two dozen county WebEOC sites broke completely down under the sheer load of requests [24].

Besides these serious load-related issues, other reports found a lack of automatic information summarization technologies implemented in WebEOC [15], which made it hard for responders to see the forest for the trees, once an incident response began growing, so that information had to be manually aggregated on paper to be useful [25]. The latter study also found "poor interoperability" within the network infrastructure [25, p. 9] resulting in poor information sharing exacerbated by ineffective ex-ante staff training and unaddressed communication gaps.

Other studies found that in order to make good use of WebEOC, the incident response had to accommodate to the "tool" rather than that the tool accommodated to the demands and needs of the response [26]. The same study also reported that WebEOC's customizability, while giving the respective agency the flexibility to tailor the tool to its specific needs, by so doing it also sacrifices standardization and compatibility with other WebEOC implementations. Many agencies, particularly resource-poor ones, may even have great difficulty with setting up WebEOC in a tailored fashion [5, 26].

When analyzing the efficacy of a particular CIMS in response to an incident, scale, scope, and duration of this particular incident present the first benchmarks to consider. As mentioned in the introduction, a CIMS, which performs reasonably well in the response to incidents of small scale, small scope, and short duration may not perform as well when scale, scope, and duration of the incident increase, let alone when catastrophic proportions are reached. However, few studies such as Son et al. on CIMS efficacy have taken this consideration into account. When, for example, taking Fischer's scale [6], which categorizes emergencies and disasters in a range from "DC (for disaster category) 1" to "DC 10" with "DC 1" standing for an everyday local and small incident and "DC 10" representing a catastrophe of extraordinary magnitude and annihilation, it appears intuitively evident that a CIMS has to be extremely scalable to cover this enormous range.

In summary, the efficacy of existing CIMS, and especially, WebEOC, in emergency and disaster response management is understudied; therefore, it has remained an open question of whether or not current CIMS, and here, WebEOC, are fit to task, in particular, when it comes to larger and dynamically growing incidents towards the upper end of the Fischer scale.

3 Research Questions and Methodology

3.1 Research Questions

As the literature review illustrated the gap of understanding with regard to the efficacy of CIMS, and specifically WebEOC, in practical disaster response management is wide. Moreover, it will be a potentially life-saving and likely disaster-mitigating contribution if this known gap in understanding could be narrowed. It also appears that the most important stakeholders, that is, disaster responders would bring first-hand practical experience to the table, when it comes to the efficacy of WebEOC, which leads to the following two research questions:

Research Question #*1* (RQ #1):

How do professional emergency responders perceive the efficacy and fitness to task of WebEOC in emergency response management?

Research Question #2 (RQ #2):

What specific, if any, concerns regarding WebEOC (and its use) do professional emergency responders express in emergency response management?

3.2 Data Selection and Analysis

Instrument. Owed to the paucity of research on the subject and the concurrent absence of a guiding theoretical framework, the inquiry had to be of exploratory nature. For this purpose, an online (Google Forms) fourteen-question survey was devised. All questions except the last were either single or multiple choice questions. The first two questions established demographics (affiliation, WebEOC licensing status). The next eleven questions queried about use and performance aspects of WebEOC. The last question was free-format and open-ended, which gave participants an additional opportunity to enter their own observations in a narrative.

Sample. The intention of the researchers was to reach out and receive feedback from both the managerial and professional levels of disaster responders around the country. As a reminder, this inquiry did not seek to statistically test any hypotheses regarding the usefulness of WebEOC in disaster response. It rather intended to explore the perception of usefulness of WebEOC on part of professional disaster responders who had gained practical experience with this particular CIMS, which suggested a convenience sample was to be used [27]. As a long-term practitioner and a leader in the field, the second author has run a regular and well-respected blog for several years, which is read by a large audience of response professionals. In order to attract responses, the survey was attached to an opinion editorial that the second author posted on his blog site [28]. The tone of the blog was critical towards WebEOC, which was hoped to prompt professional responders into reacting and taking the survey, either for reasons of strong disagreement, or for the opposite.

Data Collection. The vast majority of the data were received and collected within two and a half weeks after the publication of the opinion piece. Very few responses were entered weeks after the publication. A total of 83 responses were received, and 48 respondents also took the time to enter a narrative, some of which was extensive and rich. Half of the respondents were County-level responders, 26.3% State-level responders, 13.1% Municipal Government-level responders, just under 5% Federal-level responders, 2.4% other governmental institution-level responders, and 3.6% were non-governmental-organization-based responders. The vast majority of responders (72.6%) represented organizations that had active WebEOC licenses, and 17.9% of responders represented organizations that previously held a WebEOC license.

Data Analysis and Coding. Data were analyzed in an open coding approach [29, 30], in which tentative concept labels were attributed to chunks of texts and their particular attributes. The concept labels were connected with regard to their relationships to each other in an axial-coding exercise [31] and compared to the results of the eleven single and multiple-choice survey questions for plausibility, consistency, and further explanation.

Neutrality/Impartiality. This research has not been funded nor otherwise supported by any commercial or other vested interest.

4 Findings

In the following the findings are presented in the order of the research questions. The findings from both the single/multiple-choice questions and the free-format narratives are integrated in each findings subsection.

Ad Research Question 1 (RQ #1)—(How do professional emergency responders perceive the efficacy and fitness to task of WebEOC in emergency response management?).

The first survey question attempted to establish the overall satisfaction or dissatisfaction of survey respondents with WebEOC. Without undue speculation it was assumed that responders' satisfaction or dissatisfaction with WebEOC would largely correspond to the system's perceived efficacy and fitness to task. It was found that 33.7% of respondents were either very satisfied or at least somewhat satisfied whereas a majority of respondents (53%) across all groups were either very dissatisfied or somewhat dissatisfied, while 18.1 percent of respondents fell into neither camp. In other words, with only about one third of respondents expressing satisfaction of some kind with the system, WebEOC's efficacy and fitness to task in emergency and disaster response management appears to be called into question for the most part. However, based on the demographic and other data derived from the survey, it was possible to provide sharper contours and more granular detail for painting this mostly unfavorable overall picture of WebEOC performance in US emergency and disaster response management.

As Fig. 1 shows when breaking down the distribution of satisfaction and dissatisfaction along government levels, WebEOC-related satisfaction is strongest at Federal and State levels, whereas on County and municipal levels dissatisfaction prevails. It is noteworthy, though, that while the survey produced only four responses from the Federal level, the four responses were widely spread with regard to the degree of satisfaction, and no Federal-level response indicated the highest level of satisfaction with WebEOC.

Taking County and municipal levels together, overall dissatisfaction with WebEOC was more than twice as frequent as was overall satisfaction with the tool. Among the variables, which might influence the degree of satisfaction or dissatisfaction, the authors suspected "frequency of use," "ease of use," "functionality," and "degree of customization" (see Fig. 1). Upon inspecting the percent values, one might tend at first sight to associate, for example, far more frequent, that is, "daily use" with higher degrees of satisfaction; as Fig. 1 shows, only 17.9% of "somewhat or very dissatisfied" respondents indicated that they used WebEOC on a daily basis, while, in contrast, outright 60.7% of "somewhat or very satisfied" respondents suggested they used the system on a daily basis. One might argue that more frequent use leads to, or, at least, illustrates higher degrees of satisfaction. However, regression analyses on all independent variables specified above and their combinations did not produce any statistically significant prediction of the dependent variable (satisfaction/dissatisfaction).

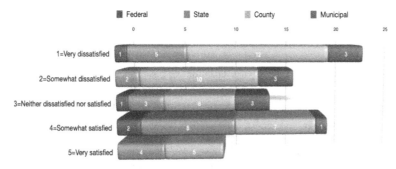

Fig. 1. WebEOC user satisfaction/dissatisfaction per government level

Table 1. WebEOC user satisfaction/dissatisfaction relative to other factors

Variable values (variables: frequency, ease of use, functionality, & customization)	Very or somewhat dissatisfied (%)	Very or somewhat satisfied (%)
Daily use	**17.9%**	**60.7%**
Weekly use	**28.2%**	**14.3%**
Monthly use	**15.4%**	**14.3%**
Infrequent use	**38.5%**	**10.7%**
Very complicated	37.5%	0.0%
Somewhat complicated	32.5%	37.0%
Neither complicated nor easy	20.0%	22.2%
Somewhat easy	10.0%	29.6%
Very easy	0.0%	11.1%
Basic functions	**26.3%**	**17.9%**
Advanced functions	**73.7%**	**82.1%**
No/Little customization	28.2%	11.1%
Some customization	25.6%	25.9%
Substantial customization	25.6%	33.3%
Extensive customization + add-ons	20.5%	29.6%

Despite this particular finding, it is noteworthy that WebEOC customization is the greater the higher the level of government (see Table 1). For the Federal level, substantial WebEOC customization was reported in all cases, on State level, customization is over 82% with half of this attributed to "extensive customization with add-ons." On County and municipal levels, customization of WebEOC is also found in or slightly above

70% the responses; however, on the municipal level no "extensive customization with add-ons" is reported.

Table 2. WebEOC customization per government level (%)

Degree of customization	Federal	State	County	Municipal
Little or no customization	0.0%	13.6%	25.6%	30.0%
Some customization	0.0%	18.2%	23.1%	50.0%
Substantial customization	100.0%	22.7%	30.8%	20.0%
Extensive customization/add-ons	0.0%	40.9%	20.5%	0.0%
Not sure	0.0%	4.5%	0.0%	0.0%
Totals	**100.0%**	**100.0%**	**100.0%**	**100.0%**

Table 3. WebEOC functionality usage per government level (%)

Functionality	Federal	State	County	Municipal
1 = Basic functions	0.0%	0.0%	30.8%	70.0%
2 = Advanced functions	100.0%	100.0%	66.7%	30.0%
3 = Not sure	0.0%	0.0%	2.6%	0.0%
Totals	**100.0%**	**100.0%**	**100.0%**	**100.0%**

With regard to functionality, again the higher the government level the more the advanced functionality of WebEOC is employed. At municipal level, overwhelmingly basic functionality of WebEOC is adopted, which illustrates an enormous gap of sophistication and experience between the local level and even the next higher level (County), let alone the State and Federal levels (see Table 2).

One of the most important, if not *the* most important task in emergency management is gaining and maintaining *Situational Awareness (SA)*, which is the prerequisite for developing and also maintaining a *Common Operating Picture (COP)*. Fully developed and vetted SA/COP are at the core of any effective and successfully targeted response to any incident [7, 32]. In this particular context, the detailed geographic location of incident-related information is essential. Many response units employ highly specialized Geographic Information Systems (GIS) such as the Environmental System Research Institute's ArcGIS. However, WebEOC also comprises a mapping component of its own and affords some GIS record integration with ArcGIS, although the WebEOC mapping component lacks the sophistication of ArcGIS.

As Table 3 demonstrates, WebEOC-based mapping is rarely if ever used at municipal level, and also at Federal level its usage is relatively low, which in this latter case is most likely attributable to the use of more powerful GIS at Federal level. But on County and State levels, this particular mapping functionality is never or rarely used in almost 70%, or almost 50%, of the cases, respectively. Similar to the Federal level, it is likely that

Table 4. Usage of WebEOC mapping per government level (%)

Usage of WebEOC mapping	Federal	State	County	Municipal
Mapping never used	75.0%	22.7%	48.7%	60.0%
Mapping rarely used	0.0%	27.3%	20.5%	40.0%
Not sure	0.0%	9.1%	2.6%	0.0%
Mapping regularly used	25.0%	22.7%	17.9%	0.0%
Mapping key functionality	0.0%	18.2%	10.3%	0.0%
Totals	**100.0%**	**100.0%**	**100.0%**	**100.0%**

both County and State responders utilize more powerful and more specialized tools like ArcGIS instead. As before, a major gap in functionality utilization, and consequently, sophistication with regard to WebEOC-based generation and preservation of SA/COP appears to exist between municipal levels of government and higher levels (Table 5).

Table 5. Intra-/extra-jurisdictional connectivity per government level (%)

Connectivity	Federal	State	County	Municipal
Not connected (intra-jurisdictional)	75.0%	15.0%	23.7%	22.2%
Some connected (intra-jurisdictional)	25.0%	65.0%	57.9%	66.7%
All connected (intra-jurisdictional)	0.0%	20.0%	18.4%	11.1%
Totals (intra-jurisdict'l connectivity)	**100.0%**	**100.0%**	**100.0%**	**100.0%**
Not connected (extra-jurisdictional)	75.0%	10.5%	30.8%	0.0%
Some connected (extra-jurisdictional)	25.0%	36.8%	43.6%	88.9%
All connected (extra-jurisdictional)	0.0%	52.6%	25.6%	11.1%
Totals (extra-jurisdict'l connectivity)	**100.0%**	**100.0%**	**100.0%**	**100.0%**
Upstream log in	n/a	40.9%	27.8%	33.3%
No upstream log in	n/a	59.1%	72.2%	66.7%
Totals (upstream log-in connectivity)	**n/a**	**100.0%**	**100.0%**	**100.0%**

Problems with connectivity have been a known WebEOC characteristic, which encompass network load issues, connection security issues, slow or no responses, connection failures, among others [22–24, 26, 33]. The survey instrument distinguished between same-jurisdiction connections (including resource requesting and tracking) and cross-jurisdictional connections (also, including resource requesting and tracking). Since most respondents were believed to be non-experts on ICT network-related matters a control question was included that prompted for the type of establishing connections to WebEOC systems in other jurisdictions (upstream log-in for access). For example, FEMA does not allow for their WebEOC implementation to directly interoperate with

States' WebEOC implementations. Rather State responders have to remotely log on to the FEMA system via a secure connection, where an account for them is maintained. Many States act likewise with their lower-ranking jurisdictions. If upstream log-in is provided as a connectivity mechanism, then in all likelihood there is no other connectivity mechanism established in that particular direction. It is obvious that this type of interoperation is anything but seamless and has to be seen as an inelegant workaround. As Table 4 shows, Federal-level respondents confirmed that most of their WebEOC implementations do not connect to other systems. In contrast, a majority of State, County, and municipal respondents corroborate that most of their WebEOC implementations interoperate in some fashion with other WebEOC systems, both intra-jurisdictionally and extra-jurisdictionally. The highest numbers of upstream log-in access were found at State level (40.9%) followed by municipalities (33.3%) and Counties (27.8%). However, that means that in most cases no upstream log-in appears to exist or to be used.

When looking at the narratives in survey responses, only a single highly positive comment stood out from a State-level responder who reported on a decade-long experience also praising the cost-benefit ratio of WebEOC. Unfortunately, the responder did not give more details, for example, regarding the use of the system across emergencies of different magnitudes, or regarding the coordination with other agencies. Another State responder stated that all lower-level jurisdictions log on to their State WebEOC system during an incident response, so that the incident is dealt with from a unified SA/COP perspective. Another State responder referring to an identical log-in-from-remote setup between the State and lower-level jurisdictions, however, remarked that the system was "clunky" and not easy to use, and unlike the other two respondents who were very satisfied with WebEOC, this respondent was somewhat dissatisfied. Some County respondents noted that their upstream log-in setup was a one-way street only for sharing State information downstream. Interestingly, WebEOC's mapping functionality was mentioned in the narrative responses only twice: Despite one County respondent's overall dissatisfaction with WebEOC, this individual was highly appreciative of the integration of ArcGIS and WebEOC, which allowed for importing some data from WebEOC into ArcGIS (sic!). Another respondent who was neither satisfied nor dissatisfied with WebEOC had not come across this integration functionality and rather urged for GIS integration. Although mildly satisfied with WebEOC, but implicitly acknowledging the system's problems, one Federal responder stated,

> "Big Tech could solve this easily; look at the interoperability within Apple or Google apps - maps, sharing, email, messaging, browsing are instinctively linked. Imagine what they could do if given the task to package existing apps into an EM layer" (quote #1—from survey responses).

In summary, dissatisfaction with WebEOC among survey respondents was found much stronger and more outspoken than satisfaction thereof, and, in particular, the "very dissatisfied" outnumbered the "very satisfied" by a margin of more than two to one in the responses. When analyzing, which (independent) variables might have influenced these particular outcomes, neither "frequency of use," nor the "functionality used" (basic or advanced), nor the "degree of customization", nor "ease of use" were found predictors for satisfaction or dissatisfaction on part of the respondents. Furthermore, WebEOC mapping was relatively sparsely used, and certainly not as a core function, but rather as an add-in, which was connected to a more powerful GIS. Finally, overall WebEOC connectivity was only moderately implemented with States most highly engaged. Given the relatively high levels of dissatisfaction in the perception of responding practitioners WebEOC's fitness to task appears to be debatable, and it appears that the reasons for this dissatisfaction are multifold.

Ad Research Question 2 (RQ #2)—(What specific, if any, concerns regarding WebEOC (and its use) do professional emergency responders express in emergency response management?).

Respondents expressed most of their concerns in the open-ended narrative at the end of the survey. However, one multiple-choice survey question was geared at eliciting potential concerns regarding moving away from WebEOC. Nine choices were given including one "other" as shown in Table 6 below. The respondents marked a total of 222 choices, or on average 2.7 per respondent. It appears that no single concern stood out above all others with the exception of "budgetary concerns" with 33.3%, which was most pronounced on Federal level than on any other government level followed equally with 16.7% each by concerns regarding "going outside the norm" (sic!), "difficulty of adopting a new system," and both the institution and its internal stakeholders too "deeply invested" into the status quo with WebEOC.

Table 6. Concerns and obstacles perceived (when switching from WebEOC – in %)

Concerns/Obstacles	Federal	State	County	Municipal
State standard	0.0%	20.6%	18.8%	18.2%
No known alternative	0.0%	16.2%	15.8%	21.2%
Budgetary concerns	33.3%	11.8%	10.9%	6.1%
New system might not be working	0.0%	4.4%	6.9%	9.1%
Changing means going outside the norm	16.7%	7.4%	9.9%	18.2%
Difficult adoption of a new system	16.7%	16.2%	6.9%	12.1%
Institution deeply invested	16.7%	13.2%	10.9%	9.1%
Internal stakeholders deeply invested	16.7%	8.8%	9.9%	6.1%
Other	0.0%	1.5%	9.9%	0.0%
Totals	**100.0%**	**100.0%**	**100.0%**	**100.0%**

In lower-ranking jurisdictions the implicit or explicit de-facto standardization on WebEOC as the emergency and disaster management system represented the most highly cited concern with 20.6%/at State, 18.8% at County, and again 18.8% at municipal levels. Furthermore, at municipal level a higher-ranking concern with 21.6% was the absence of a "known alternative" to WebEOC. Since only very few "other" concerns were specified, the first eight choices in this multiple-choice question on the subject must have covered the prevailing concerns and perceived obstacles fairly comprehensively.

On the municipal level, respondents' concerns revolved around the perceived high cost of changes in system versions, system administrators, and when adding functionality by coding and recoding. Some municipal responders felt that WebEOC was oversized for their respective needs, while others bemoaned the absence of mobile versions. Quite a number of municipal responders decried the perceived lack of ease of use and straightforward task-relevant functionality. Said one respondent,

> "Having used both <another system> and WebEOC, I have found WebEOC is clunkier and less user friendly. <The other system> is easier to build what is needed by the user." (quote #2—from survey responses).

And another municipal respondent explained,

> "WebEOC is designed for large agencies not the majority of EM offices with one or two staff" (quote #3—from survey responses).

County respondents also criticized that WebEOC's lack of intuitiveness and ease of use, which they felt did not take into account the relatively modest ICT savviness of average emergency responders, in particular, in the more typical case that responders would not use the system frequently enough to maintain familiarity. Like respondents on municipal level, the county respondents also expressed dissatisfaction with WebEOC's lack of functionality and unintuitive user interface. In this context some respondents used explicit language to illustrate their personal frustration with WebEOC ("It sucks." "Terrible old system that has become a failure." "Outdated and obtuse system that wastes an agency's limited resources." "Lots of money spent. Still doesn't work." "After using WebEOC for numerous large and small emergencies and disasters over the past years, I give WebEOC functionality and "usability" a grade of C/C-."). Respondents on this government level also pointed at compatibility and interoperability problems, which emanated in part from a lack of standards set and followed in WebEOC implementations resulting in a wide variety of organizationally incompatible implementations. Some of these incompatibilities could be attributed to different needs at different levels of government. As one County respondent shared,

> "Local EOCs who have adopted WebEOC as their software of choice in this State are buying and operating their WebEOC systems independently (State and local WebEOC systems do not interface with each other). If the locals buy their own WebEOC system, they tailor boards also to their respective EOC needs and unfortunately all the boards do no match each other at all the respective EOC levels" (quote #4—from survey responses).

On State level, the concerns of lower-ranking jurisdictions were echoed regarding the lack of "ease of use" and "functionality" as well as the high cost of maintenance including extensive training needs for coping with WebEOC's complexity. Frustration with WebEOC was also expressed on this level in no uncertain terms ("WebEOC is very clunky." "<WebEOC> has outlived its usefulness and should be trashed."). As mentioned while for States "interconnectivity" exists via secure upstream single-user log-in onto FEMA's WebEOC implementation (and not, as manifest, via a bidirectional State-WebEOC-to-FEMA-WebEOC interoperation protocol), this type of interconnection is limited in capacity and bi-directionality, which creates unpleasant bottlenecks and redundancies, in particular, in the resource request process, which employs so-called resource request forms (RRFs). As a State respondent explains,

"Throughout our response in various disasters, missions could easily get lost as hundreds of mission requests flowed into WebEOC in a short period of time. This was problematic and challenging. We created alerts if missions were time sensitive or not updated in a timely fashion. Having no interface between our State and FEMA's WebEOC platform is problematic and time consuming as we submit RRF's, we have to submit paper RRFs to FEMA which defeats the purpose of WebEOC" (quote #5—from survey responses).

Another respondent summed up the experience with WebEOC this way,

"The biggest problem with WebEOC is that emergency managers all too often have to manage WebEOC instead of using it as a tool (quote #6—from survey responses).

On Federal, respondents did not leave comments except for one (see quote #1 above). However, this respondent also highlighted the high licensing cost and the limitations ("single channel") of WebEOC.

In summary, respondents from all levels of government were critical with the relatively high cost of licenses for using and maintaining WebEOC. In particular, a dearth of functionality, a deficit in true interoperability, and a lack of ease of use were criticized on all levels of government. The terms "clunky" and "outdated" were used repeatedly.

5 Discussion, Future Research, and Concluding Remarks

5.1 General Observations

Crisis Information Management Systems (CIMS) differ from other and, particularly, non-mission critical information management systems in at least two ways: (1) With regard to their specific purpose, and even more so, with respect to their centrality in the overall critical information infrastructure, CIMS must be resilient, that is, robust, resourceful, redundant, and rapid (in operational usability and response time) [7, 34]. The findings of this study along with those of earlier academic reports, however, suggest that WebEOC would not qualify as a resilient CIMS along these lines, at least not in terms of robustness nor rapidity. It rather appears to slow down in response time and even to break down under only moderate loads, which apart from security and network safety concerns also explains the lack of true multiway interconnectivity (with FEMA presenting the most prominent example). Interconnectivity is at the core of any system's scalability. If interconnectivity is limited, then scalability is limited. With limits in scalability the respective CIMS can only be reasonably and safely used in responses to relatively small-scale incidents. (2) CIMS are supposed to be extremely easy to understand and use [7, 35], since under the typically increasingly stressful circumstances of an incident response, professional responders have no time nor do they have the stomach for struggling with idiosyncrasies and peculiarities of any given CIMS. The respective CIMS has to support the response seamlessly and without putting additional burdens on its users. However, WebEOC reportedly appears not to be in this category of seamless CIMS. Paraphrasing one respondent's words, when using WebEOC in more complex incident responses, rather frequently the tail appears to be wagging the dog.

In a nutshell, in terms of flexibility, reliability, scalability, and ease of use, WebEOC does not appear to meet the CIMS standard requirements formulated in the basic NIMS document of 2008 [7, p. 24] according to this study's findings.

5.2   The Need for a Widely Accepted, Resilient, and Scalable CIMS

In a recent study on the subject, Son and colleagues performed a meta-analysis of the literature [12] and confirmed earlier insights regarding resiliency in emergency management that highlighted factors including "collective sensemaking," "team decision making," and "interaction and coordination" (p. 10), all of which heavily rely on the availability and proper functioning of a capable and robust CIMS as a prerequisite. As has been shown elsewhere, it does not suffice that a system can actually perform certain operations under certain circumstances. It rather also matters what the respective system's overall performance expectancy is, which is colored by past and present experiences from a human agent's (and here professional responder's) perspective [5]. If human agents who have to perform together as a coordinated group grow increasingly frustrated with a system's expected performance, then the acceptance of using such a system plummets, which seems to be the case with WebEOC among numerous responders on all level of government. In other words, if WebEOC's reputation among a large group of responders is turning unfavorable through lived and repeated negative experience, then the impact on the adoption and use of the system in the larger community of responders becomes problematic through the social influence of the disenchanted group. Conversely, if a CIMS, satisfies the performance expectations of a group of human agents, then the system's adoption and use is strongly and more widely supported also through the group's social influence. As seen in the findings, some responders suggested alternative COTS CIMS, while still others preferred a national initiative and a system standardized and centrally supported for all levels of government at affordable cost. The idea of using cloud-based services and existing standard tools for such undertaking might also be a viable path, which deserves study and evaluation.

It has been argued elsewhere that scalability is not only an upward affair, but rather also includes downward capabilities in case that power and networking capabilities are completely lost for an extended period of time and low-tech solutions have to be employed temporarily. While these incident scenarios might still be rare, incidents of larger magnitude will undoubtedly encompass situations, in which, on the one hand, multijurisdictional collaboration and coordination of the response is badly needed, while, on the other hand, major portions of the critical (information) infrastructure are destroyed or degraded to an extent, which makes such coordination and collaboration extremely difficult. CIMS redundancy then means that critical functions in such scenarios need to be performable elsewhere, and logistical support for equipping responders on the ground who have limited or no direct connectivity with updated stand-alone CIMS from remote sites via appropriate means of physical transportation.

5.3 Limitations of the Study

WebEOC is a CIMS predominantly used in the United States. The results reported here may be different for other CIMS in other countries. Also, software systems undergo relatively frequent revisions. This study did not discriminate between respondents reporting on the most recent version as opposed to older versions of this particular COTS. As a result, experiences with newer versions of WebEOC might have produced more favorable results. However, the convenience sample still reports on "what is currently out there;" yet, a large random or systematic sample might have produced more accurate results. While the number of respondents (83) who fully took the survey cannot be called small, it nevertheless was not large enough to produce highly robust results, which would lend themselves subject to elaborate statistical analyses. The study attracted participation by attaching the Web survey to a subject matter blog widely read by practitioners in emergency management. This particular blog entry on WebEOC was highly critical of the system, which might have primed and incentivized more respondents with negative than positive views to also share their own mainly negative views on WebEOC. Therefore, besides the sampling situation also from this latter perspective of potential bias, no claim of results-based generalizability can be made. Furthermore, when testing for predictors for the dependent variable (satisfaction/dissatisfaction) via regression analysis, none of the independent variables was found as outcome predictors. This might change in case of a larger and systematic sample. While these limitations are acknowledged, the study nevertheless was able to document in detail considerable dissatisfaction with WebEOC on part of practitioners on all levels of government who gave ample comments in support of their views. The study, hence, represents a broader exploratory step than previous studies also geared at better understanding the current problem space involving WebEOC.

5.4 Concluding Remarks and Future Research

It has been the object of this exploration to identify and document practitioners and system users' perceptions of fitness to task of WebEOC, the leading crisis information management system (CIMS) in the United States. This study contributes to the understanding of challenges and potential pitfalls when using commercial-off-the-shelf systems (COTS) in the context of emergency and disaster response management. While WebEOC appears to have some support among practitioners (mainly on Federal and State levels), a far larger number of practitioners on all levels of government was found to be highly critical of the system with respect to its perceived high cost, difficult maintenance, low performance, insufficient functionality, limited interoperability, and weak scalability. Since CIMS are the backbone of effective all-hazard and all-magnitude incident responses, these findings, which are supported by other studies, have to prompt further research, since they suggest a serious vulnerability in the Nation's capacity to effectively cope with emergencies and disasters, which can have adverse consequences for lives and assets.

Future research therefore needs to focus on how CIMS can be devised that meet the long established criteria and performance benchmarks [7, 36] and what obstacles must be cleared in order to implement them.

References

1. Hanson, P., McDougall, C.: Enabling collaborative and resilient emergency management efforts: DFES and Western Australia's adoption of a common operating picture. In: Proceedings of the 1st International Conference on Information Systems for Crisis Response and Management Asia Pacific (ISCRAM Asia Pacific 2018), Wellington, New Zealand, pp. 75–82. 5-7 November 2018

2. Levy, J., Prizzia, R.: Customizing web-EOC crisis management software to facilitate collaboration and increase situational awareness: advances in business resource center (BRC) design for business continuity management. In: Masys, A.J. (ed.) Security by Design. ASTSA, pp. 291–316. Springer, Cham (2018). https://doi.org/10.1007/978-3-319-78021-4_14

3. Scholl, H.J.: Overwhelmed by brute force of nature: first response management in the wake of a catastrophic incident. In: Lindgren, I., et al. (eds.) EGOV 2019. LNCS, vol. 11685, pp. 105–124. Springer, Cham (2019). https://doi.org/10.1007/978-3-030-27325-5_9

4. Cawley, K.S.: Assessing the impact of age and experience on the perceived ease of use of crisis information management software (2020)

5. Prasanna, R., Huggins, T.J.: Factors affecting the acceptance of information systems supporting emergency operations centres. Comput. Hum. Behav. **57**, 168–181 (2016)

6. Fischer, H.W.: The sociology of disaster: definitions, research questions, & measurements continuation of the discussion in a post-September 11 environment. Int. J. Mass Emerg. Disasters **21**(1), 91–107 (2003)

7. Anonymous, National Incident Management System, FEMA P-501. FEMA, Washington, DC (2008)

8. Anonymous, "National Response Framework," Homeland Security, ed. FEMA, p. iv/48 (2013)

9. Kelly, J.V.: FEMA's Initial Response to the Colorado Flood. U.S. Department of Homeland Security, Office of Inspector General, Washington, DC (2014)

10. McCauley, S.F.: FEMA Faces Challenges in Managing Information Technology. Office of Inspector General, Department of Homeland Security, Washington, DC (2015)

11. Delaney, A., Kitchin, R.: Progress and prospects for data-driven coordinated management and emergency response: the case of Ireland. Territ. Politics Governance **8**(6), 1–16 (2020)

12. Son, C., et al.: Investigating resilience in emergency management: an integrative review of literature. Appl. Ergon. **87**, 1–16 (2020)

13. Hart, S.V.: Crisis information management software (CIMS) feature comparison report. National Institute of Justice, Washington, DC (2002)

14. Nikolai, C., Becerra-Fernandez, I., Johnson, T., Madey, G.: Leveraging WebEOC in support of the Haitian relief effort: insights and lessons learned. In: Proceedings of the 7th International Conference on Information Systems for Crisis Response and Management (ISCRAM 2010), pp. 1–5. 2–5 May 2010

15. Li, T., et al.: Data-driven techniques in disaster information management. ACM Comput. Surv. (CSUR) **50**(1), 1–45 (2017)

16. Barnett, D.J., et al.: An analysis of after action reports from Texas hurricanes in 2005 and 2017. J. Public Health Manag. Pract. **27**(2), E71–E78 (2021)

17. Sánchez, C.E., Sánchez, L.D.: Case study: emergency department response to the Boston marathon bombing. In: Callaway, D.W., Burstein, J.L. (eds.) Operational and Medical Management of Explosive and Blast Incidents, pp. 363–367. Springer, Cham (2020). https://doi.org/10.1007/978-3-030-40655-4_25

18. Wukich, C.: More monitoring, less coordination: Twitter and Facebook use between emergency management agencies. J. Homel. Secur. Emerg. Manag. **17**(3), 1–29 (2020)

19. Levy, J., Prizzia, R.: Building effective emergency management public-private partnerships (PPP) for information sharing. In: Masys, A.J. (ed.) Security by Design. ASTSA, pp. 375–401. Springer, Cham (2018). https://doi.org/10.1007/978-3-319-78021-4_18

20. Truptil, S., Bénaben, F., Couget, P., Lauras, M., Chapurlat, V., Pingaud, H.: Interoperability of information systems in crisis management: crisis modeling and metamodeling. In: Mertins, K., Ruggaber, R., Popplewell, K., Xu, X. (eds.) Enterprise Interoperability III, pp. 583–594. Springer, London (2008). https://doi.org/10.1007/978-1-84800-221-0_46

21. Aros, S.K., Gibbons, D.E.: Developing an agent-based simulation model of the use of different communication technologies in inter-organizational disaster response coordination. In: Proceedings of the 2018 Winter Simulation Conference (WSC), Gothenburg, Sweden, pp. 68–79. 9–12 December 2018

22. Whelan, C., Molnar, A.: Organising across boundaries: communication, coordination and conflict. In: Whelan, C., Molnar, A. (eds.) Securing Mega-Events: Networks, strategies and tensions, pp. 91–122. Palgrave Macmillan, London (2018)

23. Scholl, H.J., et al.: Informational challenges in early disaster response: the massive Oso/SR530 landslide 2014 as case in point. In: Proceedings of the 50th Hawaii International Conference on System Sciences (HICSS-50), Waikoloa, Hawaii, pp. 2498–2508 (2017)

24. Scholl, H.J., Hubbel, K., Leonard, J.: Communications and technology challenges to situational awareness: insights from the CR16 exercise. In: Proceedings of the 1st ISCRAM Asia-Pacific Conference, ISCRAM, pp. 1–15 (2018)

25. Kedia, T., et al.: Technologies enabling situational awareness during disaster response: a systematic review. Disaster Med. Public Health Prep. 1–19 (2020). https://doi.org/10.1017/dmp.2020.196

26. Misra, S., Roberts, P., Rhodes, M.: The ecology of emergency management work in the digital age. Perspect. Public Manag. Governance 3(4), 305–322 (2020)

27. Ritchie, J., Lewis, J., Gillian, E.: Designing and selecting samples. In: Ritchie, J., Lewis, J. (eds.) Qualitative Research Practice: A Guide for Social Science Students and Researchers, pp. 77–108. Sage Publications, Thousand Oaks (2003)

28. Holdeman, E.E.: Use of WebEOC is insanity defined. Emergency Management: Disaster Zone, 27 August 2020. Government Technology (2020)

29. Corbin, J.M., Strauss, A.: Grounded theory research: procedures, canons, and evaluative criteria. Qual. Sociol. 13(1), 3–21 (1990). https://doi.org/10.1007/BF00988593

30. Fereday, J., Muir-Cochrane, E.: Demonstrating rigor using thematic analysis: a hybrid approach of inductive and deductive coding and theme development. Int. J. Qual. Methods 5(1), 80–92 (2006)

31. Charmaz, K.: Constructing Grounded Theory: A Practical Guide Through Qualitative Analysis, p. xxiii/207. Sage Publications, London (2006)

32. Anonymous, National Incident Management System Supporting Evaluation Program (NIMS STEP): Guide, Report, Federal Emergency Management Agency, Washington, DC (2010)

33. Scholl, H.J., Hubbell, K., Leonard, J.G.: Information sharing and situational awareness: insights from the Cascadia rising exercise of June 2016. In: Proceedings of the 52nd Hawaii International Conference on System Sciences (HICSS-52), pp. 1–11 (2019)

34. Scholl, H.J., Patin, B.J.: Resilient information infrastructures: criticality and role in responding to catastrophic incidents. Transform. Gov. People Process Policy 8(1), 28–48 (2014)

35. Turoff, M., et al.: The design of a dynamic emergency response management information system (DERMIS). JITTA: J. Inf. Technol. Theory Appl. 5(4), 1 (2004)

36. Anonymous, Incident Decision Support Software Application Note: System Assessment and Validation for Emergency Responders (SAVER). U.S. Department of Homeland Security, Washington, DC (2010)

Open Data: Social and Technical Perspectives

A Typology of Municipalities' Roles and Expected User's Roles in Open Government Data Release and Reuse

Elisabeth Gebka$^{(\boxtimes)}$ and Annick Castiaux

Namur Digital Institute, University of Namur, 5000 Namur, Belgium
{elisabeth.gebka,annick.castiaux}@unamur.be

Abstract. The purpose of this paper is to identify the roles municipalities take when engaging in Open Government Data (OGD) and the expectations of user's roles they imply. According to the output delivered, the user can relate to data or data-based solutions. OGD is data released by public organisations to enhance government transparency, innovation, and participation. The realization of those benefits involves different roles, from providing data, developing solutions, to using them for a certain purpose. However, the definition of the municipalities' and users' roles in that context is unclear, which can impact the realization of the OGD benefits. This study uses Role Theory's concepts as an analytical lens, following the Design Science Research approach to create a typology. We conducted a hermeneutic literature review, identified, and analysed 52 papers, to build a typology of the municipalities' roles based on the goals, tasks, output delivered, and the expected users' roles they generate. It results in seven classes of roles coming in pairs. We tested the typology on empirical cases: the 28 Belgian and 158 Swedish municipalities engaged in OGD. Five role pairs were encountered in the empirical cases, and two occurred only in previous literature. The typology can help municipalities to understand how their role choice calls for a certain type of users that cannot be generalized as a "citizen". Role Theory opens new perspectives of research to understand their interdependence and raises fundamental role-related questions that should be given the same importance as technical and technological challenges.

Keywords: Open Government Data · Municipalities · User · Roles · Typology

1 Introduction

In 2013, the European Commission adopted the *Public Sector Information* (PSI) Directive (Directive 2013/37/EU), which encourages public organisations to share their information and data for reuse. The idea is that Open Government Data (OGD) is funded by public money and can generate social and economic value [1], therefore it should be made accessible to all. OGD is data released by a public organisation, the publisher, for secondary use, by a user, without any restriction or limitation in use. For a public organisation, the benefits of publishing OGD can be better transparency and accountability,

© IFIP International Federation for Information Processing 2021
Published by Springer Nature Switzerland AG 2021
H. J. Scholl et al. (Eds.): EGOV 2021, LNCS 12850, pp. 137–152, 2021.
https://doi.org/10.1007/978-3-030-84789-0_10

innovation and improved efficiency, and/or an increased engagement and participation in governance [2]. The municipalities play an important role because they own plenty of data (e.g., on transport, pollution, geographic data) [3] that can supply the regional and national portals and are amongst the most reused data sets [4].

However, publishing OGD is new for most municipalities and creates ambiguities in terms of role and scope of action, compared to their traditional role. To serve the common interest, several institutional paradigms co-exist, have different views about what is at stake, and bring different answers on how to achieve efficiency, accountability, and equity [5]. They create a variety of citizens' roles and modes of interaction [6]. In the same vein, what is included in the actors' roles to realize the OGD benefits is variable. For example, the public organisation can be limited to the publisher role [7] or considered as a data user [8, 9], a duality that is under-researched [10]. The citizen, which involvement in OGD is lacking empirical evidence [11], is broadly assimilated to a group of data users, or indirect beneficiaries (end-users) depending on intermediaries, developers or companies, to benefit from OGD [11, 12].

There are different approaches of role classifications in OGD literature: a process approach based on data value chain (e.g., [1, 7]), the data provision (e.g., [13]), the reuse process (e.g., [12, 14]) or the data ecosystems (e.g., [15]). They help to model roles to reach data value creation in an ideal world, as things happened in a continuous process and perfect interactions. However, they provide little insights about the influence of other roles (municipality *and* publisher) and projected expectations towards others. The purpose of this research is to investigate the possible roles of the municipalities, considering that they can be publisher and user, and deliver a certain type of output, data or solutions, for others to use. They generate expectations towards the user. To this end, we develop a typology of roles through the lens of Role Theory's concepts, following a Design Science Research approach. The research questions guiding the study are:

– *What are the possible municipalities' roles within OGD release and reuse?*
– *What expected users' roles are implied by the municipalities' roles?*

The typology should help to differentiate the municipalities' approaches to OGD, roles, and type of users they call for, and raise role-related issues that can impede the realization of benefits. The paper is structured as followed: the background introduces role ambiguities and the Role Theory's concepts used to develop the typology. Then, we explain the research approach, present the findings, discussion and conclusion.

2   Background

2.1   OGD Roles, Outputs, and Ambiguities

To generate benefits, the data needs to be made available. Then, it needs to be accessed by users, handled and repurposed to give it a new use and a broader value (e.g., insights, visualisations, or information solutions) [14]. Therefore, in OGD, the most comprehensive and acknowledged roles are (1) the publisher, the actor who publishes data, and (2) the user, the actor who makes a secondary use of it. Publishing and reusing data is not easy and can require new roles and intermediaries between the publisher and the user.

For example, a publisher might need the help of a portal provider to structure the data released on the web. A user might need the help of an enabler who provides tools or visualisations to facilitate data reuse in context [4]. The user can also have the expertise to develop solutions for others, make decisions, participate in governance processes, or benefit from new digitalized services. A complexity of OGD lies consequently in the role coordination around an output, to reach a higher purpose. The output delivered by the municipality can vary from raw data in an excel spreadsheet, datasets on a portal, visualisations and charts, or a complete information solution. To use the output, the user can need analytical skills or just be able to use a computer or smartphone. The expected user is moreover coloured with citizen's roles, to participate in the discussion, exchange of ideas and decision-making process with the government [16], enabled by OGD. Users can collaborate with decision-makers to create solutions based on OGD that will be implemented in the city [17] or consume the developed services.

The extent to the municipalities engage with OGD, therefore, has an impact on the user expected tasks and activities, to realize the higher purpose. When the municipalities' role and expectations are not in line with the user capabilities, resources, and motivations, there is a risk that the expected benefits will not be realized. To understand the relation of the actors through their role, Role Theory provides a relevant lens.

2.2 Role Theory

The concept of roles is widely used in the area of social sciences to explain human and organisations' behaviour patterns. It assumes that people have social positions and hold expectations for their own behaviours and those of other persons, according to their role [18]. The concept of role can be extended to the concept of actors, understood as persons, entities, or organisations. "Role Theory" is a catchphrase grouping different research streams that study roles, with different perspectives and terminologies. In our context, three approaches can complement each other to understand roles in OGD.

The *functional approach* has focused on the behaviours of individuals occupying a social position within a stable social system. This perspective suggests that individuals within their social systems are taught norms and are expected to conform to those norms and sanction individuals who do not [18]. In the traditional conception of roles of the citizens and the government, as voters vs. elected representatives, or public managers vs. users, the boundaries of the roles are shared, normative. Clear expectations prescribe and explain behaviours. In OGD, the municipality might expect the public to reuse OGD as a tool to monitor public action because it is the duty of the citizens.

The *symbolic interactionist approach* assumes that roles are not consequences of one's position in a social structure, but that an actor can change its position as roles are context-specific [19, 20]. Roles are created through interactions with others, they are emergent and negotiable [18]. Network and innovation studies have focused on a processual aspect of roles that describes what actors intend to do. It implies that actors' roles can also be used for granting access to important resources. The roles are products of actors' interpretations of situations [19]. In OGD, it explains how the publishers rely on the users to innovate, providing creativity and skills that it has not internally. They bring essential resources to realize the expected benefits. The first two approaches of Role Theory can be considered normative.

Finally, *the task-based approach*, as suggested by Nyström et al. [21] for the study of open innovation networks (in Living Labs), looks at individuals using an ideal role to achieve a certain goal. The actor's role is created through action: the goal and the related tasks determine the role, which resources are allocated, and which actors are teamed up with. The roles emerge in the innovation process and, as the process is open, roles are not predefined. The same actor can have different roles. This approach is particularly relevant for our study, as the OGD reuse is an open innovation process by principle. It gives the appropriate flexibility to create role categories, necessary in OGD, where the roles are emerging and varying with the local contexts.

In sum, the **roles** are functions, tasks, and behaviours expected of parties in particular positions and contexts [22]. A **role-set** of an actor is related to the expected acting out of a role: required duties, activities, standards, objectives and responsibilities [23]; a role-set emphasises the interdependence between the actors within a certain structure: the actor who sends the role through expectations, and the focal actor, who receives the role [24]. The **role expectations** can be explicit (e.g., job description) or not (e.g., informal notions, agreements) [22].

Herrmann et al. [22] argue that the repetition of social interaction patterns until they can be anticipated, based on patterns of expectations, gradually develops new roles. They add that the development of roles is accompanied by role-mechanisms, i.e. interaction patterns for role-taking and role-making. The role-taking is acting with respect to the expectations, which can be potentially enforced by sanctions being imposed on the role actor [22]. The role-making is how a person lives a role, and how she transforms the expectations into concrete behaviour [22]. Role expectation is, therefore, a key concept in Role Theory. In the functional approach, the focus is on the given expectations (role-taking). In the interactionist approach, roles are emergent and negotiable, consequently, the actors interpret, organise, modify the expectations (role-making). In the task-based approach, the roles are defined by the network's goal and needs depending on the situation, there are constant occurrences of role-making and role-taking [21].

The study of role-sets and expectations can help to understand dysfunctions in the role-taking or making and its impact on the process. For example, role ambiguity is the lack of clarity of role expectations and the degree of uncertainty regarding the outcomes of one's role performance [25]. Role overload occurs when a person is faced with too many expectations [18]. Role malintegration occurs when interdependent roles do not fit well together [18]. In this study, we use concepts of Role Theory to develop a typology of roles and discuss the role-related issues.

3   Research Approach

The research approach to develop the typology is based on Design Research Science (DSR). This paradigm of research aims at developing solutions (artefacts) meeting defined goals, that contribute to the scientific knowledge base (rigour) and provide utility in the environment (relevance). To reach that purpose, a research project should, in as many iteration loops as needed, follow 6 steps: *identify and motivate the problem domain (1), define the objectives of the solution (2), develop (3), demonstrate (4), evaluate (5), and finally communicate (6)* the results to the audience [26].

The problem (1) we identified is the lack of clarity in the role of the municipality and citizens identified in the literature. Accordingly, *the motivation and objective (2)* of this study are to design a typology of municipalities' roles when dealing with OGD, enlightening the expectations they project on the users. Such a typology can be used as a tool to diagnose the OGD approach of municipalities and help them to raise the critical questions of new role integration that OGD implies for all the actors.

To develop the typology (3), we used the method suggested by Nickerson et al. [27] anchored in DSR. A typology is a system of conceptually derived grouping. The method of Nickerson et al. [27] starts with the determination of the meta-characteristic, the most comprehensive characteristic that will serve as the basis for the choice of dimensions and their characteristics in the typology. In this research, it is the interdependence between the role of the municipality releasing or reusing OGD and the user of the provided output. Each characteristic should be a logical consequence of the meta-characteristic, in our case, relevant concepts from Role Theory: components of the role-set (e.g., tasks, responsibilities), output, and role expectation. The typology development, made in iterations, combined a conceptual method (deductive: conceptualizing the dimensions of the taxonomy without examining actual objects) and an empirical method (inductive: identifying a subset of objects that we want to classify).

The typology development was based on previous literature as it helped us to access more cases and potentially identify more roles than an empirical method. To review the literature, we used the hermeneutic method of Boell et al. [28], consistent with the DSR approach. It allows a progressive and critical understanding of a body of literature, through two intertwined circles of research that can be repeated several times: the searching and acquisition circle, and the analysis and interpretation circle. The software NVivo was used to store, code, analyse, and sort the selected papers. We conducted three cycles. We used the databases Google Scholar and Science Direct and, in the first cycle, the keywords "role", + "Government", + "Citizen", + "Open Government Data", then "Task", "Actors". We selected empirical papers wherein the words "role" and "open (government) data" appeared in keywords, abstract or body text, with the cities as a context. It resulted in the first iteration of the typology, with roles based on the level of engagement of the municipalities and the user's roles as citizens. For the second cycle, we extended the research with citation tracking (backward and forward literature search) and keywords of concepts discovered in the papers to find new papers. We came to the second iteration of the typology, but noticed overlaps between roles and dimensions due to conceptual ambiguities in the chosen characteristics and reuse of role classes of previous research. We detached ourselves from previous role classes and re-focused on the key concepts of Role Theory for the third iteration. We analysed one more time the goals, tasks, outputs and expectations to let emerge classes of municipalities' roles, and sort the empirical literature. In the third and last cycle of literature search, we focused on acquiring empirical and conceptual papers for the less covered roles (e.g., OGD + "commercial reuse", OGD + "citizen participation") and refined the typology in its fourth iteration. Conceptual papers helped us to strengthen the logic of the typology, i.e. its dimensions in accordance with the research purpose, and to understand the school of thoughts of the empirical studies. We coded and used 40 empirical papers and 12 conceptual papers to develop the typology. The roles are more often indirectly presented than explicitly researched in the current OGD literature. They were not found with the names and the combinations presented in the typology, as they result from the analysis and understanding of the researchers.

To consolidate the typology and demonstrate (4) its relevance in practice, we collected primary empirical data for two national cases, Belgium and Sweden, wherein we analysed the municipalities engaged with OGD. Two cases allow better generalization. Those countries were chosen for their different level of maturity in OGD, according to the European Maturity Report[1], Belgium and Sweden being respectively follower and fast-tracker. Both countries have translated the European PSI Directive into their laws and encourage their municipalities to publish data. Belgium counts 581 municipalities, and Sweden 290. By comparing national data portals and lists of publishers, we identified 28 municipalities in Belgium and 158 in Sweden publishing or reusing OGD at the time of the data collection (January-February 2021). We applied the typology to each of them and used a directed content analysis [29]. We analysed the websites, portals, and all type of reported off-line activities that constitute the output and create a channel for interaction between the municipality and the user. We identified and tabulated their stated goals, expected users, activities and tasks through the output delivered to sort them per role classes. At the end of the analysis, *we evaluated (5)* the typology based on the ending conditions of Nickerson et al. [27] and concluded that they were met. The publication of the findings in that paper is part of the *communication (6)*.

4   Analysis and Findings

This section presents the typology of the municipalities' roles and expected user's roles (Table 1). The first column lists the municipalities' role, characterized by a set of goals, tasks, and output. In pair come one or several expected users' roles that interact with the municipalities in unique ways. Key references and the number of occurrences are specified. The sum of occurrences is higher than the total number of municipalities analysed, as the combination of roles is possible, which is further presented in the findings. Each pair of role class is subsequently elaborated with empirical examples.

The compliant data provider goes for the simplest way of providing data by responding to external data demand or pressure. For example, in Sweden, municipalities can freely upload their data on a platform managed by an association (Kolada), to allow the citizens to compare their performance. Nine municipalities refer to that website under a page labelled "Open data" or "PSI data", 118 just imported a script from Kolada's website that displays a selection of datasets, and only 13 of those provided contact details. For very broad goals (e.g., "*promote participation, democracy and growth*"), the municipalities provide what is strictly necessary and create huge expectations on the users. They are true **data hunters**: to find data, they have to be ready to explore websites and dig into unstructured datasets. These roles are not very documented in research, since they bring little knowledge about OGD, but they are the case of most municipalities that have not intention to invest time and resources in OGD.

Municipalities and citizens can both be **partners** and collaborate in projects led by third parties for new service development (user-centred approaches) and governance

---

[1] https://www.europeandataportal.eu/en/dashboard/2020.

Table 1. Typology of the municipalities' roles and expected user's roles

Municipalities' role	Role-set (G: goal, T: examples of tasks and activities)	Example of output delivered to the user	Expected users' roles	Key references and number of occurrences in Belgium (BE) and Sweden (SE)
The Compliant Data Provider	G: Compliance with the law and public values (e.g., transparency) T: Answer requests; send data on demand, without specifically publishing it. Open "on-demand"	Unstructured data, formatted for internal use, delivered on-demand by email, or imported web pages showing a selection of data, with low engagement to improve it	**The Data Hunter:** The users are experts in data reuse and know what data they need to satisfy their goals (find information, innovate)	[30] BE: 0 SE: 127
The Partner	G: Support the development of new services and public value T: Participate in collaborative processes (for innovation, governance)	Client briefing, guidance and feedback, expertise for the under-development solutions, funds	**The Partner** in governance or innovation processes, as a project led by third organisations or researchers	[31–33] BE: 0 SE: 0
The Stand-Alone Publisher	G: Openness, transparency, economic growth, innovation, participation (multiple and broad goals) T: Publish data on a website or portal, with a supply-driven and often scattered approach	OGD portal or website, with data as the main content. Do not always provide contact forms	**The Rare Bird:** the users are the expert and can conduct all type of activities required to reuse data (searching, finding, cleansing, enriching, combining, visualizing, developing solutions). The provided data is believed to be enough	[34–36] BE: 23 SE: 24

(continued)

Table 1. (*continued*)

Municipalities' role	Role-set (G: goal, T: examples of tasks and activities)	Example of output delivered to the user	Expected users' roles	Key references and number of occurrences in Belgium (BE) and Sweden (SE)
The Dedicated Publisher	G: Make the data appealing to reach the above mentioned multiple goals T: Make the data easy to use, accessible, provide extra tools and resources, publicize the data released and reuses (apps), release new data on a regular basis	OGD portal with extra content and functionalities to provide support and feedback (tools, tutorial, documentation, API's, technical standards, selection of best cases of reuses, feedback form)	**The Data Analyst and Developer:** develop new applications and solutions based on data, exchange ideas with the open community members, gives feedback to the publisher, analyse data for monitoring the public action	[1, 37, 38] BE: 4 SE: 6
The Enabler	G: Make the data reused to outsource innovation, service development, or to solve identified problems T: Raise the awareness and capabilities of the ecosystem, identify public issues, provide means and call for actions	Beside the portal, organizes hackathons, training programs, workshops, ideation platforms, innovation contests, guidelines, policies, places of collaboration and exchanges (ideas, resources)	**The Ideator, Innovator, Co-producer, Co-implementer:** share community needs, provide ideas, prototypes of solutions, applications, technical know-how, creativity, solve public challenges	[39–41] BE: 4 SE: 2
The Solution Provider	G: Provide public e-services and digital tools based on data for the citizens T: (Co-)fund solutions, develop tools	Dashboards, policy evaluation tools, improved public services	**The Smart Citizen:** use enhanced public services, make informed decisions, participate in governance processes	[8, 42, 43] BE: 8 SE: 2
The Orchestrator	G: Coordinate means and strategies together to reach a vision and purpose (smart city, data ecosystem) T: Develop policies, strategies, tools	Living labs, policies, change management strategies, global approach of data production, management and reuse, pilot projects	**The Data Producer:** generate data that is reused by the municipality **Innovator, Smart Citizen**	[44, 45] BE: 0 SE: 0

(decision-making, policy-making, monitoring). As the goal of the data reuse is clear, the process led and facilitated by a third party, municipalities and users can be called for expertise other than data analytics: field knowledge, community needs, creativity, voices in public debate. The expectations are directed to a role in society (user of public service, citizen), instead of technical expertise. However, the collaborative processes identified in our literature review were research-led projects and no cases were reported in the empirical material. These roles are temporary and reactive to external impulsion.

The **stand-alone publisher**, unlike the compliant data provider, shows intentions to join the OGD movement. Still, it has either not stated or very general goals (e.g., *"foster innovation and the development of applications", "promote the participation of all"*). The output can consist of only one to five datasets on a regional or national portal, a catalogue on the website, or owned external portals. The publisher follows a supply-logic: what is in house, cleanable and openable, or thought as a priority by the municipality, is released [34]. The publisher expects the rest of the reuse to be undertaken by the user, a **rare bird**. Despite the little resources provided and lack of channels to interact with the publisher, he would navigate between portals, find and reuse data, develop new solutions, and participate in governance processes and public debate, empowered by the information he would have extracted himself [35, 36].

The **dedicated publisher** has understood data only gain value being reused and tries to make it appealing. A common strategy to enhance reuse is to publish as much data as possible on an owned portal, which accessibility and user-friendliness depend on the functionalities offered by the portal provider. Besides extra information, technical documentation, portals can also include tools to visualise data and improve the data reusability, discoverability [37], even extent the technical development of data (e.g. linked open data, 1 municipality, BE). The municipality is aware of the difficulty of reusing OGD, but the output (portals, tools), can still be complex for a lay user. Part of the support is addressed to the **developers and data analysts**, who still are expected to develop services and solutions for the community.

As an **enabler,** the municipality moves beyond the publishing activities, seeing the need for a more interventionist approach. It enables the actors of an ecosystem to realize the benefits of OGD. It has still no control over the developed services but shows more leadership because its goal is to create public value, stimulate innovation to solve public issues and meet the citizen's needs. To achieve that, the municipality undertakes an enabling role that can be oriented towards the capabilities of the actors, the functioning of the ecosystem, or the motivation to solve specific issues. This role was well documented in previous research, as it was an ideal to aim. In practice, only six municipalities took that role, and organised workshops and hackathons. They serve as places to meet, raise public needs, exchange ideas and develop prototypes based on data. The municipality expects the citizens to be an **innovator, ideator, co-creator** of new services of public interest. Interestingly, that role can be limited in time, as it relates to a specific project. Three municipalities organised a single hackathon or similar, in two cases, funded by European projects, two ran yearly hackathons but stopped due to the pandemic, and one stopped due to the lack of sustainable results but is considering new ways to energize the user community.

When the municipality reuses its data, it becomes a **solution provider**. It can improve its processes and digitalized its public services [8]. Innovation and reuse are internalized. The user is a **smart citizen** who gets tools like dashboards and visualisation of key facts to monitor the performance of the city [8, 42] (9 municipalities), make better decisions, and trust the government [43]. Municipalities try to reduce the information asymmetry and encourage "citizen participation" in the decision-making process, but in the empirical cases, dashboards do not come along with off-line governance processes. It is more an open window on key figures and performance. Information can also be developed into applications (2 municipalities, e.g., an app for parking spots, cemeteries). Open data is integrated to the municipalities' core activities, and the key outputs are tools for transparency and digitalized information services.

In the role of **orchestrator**, the municipality put means together to reach a certain purpose (under its control), the transformation of the city into a smart city [44], a smart data ecosystem [45] or a platform model of data-driven public services [46]. The municipality takes the lead to fulfil its goal and strategy. The OGD is a piece of a larger program, which can enrol any of the municipality and citizens' roles previously cited. The difference is that the goal of the municipality is clear and its maturity in reusing data enables it to make strategic choices instead of experimentations with OGD. These roles were not observed in the empirical material.

We observed municipalities **combining roles**. One municipality (SE) was a stand-alone publisher (basic data catalogue) and temporary enabler (European project addressed to the citizens), three were stand-alone publishers and solution providers (app of visualisation of the key figures). Two added to the latter combo the enabler role (organisation of single or yearly hackathon). Finally, the dedicated publisher role was combined once with temporary enabler (unique hackathon), once with solution provider (app of cemeteries, visualisation of key figures), and twice with solution provider and permanent enabler (yearly activities with the users).

5   Discussion

The purpose of this study was to create a typology of roles for the municipalities within the spectrum of data release and reuse. Previous research on OGD roles took a technical perspective, dividing them between a succession of tasks and operations to reuse data and create value (e.g., [1, 7, 12, 14, 15]). Sieber et al. [13] take a government-citizen perspective, limiting the scope to data provision. We were missing a more comprehensive definition of roles, considering that in our context the data provider is also and first a municipality. They have to define the limits of their new OGD roles, which creates expectations towards the user. In this section, we further discuss the nuances between the identified roles and role-related issues. Then, we highlight discrepancies between the given importance to the roles identified in the literature, and their occurrences in practice.

Through the lens of the Role Theory's concepts, we can highlight three ways municipalities approach the OGD roles, as shown in Fig. 1. The partner and the compliant data provider are in reality in a focal role [24]. The role sender can be a citizen asking for data, a supra-government or an institution that push the municipality in the role of data provider or partner. The stand-alone, dedicated publisher, and enabler, believe in the benefits of data and embrace a new but *distinct* role, imposed by the new activities coming along with data release. The stand-alone is doing what Sieber et al. [13] call "data-over-the-wall". The dedicated, with better tools, expects the user to provide new public services themselves ("Do-it-Yourself Government" [47]). The enabler makes its resources and knowledge available to the public, provides support to foster greater public value, embedded in an ecosystem view, but without active involvement in the development of solutions ("Government as a platform" [47]). However, the solution provider and orchestrator integrate data reuse in their operations to deliver digitalized services or improve public management.

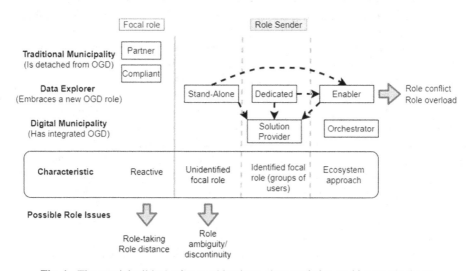

Fig. 1. The municipalities' roles combinations, characteristics, and issues (Authors)

More complex municipalities' perspectives on OGD show through the combination of roles. The stand-alone/service provider goes for the quick-wins: basic portals for the experts, easy to read visualisation for the other and transparency. The stand-alone /enabler/solution provider adds user interactions, which is interesting when the enabler role is recurrent: basic portals are balanced with regular hackathons. The stand-alone/temporary enabler is an experimenter, and the dedicated publisher/temporary enabler chooses to invest in a rich portal more than in user interaction. The dedicated publisher/solution provider is a logical combination that comes with experience and time: the more they publish data, the more they see opportunities for new services. The dedicated publisher/permanent enabler/service provider is probably the most engaged in OGD, intending to become a "data-driven" city.

Role Theory also allows identifying issues and ambiguities that can impair the realization of OGD benefits, as presented in Fig. 1. In a focal role, the municipality is in a position of role-taking that can be potentially enforced by sanctions [22] (laws regarding OGD), which can increase a role distance [22] and the absence of interest in providing data. The stand-alone publisher has an unidentified focal role ("anyone", role ambiguity), without interaction with the user. Consequently, the output might meet the requirements of no one: there can be a role discontinuity [18] between the publisher and the user in terms of skills, objectives, and data available. The stand-alone, dedicated publisher, and enabler can raise a role conflict [25] for the municipality. If the data reuse is entirely delegated to independent users, can the public interest be guaranteed? Who is responsible for? The provided data (limited in quality, interoperability) combined with the high expectations (create applications for the citizens) can also generate role overload [18], a role wherein few users recognize themselves. In the context of OGD, where roles develop and are performed through the provision and the use of a complex output, a functional approach, which can fit with the organisational culture of traditional public organisations, can impede the OGD reuse and realization of its benefits.

In terms of occurrences, five of the seven roles were taken by the municipalities. The most represented role is the compliant data provider, in Sweden. Importation of Kolada's datasets on their website is considered sufficient to comply with their obligation of delivering data for transparency. It is reasonably arguable, however, that this operation results in the claimed objectives (*"promote participation, democracy and growth"*), as none of these pages reported initiatives making use of the data.

The most documented role, in our literature review, is the enabler (13 papers identified). According to research, the municipalities can, among others, provide training to build data-literacy [39], hackathons, workshops, understand the needs of the users [41], develop policies that focus on the availability of resources and good governance [48], encourage participation and balance the benefits of all type of users (companies, citizens, social organisations) [37]. In practice, the instances of enabler's roles are focused on the organisation of hackathons, which remained a unique or abandoned experiment for four cities. The lack of resources can be a reason, as two projects relied on external funding, but also the question of the role attribution: is that the role of the municipality?

Finally, the roles of partners and orchestrators did not occur. The partner, as understood in the literature, is, in fact, a reactive role: the municipality joins an experimental process that intends to create value with data, led by other organisations. It depends therefore on external impulsion. The orchestrator is a role that requires a certain maturity with data and digitalization, together with ambition, vision, and resources. Capitals can more easily gather these conditions, such as London [45]. Brussels and Stockholm appear to be dedicated publishers. They invest more in appealing and well-provided portals than in the integration of the data in their operations with a coordinated vision.

The "citizen" turns out to be an elusive role that does not help to grasp the nuances between the expectations generated by the different municipalities' roles. This lack of clarity is substantial in the empirical material. The citizen's role is not stated (*"Open data is available for anyone"*) or implied (transparency for the citizen to monitor) by the compliant data provider. For the stand-alone publisher, the citizen is the data user or user of future applications. The dedicated publisher addresses clearly its output to experts, while the enabler can see the citizens as idea providers. Solution provider and orchestrator, on the other hand, have a clear objective and output, and therefore defined user groups of democratic processes or digitalized services.

Implications for practice are that an interactionist and task-based approach would enable the actors to shape their role in relation to each other and the resources available, through time and experience. "Open" should not mean "abandon" of and disconnection with the users. Until then, if the municipality can combine the role of solution provider with other roles, it can increased the perceived value of OGD for both municipalities and lay users, and avoid a role conflict that could cease the municipality's engagement in OGD. For research, Role Theory offers a new perspective to understand the difficulties and barriers faced by the actors in OGD. It raised fundamental role-related questions that should be given the same importance as technical and technological challenges.

6 Conclusion

Municipalities are encouraged to publish OGD, which is for most, a new role. There is no definition or limits regarding what a municipality is supposed to do and deliver to the user. However, the way they frame their role creates expectations towards the user. The interdependence between roles and generated expectations is not researched in previous literature, as roles are defined from technical and process perspectives. The expectations are ironed out or ignored, although it is a central concept in Role Theory. This study is the first to use Role Theory's concepts in the OGD field. With that theoretical lens, we develop a typology of municipalities' roles, coming in pair with expected users' roles. The way each pair interacts is unique. Seven pairs were identified and applied to the municipalities of two national cases, Belgium and Sweden. One of the main findings is that municipalities can detach themselves from the OGD roles, create new ones focussing on the provision of data and support for the user, or integrate OGD as part of their main operations. The aim of the typology is not to suggest an ideal-type role or path to follow, but to allow identifying municipal approaches to OGD and highlighting the possible role-related issues that could impede the realization of OGD benefits. The main contribution lies in the originality of the theoretical lens used, which opens a new perspective to understand the difficulties and barriers faced by the actors in OGD.

The study has limitations. It has focused on the municipalities and their users. It is however evident that they do not work in closed environments and other factors and actors influence the way they perceive and deliver output. The analysis of the data, information, tools and activities provided by the municipalities, pictures a situation at a time. It does not reveal uncommunicated intentions or future projects that could affect the role classification of the cases.

Future research could use the typology to conduct case studies and explore the factors or conditions that encourage the municipalities to take certain roles. With a time perspective, future research could explore what experiences and learnings make them evolve between roles, combine them, or stop and leave OGD. The typology could also be compared with the user perception of the municipality role, and explore how role-making interplays with role-taking for both users and municipalities.

Acknowledgements. The study was performed with financial support by the FEDER and the Walloon Region (H2020), as part of the project "Wal-e-cities".

References

1. Attard, J., Orlandi, F., Scerri, S., Auer, S.: A systematic review of open government data initiatives. Gov. Inf. Q. **32**, 399–418 (2015)
2. Charalabidis, Y., Zuiderwijk, A., Alexopoulos, C., Janssen, M., Lampoltshammer, T., Ferro, E.: The open data landscape. In: The World of Open Data. PAIT, vol. 28, pp. 1–9. Springer, Cham (2018). https://doi.org/10.1007/978-3-319-90850-2_1
3. Berends, J., Carrara, W., Vollers, H.: Analytical Report 6: Open Data in Cities 2., Luxembourg (2020)
4. Berends, J., Carrara, W., Engbers, W., Vollers, H.: Re-Using Open Data: A Study on Companies Transforming Open Data into Economic & Societal Value (2017)
5. Stoker, G.: Public value management: a new narrative for networked governance? Am. Rev. Public Adm. **36**, 41–57 (2006)
6. Vigoda, E.: From responsiveness to collaboration: governance, citizens, and the next generation of public administration. Public Adm. Rev. **62**, 527–540 (2002)
7. Carrara, W., Chan, W.S., Fischer, S., van Steenbergen, E.: Capgemini Institute, European Commission: Creating Value Through Open Data: Study on the Impact of Re-Use of Public Data Resources (2015)
8. Mergel, I., Kleibrink, A., Sörvik, J.: Open data outcomes: U.S. cities between product and process innovation. Gov. Inf. Q. **35**, 622–632 (2018)
9. Pereira, G.V., Macadar, M.A., Luciano, E.M., Testa, M.G.: Delivering public value through open government data initiatives in a smart city context. Inf. Syst. Front. **19**(2), 213–229 (2016). https://doi.org/10.1007/s10796-016-9673-7
10. Mesquita, M.A., Luciano, E.M., Rafael, M., Wiedenhöft, G.C.: Discussing the twofold role of government - provider and user - in the open government data ecosystem. In: EGov-CEDEM-EPart Conference Proceedings. Linköping (2020)
11. Safarov, I., Meijer, A., Grimmelikhuijsen, S.: Utilization of open government data: a systematic literature review of types, conditions, effects and users. Inf. Polity. **22**, 1–24 (2017)
12. Abella, A., Ortiz-de-Urbina-Criado, M., De-Pablos-Heredero, C.: The process of open data publication and reuse. J. Assoc. Inf. Sci. Technol. **70**, 296–300 (2019)
13. Sieber, R.E., Johnson, P.A.: Civic open data at a crossroads: dominant models and current challenges. Gov. Inf. Q. **32**, 308–315 (2015)
14. Lassinantti, J.: Re-use of public sector open data. Int. J. Enterp. Inf. Syst. **1**, 1–29 (2019)
15. Dawes, S.S., Vidiasova, L., Parkhimovich, O.: Planning and designing open government data programs: an ecosystem approach. Gov. Inf. Q. **33**, 15–27 (2016)
16. Harrison, T.M., et al.: Open government and e-government: democratic challenges from a public value perspective. Inf. Polity. **17**, 83–97 (2012)
17. Noveck, B.S.: Wiki government: How technology can make government better, democracy stronger, and citizens more powerful., Washington DC (2009)
18. Biddle, B.: Recent developments in role theory. Annu. Rev. Sociol. **12**, 67–92 (1986)
19. Anderson, H., Havila, V., Andersen, P., Halinen, A.: Position and role-conceptualizing dynamics in business networks. Scand. J. Manag. **14**, 167–186 (1998)
20. Ashforth, B.E.: Role Transitions in Organizational Life: An Identity-Based Perspective. Lawrence Erlbaum Associates, Mahwah (2000)
21. Nyström, A.G., Leminen, S., Westerlund, M., Kortelainen, M.: Actor roles and role patterns influencing innovation in living labs. Ind. Mark. Manag. **43**, 483–495 (2014)
22. Herrmann, T., Jahnke, I., Loser, K.U.: The Role Concept as a Basis for Designing Community Systems. In: Francoise, D., Rose, D., Carla Sand Manuel, Z. (eds.) Cooperative Systems Design Scenar, pp. 163–178, IOS, Amsterdam (2004)

23. Heikkinen, M.T., Mainela, T., Still, J., Tähtinen, J.: Roles for managing in mobile service development nets. Ind. Mark. Manag. **36**, 909–925 (2007)

24. Kahn, R.L., Wolfe, D.M., Quinn, R.P., Snoek, J.D., Rosenthal, R.A.: Organizational Stress: Studies in Role Conflict and Ambiguity. John Wiley, New York (1964)

25. Miles, R.H.: Role-set configuration as a predictor of role conflict and ambiguity in complex organizations. Sociometry **40**, 21 (1977)

26. Peffers, K., Tuunanen, T., Rothenberger, M.A., Chatterjee, S.: A design science research methodology for information systems research. J. Manag. Inf. Syst. **24**, 45–77 (2014)

27. Nickerson, R.C., Varshney, U., Muntermann, J.: A method for taxonomy development and its application in information systems. Eur. J. Inf. Syst. **22**, 336–359 (2013)

28. Boell, S.K., Cecez-Kecmanovic, D.: A hermeneutic approach for conducting literature reviews and literature searches. Commun. Assoc. Inf. Syst. **34**, 257–286 (2014)

29. Hsieh, H.-F., Shannon, S.E.: Three approaches to qualitative content analysis. Qual. Health Res. **15**, 1277–1288 (2005)

30. Agrawal, D., Kettinger, W.J., Zhang, C.: The openness challenge: why some cities take it on and others don't. In: Twentieth Americas Conference on Information Systems, pp. 1–7. Savannah (2014)

31. Ruijer, E., Grimmelikhuijsen, S., Meijer, A.: Open data for democracy: developing a theoretical framework for open data use. Gov. Inf. Q. **34**, 45–52 (2017)

32. Conradie, P., Mulder, I., Choenni, S.: Rotterdam open data: exploring the release of public sector information through co-creation. In: 2012 18th International ICE Conference on Engineering, Technology and Innovation, pp. 1–10. IEEE (2012)

33. Toots, M., et al.: A framework for data-driven public service co-production. In: Janssen, M., et al. (eds.) EGOV 2017. LNCS, vol. 10428, pp. 264–275. Springer, Cham (2017). https://doi.org/10.1007/978-3-319-64677-0_22

34. Ham, J., Koo, Y., Lee, J.: Provision and usage of open government data: strategic transformation paths. Ind. Manag. Data Syst. **119**, 1841–1858 (2019)

35. Attard, J., Orlandi, F., Auer, S.: Data driven governments: creating value through open government data. In: Hameurlain, A., et al. (eds.) Transactions on Large-Scale Data-and Knowledge-Centered Systems XXVII, pp. 84–110. Springer, Berlin (2016)

36. Attard, J., Orlandi, F., Auer, S.: Value creation on open government data. In:Proceedings of the Annual Hawaii International Conference on System Science March, 2016, pp. 2605–2614 (2016)

37. Abella, A., Ortiz-de-urbina-criado, M., De-pablos-heredero, C.: A model for the analysis of data-driven innovation and value generation in smart cities ' ecosystems. Cities **64**, 47–53 (2017)

38. Khayyat, M., Bannister, F.: Towards a model for facilitating and enabling co-creation using open government data. Inf. Polity. **22**, 211–231 (2017)

39. Foulonneau, M., Martin, S., Turki, S.: How open data are turned into services? In: Snene, M., Leonard, M. (eds.) IESS 2014. LNBIP, vol. 169, pp. 31–39. Springer, Cham (2014). https://doi.org/10.1007/978-3-319-04810-9_3

40. Sangiambut, S., Sieber, R.: The civic open data and crowdsourcing app ecosystem: actors, materials, and interventions. URISA J. **28**, 49–62 (2017)

41. van Loenen, B.: Towards a user-oriented open data strategy. In: van Loenen, B., Vancauwenberghe, G., Crompvoets, J. (eds.) Open Data Exposed. Information technology and Law Series, vol. 30, pp. 33–53.T.M.C. Asser Press, The Hague (2018). https://doi.org/10.1007/978-94-6265-261-3_3

42. Barns, S.: Smart cities and urban data platforms: designing interfaces for smart governance. City, Cult. Soc. **12**, 5–12 (2018)

43. Matheus, R., Janssen, M., Maheshwari, D.: Data science empowering the public: data-driven dashboards for transparent and accountable decision-making in smart cities. Gov. Inf. Q. **37**, 101284 (2018)
44. Bakici, T., Almirall, E., Wareham, J.: A smart city initiative: the case of Barcelona. J. Knowl. Econ. **4**, 135–148 (2013)
45. Gupta, A., Panagiotopoulos, P., Bowen, F.: An orchestration approach to smart city data ecosystems. Technol. Forecast. Soc. Change **153**, 119929 (2020)
46. Cordella, A., Paletti, A.: Government as a platform, orchestration, and public value creation: the Italian case. Gov. Inf. Q. **36**, 101409 (2019)
47. Linders, D.: From e-government to we-government: defining a typology for citizen coproduction in the age of social media. Gov. Inf. Q. **29**, 446–454 (2012)
48. Zuiderwijk, A., Janssen, M., Van De Kaa, G., Poulis, K.: The wicked problem of commercial value creation in open data ecosystems: policy guidelines for governments. Inf. Polity. **21**, 223–236 (2016)

A Digital Game to Learn About Open Data

Davide Di Staso[1]([✉]) [ID], Fernando Kleiman[1] [ID], Joep Crompvoets[2] [ID],
and Marijn Janssen[1] [ID]

[1] Faculty of Technology, Policy and Management, Delft University of Technology,
Delft, The Netherlands
{d.distaso,f.kleiman,m.f.w.h.a.janssen}@tudelft.nl
[2] Public Governance Institute, KU Leuven, Leuven, Belgium
joep.crompvoets@kuleuven.be

Abstract. The implementation of open data policies requires the efforts of many public employees across different levels of government, who may be unaware of the benefits and risks of open data. Serious games have demonstrated potential for training in a professional environment. For this research, a collaborative digital serious game about open data was developed. A sample of 24 civil servants played the game. Pre-test and post-test surveys were used to evaluate the effects of the game on participants' perception of open data. Likert score changes between pre-test and post-test indicated that the game had a positive effect on the willingness to share public sector data. By simulating the setting of a public office and by having players make decisions about whether to open certain datasets, the game facilitated learning about the benefits and disadvantages of opening data.

Keywords: Serious games · Gaming · Open data · Open data policy · Covid-19

1 Introduction

Open government data is data produced by governmental organisations and released to the public without any limitations on its use and redistribution [12,13]. Open data can be released either as dynamic APIs or as static datasets [21], which can be accessed via web-portals such as data.europa.eu. A number of stakeholders, such as transparency activists, entrepreneurs and government employees need open data to increase accountability, deliver better services, or support new business models [22]. Open data is one of the pillars of open government, which promotes the release of public sector data in order to enable public oversight into the government [12]. The release of open data ultimately rests on

H. J. Scholl et al. (Eds.): EGOV 2021, LNCS 12850, pp. 153–164, 2021.
https://doi.org/10.1007/978-3-030-84789-0_11

the decisions made by civil servants across different levels of government, from municipalities, to central government institutions. Public employees involved in the release of open data need to be willing to publish datasets, while at the same time being aware of the risks and benefits of doing so. Several behavioral factors can affect a civil servants' willingness to release data, such as a limited understanding of its benefits, the perception that it might be useless, and a general risk aversion and overestimation of security risks [16]. Serious games are a possible solution, as they offer a powerful tool to implement policies and create behavioral change [7]. They also offer a safe environment for players to experience decision-making and policies in a practical way [7]. In the context of open data, serious games can facilitate learning about how data is generated [24], show ways in which datasets can be combined to provide services [4,11] or have players decide whether or not to share certain datasets and provide feedback on their decision [14]. Winning Data by Kleiman et al. [14] was successful in changing civil servants' attitudes towards open data, but requires the presence of 4 people in the same room, which is temporarily prohibitive during the COVID-19 pandemic. Beyond the pandemic, this limitation will remain relevant for governmental teams working remotely or following a hybrid model. Therefore, there is a need for an online game that lets public employees learn about the opening of data. For this research, a collaborative digital serious game was developed, called Data Belt. By digitalising the game and observing the online gameplay it is possible to produce new insights and knowledge about open data gaming interventions. Data Belt is based on the in-person role-playing game Winning Data [14]. Like its in-person counterpart, Data Belt allows participants to make decisions on whether or not to open certain datasets and encourages them to evaluate the benefits and risks of opening data. However, in Data Belt, participants can play via video conference, instead of being in the same room. No other game designed for online multiplayer interaction on the topic of open data was found in the literature review. The game's multiplayer interactions are designed to foster knowledge sharing and create new insights about open data among players. A sample of 24 civil servants played remotely and the effects of the game were observed by measuring changes in responses to pre-test and post-test questionnaires. This research presents a preliminary analysis of the responses to the most relevant survey items, together with statements made by players during the game session debrief.

In the next section, barriers to open data are presented, along with examples of the use of serious games in government and serious games for open data. Next, the methodology for the game and experiment design are presented. Differences between pre-test and post-test survey responses are shown and discussed, before presenting the conclusions and limitations of this research.

2   Theoretical Background and Literature Review

By opening public sector data, governments can become open systems and engage in feedback loops with citizens, thereby becoming more responsive to their needs [12]. Opening data can also facilitate the creation of citizen-made digital tools for public use, such as portals to monitor lobbying activities, or even email notifications to avoid parking violations [13]. Still, a number of barriers and myths still exist around open public sector data [12]. Barriers to the opening of data affect the identification of suitable datasets, the decision to release, the publication process, usage of the dataset and the evaluation of its impact [6]. For example, when trying to decide whether or not to release data, public employees might not see the value of sharing a certain dataset or might overestimate the privacy risks [12,16]. In the same context, civil servants might fear "unexpected and unwanted responsibilities" [6] due to unclear liabilities for the consequences of opening a dataset [6]. It should also be noted that open data decision-making does not happen in a vacuum; civil servants might be confronted with risk-averse stakeholders (politicians, administration officers) or they might lack the necessary tools and resources to open data [17]. On the other hand, the benefits of open data might also be exaggerated, as in the myth that releasing data will create immediate and automatic benefits or that it is good practice to release any sort of data unrestrictedly [12]. The barriers listed are ultimately common issues arising from policy implementation, and the consequent need for a change in behaviour, which serious games can facilitate [7].

2.1 Serious Games in Government

Games are uniquely positioned to facilitate learning in governmental organisations. When games are used for policy implementation, they can contribute to "sense giving" and facilitate the understanding of policy documents and guidelines that otherwise might not have clear operational value or actionable elements [7]. By playing a game, participants can experience exactly what the policy is about on a practical level and understand it more deeply [10]. Moreover, players are presented with a safe space, which they can use to experiment new ideas and behaviors, some of which may be unexpected to the game designer or facilitator [7]. Learning outcomes are deeply connected to the use of game mechanics [2]. Game mechanics encompass "everything that affects the operation of the game" [1], including how players can behave within the game and the tools, items and attributes that they can use, such as bonus cards, incentives and penalties [1]. Game mechanics are also media-independent, that is, one mechanic can be brought over from a physical game to virtual one [1], as was done for this study. The use of serious games in government is not new [19]. For example, Bharosa et al. [3] developed an in-person role-playing game for civil servants aimed at synthesising principles for service delivery. Players interacted in the role of customer, front-office and back-office employees according to purposefully flawed scripts. Participants could relate to the role they were playing and, after the game session, identified insightful principles and rationales which can improve professional interactions. Open data policies can benefit from a similar bottom-up approach to explain policy contents to civil servants from different levels of government.

2.2   Games About Open Data

There are several serious games dealing specifically with the topic of open data. Datopolis [4] is a board game in which players need to negotiate with each other in order to make data open and in turn build services. The game can be played in its physical version, as well as in an online environment for virtual tabletop games. While Datopolis can technically be played online, it was not initially designed for this mode of interaction and the digital version is simply a simulation of a tabletop environment. The Open Data Card Game [11] is another game about open data in which players are divided into groups of three, asked to freely combine different cards representing datasets, and think about ideas for the services that can be built using the data at hand. In Datascape [24], players are presented with a map showing different features and data sources. They are then asked to identify the data sources that can answer the questions they are presented with. Winning Data by Kleiman et al. [14] is an in-person role-playing game in which one player acts as the citizen and the other three as government employees. By processing the citizen's requests, government employees generate datasets and decide whether or not to open them by evaluating the sensitivity of their contents.

The examples of open data games listed until now all require the participation of multiple players. Still, none of these group games were designed for digital gameplay, and, with the COVID-19 pandemic, in-person participation has temporarily become prohibitive. A solution is also needed for remote or hybrid teams which have limited opportunities for in-person training. Multiplayer serious games are hard to find, in part due to the additional challenges posed by concurrent gaming and player interaction [23]. A multiplayer game is useful to exploit the effectiveness of collaborative learning [9] and its ability to leverage pooled knowledge and observational learning [20]. In the context of governmental organisations, a multiplayer game can also better reflect the reality of a public office. At the time of writing, no collaborative digital serious game on open data could be found in the literature. This research attempts to address this gap by creating a new game about open data for civil servants which makes extensive use of concurrent gaming and player interaction. The methodology used to design the game and to test its effectiveness are presented in the following section.

3   Methodology

3.1   Game Design

By looking at the already existing Winning Data [14], which has proved to be effective at changing civil servants' attitudes [15], a list of essential features that had to be brought into the new, digital version of the game was drafted: (1) players must be situated in a fictional municipal office where they (2) rotate between different roles, each of them having a specific skill, (3) at the office, players need to process the citizen's demands, in turn generating datasets that can be opened, partially shared, or kept closed, (4) players must receive a reward by the game if their decision to open or close datasets matches the recommendations found in the literature. The four essential features found in Winning Data also converge with the seven lessons learned from board games found in Zagal et al. [25]. In order to bring these dynamics into the digital game, the user interface and flow of the game were sketched and a basic prototype was developed. The prototype was then tested with university students and incremental changes were made after each game session, with more than a dozen different iterations.

3.2 Game Mechanics

Fig. 1. Screenshots representing what each player sees during gameplay. From left to the right, the civil servant, citizen, colleague, and boss. Reprinted from Di Staso, D., Kleiman, F., Crompvoets, J., Janssen, M.: Changing Civil Servants' Awareness about Open Data Using a Collaborative Digital Game. In: DG.O2021: The 22nd Annual International Conference on Digital Government Research [In Press]. ACM, Omaha, NE, USA. Copyright 2021 Di Staso et al.

As already described in [8], in the version played by civil servants for this research, Data Belt requires the participation of exactly four players, connected via video conference, who are assigned to the roles of civil servant, colleague, boss and citizen. Each of these roles have specific abilities which are needed by the team to complete their tasks, therefore forcing players to collaborate. The game is divided into four rounds, at the end of which players rotate into a different role; participants never play in the same role more than once. During each round, the civil servant and colleague need to process the five files brought to them by the citizen (data processing). Each correctly processed file generates a dataset, which can be released to the public to different degrees or kept closed. For each dataset, the citizen, civil servant and colleague are shown a description and asked to suggest the boss what to do with the dataset (data labelling). The suggestion is synchronised across the three devices, meaning that any of the three players can see the current pick and change it, if they want to. For example, the dataset on budget, adapted from [14], reads:

By assessing public lawsuits, citizens can monitor problems related to public life. Tax evasion, misuse of public assets could be shared with citizens? Are there risks for individuals or security?

Through a synchronised checkbox, the citizen, civil servant, and colleague can suggest as a group to either open the dataset as is, anonymise it and then share it or keep it closed. The datasets and the labelling suggestions will be passed to the boss, who will make the final decision. The boss does not receive any special guidance or instructions; this role was created in order to place the burden of the final decision-making process on each player at least once during the game session (as noted earlier, players rotate among roles). Lastly, all players are brought to a summary screen, where they can see the datasets they processed, how the boss decided to label them, and the correct labelling according to the literature review. The dataset descriptions and labelling were adapted from Kleiman et al. [14]. In case a dataset has been labelled incorrectly, a penalty is given by the game, and the facilitator gives feedback on why the literature indicates a different labelling.

While porting the game to a digital environment, several adaptations had to be made. For example, in the data processing phase of Winning Data, the player with the role of civil servant walks to the other players' desks and passes them the files that need processing. In Data Belt, when players want to pass a file, the sender reads the file's unique code out loud and the addressee transcribes it into a keypad. In Fig. 1, the civil servant (second screen from the left) retrieved file 1451 (Budget) from the citizen and is processing it by putting stamps. The keypad used to retrieve files is visible in the colleague's screen (third screen from the left), who has used it to retrieve two files that will need to be opened and processed as well.

3.3 Pre-experiments

This research focuses on evaluating the effects of the game on participants' perception of open data in a pre-experimental setting. Having already established that a game has the potential to impact players' behaviour, there is a need to evaluate its specific effects [18]. Because the game was tested with a non-random sample participating remotely and because there was no control group, the setting in which the game was tested is a pre-experiment [5]. Data Belt aims at changing perceptions of players, which demands experimentation. A pre-experimental set-up can be appropriate to conduct a preliminary investigation of the effects of the game on its players. It converges with de Caluwé et al. [7], who identified that gaming or simulation solely developed for research purposes can leverage the benefits of experimental research, such as "the possibility of applying statistical methods in a study that is, in essence, a qualitative project" [7]. Additionally, games can offer insights into decision-making processes that are usually kept private and obscure and could not otherwise be studied [7].

3.4   Game Sessions and Surveys

Questionnaires from the existing literature [14] were adapted to an online environment so that they could be used for this research. Participants were arranged in groups of four people and sent the pre-test survey, which they filled some time before the game session. At the beginning of the session, players connected via video conference and were invited to briefly introduce themselves. The facilitator then gave a 10 to 15 min presentation explaining the game's rules and interface. Participants then played together using smartphones, with the actual gameplay lasting 30–40 min. At the end of the gameplay, participants filled the post-test questionnaire, were debriefed and asked to provide their impressions about the experience. Most game sessions were organised and scheduled with governmental organisations in the Netherlands: Digicampus (12 participants), Provincie Zuid-Holland (4), ICTU foundation (4). One game session was organised as part of Brazil's National School of Public Service Innovation Week (4 participants).

The dataset used for this research only includes participants who played the finalised version of the game and who successfully completed the session without encountering game-breaking bugs or complete disconnections. This research presents responses to the items of the questionnaires focused on the learning aspect, which could be answered using a Likert scale going from one (strongly disagree) to seven (strongly agree). The idea is that the loop of processing data, deciding whether or not to open it and then receiving feedback for that decision leads to civil servants being more willing share public sector data, while at the same time knowing more about the possible benefits of doing so (Q1, Q5) and feeling that the process is less threatening (Q6). When participants released a sensitive dataset which should have been kept private or anonymised before publishing, the game assigned a penalty and the facilitator explained the associated issues, which would often include privacy. Therefore, a change in awareness about privacy issues (Q4) was expected. Some of the items presented (Q2, Q3) ask about participants' knowledge on how to open datasets. The game represented this process in a very abstract way, and therefore we did not expect a significant effect on these items.

4   Results and Discussion

The game was played with 24 civil servants, pre-test and post-test surveys were distributed some time before the session and immediately after the gameplay was completed. Data Belt was effective in increasing civil servants' willingness to release datasets and in facilitating learning about the general risks and benefits involved. However, findings suggest that there was no significant effect on participant's knowledge about how to open datasets. The game invited players to collaboratively decide whether or not to share some public sector data and gave feedback on their choice. Table 1 summarises the initial results of the pre-experiment. Respondent's age ranged from 25 to 53 years old, with an average of 41.6; 15 subjects were male and 9 female. A paired sample t-test was performed on each individual item, comparing pre-test and post-test responses.

The results of this analysis are shown in Table 1. The following paragraphs present the change observed between pre-test and post-test, discuss whether this change is consistent with our expectation and present a possible explanation behind it. Quotes from the players during the debrief session are also presented to support the explanations.

Table 1. Most relevant survey items selected from the preliminary data analysis

	Description	n	Pre-test		Post-test		$\Delta\bar{x}$	p
			$\bar{x}$	σ	$\bar{x}$	σ		
Q1	Some public sector data can be shared	24	5.08	1.91	5.88	1.36	0.79	0.02
Q2	I know how to make public sector data available for others to access	24	4.12	1.75	4.21	1.72	0.08	0.79
Q3	People in my office know how to make public sector data available for others to access	24	4.79	1.86	4.83	1.27	0.04	0.91
Q4	Public sector data that results from my work cannot be shared for privacy issues	24	3.42	1.53	3.12	1.26	−0.29	0.37
Q5	Providing open public sector data has benefits which are difficult to explain	24	3.75	1.73	4.62	1.71	0.88	0.02
Q6	Providing public sector data is a threat	24	1.96	0.91	2.83	1.52	0.88	0.01

Q1 - Some Public Sector Data Can Be Shared. The average score went from 5.08 to 5.88 in a statistically significant way ($p = 0.02$). A positive increase was expected for this item and it indicates that playing Data Belt had a positive impact on players' perceptions of data sharing. This effect can be explained by the fact that players, while labelling together each dataset, became more confident about releasing some public sector data. As stated by one of the players:

> ...it's spot on really...the questions...I can recognise immediately what it's about. The fact from the game...it's a bit overwhelming because of the information. There is no difference in real life, too many questions, too much information, hard, partial information, and I have to make a decision and plan some action and I'm not really confident. That's real life.

Q2 - I Know How to Make Public Sector Data Available for Others to Access. The average Likert score went from 4.12 to 4.21 and the change was not statistically significant ($p = 0.79$). A significant change was not expected for this item, as the game did not address the real-world procedures involved with making data available to others.

Q3 - People in My Office Know How to Make Public Sector Data Available for Others to Access. For this item, the mean score went from 4.79 to 4.83 with no statistical significance ($p = 0.91$). For this item, just like for the previous one, a significant change was not expected.

Q4 - Public Sector Data that Results from My Work Cannot Be Shared for Privacy Issues. The mean Likert score went from 3.42 to 3.12 with no statistical significance ($p = 0.37$). The expectation was to see a statistically significant increase caused by players becoming more accustomed to managing privacy risks. Instead, it appears the in-game content about privacy did not affect participants' perceptions. While more research is needed to confirm this outcome, it is possible that the penalties given by the game for privacy violations were not evident enough.

Q5 - Providing Open Public Sector Data Has Benefits Which Are Difficult to Explain. This item saw a positive increase from 3.75 to 4.62, which was statistically significant ($p = 0.02$). Open data is seen as a complex topic, and the game provided reinforcement on this aspect, therefore a positive change on this item was expected. During the debrief, one of the players said that the feedback given by the facilitator at the end of each round (when looking at the results) was helpful:

> ...the explanation you [the facilitator] gave was sometimes helpful, like why some data can be shared or cannot be shared, can be open or cannot be open. I think we can learn from that, because a lot of times people ask me to provide data, and a lot of times I cannot explain why it should be open or not.

The feedback provided by the facilitator is a fundamental aspect of the game. At the end of each round, the facilitator explains why a certain dataset might be too sensitive to be shared or why it does not actually pose a threat. The feedback highlighted hidden risks, such as data becoming personally identifiable in small datasets, even when anonymised, or hidden benefits, such as how a dataset is used by private entities or other governmental organisations.

Q6 - Providing Public Sector Data Is a Threat. The mean Likert score for this item went up from 1.96 to 2.83 in a statistically significant way ($p = 0.01$). This change seems to contradict the effects observed for Q1 and Q5. The assumption was that, by experiencing the process of opening data, players would perceive it as less of a threat, therefore an increase in this item's score was not expected.

Overall, changes in the responses between pre-test and post-test are coherent with the game's main focus, which is to collectively decide whether or not to open a certain dataset and then receive feedback on the decision. From the observations that player made during the debrief, it appears that game was generally well received.

5 Conclusion

The purpose of this research was to design a collaborative digital serious game about open data and measure its effects on civil servants. As there was no prior work on a game for open data designed for the online environment, we derived the game mechanics from another game and conducted game sessions with participants connected remotely. One of the requisites was for the new game to allow for remote participation via video conference, both due to the temporary restrictions imposed to contrast the COVID-19 pandemic and due to the need for a game than can be used by remote or hybrid government teams. Based on the in-person game Winning Data [14], the requirements and characteristics for the new, digital game were listed, and a prototype was developed. The new game, called Data Belt, was played by civil servants, who filled pre-test and post-test surveys to measure learning about open data. Data Belt used game mechanics such as collaboration, time pressure, and feedback loops to facilitate learning. Findings indicate that these game mechanics were suitable to enable learning about open data. Having multiple players collaborate to satisfy citizen's requests more closely reflected the environment of a real public office. Moreover, forcing players to make one common choice about data release fosters discussion and reflection on the contents of each dataset and on whether or not it can be shared. However, it appears that the game did not have significant effects on civil servants' concerns about privacy issues. This result is possibly explained by the penalty for sharing too much being too weak or not evident enough. After playing the game, participants were more inclined to believe that some public sector data can be shared and seemed to be more aware about the hidden benefits of opening data. At the same time, it seems that, after playing the game, participants perceived the provision of public sector data as more of a threat, a finding which seems contradictory and which requires further research. The game was designed to be played only once, therefore its scope is limited by the short gameplay time. For example, the game does not address the specific procedures and tools needed to open data, and, accordingly, there was no significant change in participant's self-reported knowledge about how to open data. Since Data Belt was designed to be played by civil servants working for different organisations in different countries, it did not detail the technical aspects involved in the opening of data, which might change from one department to another. The conclusions presented in this study are limited by the small sample size, lack of a control group and lack of data to establish if the effects of the game are still present after an extended period of time. Future research should further investigate the effects of the game, including the contradiction observed for some of the survey items. More research is also needed to compare the outcomes of the in-person game with Data Belt. Finally, improvements to the game could be explored, such as removing the requirement for a facilitator by introducing a tutorial mode, introducing new game modes to allow smaller or larger groups to play together, and including new game mechanics describing some of the most common procedures involved in opening datasets.

References

1. Adams, E., Dormans, J.: Game Mechanics: Advanced Game Design. New Riders, Berkeley (2012)
2. Arnab, S., et al.: Mapping learning and game mechanics for serious games analysis. Br. J. Educ. Technol. **46**(2), 391–411 (2015)
3. Bharosa, N., Janssen, M., Klievink, B., van Veenstra, A.F., Overbeek, S.: Guiding integrated service delivery: synthesizing and embedding principles using role-playing games. Electr. J. e-Gov. **8**(2), 83–92 (2010)
4. Broad, E., Tennison, J.: Datopolis board game, March 2015. http://datopolis.theodi.org/about/
5. Campbell, D.T.: Experimental and quasi-experimental designs for research on teaching. Handbook Res. Teach. **5**, 171–246 (1963)
6. Crusoe, J., Melin, U.: Investigating open government data barriers. In: Parycek, P., et al. (eds.) EGOV 2018. LNCS, vol. 11020, pp. 169–183. Springer, Cham (2018). https://doi.org/10.1007/978-3-319-98690-6_15
7. de Caluwé, L., Geurts, J., Kleinlugtenbelt, W.J.: Gaming research in policy and organization: an assessment from the Netherlands. Simul. Gaming **43**(5), 600–626 (2012)
8. Di Staso, D., Kleiman, F., Crompvoets, J., Janssen, M.: Changing civil servants' awareness about open data using a collaborative digital game. In: DG.O2021: The 22nd Annual International Conference on Digital Government Research [In Press]. ACM, Omaha. https://doi.org/10.1145/3463677.3463684
9. Dillenbourg, P., Schneider, D.: Mediating the mechanisms which make collaborative learning sometimes effective. Int. J. Educ. Telecommun. **1**(2), 131–146 (1995)
10. Duke, R.D.: Gaming: The Future's Language. Sage Publications, Beverly Hills (1974)
11. Goraya, J.: Open Data Card Game, October 2015. https://github.com/Atomland/open-data-card-game
12. Janssen, M., Charalabidis, Y., Zuiderwijk, A.: Benefits, adoption barriers and myths of open data and open government. Inf. Syst. Manage. **29**(4), 258–268 (2012)
13. Kassen, M.: A promising phenomenon of open data: a case study of the Chicago open data project. Gov. Inf. Q. **30**(4), 508–513 (2013)
14. Kleiman, F., Janssen, M., Meijer, S.: Evaluation of a pilot game to change civil servants' willingness towards open data policy making. In: Simulation and Gaming: Through Times and across Disciplines, pp. 286–297. Kozminski University, Warsaw, December 2019
15. Kleiman, F., Janssen, M., Meijer, S., Jansen, S.J.: Changing civil servants' behaviour concerning the opening of governmental data: evaluating the effect of a game by comparing civil servants' intentions before and after a game intervention. Int. Rev. Admin. Sci. 002085232096221 (2020). https://doi.org/10.1177/0020852320962211
16. Kleiman, F., Meijer, S., Janssen, M.: Behavioral factors influencing the opening of government data by civil servants: initial findings from the literature. In: Proceedings of the 13th International Conference on Theory and Practice of Electronic Governance, pp. 529–534 (2020)
17. Luthfi, A., Janssen, M., Crompvoets, J.: Stakeholder tensions in decision-making for opening government data. In: Shishkov, B. (ed.) BMSD 2020. LNBIP, vol. 391, pp. 331–340. Springer, Cham (2020). https://doi.org/10.1007/978-3-030-52306-0_23

18. Mayer, I., et al.: The research and evaluation of serious games: toward a comprehensive methodology: the research and evaluation of serious games. Br. J. Educ. Technol. **45**(3), 502–527 (2014)

19. Mayer, I.S.: The gaming of policy and the politics of gaming: a review. Simul. Gam. **40**(6), 825–862 (2009)

20. Nokes-Malach, T.J., Richey, J.E., Gadgil, S.: When is it better to learn together? Insights from research on collaborative learning. Educ. Psychol. Rev. **27**(4), 645–656 (2015)

21. Tamberer, J.: Bulk data or an API? In: Open Government Data: The Book, 2nd edn. (2014). https://opengovdata.io/2014/bulk-data-an-api/

22. Ubaldi, B.: Open Government Data: Towards Empirical Analysis of Open Government Data Initiatives. OECD Working Papers on Public Governance 22, OECD, May 2013

23. Wendel, V., Gutjahr, M., Göbel, S., Steinmetz, R.: Designing collaborative multiplayer serious games: escape from Wilson Island—A multiplayer 3D serious game for collaborative learning in teams. Educ. Inf. Technol. **18**(2), 287–308 (2013)

24. Wolff, A., Barker, M., Petre, M.: Creating a Datascape: a game to support communities in using open data. In: 8th International Conference on Communities and Technologies, pp. 135–138. ACM, New York, June 2017

25. Zagal, J.P., Rick, J., Hsi, I.: Collaborative games: lessons learned from board games. Simul. Gam. **37**(1), 24–40 (2006)

Ronda: Real-Time Data Provision, Processing and Publication for Open Data

Fabian Kirstein[1,2]([⊠]), Dario Bacher[1], Vincent Bohlen[1], and Sonja Schimmler[1,2]

[1] Fraunhofer FOKUS, Berlin, Germany
{fabian.kirstein,dario.bacher,vincent.bohlen,
sonja.schimmler}@fokus.fraunhofer.de
[2] Weizenbaum Institute for the Networked Society, Berlin, Germany

Abstract. The provision and dissemination of Open Data is a flourishing concept, which is highly recognized and established in the government and public administrations domains. Typically, the actual data is served as static file downloads, such as CSV or PDF, and the established software solutions for Open Data are mostly designed to manage this kind of data. However, the rising popularity of the Internet of things and smart devices in the public and private domain leads to an increase of available real-time data, like public transportation schedules, weather forecasts, or power grid data. Such timely and extensive data cannot be used to its full potential when published in a static, file-based fashion. Therefore, we designed and developed Ronda - an open source platform for gathering, processing and publishing real-time Open Data based on industry-proven and established big data and data processing tools. Our solution easily enables Open Data publishers to provide real-time interfaces for heterogeneous data sources, fostering more sophisticated and advanced Open Data use cases. We have evaluated our work through a practical application in a production environment.

Keywords: Open Data · Big data · Real-time

1 Introduction

The ongoing digitization leads to a growing availability of real-time or very frequently updated data sources. This process is supported by the increasing adoption of smart devices and the growth of the Internet of things. Many of these original data sources are strongly connected to public organizations and administrations, such as urban, energy, transportation, or environment data. Therefore, plenty of such data will be and is supposed to be available as Open Data. This requires to facilitate the technical means and processes to enable the publication of real-time Open Data. Popular open source solutions for Open

© The Author(s) 2021
H. J. Scholl et al. (Eds.): EGOV 2021, LNCS 12850, pp. 165–177, 2021.
https://doi.org/10.1007/978-3-030-84789-0_12

Data, such as CKAN[1], are mainly designed to serve static metadata and file downloads, usually containing aggregated information over a past period of time. However, the timely and raw provision of data is one central requirement in Open Data [1], which cannot be satisfied with the current solutions. Especially the demand in volume and velocity cannot be handled by plain file downloads. From a technical point of view this creates an intersection between aspects of Open Data and big data. Among other things the field of big data provides concepts and tools to handle data, which cannot be managed by traditional methods. [1] Therefore, our general hypothesis is that, *established open source big data technologies and practices constitute a proper foundation for enabling Open Data portals and ecosystems to consume, process and provide (near) real-time data.*

The focus of our work is the architectural design and implementation of a reusable and extendable big data platform which can hold Open Data collected from heterogeneous data sources. The platform is capable of dynamically analyzing, processing and, if needed, anonymizing the incoming data, which can be supplied as streams or batches. To achieve this, big data methods and architectures are analyzed and selected. Our core contributions are:

(1) We designed a comprehensive architecture for retrieving, processing and providing real-time Open Data based on open source software, well-known industry standards, and established big data architecture paradigms.
(2) We developed a fully working prototype to harvest and disseminate real-time data in the context of a production smart city project. Our solution is available as open source and can be easily applied and extended in various Open Data domains.
(3) Our architecture and prototype can serve as a blueprint for similar real-time Open Data projects, demonstrating a path for the next generation Open Data portals, which act as real-time data hubs, instead of simple file servers.

The remaining part of this paper is structured as follows: Sect. 2 reviews related work in the field of Open Data and big data. Section 3 presents the requirements for real-time Open Data, which are transformed into a system design in Sect. 4. Section 5 presents the implementation and evaluates our approach. In Sect. 6 we draw our conclusions and discuss our findings.

2   Related Work

Our work covers the fields of big data, i.e. real-time data streams, and (linked) open (government) data along with related standards and technologies. Charalabidis et al. [1] survey the domain of Open Data and describe differences and similarities to government data, big data and linked data. Government agencies have a long history of publishing their data as open government data and Open Data portals have adopted linked data principles and serve linked open data on

---

[1] https://ckan.org/.

a large scale [11,12]. This makes linked open government data an established part of data published on the Web.

Governments or companies operating in the public sector already produce real-time data such as traffic, transport or weather data [7]. This data is often not directly accessible, but used in public use cases, e.g. billboards, displays or web applications, or require registration to access it. There exist a variety of different solutions for building Open Data portals. Some of them, such as CKAN are open source, while others, such as OpenDataSoft[2] are closed source [3]. CKAN provides real-time data features through an extension. At the time of writing, this extension was not updated since 2014. OpenDataSoft provides the possibility to push real-time data to previously uploaded datasets or schedule updates for them. These datasets can be exported by users or visualized in graphs, tables or maps. The open government data platform OGoov allows the communication with different data sources via its Real Time Open Data module[3]. Among other sources, it offers an integration to the publish/subscribe endpoint of the FIWARE Orion Context Broker[4] and allows exposing real-time snapshots as well as historical views of that data. Lutchman et al. [15] describe an architecture for a real-time Open Data portal. Data providers register their data streams to the portal's REST endpoints and periodically push data to the server. Data consumers access the data via dedicated REST endpoints and specify the rate with which updates are received. All of the solutions described above rely on the data publisher pushing data to an existing endpoint. To the best of our knowledge, there exists no open source solution, which registers to existing (real-time) data streams and relies on big data technologies.

The WebSocket[5] protocol is standardized by the IETF as RFC 6455 and allows for bidirectional communication between two applications over TCP. The protocol sequence consists of an opening handshake followed by a bidirectional message exchange. WebSockets are primarily targeted at web applications that need two-way communication without opening multiple HTTP sessions. MQTT[6] is a lightweight publish/subscribe message transport protocol designed for communication in constrained environments such as Internet of things or machine to machine communication. The light-weight nature and low packet overhead compared to HTTP makes it especially suited to be used in environments where space or bandwidth limitations apply.

Big data technologies distinguish between stream and batch processing. In batch processing, data is stored in non-volatile memory before it is processed. This has the advantage that a big amount of data can be processed. In contrast, stream processing uses volatile memory before processing and therefore achieves better performance in time aspects. Yet, only a small amount of data

---

[2] https://www.opendatasoft.com.

[3] https://www.ogoov.com/en/rtod/.

[4] https://fiware-orion.readthedocs.io/en/master/.

[5] https://tools.ietf.org/html/rfc6455.

[6] https://mqtt.org/.

can be grouped for processing [16]. Two of the most popular big data analysis frameworks are Apache Spark[7] and Apache Flink[8]. They both support batch and stream processing. Using batch processing on datasets, Spark achieves better results in terms of processing time [18]. Comparing stream performance, Flink performs better regarding latency [9,10], while Sparks streaming features show better results in terms of throughput [2]. Hadoop Distributed File System (HDFS) and Apache Cassandra are both commonly used in combination with big data analysis frameworks. While Cassandra acts as a distributed database with its querying language (CQL) [4], HDFS is a distributed file system. Cassandra performs better on highly time-based, structured data, whereas HDFS is used for big files and unstructured data [5,8]. Messaging systems provide the means to manage and organize data feeds between applications in a distributed system [13]. Two of the most common messaging systems are Apache Kafka and RabbitMQ. Both use the publish/subscribe pattern to distribute messages and offer scalability using clusters [6]. Kafka focuses on concurrency and fault-tolerance, and can be used as a persistence unit, and to store long term messages without compromising performance. This makes it a good fit for connecting various batch and streaming services. RabbitMQ uses a lightweight, disk-less approach, which makes it a particular fit for embedded systems [6].

3   Requirements for a Real-Time Open Data Platform

In the following, we describe six high-level requirements of our real-time Open Data platform. They are derived from practical functional and non-functional requirements, and form the basis of our work. They are inspired by established Open Data methodologies, and cover the entire process from acquisition, processing and provision of the data.

(1) **Compliance with Open Data standards and best practices:** The publication of data has to follow established Open Data standards and best practices. This includes the application of the DCAT-AP [17] specification for creating metadata and the facility to publish the metadata on existing Open Data portal solutions. Historic aggregations have to be available in an open and machine-readable format, such as CSV or JSON.

(2) **Throughput and scalability:** Ronda has to support a sufficient throughput, which at least fits to typical Open Data access loads. This holds true for data acquisition, processing and provision.

(3) **Support for different data sources:** Open Data is mostly generated from raw data, which is provided by various types of interfaces and in a plethora of data formats. Hence, Ronda needs to support this variety through expandable and custom connectors and transform it into harmonized representations.

(4) **Support for data processing and analysis:** In many cases, the raw data needs to be processed, aggregated and cleaned before publishing. Especially,

---

[7] https://spark.apache.org/.

[8] https://flink.apache.org/.

if the raw data includes sensitive or personal information, an appropriate pre-processing is indispensable to comply with regulations and privacy policies. Therefore, Ronda needs to support arbitrary and flexible data processing and analysis.

(5) **Real-time access:** The entire data processing has to be performed in real-time, hence, the data has to be available to the user almost immediately (within seconds) after its retrieval from the original source. A suitable protocol for the machine-readable user interface is required. This constraint does not cover the actual timeliness of the source data, which is out of control for our solution.

(6) **Historic and aggregated access:** The collected data should be preserved to allow for a retrieval of historic information. Hence, the real-time data needs to be aggregated over configurable time periods and bundled into downloadable static batches. This makes the data available for non real-time use and creates a transparent log of the data.

4   Designing a Real-Time Open Data Platform

Based on the high-level requirements and the related work in big data, we present the design and technological base of our solution. It is designed to be operated alongside an Open Data portal. Hence, it does not provide the typical functionalities of an Open Data portal, but extends them. The foundation of our design is the so-called lambda architecture, which combines the advantages of batch and stream processing techniques and consists of three layers: a batch layer, a speed layer and a serving layer [14]. This supports the requirement to offer both, real-time and historical data. Incoming data is fed to the batch and speed layer. The batch layer appends all incoming data to an immutable master and computes batch views by analyzing the incoming data. This allows the analysis of historic, not time-critical data and especially improves the analysis for big datasets. The speed layer analyzes only the most recent data and provides the real-time capabilities. In order to realize this architecture the solutions Spark, HDFS and Kafka are selected as core technologies. As indicated in Sect. 2 Spark serves as batch and speed layer, and provides efficient and scalable analysis and manipulation functionalities for big datasets. HDFS is used as the persistence system, since it works well with unstructured and big data and is integrated into Spark's core library. It is provided via Apache Hadoop and acts as serving layer for batch data. Kafka acts as the principal messaging bus to serve data from and to Spark and can easily be connected to it through an official library. In addition, it offers an additional layer of persistence, which improves the fault-tolerance of the system (see Sect. 2) and operates as the serving layer for real-time data.

In order to achieve a clear separation of concerns, simple extensibility, and developer friendliness, the system is divided into five modules. Each module fulfills a distinct task within the data processing chain and in combination with Spark, Kafka and HDFS they depict the lambda architecture. In the following, they are described. Figure 1 illustrates the entire design.

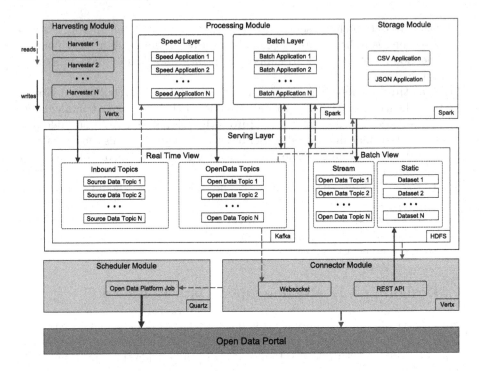

Fig. 1. Architecture overview

The **harvesting module** constitutes the connection to external data sources and main entry point for the data processing. It is responsible for retrieving data from external interfaces, transforming it to an internal representation and injecting it into the Kafka messaging bus. The module offers a flexible extension mechanism to support a broad variety of interface standards. Each data source is mapped to a distinct topic (aka a kind of category) in Kafka.

The **processing module** offers arbitrary and extensive features to alter the source data in real-time. Hence, aggregation, modification, normalization and cleaning tasks are executed here. This also covers any privacy preserving alterations, such as anonymization or data removal. The result of the processing is again stored in a Kafka topic, applying a pre-defined data structure.

The **storage module** is responsible for periodically batching and storing the real-time data. The resulting datasets are chronologically organized and saved in structured data formats, such as CSV and JSON. Frequency, size and resolution of the batches can be individually configured.

The **connector module** represents the public interface of the system, by giving access to the real-time and historic data. Real-time access is provided via the popular and versatile WebSocket protocol. Whereas the static historic data is served via HTTP, supporting content negotiation and query parameters to serve the data in different serialization formats and granularities. The connector module directly subscribes to the topics in Kafka, which allows for real-time forwarding of the data to the client.

The **scheduler module** functions as a job scheduling system for reoccurring tasks. It is mainly used to connect the system to Open Data portals. Therefore, it can be configured to periodically create metadata (e.g. DCAT-AP-compliant) about available real-time and historic data. In addition, it can be applied for other periodic tasks, such as triggering Spark applications.

5 Evaluation

Based on our design we implemented Ronda as a fully working prototype and evaluated it in two stages: (1) We verified the functional requirements in a real-world production use case, and (2) conducted a comprehensive performance assessment in order to evaluate functionality and scalability.

5.1 Implementation

The practical realization of our design includes the deployment and configuration of the underlying big data tools, and the implementation of the five modules. The harvesting, connector and scheduler modules are custom implementations based on the event-driven and non-blocking Java framework Vert.x[9]. This high-performance framework supports the requirement for scalability and has a strong concept for concurrency and modularization (called Verticles). Moreover, it acts as the main web server to provide the WebSocket and HTTP interfaces. The processing and storage modules are naturally implemented as Spark applications, since they are executed as distributed Spark jobs. The entire system is containerized with Docker and can be easily deployed. In addition, it has support for Kubernetes orchestration[10]. In general, all modules communicate with each other via the Kafka messaging bus. For each data source a separate topic is created, which is used throughout the entire processing chain for a particular source. This horizontal separation for each data source is also represented in each module. For instance the harvesting module is split into distinct submodules for each data source. Furthermore, a common library is available to all modules, providing shared functionalities, such as topic descriptions. The scheduler module makes extensive use of the Quartz scheduling library[11]. The implementation is available as open source[12], which supports a broad application in the Open Data domain.

---

[9] https://vertx.io/.
[10] https://kubernetes.io/.
[11] http://www.quartz-scheduler.org/.
[12] https://gitlab.com/piveau/piveau-ronda.

5.2 Smart City Use Case

The solution was tested within the research project QuarZ[13], which aims to enable the development of new and innovative smart services for urban districts. The software is being developed for and tested in an urban district in the city of Rüsselsheim am Main that encompasses about 100 homes. As part of the project, households and the surrounding outdoor area were equipped with various sensors and smart devices. The households were provided with smart meters, collecting data about power, gas and water consumption in real-time. Additionally smart home components were offered to all households. In the vicinity, outdoor sensors, collecting temperature, humidity, solar radiation and noise levels were setup. Residents also got access to an electric rental car.

The aim of the project is to collect the generated data into a central data hub. Smart services can then make use of that data while strictly considering the data sovereignty of the individual resident. The central data hub includes an internal storage, as well as an Open Data portal. The internal data hub stores data, emitted by the various sensors and provides the smart services with the desired data. The Open Data portal harvests and integrates traditional Open Data of the region, but in addition publishes real-time data generated in the district for public use. For the latter the internal real-time data streams are retrieved, processed, anonymized, and finally published. We successfully used Ronda for that purpose, by processing data about the power, gas and water consumption of each household, which generates new data points every couple of seconds. In the future, aggregated usage data of the smart home components, the electric rental car and other sources will be integrated too. Based on this data, residents and other interested parties are enabled to create derived services or simply compare their resource consumption with the public.

5.3 Performance Evaluation

We conducted a thorough load test in order to evaluate the performance of Ronda under typical hardware requirements. Therefore, the system was deployed on a Kubernetes cluster. The cluster uses Intel Xeon processors of type E5520 with a base frequency of 2.27 GHz. Table 1 shows the resource consumption for each component.

For HDFS, one name node and four data nodes are deployed as pods on Kubernetes. For Kafka, three Apache Zookeeper instances are required and three Kafka instances are deployed. Zookeeper is a service to provide coordination between the implemented Kafka instances and is mandatory for using Kafka. Spark uses one cluster manager in standalone mode and three worker nodes. The harvesting, processing, storage and scheduler modules are each using one pod. In addition to the Kubernetes cluster deployment, Apache JMeter[14] was installed on a separate client system and used to execute the load tests. Two test

---

[13] https://www.quartier-der-zukunft.de/ (only available in German).
[14] https://jmeter.apache.org/.

Table 1. System deployment

Component	Instances	RAM	Peek CPU	Volume
HDFS namenode	1	0.8 GB	14 milliCPU	128 GB
HDFS datanode	4	1.2 GB	11 milliCPU	32 GB
Zookeeper	3	0.5 GB	11 milliCPU	–
Kafka	3	3.5 GB	100 milliCPU	16 GB
Spark manager	1	0.5 GB	1 milliCPU	–
Spark worker	3	4.3 GB	22 milliCPU	–
Processing	1	2.4 GB	180 milliCPU	–
Storage	1	1.5 GB	8 milliCPU	–
Connector	5	1 GB	8 milliCPU	–
Harvesting	1	1 GB	6 milliCPU	–
Scheduler	1	0.5 GB	2 milliCPU	–
PostgreSQL	2	0.05 GB	25 milliCPU	5 GB

plans were created within Apache JMeter to measure the performance for both, the user and the data provider view. Suitable test data was programmatically mocked with JavaFaker[15] to create a provider data source. To the best of our knowledge, there does not exist a baseline about expected loads and frequencies on real-time Open Data in the literature. Therefore, we applied the general use statistics of the European Data Portal (EDP) as a rough baseline. The EDP is one of the biggest Open Data portals in the world and in 2018 an average of 1.300 visitors per day was measured [11]. We liberally assume that around 10% of these users will constantly subscribe to a real-time data stream, leading to a threshold of 100 simultaneous requests. Furthermore, we assume a high frequency of incoming data of four values per second.

(1) **Data user view:** The user test plan executed 100 simultaneous HTTP and WebSocket requests for the collected test data. HTTP requests were made on the collected historic test data after two hours of collecting and WebSocket requests were made on the test data source. WebSocket connections remained open as long as no data arrived, afterwards the connections were closed and the time was measured. For HTTP requests, the time was measured after receiving a successful response. The results in Table 2 show an average response time of around 1000 ms and a maximum response time of around 2100 ms, whereas 99% of requests are under 2000 ms. Hence, the system is capable of handling 100 simultaneous WebSocket requests. The HTTP response time was around 1000 ms with 99% under 1929 ms.

(2) **Data provider view:** The test data source sends messages every 250 ms. Four messages per second and 240 messages per minute should be received if the system can process every sent message quickly enough. For this test, the

---

[15] http://dius.github.io/java-faker/.

connected WebSocket client counted the messages over a period of 10 min. The results are displayed in Table 3. After 600 s all expected 2400 messages are received by the client. This results in a throughput of four messages per second (240 messages per minute).

Table 2. Results of simultaneous requests test

Request	Samples	AVG	95%	99%	Min	Max	Throughput
HTTP	1000	1091 ms	1759 ms	1929 ms	153 ms	2190 ms	48,24159
Websocket	1000	1354 ms	1734 ms	1953 ms	66 ms	2139 ms	49,63518

Ronda is capable of processing the expected 100 simultaneous requests for real-time as well as batch data. Furthermore, the system is capable to support 240 messages from data providers per minute, which is sufficient for typical use cases. However, the evaluation was performed on a specific set of hardware and the underlying architecture scales easily, to ensure the support for much higher amounts of data.

Table 3. Results of processed message test

Request	Estimated time	Messages	Throughput
Websocket	600 s	2400	4

6   Conclusions, Discussion and Future Work

In this paper we have presented Ronda, an open source solution for gathering, processing and publishing real-time Open Data. We have shown that established and industry-proven big data and data processing solutions constitute a proper foundation to enable Open Data publishers to provide and manage real-time interfaces for heterogeneous data sources. Established solutions, such as CKAN, focus on the provision of static file downloads and have little support for real-time data and respective interfaces. Yet, the increased availability of smart devices leads to a rising relevance to provide real-time Open Data, such as weather reports, public transport data, or energy consumption information. Ronda is inspired by the big data lambda architecture and Apache Spark, Kafka and HDFS are used as technological basis. The solution is divided into five highly extendable modules: harvesting, processing, storage, connector, and scheduler. Those modules allow integrating and managing arbitrary real-time sources for Open Data portals and supports the scheduled provision of corresponding metadata. We applied Ronda in a production smart city use case, where residential power, gas and water consumption data is processed, anonymized and published via a DCAT-AP-compliant Open Data portal. In addition, we conducted a thorough performance evaluation under average hardware requirements. It demonstrated that Ronda can cope with up to 100 simultaneous data consumers for real-time and historic data, while allowing the data providers to push 240 messages per minute. This is sufficient with regard to typical volume, velocity and veracity in the Open Data domain. Therefore, we have shown, that our solution is in compliance with existing Open Data standards, offers sufficient throughput and scalability, supports a variety of data sources, is capable of data processing and analysis, and offers real-time and historic data interfaces.

We are confident, that the Open Data domain will highly benefit from the increasing availability of real-time data sources, since they enable more advanced use cases and business models. Applications and derived products can deliver an advanced experience and functionality over traditional static data. For instance real-time public transportation or traffic applications. Yet, timeliness plays a crucial role, since in many cases the data quickly loses value over time. This clearly shows the relevance to extend the technological foundations of Open Data portals with big data artefacts and establish it as a standard for future implementations. The maturity and capabilities of these industry-proven tools allow a quick transformation of the Open Data domain towards the next level: Open Data portals become powerful data hubs, instead of merely collections of outdated static files. In addition, they provide a variety of features out-of-the-box, such as excellent scalabilty, community support, and a rich extension ecosystem. Beyond that, big data tools constitute a solid basis for even more progressive Open Data applications, such as machine learning or artificial intelligence to further refine the datasets and/or derive additional insights. However, big data tools are complex software artefacts, which add a new level of complexity to Open Data, and currently require more hardware and especially human resources to be implemented and maintained. A joint effort of Open Data developers and publishers is required to establish a common baseline and software recommendations. Ronda can act as a first enabler and starting point for that effort, since it already considers the requirements for real-time Open Data.

In the future, we are planning to extend Ronda with various features and expand our production use case. The actual data streams will be enriched with semantic details, which will increase reusability further. As a showcase, we will provide a data visualization tool, which allows to monitor the real-time data without any detailed technical knowledge. Finally, we aim to further analyze the economic, organizational and social implications of real-time Open Data.

Acknowledgments. This work has been partially funded by the Federal Ministry for Economic Affairs and Energy of Germany (BMWi) under grant no. 01MD18009A ("QuarZ") and by the Federal Ministry of Education and Research of Germany (BMBF) under grant no. 16DII117 ("Deutsches Internet-Institut").

References

1. Charalabidis, Y., Zuiderwijk, A., Alexopoulos, C., Janssen, M., Lampoltshammer, T., Ferro, E.: The open data landscape. In: The World of Open Data. PAIT, vol. 28, pp. 1–9. Springer, Cham (2018). https://doi.org/10.1007/978-3-319-90850-2_1
2. Chintapalli, S., et al.: Benchmarking streaming computation engines: Storm, Flink and spark streaming. In: 2016 IEEE International Parallel and Distributed Processing Symposium Workshops (IPDPSW), pp. 1789–1792, May 2016. https://doi.org/10.1109/IPDPSW.2016.138
3. Correa, A.S., Zander, P.O., da Silva, F.S.C.: Investigating open data portals automatically: a methodology and some illustrations. In: Proceedings of the 19th Annual International Conference on Digital Government Research: Governance in the Data Age, pp. 1–10. dg.o 2018, Association for Computing Machinery, Delft, The Netherlands, May 2018. https://doi.org/10.1145/3209281.3209292
4. Dede, E., Sendir, B., Kuzlu, P., Hartog, J., Govindaraju, M.: an evaluation of cassandra for Hadoop. In: 2013 IEEE Sixth International Conference on Cloud Computing, pp. 494–501, June 2013. https://doi.org/10.1109/CLOUD.2013.31. iSSN 2159-6190
5. Dhruba, B.: HDFS Design (2008). http://svn.apache.org/repos/asf/hadoop/common/tags/release-0.19.2/docs/hdfs_design.pdf. Accessed 01 Mar 2021
6. Dunne, M., Gracioli, G., Fischmeister, S.: A comparison of data streaming frameworks for anomaly detection in embedded systems. In: Proceedings of the 1st International Workshop on Security and Privacy for the Internet-of-Things (IoTSec), Orlando, FL, USA (2018)
7. Janssen, M., Matheus, R., Zuiderwijk, A.: Big and open linked data (bold) to create smart cities and citizens: Insights from smart energy and mobility cases. In: International Conference on Electronic Government. pp. 79–90. Springer (2015)
8. Kala Karun, A., Chitharanjan, K.: A review on Hadoop – HDFS infrastructure extensions. In: 2013 IEEE Conference on Information Communication Technologies, pp. 132–137, April 2013. https://doi.org/10.1109/CICT.2013.6558077
9. Karimov, J., Rabl, T., Katsifodimos, A., Samarev, R., Heiskanen, H., Markl, V.: Benchmarking distributed stream data processing systems. In: 2018 IEEE 34th International Conference on Data Engineering (ICDE), pp. 1507–1518, April 2018. https://doi.org/10.1109/ICDE.2018.00169. iSSN 1063-6382
10. Kipf, A., Braun, L., Pandey, V., Neumann, T., Böttcher, J., Kemper, A.: Analytics on Fast Data: Main-Memory Database Systems versus Modern Streaming Systems, p. 12 (2017)
11. Kirstein, F., Dittwald, B., Dutkowski, S., Glikman, Y., Schimmler, S., Hauswirth, M.: Linked data in the european data portal: a comprehensive platform for applying DCAT-AP. In: Lindgren, I., et al. (eds.) EGOV 2019. LNCS, vol. 11685, pp. 192–204. Springer, Cham (2019). https://doi.org/10.1007/978-3-030-27325-5_15
12. Kirstein, F., Stefanidis, K., Dittwald, B., Dutkowski, S., Urbanek, S., Hauswirth, M.: Piveau: a large-scale open data management platform based on semantic web technologies. In: Harth, A., et al. (eds.) ESWC 2020. LNCS, vol. 12123, pp. 648–664. Springer, Cham (2020). https://doi.org/10.1007/978-3-030-49461-2_38
13. Korhonen, T.: Using Kafka to Build Scalable and Fault Tolerant Systems, p. 26 (2019)
14. Kumar, Y.: Lambda Architecture – Realtime Data Processing. SSRN Electron. J. (2020). https://doi.org/10.2139/ssrn.3513624

15. Lutchman, S., Hosein, P.: An open source real-time data portal. J. ICT Stand. **2**, 269–302 (2015). https://doi.org/10.13052/jicts2245-800X.235
16. Miloslavskaya, N., Tolstoy, A.: Big data, fast data and data lake concepts. Procedia Comput. Sci. **88**, 300–305 (2016). https://doi.org/10.1016/j.procs.2016.07.439
17. Nuffelen, B.V.: DCAT Application Profile for data portals in Europe (Jun 2020), https://joinup.ec.europa.eu/sites/default/files/distribution/access_url/2020-06/e4823478-4458-4546-9a85-3609867ad089/DCAT_AP_2.0.1.pdf. Accessed 01 Mar 2021
18. Veiga, J., Expósito, R.R., Pardo, X.C., Taboada, G.L., Tourifio, J.: Performance evaluation of big data frameworks for large-scale data analytics. In: 2016 IEEE International Conference on Big Data (Big Data), pp. 424–431, December 2016. https://doi.org/10.1109/BigData.2016.7840633

The Potential of BOLD in National Budget Planning: Opportunities and Challenges for Kosovo

Mentor Geci[✉] and Csaba Csáki

Corvinus University of Budapest, Budapest, Hungary
csaki.csaba@uni-corvinus.hu

Abstract. Kosovo is a relatively new country with short history in terms of national budget planning. Budget preparation dates back to the year of 2000 when it was started under international support. Therefore, even now budget planning is done in line with international practices and standards. This implies exponential increase in the volume of budget data and at the same time resulted in a need for data openness and linking. This paper sheds some light on opportunities and challenges of using Big Open Linked Data (BOLD) in helping budgetary transparency of this developing country. In order to get insights about the status of using BOLD in national budget planning in Kosovo, interviews are conducted with public sector servants, covering different ministries and levels (from technical staff up to ministerial level). In addition, local NGOs are also contacted. This paper points out that the strategic approach developing countries are following in relation to the transparency of their BOLD open budget data and the attitude of public servants involved are more important determinants of future potentials than simple quantity or quality concerns in themselves.

Keywords: National budget planning · Open data · Big data · Big Open Linked Data · Data quality

1 Introduction

With the rise of open government [18] issues of public sector transparency and open data quality has gained renewed attention [15]. This has a special connotation in the context of national budget planning – especially in developing countries where accountability and even the practice of open data might face difficulties [6].

Transparency of processes related to the national budget (including planning, spending, and reporting) may be supported by open data [10, 15]. However, considering the nature of such data – as follows from its management process and the feedback associated with it – is not only open, but may be categorized as Big Data [8]. Furthermore, to understand, analyze and apply budgetary data in public sector activities, connection of it to other data sets is crucial as well – all in all making budgetary data to meet the characteristics of Big Open Linked Data (BOLD). BOLD refers to a diverse collection

© IFIP International Federation for Information Processing 2021
Published by Springer Nature Switzerland AG 2021
H. J. Scholl et al. (Eds.): EGOV 2021, LNCS 12850, pp. 178–189, 2021.
https://doi.org/10.1007/978-3-030-84789-0_13

of data that needs to be formally combined to be effectively utilized or generate new insights [13].

The influence of the national budget cannot be underestimated as it typically touches on or influences almost all entities in the public sector. The public sector is composed of various governmental layers with all resident institutional units controlled directly or indirectly by resident government units having their specific roles and positions – which, of course may differ from country to country. Nevertheless, those units each have their own budgetary plan and collect data about their expenditures [11]. Planning the budget and controlling spending is, therefore, a complex task and could bear civil oversight usually taken on by NGOs and other non-public entities [7].

Questions of Big Data in budgeting as well as BOLD in more developed countries have received reasonable attention [13, 14]. Processes of budget planning and execution does provide large volumes of data that can be analyzed to detect patterns, which can be used to improve related decision making when creating future budgets [10]. However, there is little evidence about the use and usability of BOLD in national level budgeting of less developed countries with usually more relaxed policy making procedures. Therefore, the main goal beyond this research was to investigate how BOLD may be utilized to improve the national budget planning process of Kosovo as a newly formed country with a short twelve years of history. To that end the state of open data was assessed and views of various stakeholders on the current and potential role of BOLD was investigated. Kosovo has provided a rare opportunity to look at such a situation from scratch: to create a program how BOLD may be used in the planning and execution of the budget the country may build on international experiences and consider best practices of other developing countries.

The paper is organized as follows. First key concept behind BOLD is presented followed by a review of the area of national budget planning. Then cases of the use of BOLD in the budget planning of other developing countries is reviewed to create a background. The methodology section is followed by the introduction of Kosovo as a special case. After the analysis and the discussion of above goals the final section presents the conclusion and offers direction for future research.

2   Big Data, Open Data, Linked Data

Big Open Linked Data (BOLD) is a broad concept that typically refers to the big data aspect of open data combined with the need to relate and integrate diverse datasets using accepted standards and it has a special relationship to the public sector [14]. The term 'open data' assumes that it is accessible for free or at minimal cost, and thus can be reused by anybody for any purpose [9]. The opening of public sector data promotes more transparency and accountability [12] but it may also drive innovation [17]. Big data is about large volumes of data from a multiplicity of sources that needs to be processed to provide value [19]. It might be non-numerical data without context or large volumes of structured or unstructured data [30]. While linked data refers to the possibility (and often requirement) of connecting different datasets through direct links or metadata (using dedicated solutions) in order to provide richer context and to allow for complex reuse in new services: it is about structured and machine readable data that can be semantically queried [32]. The term is used not only to indicate connections between datasets from various sources but also to imply the presence of provenance (traceability) information [23].

BOLD is often used to harness the potential of existing systems, generate new insights, or even to create new services. A concrete example of utilizing BOLD in the public sector is its use to improve fraud detection by customs and tax organizations [16]. However, the relationships between big and open linked data for use by policy-makers and researchers are less explored [14]. While research in open data has shown that quality rather than the quantity of data matters for service and digital innovation 17], there is still a growing global trend for more and more government data to be released to the public as 'open data'. As a result, the Big and Linked aspect has grown as well over the last decade or so. BOLD is gaining attention in developing countries too, and it is especially true for the planning (and execution) of national budgets [8, 20, 29]. Availability of more data, especially when budgetary data are linked to other data sets (such as project, policy, geographical, or local government related ones) may allow for the creation of evaluation frameworks enabling a national budget that could funnel resources to where they are needed most [10]. This, of course also assumes analytical capabilities being available and utilized at all levels.

3 National Budget Planning

The national budget is the most important economic policy instrument of any government, and as such it reflects its development priorities. From the point of view of financing, general governments are typically composed of four components (also called subsectors): (i) central government; (ii) state government; (iii) local government; and (iv) social security funds. The general government itself includes all government units and all nonmarket or nonprofit institutions (NPI) that are controlled by government units and they fulfil the functions of government as their primary activity. The central government has the authority to incur expenditure on public administration, defence, education, health, and the provision of other services. It may also make transfers to other institutional units, including other levels of government. In all countries, the budgetary central government, as an institutional unit of the general government sector, has the power to exercise certain, fiscal control over many other units and entities. This single unit of the central government encompasses the fundamental activities of the national executive, legislative, and judiciary powers regarding fiscal matters [11]. Budgetary units (such as ministries, agencies, boards, commissions, judicial authorities, legislative bodies, and other entities that make up the budgetary central government) are not separate institutional units for financial purposes. This is because they generally do not have the authority to own assets, incur liabilities, or engage in transactions on their own right. General government entities with individual budgets not fully covered by the main (or general) budget are considered extra budgetary. Extra budgetary entities may have their own revenue sources, which may be supplemented by grants (transfers) from the general budget or from other sources.

Budget plans are based on past budgets, past experience and current revenue projections. While the budget typically regulates the revenue and expenditure over one fiscal year, the budget process is continuous and circular. Financial data should be compiled for the general government and public sectors, as well as for all the subsectors of the general government (and the public corporations subsector).

4   BOLD in the Budget Planning of Developing Countries

The idea of open data and the potential of BOLD in helping both transparency and the economy has been considered by less developed countries as well. Accordingly, the strategies adopted and the projects that ensued have been reported in the literature. Well documented cases represent emerging economies such as Brazil, Turkey, or South Africa, while notable reports on developing countries cover Saudi Arabia, Chile, Indonesia, Mozambique, or Thailand among others. Some of these cover general BOLD initiatives while a few has dedicated focus on national budget related open data programs. Out of the above list, four countries have been well documented in the literature and those reports offer some background to help explore the Kosovo case.

It is easy for typical eGovernment programs to focus on the technology needed to support the usability and accessibility of data and services. While the open government initiative embraced by Saudi Arabia as Saudi Vision 2030 [21] was more generic (not specifically budgeting) it is still interesting as the goal set by the government was considering both the development of technological capacity as well as the task of increasing citizen awareness and use of open government data in order to promote transparency, trust, and accountability. However, actual actions by government actors and thus awareness of the program has been questioned and it was also revealed that the capabilities of the existing portal was fairly limited [1]. Analyses of the openness and citizen use of the country's Open Data Portal later underlined [2] that further increasing citizen engagement would require more technical integration (such as smart endpoints, a common format framework and a linked data cloud). The results suggest iterative cycles of technology development, practice improvement and marketing engagement.

Brazil, as a large emerging economy has put data standardization into the forefront of their program. To reach effective transparency, the country has a legal framework that enforces all public entities to publish detailed budgetary data on the web in real time [25]. The challenges of such an approach highlight the importance of the standardization of open budgetary data [28]. In response [28] derive a set of requirements to be addressed. Most importantly, attention is directed to the need of interoperability that requires the integration of federal, state and municipal contexts (which in turn assumes an appropriate level of information available to each public organization). Furthermore, from the eighteen criteria proposed, it appears that only three are fully met. The conclusion is that while the legal system is forward-looking, it still lacks regulations that clarifies how to 'identify things' in a digital world and requires reports being presented in a uniform way.

During the last decade serious effort was directed at open data initiatives concerning national budget data in Indonesia [24]. While budget transparency initiatives have gained attention, including political support in the form of a new policy framework and interest of involved actors from the demand side, actual utilization of open budget data is slow to follow [5]. Although there is a new dedicated data portal, the ability of potential users to relate datasets is limited mostly due to the way data is presented [3]. To overcome the limited utilization of open data by civic actors, there is a host of NGOs that serve as intermediaries in budget issues: on the demand side they help potential users to understand the concept of open data, while on the supply side they work on improving the transformation of the open data program from conception to adoption.

While the government of Thailand had an open data program, it did not gain momentum with respect to utilization of the data primarily due to difficulties with easy access and lack of examples demonstrating the power of open data. There were two projects reported both offering solutions that not only help public sector entities, but also considered citizens as potential users. An analytical system was developed to help the identification of irregular spending or request patterns [27]. The project can be considered BOLD utilization as it covered and linked a vast amount of data for fiscal years 2013–2017 from two different sources: budget requests of government agencies (collected by the Bureau of the Budget), and procurement records of government agencies (stored by the Comptroller General's Department). In addition to supporting budgetary decision making through visualization, the tool had an open interface. Local governments in Thailand also store a significant amount of data in disperse relational databases. Even though the data may be accessed through a Web application (called e-Plan), this solution is not suitable to distribute and reuse that vast amount of data. Using a linking tool [4] that is also able to highlight interesting patterns and hidden linkages Sub-district Administrative Organizations (SAO) are able to make decisions for their strategic and project plans using experiences based on data of other SAOs.

These examples demonstrate different approaches of governance to direct efforts towards utilizing open data in general or in budget planning in particular and they represent different possible viewpoints on related national strategy. Choices made reflect the economic development of the country and the approach of its government to the idea of open data. They serve as examples for countries that are more behind in embracing or cultivating open data opportunities. However, it appears that studies tend to address negative issues faced, which could only serve as guidance what to avoid. One promising approach could be for the government of such countries to jump ahead and instead of looking at open data opportunities only, they could explore the option of BOLD right away. This appeared to be a possibility for Kosovo in the context of their open budget initiative. Therefore, the goal of this study was to look at what stakeholders in the open budget data program the recently formed country of Kosovo think about the potential benefits of BOLD and how the country could take advantage of existing practices.

5   Research Questions and Methodology

The research reported here is essentially a case-study [31], where the case is a so called intrinsic [22] or special [26] case since it is rare to see a new country building up budget and transparency practices from scratch. As Kosovo may build its BOLD initiative from ground up it is a unique opportunity to watch its government officials and the public to work this out. In order to understand the current state of national budget planning and find ways for improvement, the following Research Questions have been posed: 1) How do regulations deal with transparency related to fiscal data and is there a role envisioned for BOLD in this context? 2) What is the quality of the fiscal data published? 3) What is the knowledge and expectations of stakeholders involved in national budget planning regarding BOLD? 4) How may Kosovo take advantage of experiences and best practices of other developing countries?

Data collection is done using a mixture of methods including deskwork (exploration of the background of the Kosovo case such as legal documents, websites and data published) and fieldwork (interviews with government officials at various levels of the Kosovo government and with NGOs). The goal of the semi-structured interviews was three-fold: a) understand the process beyond the law; b) set a baseline for the quality of fiscal data; and c) understand the opinion and level of understanding of state officials as well as the view of civil groups on the applicability BOLD in the national budget planning process. Content of interview questions was based on the experiences collated from the international case studies (see above). Questions were structured into four sections: (i) basic (e.g. demographic) information; (ii) the budgeting process and the role of open data in it; (iii) opinion about quality of fiscal data (using a 5-level Likert scale along six dimensions – see Fig. 1); and (iv) open questions about specific (individual) views on BOLD. Interviews were executed February-June 2020 and interview respondents were asked to verify interview transcripts. Interviewees were selected using stratified sampling. Selection thus covered three layers, namely Political level; Middle management (i.e. department heads) and Staff with 2, 3, and 2 interviewees respectively. Entities approached included Ministry of Finance and Transfers (2), Ministry of Economy (2), and Ministry of Agriculture, Forestry and Rural Development (3). On top of state institutions, stakeholders approached included heads of 3 NGOs. In terms of time in office, respondents were quite experienced ranging from 3 up to 20 years of experience (with the majority of public servants, 47% having at least 15 years, while NGO personnel had less than 5 years of experience). Number of subordinates of non-staff ranged from 5 to 22 in total.

6 The Case of Kosovo

6.1 Kosovo History of National Budget Preparation

Kosovo has a short history in terms of budget preparation, following the declaration of independence in 2008. Since then, there were several developments in terms of modalities of budget preparation, its execution, as well as transparency issues. Following the approval of the annual Law on Budget, the fiscal year covers the period January to December. The provisions of the respective law are compulsory for all institutions and their respective units, which fall within the scope of the Budget of the Republic of Kosovo. As there was more and more public demand for government data in terms of budget execution compared to the planned one, Kosovo governments were pushed to increase budget transparency. Indeed, amidst the evolution of the country's budgetary process, the purpose of this research was to get better insights in terms of the potential application of BOLD in budget planning in comparison to international standards.

6.2   The Budget Planning Process in Kosovo

The budget process in Kosovo goes through four stages: 1) budget formulation; 2) enactment, 3) execution, and 4) oversight (including auditing). In this paper the focus is primarily on formulation and oversight (to a certain extent). In addition to the annual budget, the government develops the Medium-Term Expenditure Framework (MTEF), which seeks to improve the predictability and sustainability of the budget, covering the coming fiscal year and estimates of the two following fiscal years.

When preparing the next annual budget, each April the Ministry of Finance (MoF) issues so-called budget circulars, which provide information and instructions on the expenditure ceiling for the next fiscal year and specify the coordination process of budget organizations with the MoF. The requests are checked and are corrected if necessary. The requests are collated, and the draft budget is opened up for public hearings in July and August. Based on the resulting budget proposals, the Minister of Finance prepares the Proposed Kosovo Budget and Proposed Appropriations Law for consideration by the government in September. The government adopts the proposed budget in October, while the Assembly approves by December. In terms of following budget spending, whenever the Assembly requests it, the Minister of Finance shall, on behalf of the Government, present to the Assembly a comprehensive report detailing and reconciling the approved budget spending and appropriations, all subsequent transfers and other changes. Participants and their roles are thus as follows: Ministry of Finance (preparation, guidelines, and consultation), Budgetary organizations (proposals for expenditure), public including NGOs (attends hearings and comments by raising issues), central government (approval), Assembly (final approval). For the purposes of ensuring that the budget is implemented according to the approved budget law, the Assembly exercises budget oversight and to do this the Assembly requires extensive reporting from the government.

The question is then, how data is utilized in the various steps of this process and whether the BOLD nature of the data is considered during Steps 1) and 4).

6.3   Data Quality of Budgetary Open Data in Kosovo

Questions about quality received quite diverse responses as the role of ministries in budget preparation was quite different compared to NGOs. While ministries had to follow specific templates according to the Law on Budget, the main aim of NGOs according to the responses received was to comment in terms of economic reasoning of specific budgetary items and regarding data quality as well.

In terms of composition of data used in budgeting, the main sources are public institutions. As it is a standard procedure using set templates, data are sourced from the Free Balance software officially used across all the ministries in the country. Data disposed are at granular level, by counterparts and type of expenses. This data is supplemented with private sector data, mainly in relation to capital investment projects of the private sector (such as highway constructions, etc.), where deployment of specific questionnaire or survey is needed to collect information. This is also confirmed from the respondents that apart from the expected 86% that is public sector data, the remaining 14% comes from private sector sources.

On the questions concerning the quality of budgetary data, where answers ranged from 1-worst to 5-best, the average was 2.63: this implies that there is room for improvements. Individual areas covered opinion on accessibility, transparency, usable format, relevance, metadata, and potential privacy violations. As may be concluded from Fig. 1, there is a marked difference between the view of NGOs (representing the public) and that of the public servants: the latter group is consistently more optimistic in every dimension. While representatives of ministerial agencies claimed that the budget preparation, execution and data disclosure are quite transparent and they follow international standards, the main claim of NGO personnel was that data are published with certain delay, format is not user friendly so they need to do additional data manipulation, and there are no specific explanations for certain items.

Civil group representatives claim that the data should be published in machine readable format suitable for statistical analysis and handling purposes and it should be published at a more granular level. They recommend that publication of the chart of accounts must be mandatory. Another reasoning for the lack of public sector qualitative data is about the absence of metadata (use of provenance data is limited and clarifications are lacking). This increases the risk of error when transposing them into readable formats. On the other hand, public sector servants' responses rely on current legislative requirements in terms of compilation (preparation) and dissemination. Still, 29% of them responded that the quality is on average and there is space for improvement. Some of the reasoning was that the average quality of public sector data is due to constant increase in the amount of public sector data.

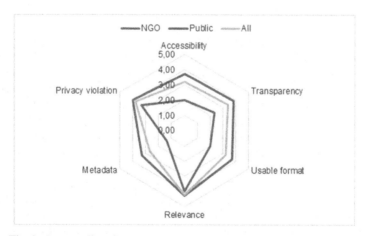

Fig. 1. Data quality of open government data in Kosovo (Source: Authors)

Although budget data is publicly available free of charge, Kosovo is still ranked only 76th out of 79 countries according to the international Global Open Data Index (https://index.okfn.org/). What the index recognizes is that in case of Kosovo government data are not in fully machine-readable format and are not downloadable at once. Therefore, recently, the Ministry of Finance introduced a Transparency Portal within its website (https://ptmf.rks-gov.net/page.aspx?id=2,1), but it still offers only a snapshot of budget spending by ministries covering the period 2015–2020. Absence of time series, along with two key parameters specified by Global Open Data Index, are still to be addressed.

6.4 Respondents' Views on BOLD and Its Role in National Budget

Section 4 dealt with respondents' individual views on BOLD. Regarding personal experience, almost all of the respondents confirmed they had little direct exposure to BOLD before. The opinion was that the main precondition to apply BOLD was to increase the quantity of government data compiled and published in relation to the budgeting process. In addition, formally linking planning data (as approved) to spending details would be necessary. Even more crucial is to link spending to economic and other output results (such as social, health, and other societal and statistical data collected).

Interview responses have also touched on the applicability of BOLD in the daily work of interviewees. Respondents were quite optimistic on the role of BOLD in performing their tasks in relation to the national budget. Both public and NGO officials agreed that it would have major impact if done properly, due to the constant increase in the volume of data. BOLD approaches and tools would also assist in extracting the necessary information to analyse the design and orientation of the state budget and would enable the monitoring of the implementation of the planned budget. In addition to that, higher data volume contributes directly to forecasting of macro-fiscal trends, namely, in producing the Medium-Term Expenditure Framework.

7   Discussion

In comparison to practices of other developing countries and based on these research results it is clear, that there is major room for improvement on open government data in Kosovo in order to meet BOLD standards. In general, the agreement seemed to be that BOLD is an important concept but not yet applicable in Kosovo budgetary practices. Immediate preconditions for its applicability concern both quantity and quality of data published. Kosovo is at a very early level of development regarding openness of government data. Comparing Kosovo to specific countries mentioned earlier, beyond issues related technical features of open data expected results heavily depend on the lack of abilities to link data that is available. However, there was common agreement (including all levels from staff up to ministerial level) that application of BOLD would be very beneficial to all stakeholders as they could use their resources more efficiently by focusing on real social and economic issues based on more advanced analysis.

While increasing the availability, quality and understandability of data is an obvious condition, improvement in other areas are also required. What should be considered includes education about BOLD (of both public servants and civil stakeholders), improved technological capabilities (such as better platforms) and tools (e.g. portals with semantic abilities). This, of course, assumes a forward looking legal framework with supportive regulations based on a national strategy. Finally, the ecosystem view could be applied by encouraging various intermediaries to come forward who can promote actual utilization through various services offered to specific, targeted user groups.

Although BOLD does not seem to be an applicable concept in Kosovo budgetary data, yet stakeholders do realize the potential benefits. However, they do not think the time has come for a full application – neither they seem to be willing to and, consequently, ready to handle it. This is underscored by the vastly diverging views of public servants from that of the NGO representatives over a few key points (such as judgement of quality performance). Public servants are satisfied with the current direction and speed of the changes in this matter, while NGOs have little influence on the outcome and are quite occupied with dealing with the actual budget and spending in order to be able to provide feedback.

To what extent these findings can be applied to other countries depends on (i) the approach countries are following in relation to transparency through open government data; (ii) their willingness to broaden the scope of stakeholders, especially to those with more critical views on budget issues; (iii) committed economic capacities to develop new tools; and (iv) improvement of management solutions.

8   Conclusions and Future Research

Based on the responses received so far, main conclusion is that BOLD is still not applicable to Kosovo, among others due to short budgetary data history, and, apart from that, due to limited data sources. In addition, users are still not so much aware about BOLD, but they do believe there is opportunity for the application of BOLD in Kosovo budgetary data. Apart from the technological part of BOLD, special attention should be given to users' awareness about open government data in general, and to the training of staff in particular. In the meantime, other factors highlighted by earlier research on national budgeting may be considered such as strong checks and balances by audit institutions, data standardization (at least machine readable syntax), and automated data controls as these could be be quite instrumental in improving the quality of national budgeting and transparency practices.

In terms of limitations, this research on BOLD in Kosovo had a special focus on data quality and views of stakeholders, while technological conditions and related costs were not directly investigated. Future research should follow up on improvements of quantity, quality, and transparency issues, including their impact on budgetary execution. For future considerations, results of this research could help responsible stakeholders to better identify issue to be addressed regarding the openness of open government data, access timeline, as well as broader inclusion of non-governmental bodies in budget preparation and execution. Apart from that, other country practices as depicted in this paper could be followed in order to build on their best practices.

References

1. AlRushaid, M.W., Saudagar, A.K.J.: Measuring the data openness for the open data in Saudi Arabia e-government-a case study. Int. J. Adv. Comput. Sci. Appl. **12**, 113–122 (2016)
2. AlSukhayri, A.M., Aslam, M.A., Arafat, S., Aljohani, N.R.: Leveraging the Saudi Linked open government data: a framework and potential benefits. Int. J. Mod. Educ. Comput. Sci. **11**(7), 14 (2019)

3. Aryan, P.R., Ekaputra, F.J., Sunindyo, W.D., Akbar, S.: Fostering government transparency and public participation through linked open government data: Case study: Indonesian public information service. In: 2014 International Conference on Data and Software Engineering (ICODSE), pp. 1–6. IEEE (2014). https://doi.org/10.1109/ICODSE.2014.7062655

4. Boonlamp, L.: A linked data approach to planning collaboration amongst local governments in Thailand. In: 2017 2nd International Conference on Information Technology (INCIT), pp. 1–5. IEEE (2017). https://doi.org/10.1109/INCIT.2017.8257850

5. Davies, T.: Open data in developing countries: Emerging insights from phase I (ODDC Report). (2014)

6. Dawes, S.S., Vidiasova, L., Parkhimovich, O.: Planning and designing open government data programs: an ecosystem approach. Gov. Inf. Q. **33**(1), 15–27 (2016)

7. Gaventa, J., McGee, R.: The impact of transparency and accountability initiatives. Dev. Policy Rev. **31**, s3–s28 (2013)

8. Gray, J.: Open Budget data: mapping the landscape, Open Knowledge (2015). https://doi.org/10.2139/ssrn.2654878

9. Hardy, K., Maurushat, A.: Opening up government data for big data analysis and public benefit. Comput. Law Secur. Rev. **33**(1), 30–37 (2017)

10. Höchtl, J., Parycek, P., Schöllhammer, R.: Big data in the policy cycle: policy decision making in the digital era. J. Org. Comput. Elect. Comm. **26**(1–2), 147–169 (2016)

11. IMF GFSM: International Monetary Fund - GFSM. International Monetary Fund, Washington, D.C (2014)

12. Janssen, K.: Open government data and the right to information: Opportunities and obstacles. J. Commun. Inf. **8**(2), (2012)

13. Janssen, M., van den Hoven, J.: Big and open linked data (BOLD) in government: a challenge to transparency and privacy? Govt. Inf. Q. **32**(4), 363–368 (2015)

14. Janssen, M., Kuk, G.: Big and open linked data (BOLD) in research, policy, and practice. J. Organ. Comput. Electron. Commer. **26**(1–2), 3–13 (2016)

15. Kasymova, J., Ferreira, M.A.M., Piotrowski, S.J.: Do open data initiatives promote and sustain transparency? A comparative analysis of open budget portals in developing countries. In: Zhang, J., Luna-Reyes, L.F., Pardo, T.A., Sayogo, D.S. (eds.) Information, Models, and Sustainability. PAIT, vol. 20, pp. 137–155. Springer, Cham (2016). https://doi.org/10.1007/978-3-319-25439-5_7

16. Klievink, B., Zomer, G.: IT-enabled resilient, seamless and secure global supply chains: introduction, overview and research topics. In: Janssen, M., et al. (eds.) I3E 2015. LNCS, vol. 9373, pp. 443–453. Springer, Cham (2015). https://doi.org/10.1007/978-3-319-25013-7_36

17. Kuk, G., Davies, T.: The roles of agency and artifacts in assembling open data complementarities. In: Thirty Second International Conference on Information Systems (ICIS), Shanghai, China. 04–07 December 2011, pp. 1–16 (2011)

18. Luna-Reyes, L.F., Bertot, J.C., Mellouli, S.: Open government, open data and digital government. Govt. Inf. Q. **1**(31), 4–5 (2014)

19. McAfee, A., Brynjolfsson, E.: Big data: the management revolution. Harv. Bus. Rev. **90**(10), 60–68 (2012)

20. Musyaffa, F.A., Lehmann, J., Jabeen, H.: IOTA: Interlinking of heterogeneous multilingual open fiscal data. Exp. Syst. Appl. **147**, 113135 (2020). https://doi.org/10.1016/j.eswa.2019.113135

21. Nurunnabi, M.: Transformation from an oil-based economy to a knowledge-based economy in Saudi Arabia: the direction of Saudi vision 2030. J. Knowl. Econ. **8**(2), 536–564 (2017)

22. Patton, M.: Qualitative Research and Evaluation Methods. Sage, Thousand Oaks (2002)

23. Pignotti, E., Corsar, D., Edwards, P.: Provenance Principles for Open Data. Digital Engagement 2011, pp. 1–6. Newcastle, UK,–6 (2011). http://de2011.computing.dundee.ac.uk/wp-content/uploads/2011/10/Provenance-Principles-for-Open-Data.pdf

24. Rendra, M., Cendekia, I.: The national budget transparency initiative at ministry of finance in open government data. In: 2015 3rd International Conference on Information and Communication Technology (ICoICT), pp. 522–527. IEEE, Nusa Dua, Bali, Indonesia (2015). https://doi.org/10.1109/ICoICT.2015.7231479

25. da Silva Craveiro, G., de Santana, M.T., de Albuquerque, J.P.: Assessing open government budgetary data in Brazil. In: 7th International Conference on Digital Society, pp. 20–27. The International Academy Research and Industry Association, Nice, France (2013)

26. Stake, R.E.: The Art of Case Study Research. Sage, Thousand Oaks (1995)

27. Surasvadi, N., Saiprasert, C., Thajchayapong, S.: Budget and procurement analytics using open government data in Thailand. In: 2017 10th International Conference on Ubi-Media Computing and Workshops (Ubi-Media). pp. 1–6. IEEE, Pattaya, Thailand (2017). https://doi.org/10.1109/UMEDIA.2017.8074079

28. Tavares de Santana, M., da Silva Craveiro, G.: Challenges and requirements for the standardisation of open budgetary data in the Brazilian public administration. In Informatik Angepasst an Mensch, Organisation und Umwelt (INFORMATIK 2013). Gesellschaft für Informatik e.V., Bonn, Germany (2013)

29. Tygel, A.F., Attard, J., Orlandi, F., Campos, M.L.M., Auer, S.: How much? Is not enough: an analysis of open budget initiatives. In: Proceedings of the 9th International Conference on Theory and Practice of Electronic Governance, pp. 276–286. ACM (2016). https://arxiv.org/abs/1504.01563

30. Wigan, M.R., Clarke, R.: Big data's big unintended consequences. Computer **46**(6), 46–53 (2013)

31. Yin, R.: Case Study Research-Design and Methods. Sage, Thousand Oaks (2003)

32. Bizer, C., Heath, T., Berners-Lee, T.: Linked data - The story so far. Int. J. Semant. Web **5**(3), 1–22 (2009)

Smart Cities

Policy Recommendations for Promoting Touristic Attractivity from Local Government Perspective in Innovative Environments

Manuel Pedro Rodríguez Bolívar[1]([✉]) [iD], Fabiana Roberto[2] [iD], and Rosa Lombardi[3] [iD]

[1] University of Granada, 18071 Granada Andalusia, Spain
manuelp@ugr.es
[2] University of Naples Federico II, 80126 Naples Campania, Italy
[3] Sapienza University of Rome, 00161 Rome Lazio, Italy

Abstract. The COVID-19 pandemic situation has had unprecedented negative consequences in the tourism sector, especially in the hotel industry, which has implied negative shocks directly and indirectly in city revenues, employment and economy. Recent research has indicated that technology is becoming central in finding solutions for tourism recovery through the development of new or improved ICT-enabled tourism services, which could help to achieving a higher attraction of tourists and other sources of foreign investments to cities. This paper therefore seeks to analyse the impact of blockchain technologies (BCT) on the tourism business for attracting new customers to cities with the aim at gaining insights regarding public policies to be taken by local governments for improving tourism business in their city. To achieve this aim, this paper provides an empirical research on the impact of BCT on both lowering prices and improving service quality of lodging accommodations by a sample of lodging accommodations in different Italian cities, providing insights to know if the implementation of BCT on hospitality business, can help city governments to improve smart living into the urban space, deriving some recommendations for city government to take public policies to favour the implementation of these technologies into the hospitality industry.

Keywords: Smart cities · Touristic attractivity · Blockchain · Hospitality industry

1 Introduction

The COVID-19 pandemic situation has made central governments of countries across the world to implement lockdown measures and border closures to save lives. These public policies have caused business closures due to the downwards of the income and continued uncertainty affecting negatively both the domestic and international tourism notably, especially in the hotel industry [1].

Indeed, the hospitality industry is into danger to survive in a post-COVID-19 world and it has had significant negative shocks in the short run -and it is expected in the long

© IFIP International Federation for Information Processing 2021
Published by Springer Nature Switzerland AG 2021
H. J. Scholl et al. (Eds.): EGOV 2021, LNCS 12850, pp. 193–204, 2021.
https://doi.org/10.1007/978-3-030-84789-0_14

run too- in city revenues, employment and economy [2]. There is therefore a need for city governments to accelerate the recovery of the tourism industry, preparing tourism activities for a stronger, more sustainable and resilient tourism economy, within the new post-COVID-19 context [3].

These strategies require ongoing tourism service innovations grounded in the promotion of the digital transition of the hospitality industry [4], mainly to both introduce product adjustments -for example, non-contact, automated check-in/out processes-, and support smaller local businesses that are more potentially exposed to the negative effects of this crisis scenery [5]. Technology has therefore become a central role in finding solutions for tourism recovery through the development of new or improved ICT-enabled hospitality services [6]. Technology could also make a destination more attractive to visitors impacting on their experiences and satisfaction [7]. Hospitality firms are therefore pushed to have an innovative perspective to both recover their business and compete in the short, medium and long-term in the hospitality market [8].

The fast-track implementation of disruptive technologies like that proposed by Blockchain technology (BCT) could help them to radically transform the traditional realm of their hospitality operations [9] with a clear impact on room rates and innovated services. In fact, due to main BCT characteristics (decentralization, transparency, proof of work, immutability and security), this technology provides faster and anytime transactions, better security and privacy, reduced costs, automatization and higher confidence in the process [10]. All these advantages of BCT are not only beneficial for hospitality owners but also for improving customer experiences reducing both room prices and waiting time for checking-in and out processes.

Under this framework, hospitality industry is actively investing in BCT-based start-ups or platforms (decentralized Apps -DApps-) with the aim of better connecting/interacting with the customers [11] with the offer of lower room rates and better hospitality services -rated into the DApps platforms-, due to its capacity for better understanding of tourist preferences [12].

Nonetheless, in general, despite the growing importance of BCT for city developments and the growing BCT-based hotels booking platforms launched, only a few researchers have done empirical studies with respect to BCT applications in tourism and travel industry [13]. It denotes an absolute need for more research to advance the understanding of the nature and functioning of this emerging technology (ETs) in tourism sector, since literature in the subject is still making its first steps [14]. In addition, this research could help cities to wonder the need of undertaking strategies for promoting new technological infrastructure and innovative spaces for the introduction of ETs in smart tourism business into the city, expediting the widespread deployment of the BCT [9].

Under this context, this paper therefore seeks to analyse the impact of BCT on the tourism business for attracting new customers to cities with the aim at gaining insights regarding measures to be taken by local governments for improving smart tourism business into their cities. To achieve this aim, this paper is focused on the impact of BCT on both lowering prices and improving service quality of lodging accommodations.

The remainder of this paper is as follows. The next section describes the need for enhancing smart business in the hospitality industry in cities for improving urban areas, analysing the impact of tourism activities on city revenues and the innovation role on touristic attractivity, deriving some hypotheses formulation. Then, the empirical research is undertaken describing the sample selection, the research methodology used to test the hypotheses proposed and the analysis of results. Finally, the discussion and conclusion section highlights the main findings and brings the paper to an end.

2   The Need for Enhancing Smart Business in the Hospitality Industry for Improving Smart Tourism in Cities

Prior research has traditionally indicated that governments at National and/or Regional level are responsible of tourism development through the issuance of regulations, tourism planning and development [15]. However, in the last years, the focus put on the smart city movement has made tourism both to be increasingly linked to the urban area and to require cities to improve their attractiveness and functioning of visiting areas [16]. Nowadays, city governments need to put cities into action transforming places of cultural significance into places of consumption, and requiring city government investments in infrastructure facilities [17], technology and innovation to better cope with increasing tourist numbers and expectations [18] with the aim at attracting sustainable revenues to their cities [19].

According to prior research, technological and innovative environments produced into the smart tourism contexts are the major factors for destinations to become more competitive and sustainable [20]. Innovation is especially essential for hospitality organizations' success because it allows gaining a greater market share, competition and differentiating themselves from competitors [21] and let them to generate innovative services that generate customer value co-creation process [22].

In the last years, BCT has opened new opportunities for hotel competition in the market based on the level of differentiation, mainly taking the approach of both room rates [23] and the production of innovative services [24]. Small and medium enterprises (SMEs) on lodging accommodations -b&b, hostels or apartments- being early adopters can improve their position in the hospitality market if disruptive technological innovations are implemented, obtaining commercialisation flexibility advantages over rivals [25].

Under this framework, pricing strategies of lodging accommodations are relevant when examining the impact of radical technological innovations [26]. As these technological advances are immersed into the smartness of the urban area, many cities are putting a lot of effort into the digital transformation of the entire tourism value chain [27].

Therefore, it is expected that cities located on innovative regions could help the hospitality industry to embrace emerging IT prior to other different destinations [28]. An important effect of BCT implementation in the hospitality industry is the fix of different room rates in lodging accommodations located in cities in innovative regions *vs* non-innovative cities based on their current market based on online travel agencies (OTAs). The following hypothesis is thus derived:

H1. There are no differences on dynamic price dispersion among the lodging accommodations located in innovative *versus* non-innovative cities with the implementation of BCT markets regarding those based on traditional OTAs markets.

On another hand, service innovation matters when guests are selecting a hotel, making necessary the implementation of metrics for impact and outcome assessment [29]. Prior research has indicated that online reviews provide feedback on service innovation helping firms in service improvement [30] and are used by tourists to select an accommodation, mainly when they are disclosed together with numerical rating details because it increases both booking intentions and consumer trust [31]. Also, in the OTAs market, customers providing a holistic evaluation of all the hospitality service attributes has different influence on choices according to hotel star ratings [32].

BCT is a technology capable to ensure genuine and trustworthy online reviews creating a unique private key for each identity with several independent verification processes embedded into ranking and review systems [33], which ensures reduced rates of manipulation or duplication of reviews in the OTAs market [34]. Therefore, online reviews using BCT in hospitality seem to be more trusted than those posted using OTAs and could differ from them. Nonetheless, as far as we know, there are no studies testing online reviews and ratings on the hospitality BCT market and its comparison with those based on the OTAs markets. Therefore, the following hypothesis is derived:

H2. There are no differences on online ratings among the lodging accommodations with the implementation of BCT markets regarding those based on traditional OTAs markets.

In brief, there is a need for empirical evidence to understand the impact of BCT on room rates and service innovation, which affects the visitor attraction to cities. It should be a driver for city government to take public policies fostering technological environments for the hospitality industry. Therefore, an empirical research on sample Italian cities is undertaken in the next section of this research.

3   Empirical Research

3.1   Sample Selection

EU Member States are among the world's leading tourist destinations, contributing 10% to EU GDP and creating jobs for 26 million people [35]. This paper is focused on Italy, which is one of the most representative EU countries in terms of destinations for non-residents (217 million nights) and global tourism destinations [36]. In addition, in recent years Italy has enhanced online sales, being the 2nd European country by revenues obtained through online booking platforms and is one of the countries in which hospitality competition is higher [37] and the share of medium size hotels (25–99 rooms) in relation to the share of bed-place capacity (in all types of establishments) is higher [35]. Finally, Italian governments and tourism business are now seriously considering how ETs -especially BCT- can contribute to their growth and create new opportunities for post-COVID 19 outbreak recovering [38]. Thus, Italy fits well with the aim of this research.

The empirical research was conducted selecting accommodation in 4 Italian cities included into the latest official touristic report provided by the Italian Institute of Statistics [39] -the two most touristic cities (Rome and Milan) and the two less touristic cities which are not considered as "smart cities" (Rosolina and Sorrento)- [28]. These cities are located in innovative (Milan and Rosolina) and non-innovative regions (Rome and Sorrento). Consistently with the aim of this study, all sample lodging accommodations located in these sample cities are using DApps for capturing tourists to their accommodations and have implemented BCT for operational processes such as, for example, automated check-in and check-out systems [40], which could have an impact on room booking prices and service quality. Thus, this sample selection fits well with the aim of the paper and the hypotheses testing proposed in this research.

3.2 Methodology of Research

Our empirical research selected 3 leading OTAs by revenues in 2019 according to the companies' financial statements (Booking Holdings, Expedia Group and Ctrip) and 4 Blockchain DApps based on the possibility of paying through a specific token owned by the platform (LockTrip, Trippki, Travala and Xceltrip).

The three sample OTAs are the main ones in its sector by turnover [41] and hold 86% of the total revenues [42], whereas the four sample DApps create a model with 0% or very low commissions, allowing accommodation owners and users to obtain different benefits from the use of BCT.

On each of the platforms and for each sample destination, we selected 6 different types of accommodation facilities: a) 5 *, 4 * and 3 * hotels; and b) b&b, apartment and hostel, which represent the main non-hotel categories [43].

The selection was made according to the following criteria, verified at the time of the search: 1) evaluation of the property by Booking.com guests, which is OTAs market leader; 2) presence of the structure on at least 2 platforms and 3) distance from the city center less than 5 km. Table 1 displays the sample accommodation facilities selected.

Table 1. Accommodation selected.

Italian Regions	Innovative		Non-innovative	
	Lombardy	Veneto	Lazio	Campania
Type/City	Milan	Rosolina	Rome	Sorrento
5* Hotel	Hotel Pierre	N.A.	Palazzo Naiadi, The Dedica Anthology, Autograph Collection	Parco dei Principi
4* Hotel	Hotel Berna	Hotel Formula international	Hotel Artemide	Grand Hotel Aminta
3* Hotel	Ibis Milano Centro	Hotel formula and puravita SPA	Hotel Santa Maria	Comfort Hotel Gardenia Sorrento Coast
B&B	Libeccio	La Corte	Ventisei Scalini A Trastevere	Palazzo Tasso
Apartment	Vitruvio 43	N.A.	Palazzo Al Velabro	Agora
Hostel	Babila Hostel & Bistrot	N.A.	Hostel Beauty	Ulisse deluxe hostel

Source: author's elaboration.

Legend: N.A. means not available.

On each of the selected OTAs and DApp platforms and for each sample accommodation, we collected information about token prices (and Bitcoin prices) during the period Oct-Nov 2019 (before the COVID-19 pandemic) and the quantity of rooms offered in each structure.

All information was collected by simulating the booking of a room at the date of the search and at 1, 3 and 6 months before the check-in date. This information provides the support for hypothesis testing (H1). In addition, we gathered data about ratings of both the general service of each one of sample accommodations and the services provided by each one of them (location, staff, cleanliness, comfort, value for money, facilities, free WiFi, amenities, vibe, bar, breakfast, food, room and wellness area). This information was useful for testing hypothesis 2.

The data are shown displaying descriptive statistics. Hypotheses have been tested using Wilcoxon test due to violation of normality assumption [44]. The Wilcoxon paired-sample test could be a powerful test of the null hypothesis of differences between paired attributes of the dynamic price dispersion of room bookings and rating differences based on BCT *vs* OTAs [45].

3.3 Analysis of Results

Descriptive Statistics. Descriptive statistics for price dispersion (see Table 2) show that price dispersion is generally higher in BCT markets for all cities and booking horizons analysed in this study. There are some particular exceptions in which price dispersion is slightly higher, but not significant, in OTAs markets (for example, at 6-months prior the check-in date, hotel price dispersion in Rosolina). Price dispersion is also generally higher in both the most touristic cities (Rome -mainly focused on b&b and hotels- and Milan) and the b&b lodging accommodations, than in the less touristic cities (Sorrento and Rosolina) or in hotels and apartments in all the booking horizons.

Table 2. Descriptive statistics in price dispersion between OTAs and BCT DApps (H1).

| | | | PRICE DISPERSION | | | | | | | | | | | | Mean |
| | | | At the date of the search | | | At 1-month window prior to the check-in | | | At 3-months window prior to the check-in | | | At 6-months window prior or to the check-in | | | |
			OTAs Ratio	BCT Ratio	%	OTAs Ratio	BCT Ratio	%	OTAs Ratio	BCT Ratio	%	OTAs Ratio	BCT Ratio	%	
INNOVATIVE CITIES	Milan	Hotels	1.083	1.536	41.82%	1.126	1.382	22.68%	1.110	1.525	37.45%	1.112	1.108	-0.43%	25.38%
		Apartments	N.A.	N.A.	N.A.	1.080	1.168	8.10%	1.031	1.257	21.93%	N.A.	N.A.	N.A.	15.02%
		B&B	1.054	1.089	3.29%	1.086	N.A.	N.A.	1.024	1.132	10.53%	N.A.	N.A.	N.A.	6.91%
		Hostels	1.108	1.182	6.71%	1.096	1.469	34.06%	1.076	1.248	16.01%	1.120	1.171	4.61%	15.35%
		TOTAL	1.087	1.321	21.48%	1.111	1.382	24.45%	1.079	1.345	24.67%	1.115	1.133	1.61%	18.05%
	Rosolina	Hotels	1.083	1.536	41.82%	1.126	1.382	22.68%	1.110	1.525	37.45%	1.112	1.108	-0.43%	25.38%
		Apartments	N.A.	N.A.	N.A.	N.A.	N.A.	N.A.	N.A.	N.A.	N.A.	N.A.	N.A.	N.A.	N.A.
		B&B	N.A.	N.A.	N.A.	N.A.	N.A.	N.A.	N.A.	N.A.	N.A.	N.A.	N.A.	N.A.	N.A.
		Hostels	N.A.	N.A.	N.A.	N.A.	N.A.	N.A.	N.A.	N.A.	N.A.	N.A.	N.A.	N.A.	N.A.
		TOTAL	N.A.	N.A.	N.A.	1.082	1.475	36.30%	1.298	1.054	-18.81%	1.055	1.046	-0.88%	5.54%
NON-INNOVATIVE CITIES	Rome	Hotels	1.020	1.376	34.87%	1.060	1.347	27.16%	1.059	1.330	25.51%	1.036	1.558	50.37%	34.48%
		Apartments	1.382	1.718	24.36%	1.165	1.494	28.26%	1.153	1.420	23.15%	1.138	1.409	23.79%	24.89%
		B&B	1.101	1.106	0.49%	1.047	1.943	85.50%	1.073	2.143	99.65%	1.154	1.070	-7.25%	44.60%
		Hostels	1.460	1.183	-19.00%	1.263	1.137	-10.02%	1.386	1.258	-9.27%	1.630	1.636	0.35%	-9.49%
		TOTAL	1.240	1.379	11.22%	1.110	1.402	26.33%	1.143	1.426	24.84%	1.191	1.526	28.07%	22.61%
	Sorrento	Hotels	1.284	1.596	24.31%	1.184	1.389	17.37%	1.116	1.280	14.70%	1.156	1.253	8.33%	16.18%
		Apartments	1.068	1.193	11.70%	1.073	1.122	4.50%	1.111	1.222	9.99%	1.097	1.354	23.43%	12.40%
		B&B	1.514	1.454	-3.93%	1.110	1.063	-4.23%	1.155	1.225	6.08%	1.139	2.056	80.48%	19.60%
		Hostels	1.373	N.A.	N.A.	1.040	1.127	8.41%	1.079	1.368	26.72%	1.080	1.215	12.46%	15.86%
		TOTAL	1.279	1.503	17.57%	1.141	1.284	12.51%	1.116	1.275	14.31%	1.133	1.376	21.47%	16.47%
	Total	Hotels	1.129	1.503	33.09%	1.113	1.398	25.64%	1.146	1.297	13.22%	1.090	1.241	13.86%	21.45%
		Apartments	1.225	1.455	18.84%	1.106	1.261	14.01%	1.098	1.300	18.33%	1.118	1.382	23.61%	18.70%
		B&B	1.223	1.216	-0.53%	1.081	1.503	39.02%	1.084	1.500	38.36%	1.146	1.563	36.34%	28.30%
		Hostels	1.313	1.182	-9.98%	1.133	1.244	9.84%	1.181	1.291	9.38%	1.277	1.341	5.01%	3.56%
		TOTAL	1.202	1.401	16.57%	1.111	1.386	24.74%	1.159	1.275	10.04%	1.124	1.270	13.04%	16.10%
				Mean	12.46%		Mean	20.17%		Mean	20.28%		Mean	17.75%	

Source: author's elaboration.

Legend: N.A. means not available.

Finally, results do not show a clear trend regarding price dispersion in innovative cities (Milan and Rosolina) *vs* non-innovative cities (Rome and Sorrento). Also, hostels in innovative cities generally obtain higher price dispersion in OTAs markets whereas this is not true in non-innovative cities. Lastly, whereas price dispersion for apartments and b&b is increasingly positive when the booking horizon is longer, price dispersion in hotels decreases as the booking horizon is longer.

Regarding rating scores, Table 3 shows that rating scores included in OTAs platforms are generally both higher than those in BCT DApps (see mean scores) and more homogenous (see standard deviation scores).

Table 3. Descriptive statistics in online ratings between OTAs and DApps (H2).

		Rating OTAs					Rating BCT				
		Mean	SD	Max	Min	Range	Mean	SD	Max	Min	Range
Score by	Hotel 3*	5.83	2.35	3.80	9.50	5.70	5.02	1.57	3.90	7.80	3.90
	Hotel 4*	6.18	2.54	4.50	9.50	5.00	6.56	2.52	4.40	9.60	5.20
	Hotel 5*	5.87	2.42	4.30	8.80	4.50	6.13	2.66	4.50	9.20	4.70
	Apartments	5.70	2.27	4.30	8.50	4.20	4.50	N.A.	4.50	4.50	0.00
	B&B	5.70	1.64	4.10	8.30	4.20	N.A.	0.00	0.00	0.00	0.00
	Hostels	4.20	0.00	2.60	6.40	3.80	N.A.	0.00	0.00	0.00	0.00
Hotel 3*	Location	6.64	2.36	4.30	9.80	5.50	5.47	1.93	4.00	9.00	5.00
	Staff	6.03	2.26	3.90	9.90	6.00	5.29	1.80	3.50	9.40	5.90
	Cleanliness	6.01	0.79	4.00	9.70	5.70	5.20	1.82	3.90	9.60	5.70
	Comfort	8.38	0.83	7.70	9.40	1.70	3.66	1.08	2.00	5.00	3.00
	Value for money	8.15	2.25	7.50	9.30	1.80	4.33	1.22	2.60	6.00	3.40
	Facilities	6.00	0.73	3.70	9.30	5.60	N.A.	0.00	0.00	0.00	0.00
	Free WiFi	7.95	0.52	7.20	8.80	1.60	3.60	1.08	2.50	5.00	2.50
	Amenities	4.15	0.00	3.50	4.70	1.20	6.40	2.77	4.80	9.60	4.80
Hotel 4*	Location	6.59	2.44	3.60	9.50	5.90	6.66	2.69	4.50	9.60	5.10
	Staff	6.34	2.36	3.60	9.70	6.10	6.76	2.60	4.70	9.80	5.10
	Cleanliness	6.21	1.28	3.60	9.70	6.10	6.03	2.39	4.70	9.60	4.90
	Comfort	8.68	1.21	6.80	9.60	2.80	4.77	1.72	3.20	6.60	3.40
	Value for money	8.28	2.31	6.50	9.10	2.60	6.26	2.41	4.50	9.00	4.50
	Facilities	6.91	0.36	4.50	9.50	5.00	N.A.	0.00	0.00	0.00	0.00
	Free WiFi	9.10	0.41	8.80	9.50	0.70	7.03	2.75	4.50	9.60	5.10
	Amenities	4.44	0.00	3.60	4.80	1.20	5.25	2.63	2.50	8.80	6.30
Hotel 5*	Location	6.65	2.28	4.10	9.40	5.30	6.43	2.37	4.50	9.60	5.10
	Staff	5.79	2.35	3.80	9.10	5.30	5.90	2.42	3.50	9.40	5.90
	Cleanliness	5.93	0.58	4.10	9.40	5.30	5.25	1.82	3.50	8.40	4.90
	Comfort	8.87	0.30	8.20	9.20	1.00	4.00	0.50	3.50	4.50	1.00
	Value for money	8.00	2.37	7.70	8.30	0.60	4.25	1.25	2.60	5.40	2.80
	Facilities	6.35	0.50	3.80	8.90	5.10	4.00	N.A.	4.00	4.00	0.00
	Free WiFi	8.60	0.23	8.10	9.10	1.00	N.A.	0.00	0.00	0.00	0.00
	Amenities	4.30	0.00	4.00	4.60	0.60	5.56	2.55	2.50	8.40	5.90
Apartments	Location	9.45	2.51	9.40	9.50	0.10	N.A.	0.00	0.00	0.00	0.00
	Staff	6.20	2.60	4.30	9.10	4.80	N.A.	0.00	0.00	0.00	0.00
	Cleanliness	6.22	0.49	4.30	9.40	5.10	N.A.	0.00	0.00	0.00	0.00
	Comfort	8.85	0.49	8.50	9.20	0.70	N.A.	0.00	0.00	0.00	0.00
	Value for money	8.45	2.54	8.10	8.80	0.70	N.A.	0.00	0.00	0.00	0.00
	Facilities	6.06	0.92	4.20	9.40	5.20	N.A.	0.00	0.00	0.00	0.00
	Free WiFi	9.35	2.23	8.70	10.00	1.30	N.A.	0.00	0.00	0.00	0.00
	Amenities	2.57	0.00	0.00	4.00	4.00	N.A.	0.00	0.00	0.00	0.00
B&B	Location	8.43	2.52	4.70	9.80	5.10	4.90	0.14	4.80	5.00	0.20
	Staff	6.59	2.41	4.10	9.70	5.60	4.35	0.21	4.20	4.50	0.30
	Cleanliness	6.56	0.87	4.30	9.70	5.40	4.15	1.20	3.30	5.00	1.70
	Comfort	8.90	0.61	7.90	9.50	1.60	3.80	0.99	3.10	4.50	1.40
	Value for money	8.70	2.50	8.00	9.10	1.10	4.50	N.A.	4.50	4.50	0.00
	Facilities	6.58	0.76	3.80	9.60	5.80	N.A.	0.00	0.00	0.00	0.00
	Free WiFi	8.03	0.37	7.50	8.90	1.40	3.50	N.A.	3.50	3.50	0.00
	Amenities	4.50	0.00	4.10	4.90	0.80	N.A.	0.00	0.00	0.00	0.00
Hostels	Location	6.35	2.33	3.40	9.00	5.60	5.60	2.27	4.40	9.00	4.60
	Staff	5.47	2.20	2.90	9.00	6.10	5.45	2.70	3.30	9.40	6.10
	Cleanliness	5.29	1.57	2.60	9.00	6.40	4.38	2.48	1.60	7.60	6.00
	Comfort	7.70	1.00	5.90	8.80	2.90	4.40	1.45	2.90	5.80	2.90
	Value for money	7.83	2.50	6.70	8.60	1.90	4.15	1.41	3.00	6.00	3.00
	Facilities	5.67	0.81	2.40	8.90	6.50	N.A.	0.00	0.00	0.00	0.00
	Free WiFi	7.93	0.83	7.00	8.50	1.50	4.73	2.64	2.40	7.60	5.20
	Amenities	3.73	0.00	2.20	4.40	2.20	N.A.	0.00	0.00	0.00	0.00

Source: author's elaboration.
Legend: N.A. means not available.

However, although general ratings are similar on OTAs *vs* BCT platforms, there are differences mainly focused on some services provided by the lodging accommodations. To begin with, OTAs platforms do not display rating scores about lodging services provided by apartments. Also, additional services like vibe, bar, breakfast, food, room or wellness area are not scored in lodging accommodations that provide these services. Finally, the main differences are focused on both additional services like cleanliness, facilities and free WiFi, and on aspects like comfort or value for money.

Finally, maximum and minimum rating scores are usually higher in OTAs market than in BCT DApps, mainly in the cheapest lodging accommodations (3-star hotel, apartments, b&b and hostels), where differences are higher see Table 3.

Hypotheses Testing. Table 4 collects information regarding dynamic price dispersion between OTAs and DApps in cities located in innovative *vs* non-innovative regions. Results show that price dispersion in cities located in innovative regions is often higher than in non-innovative cities except for hostels. This difference is significant in Wilcoxon test at 1% of significance level ($p < 0.01$), which means that the mean values of price dispersion are not the same into the sample cities located in innovative *vs* non-innovative regions. Therefore, the attributes compared are significantly different and hypothesis 1 cannot be supported.

Table 4. Hypotheses testing using the Wilcoxon test (H1 and H2).

	Negative range			Positive range			Balanced			Test statistics (J)	
	N	Average range	Sum of ranges	N	Average range	Sum of ranges	N	Average range	Sum of ranges	z	Sig. asint. (2-tailed)
H1. No differences on dynamic price dispersion among the lodging accommodations located in Italian innovative versus non-innovative cities between OTAs and BCT markets											
Innovative cities OTAs - Innovative cities BCT	13	24.96	324.50	40ª	27.66	1106.50	0ᵛ			-3.461	0.001
Non-innovative cities OTAs - Non-innovative cities BCT	39	66.44	2591.00	127	88.74	11270.00	0ᵛ			-6.997	0.000
H2. No differences in accommodation ratings on OTAs and BCT platforms											
Rating OTAs - BCT	2ª	3,50	7,00	2ᵇ	1,50	3,00	4			-,730ᶜ	0,465
Rating H 3* OTAs - H 3* BCT	6ᵈ	4,00	24,00	1ᵉ	4,00	4,00	7			-1,690ᶜ	0,091
Rating H 4* OTAs - H 4* BCT	4ᵍ	5,00	20,00	3ʰ	2,67	8,00	7			-1,014ᶜ	0,310
Rating H 5* OTAs - H 5* BCT	5ʲ	4,60	23,00	2ᵏ	2,50	5,00	7			-1,521ᶜ	0,128
Rating APT OTAs - APT BCT	N.A	N.A.	N.A.	N.A.	N.A.	N.A.	N.A.			N.A.	N.A.
Rating BB OTAs - BB BCT	6ᵐ	3,50	21,00	0ⁿ	0,00	0,00	6			-2,201ᶜ	0,028
Rating HOST OTAs - HOST BCT	6ᵖ	3,50	21,00	0ᵠ	0,00	0,00	6			-2,201ᶜ	0,028

Source: author's elaboration.
Legend: a. RatingBCT < RatingOTAS; b. RatingBCT > RatingOTAS; c. RatingBCT = RatingOTAS; d. THREERATBCT < THREERATOTAS; e. THREERATBCT > THREERATOTAS; f. THREERATBCT = THREERATOTAS; g. FOURRATBCT < FOURRATOTAS; h. FOURRATBCT > FOURRATOTAS; i. FOURRATBCT = FOURRATOTAS; j. FIVERATBCT < FIVERATOTAS; k. FIVERATBCT > FIVERATOTAS; l. FIVERATBCT = FIVERATOTAS; m. BBRATBCT < BBRATOTAS; n. BBRATBCT > BBRATOTAS; o. BBRATBCT = BBRATOTAS; p. HOSTELRATBCT < HOSTELRATOTAS; q. HOSTELRATBCT > HOSTELRATOTAS; r. HOSTELRATBCT = HOSTELRATOTAS; s. is based on negative range; t) H3INNOVABCT < H3INNOVAOTAs; u) H3INNOVABCT > H3INNOVAOTAs; v) H3INNOVABCT = H3INNOVAOTAs; w) H3NOINNOVBCT < H3NOINNOVOTAs; x) H3NOINNOVBCT > H3NOINNOVOTAs; y) H3NOINNOVBCT = H3NOINNOVOTAs. N.A. means Non-available data.

As for the analysis of the rating scores, Wilcoxon test confirms the existence of differences in the services provided by lower-quality lodging accommodations. Except for apartments which are not scored in the OTAs platforms, hypothesis 2 cannot be supported for the particular case of 3-star hotels (significance level at 10% -p > 0.1-), b&b (significance level at 1% -p > 0.01-) and hostels (significance level at 5% -p > 0.05-). The highest differences in the rating scores of the services provided are focused on b&b and hostels accommodations. By contrast, differences for general rating scores in all sample accommodations are not statically different.

4 Discussion and Conclusions

The effective development of new innovative services will be increasingly important for the hospitality industry to recover its financial health in the post-COVID19 period, especially as a result of not only rapid developments in new technologies but also the changes in customer needs or preferences [46]. This research has put the focus on the implementation of DApps for room booking services, analysing the impact of these technologies on both market competition and attraction of new customers to lodging accommodation, which will increase the city revenues. The empirical analysis has been scrutinised in Italian sample cities examining price dispersion in room bookings and service quality of lodging accommodations measured by customers' ratings of the different hospitality services provided.

On the whole, findings demonstrate that BCT implementation can help lodging accommodations to attract a higher number of visitors to the city, lowering room prices and improving the service quality. In particular, price dispersion is generally higher in BCT markets in all sample cities and booking horizons. Therefore, the implementation of BCT helps tourism business to increase competition into the market and, could help SMEs to survive and recover their financial health in the post-COVID19 situation. This finding requires city governments to support the implementation of this ET which will allow the economic recovery of the city: a) supporting SMEs to be competitive in the hospitality market; and b) attracting more visitors to the city increasing the business into the city and city revenues.

Future research should therefore analyse the different technological investments of city governments and its impact on both the economy and, the social area of the urban context. Also, city governments could promote the implementation of ETs through rewarding programs. For example, interested city governments could provide financial compensations to citizens that comply some sustainable practices. The required transactions for these compensations could be carried out by blockchain to meet trust, security and timeliness [47]. This way, ETs could be introduced into the culture of the city (business and citizens) becoming it smart.

On another hand, findings demonstrate that high-quality hotels obtain no differences in their rating scores comparing OTAs *vs* BCT hospitality markets, mainly due to the high-quality accommodation services they provide. Nonetheless, the lower quality in lodging accommodations, the higher differences regarding rating scores. It could indicate that the perceptions of customers about accommodation service quality are only clearly different when a determinate level of service quality is not reached.

Besides, findings indicate that main differences in rating scores among sample lodging accommodations (higher rating scores in OTAs markets) are based on both the additional services they provide (cleanliness, facilities and free WiFi) and on aspects like comfort or value for money. This is especially true for lower-quality accommodations, indicating that customers searching lower-quality accommodations using DApps could be perhaps more focused on chosing their lodging accommodation by room price than on the additional services provided by the lodging accommodation.

Therefore, it would be relevant for city governments to create innovative hubs into the city for implementing ETs in tourism business with the aim at increasing the service quality and innovation, as a main source for higher competition and touristic attractivity. Future research could thus analyse whether innovation hubs in smart cities have led to quality improvement in tourism services and its impact on the economy of the urban context.

In brief, ETs have come to be main drivers for service innovation and service quality in the urban context. City management should put attention to these technologies to increase the smartness of the city and improve the resilience of cities to face disasters like the COVID19 pandemic situation, preparing business to fast-track recover their financial health and the normal business activity of the city.

References

1. Jiang, Y., Wen, J.: Effects of COVID-19 on hotel marketing and management: a perspective article. Int. J. Contemp. Hosp. Manag. **32**(8), 2563–2573 (2020)
2. Škare, M., Soriano, D.R., Porada-Rochoń, M.: Impact of COVID-19 on the travel and tourism industry. Technol. Forecast. Soc. Change **163**, 120469 (2021)
3. OECD Homepage. https://read.oecd-ilibrary.org/view/?ref=124_124984-7uf8nm95se&title=Covid-19_Tourism_Policy_Responses. Accessed 26 Feb 2021
4. WTTC Homepage. https://wttc.org/Portals/0/Documents/Reports/2020/To%20Recovery%20and%20Beyond-The%20Future%20of%20Travel%20Tourism%20in%20the%20Wake%20of%20COVID-19.pdf?ver=2021-02-25-183120-543. Accessed 10 Feb 2021
5. Knight, D.W., Xiong, L., Lan, W., Gong, J.: Impact of COVID-19: research note on tourism and hospitality sectors in the epicenter of Wuhan and Hubei Province, China. Int. J. Contemp. Hosp. Manag. **32**(12), 3705–3719 (2020)
6. Romão, J.: Variety smart specialization and tourism competitiveness. Sustainability **12**(14), 5765 (2020)
7. da Costa Liberato, P.M., Alén-González, E., de Azevedo Liberato, D.F.V.: Digital technology in a smart tourist destination: the case of Porto. J. Urban Technol. **25**(1), 75–97 (2018)
8. Rodríguez-Antón, J.M., Alonso-Almeida, M.D.M.: COVID-19 impacts and recovery strategies: the case of the hospitality industry in Spain. Sustainability **12**(20), 8599 (2020)
9. Bagloee, S.A., Heshmati, M., Dia, H., Ghaderi, H., Pettit, C., Asadi, M.: Blockchain: the operating system of smart cities. Cities **112**, 103104 (2021)
10. Flecha-Barrio, M.D., Palomo, J., Figueroa-Domecq, C., Segovia-Perez, M.: Blockchain implementation in hotel management. In: Neidhardt, J., Wörndl, W. (eds.) Information and Communication Technologies in Tourism 2020, pp. 255–266. Springer, Cham (2020). https://doi.org/10.1007/978-3-030-36737-4_21
11. Nam, K., Dutt, C.S., Chathoth, P., Khan, M S.: Blockchain technology for smart city and smart tourism: latest trends and challenges. Asia Pac. J. Tour. Res. **26**, 1–15 (2019)

12. Seigneur, J.M.: Towards Geneva crypto-friendly smart tourism. https://archive-ouverte.unige. ch/unige:103406. Accessed 15 Mar 2015
13. Ozdemir, A.I., Ar, I.M., Erol, I.: Assessment of blockchain applications in travel and tourism industry. Qual. Quant. **54**(5–6), 1549–1563 (2019). https://doi.org/10.1007/s11135-019-009 01-w
14. Antoniadis, I., Spinthiropoulos, K., Kontsas, S.: Blockchain applications in tourism and tourism marketing: a short review. In: Kavoura, A., Kefallonitis, E., Theodoridis, P. (eds.) Strategic Innovative Marketing and Tourism. SPBE, pp. 375–384. Springer, Cham (2020). https://doi.org/10.1007/978-3-030-36126-6_41
15. Kubickova, M.: The impact of government policies on destination competitiveness in developing economies. Curr. Issue Tour. **22**(6), 619–642 (2017)
16. Brent, J.R., Ritchie, J.R.B., Crouch, G.I.: The competitive destination: a sustainability perspective. Tour. Manage. **21**(1), 1–7 (2000)
17. Russo, A.P., Scarnato, A.: "Barcelona in common": a new urban regime for the 21st-century tourist city? J. Urban Aff. **40**(4), 455–474 (2018)
18. Rucci, A.C.: Accessibility as a competitive factor in touristic smart cities. In: 7th Conference of the International Association for Tourism Economics Proceedings, 3–6 September 2019, pp. 9–10, Universidad Nacional de La Plata, La Plata, Argentina (2019)
19. Faraji, A., Khodadadi, M., Nematpour, M., Abidizadegan, S., Yazdani, H.R.: Investigating the positive role of urban tourism in creating sustainable revenue opportunities in the municipalities of large-scale cities: the case of Iran. Int. J. Tour. Cities **7**(1), 177–199 (2020)
20. Buhalis, D., Amaranggana, A.: Smart tourism destinations. In: Xiang, Z., Tussyadiah, I. (eds.) Information and Communication Technologies in Tourism 2014, pp. 553–564. Springer, Cham (2014). https://doi.org/10.1007/978-3-319-03973-2_40
21. Teixeira, R.M., Andreassi, T., Köseoglu, M.A., Okumus, F.: How do hospitality entrepreneurs use their social networks to access resources? Evidence from the lifecycle of small hospitality enterprises. Int. J. Hosp. Manag. **79**, 158–167 (2019)
22. Lee, H.C., Pan, H.L., Chung, C.C.: The study of destination image, service quality, satisfaction and behavioral intention–an example of Dapeng Bay National Scenic Area. Int. J. Organ. Innov. **11**(3), 25 (2019)
23. Becerra, M., Santaló, J., Silva, R.: Being better vs. being different: differentiation, competition, and pricing strategies in the Spanish hotel industry. Tour. Manage. **34**, 71–79 (2013)
24. Hollebeek, L., Rather, R.A.: Service innovativeness and tourism customer outcomes. Int. J. Contemp. Hosp. Manag. **31**(11), 4227–4246 (2019)
25. Zach, F.J., Nicolau, J.L., Sharma, A.: Disruptive innovation, innovation adoption and incumbent market value: Case Airbnb. Ann. Tour. Res. **80**, 102818 (2020)
26. Hill, C.W., Rothaermel, F.T.: The performance of incumbent firms in the face of radical technological innovation. Acad. Manag. Rev. **28**(2), 257–274 (2003)
27. WTCF Homepage. https://prefeitura.pbh.gov.br/sites/default/files/estrutura-de-governo/bel otur/2020/wtcf-global-report-on-smart-tourism-in-cities.pdf. Accessed 21 Mar 2021
28. Leydesdorff, L., Cucco, I.: Regions, innovation systems, and the North-South divide in Italy. El profesional de la información **28**(2), 1–15 (2018)
29. Durst, S., Mention, A.L., Poutanen, P.: Service innovation and its impact: what do we know about? Investigaciones europeas de dirección y economía de la empresa **21**(2), 65–72 (2015)
30. Eloranta, T.: Online review site data on service innovation. Int. J. E-Serv. Mobile Appl. **8**(4), 20–34 (2016)
31. Fang, B., Ye, Q., Kucukusta, D., Law, R.: Analysis of the perceived value of online tourism reviews: influence of readability and reviewer characteristics. Tour. Manage. **52**, 498–506 (2016)
32. Sparks, B.A., Browning, V.: The impact of online reviews on hotel booking intentions and perception of trust. Tour. Manage. **32**(6), 1310–1323 (2011)

33. Ye, F., Xia, Q., Zhang, M., Zhan, Y., Li, Y.: Harvesting online reviews to identify the competitor set in a service business: evidence from the hotel industry. J. Serv. Res. 1–27 (2020)
34. Kizildag, M., et al.: Blockchain: a paradigm shift in business practices. Int. J. Contemp. Hosp. Manag. **32**(3), 953–975 (2019)
35. UNTWO Homepage. https://www.e-unwto.org/doi/pdf/10.18111/9789284419470. Accessed 19 Mar 2021
36. European Commission Homepage. https://ec.europa.eu/eurostat/statistics-explained/index. php?title=Tourism_statistics_-_nights_spent_at_tourist_accommodation_establishments. Accessed 19 Mar 2021
37. Sánchez-Pérez, M., Illescas-Manzano, M.D., Martínez-Puertas, S.: Modeling hotel room pricing: a multi-country analysis. Int. J. Hosp. Manag. **79**, 89–99 (2019)
38. WTTC Homepage. https://www.oliverwyman.com/content/dam/oliver-wyman/v2/pub lications/2020/To_Recovery_and_Beyond-The_Future_of_Travel_and_Tourism_in_the_ Wake_of_COVID-19.pdf. Accessed 19 Mar 2021
39. National Institute of Statistics Homepage. https://www.istat.it/it/files/2018/11/report-movime nto-turistico-anno-2017.pdf. Accessed 15 Sep 2021
40. Foris, D., Crihălmean, N., Pănoiu, T.M.: The new technologies and sustainable practices in hospitality. Bull. Transilv. Univ. Brasov Econ. Sci. Ser. V **13**(2), 65–74 (2020)
41. Statista Homepage. https://www.statista.com/statistics/647374/worldwide-blockchain-wal let-users/. Accessed 15 Sep 2021
42. Prieto, M.: The State of Online Travel Agencies. https://medium.com/traveltechmedia/the-state-of-online-travel-agencies-2019-8b188e8661ac. Accessed 15 Sep 2021.
43. Confesercenti Homepage. http://www.assohotelconfesercenti.it/allegati/4/2/426/allegati/Ind agine%20Ufficio%20Economico.pdf. Accessed Accessed 15 Sep 2021
44. Good, P.: Permutation, Parametric, and Bootstrap Tests of Hypotheses 3. Springer, New York (2005)
45. Wilks, S.S.: Mathematical Statistics. John Wiley & Sons, Inc., New York (1962)
46. Kitsios, F., Kamariotou, M.: Service innovation process digitization: areas for exploitation and exploration. J. Hosp. Tour. Technol. **12**(1), 4–18 (2019)
47. Gupta, Y.S., Mukherjee S.: A study on smart cities using blockchain. In: Dawn, S., Balas, V., Esposito, A., Gope, S. (eds.) Intelligent Techniques and Applications in Science and Technology. ICIMSAT 2019. Learning and Analytics in Intelligent Systems, vol. 12, pp. 111–118. Springer, Cham (2020). https://doi.org/10.1007/978-3-030-42363-6_13

Understanding the Factors that Affect Smart City and Community Initiatives: Lessons from Local Governments in the United States

Xiaoyi Yerden[1] , J. Ramon Gil-Garcia[1,2](✉) , Mila Gasco-Hernandez[1] , and G. Brian Burke[1]

[1] University at Albany, State University of New York, Albany, NY 12222, USA
{xzhao6,jgil-garcia,mgasco,gburke2}@albany.edu
[2] Universidad de Las Americas Puebla, Cholula, Puebla, Mexico

Abstract. With urbanization, cities around the world have experienced increasingly complex issues that are difficult to solve using traditional strategies. So, many local governments have started smart city initiatives in order to address community issues, improve quality of life, achieve sustainable development, and, overall, make their cities smarter. As a multidimensional concept, smart city contains different components. In addition, to successfully implement smart city initiatives, local governments need to take multiple factors into consideration. Based on a survey of local governments in the United States, this article identifies what factors affect smart city and community initiatives. Overall, the analysis shows that the level of economic development, the existence of a smart city office, the availability of local government funding, the skill level of local government staff, adopting a collaborative approach, and citizens' current IT skills all have a significant positive impact on the extent that a local government invests in smart city projects. In addition, city governments invest in significantly more types of smart city projects than villages.

Keywords: Smart city · Local government · Influential factors · Governance · Citizen

1 Introduction

With increasing urbanization, cities have experienced new issues that could be described as wicked or tangled and that are difficult to address using traditional models and strategies [1, 23]. The smart city concept has emerged and been adopted by many local governments as a strategy to look for alternative solutions to better address community issues, improve quality of life, achieve sustainable development, and, overall, make cities smarter. In the last two decades, when talking about smart city development, it mainly emphasized the utilization of information and communication technologies (ICTs) to improve city infrastructures and services, and most of the existing definitions then viewed technology as one of the main components of smart cities [2]. More recently, researchers have started to recognize the importance of social aspects in smart cities and advocate to adopt a socio-technical view [3–5]. Currently, even though there is still no consensus on the definition of smart city, it seems that there is an agreement that smart city is a multidimensional and multifaceted concept [3, 6, 21].

Recognizing the different contexts in which smartness development occurs (villages, towns, cities and megacities, etc.) and conceptualizing smartness beyond technology and closely related to people's living in different communities, the discussion of smartness development has not been limited to the urban environment [18, 22], the concept of smart community has been more discussed and was defined by Nam & Pardo [3] as "a community broadly ranging from a small neighborhood to a nation-wide community of common or shared interest, whose members, organizations, and governing institutions are working in partnership to use IT to transform their circumstances in significant ways" [pp. 286].

In addition to research that discusses the characteristics of smart cities and smart communities, more recent studies have focused on how to develop smart cities and communities. For example, Oktaria et al. [7] concluded that services in different aspects, such as transportation, health, safety, education, and housing are all needed in the development of smart cities. Mora and colleagues [8, 9], based on an extensive literature review, summarized a set of dichotomies that question whether smart city development should be based on: (1) a technology-led or holistic strategy, (2) a double or quadruple-helix model of collaboration, (3) a top-down or bottom-up approach, and (4) a mono-dimensional or integrated intervention logic. However, there is still a need for empirical studies that focus on the factors that influence smart city development across a wide range of cities and communities. This article contributes to filling this gap by surveying local governments in the United States and analyzing their perspectives on what factors are affecting smart city development in their communities.

This paper is organized into six sections, including the foregoing introduction. Section two presents our review of existing literature, which includes a conceptual model of smart city and community development and presents the hypotheses of this study. Section three briefly describes the research approach used in this paper, including the design and administration of a national survey to local governments across the United Sates. The section also provides some details about the survey responses and our analysis approach. Section four presents our main results as a regression analysis on the impact of multiple factors on the development of smart cities and communities. Section five discusses some of our main findings and compare them with previous research. Finally, section six presents some concluding remarks and suggests ideas for future research.

2   Factors that Affect Smart City Development

The development of smart cities and communities is affected by multiple success factors and several studies have explored some of those factors of smart city and community development. For example, recognizing the uniqueness of different cities, Harms [10] proposed six critical success factors that can be used when developing a smart city strategy, which go from a clear vision to a city-wide smart strategy. Sujata and colleagues [11] designed a framework of developing smart city initiatives with identify six significant pillars: social, management, economic, legal, technology and sustainability. Myeong and colleagues [12] examined the internal and external determinants of smart cities and their priorities through an analytic hierarchy process analysis, they suggested that citizen participation with multi-communication channels should be included in the process of smart city development. Based on a few of these previous studies [11, 12, 14], we are grouping the factors into five categories: 1) external environment; 2) organization; 3) governance; 4) technology; and 5) citizen. In addition, to strengthen our model, we are also considering literature on the development of e-government at the local level [13–15, 17]. Figure 1 shows the conceptual model that guides our study.

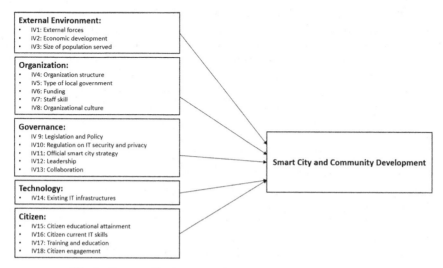

Fig. 1. Factors affecting smart city and community development

External Environment. With the urbanization, cities and communities are facing great challenges in solving complex and diverse urban problems [12]. In the meantime, government are also facing increasing and changing demands from the citizens [13], both external pressures force the government to change its traditional working methods and start to adopt smart city approach to address community issues and better serve the citizens [1, 12, 23]. Previous research also mentioned that the diversity in cities and communities, especially the level of economic development (usually refers to the citizen median household income [14]), greatly impacts the opportunities for developing and implementing new government initiatives, in this case, the implementation of the smart city initiatives [1, 14-15]. Communities that are in disadvantage of economic development, may be more eager to start smart city development but may face more challenges in doing so due to limited resources compared to the communities who are rich in funding and resources. The size of population served by the local government is another factor that was mentioned to have an impact on adopting IT innovation [14]. Based on this, we hypothesize that:

H1. Pressures to solve complex problems and increasing demands from citizens positively influence the development of smart cities and communities.

H2. A higher level of economic development positively influences the development of smart cities and communities.

H3. The size of the population served by a local government influences the development of smart cities and communities.

Organization. Local government is the main actor that leads the smart city and community development. The diversity of local governments in different cities and communities is found to have an influence in smart city and community development. The diversity mainly shows in the organization structure, the types of local governments, funding, staff skills, and organization culture. First, creating a dedicated and high-power smart city office helps form and lead collaborative efforts among different stakeholders in developing smart cities and communities [16]. Type of local government refers to whether the local government is in a county, a city, a town, a village, etc. It is a factor that was found to have an impact on adopting IT innovation [14, 22], which could be seen as related to smart city initiatives. Funding is an important and necessary financial resource that supports smart city and community development. The availability of funding on smart city development influences the available options and possibilities in implementing smart city initiatives [14-15, 17]. Project leaders and team members with strong technical skills and expertise were identify as important factors in adopting IT innovation [16-17]. Organization culture that is in favor of innovation is also mentioned as a facilitator in government innovation [15]. Based on this, we hypothesize that:

H4. The existence of a smart city office within the local government positively influences the development of smart cities and communities.

H5. The type of local government influences the development of smart cities and communities.

H6. The availability of local government funding positively influences the development of smart cities and communities.

H7. A higher skill level of local government staff positively influences the development of smart cities and communities.

H8. An innovative organization culture in a local government positively influences the development of smart cities and communities.

Governance. Governance is defined as "regimes of laws, administrative rules, judicial rulings, and practices that constrain, prescribe, and enable government activity, where such activity is broadly defined as the production and delivery of publicly supported goods and services." (p. 235) [1]. Among previous studies, legislation and policy, official strategy, leadership, and collaboration are the most mentioned factors related to governance that will influence the development of smart city and community. To smooth the implementation of smart city initiatives, it is important to remove legal and regulatory barriers and establish up-to-date legal framework and supportive policies to guide the practice of smartness development [1, 13–15, 17]. The adoption of ICTs in smart city development provides opportunities for innovation, but could also raise people's concerns about privacy and information security. The availability of appropriate regulations and policies could help alleviate this problem [1, 15, 17]. The existence of an official strategy provides a clear vision that helps maintain the direction of smart city development and specific plans on how cities use their resources to achieve their goals of smart city development [10, 13, 15, 17]. The presence of formal and informal leadership is important for good governance and the top management support is important for government innovation [1, 14]. Supportive leadership in leading smart city development is related to good ICT knowledge and great social skills [12, 13, 16, 17, 22]. Collaboration among different stakeholders is important to smart city development. Adopting a participative approach that encourages co-creation and co-development could be seen as key to the success of smart city initiatives [13, 15, 16]. Based on this, we hypothesize that: H9. The existence of supportive legislation and policy positively influences the development of smart cities and communities.

H10. The existence of regulations and policies that protect information privacy and security positively influences the development of smart cities and communities.

H11. The existence of an official smart city strategy positively influences the development of smart cities and communities.

H12. Supportive leadership in a local government positively influences the development of smart cities and communities.

H13. A collaborative approach positively influences the development of smart cities and communities.

Technology. The development of ICTs is the foundation of smart city development. Using ITCs to address urban problem is the major task in development smart cities and communities. The existence of a reliable ICT infrastructure makes it easier to successfully implement innovative initiatives, because it provides supports to further developing existing systems and services [1, 12, 15]. Based on this, we hypothesize that:

H14. The existence of a reliable ICT infrastructure positively influences the development of smart cities and communities.

Citizen. In addition to beneficiaries of smart city development, citizens should also be seen as important actors in the design of those initiatives [19, 20]. Citizen's educational attainment and IT skills are often mentioned as factors that influence citizen's acceptance and adoption of government innovative services. In the context of smart city development, these two factors may also affect citizen's abilities to participate in the development of smart cities and communities [14, 15, 17, 23]. Training and education are also important strategies to improve citizens' readiness in understanding and participating in developing smart cities and communities [15, 18]. Increased citizen participation could also be seen as essential to enhance democracy, since citizens are able to express their needs and opinions for smart city initiatives to truly address community needs [1, 12]. Based on this, we hypothesize that:

H15. A higher citizen educational attainment positively influences the development of smart cities and communities.

H16. A higher level of citizen IT skills positively influences the development of smart cities and communities.

H17. The availability of training and education opportunities for citizens positively influences the development of smart cities and communities.

H18. Citizen engagement positively influences the development of smart cities and communities.

3   Research Approach

3.1   Survey Design

For testing these hypotheses, a survey was designed and distributed to local government leaders and IT professionals across the United States, since these are the type of actors that are often involved in the development of smart cities and communities. The survey was sent through a SurveyMonkey email invitation from September to October, 2020. Reminders were sent to non-responders on a weekly basis, and follow-up phone calls were conducted with 10% of the sample randomly. Later, we also shared the survey link with local government associations across the United States and asked them to share the survey link with their local government members on our behalf (from November to December, 2020). In total, we received 167 responses. Before we distributed the survey, we conducted two pretests and one pilot test with 5% of the sample (N = 243) to assess and adjust the survey instrument and administration process.

The questions included in the survey were based on the model presented in Fig. 1. Among the independent variables, some were measured using scaled-response questions (Likert scale 1–10). The value of external forces is the average score of its two indicators, namely urban problem and citizen demand. Funding (availability) was measured by the extent of adequate funds for smart city development. Staff skill was measured by the level of skills and knowledge of the local government staff that support smart city development. Organization culture was measured by how much it supports innovation. Legislation and policy was measured as the average score of the availability of formal, clear, up-to-date laws and specific policies. Regulation on IT security and privacy was measured as the average score of protective regulation on IT security and privacy. Leadership was measured as the average score of leaders' ICTs knowledge, how much he/she was respected within the local governments, and the existence of informal leaders. Collaboration was measured as the average score of internal collaboration among local government departments, and external collaboration between the local government and other community stakeholders. Existing IT infrastructure was measured as the availability of reliable and integrated technology infrastructures. Citizen current IT skills was measured by the level of citizens' digital literacy and skills. Training and education was measured as the availability of training opportunities for citizens to improve their digital skills. Citizen engagement were measured using the extent that citizen participate in designing and implementing smart city initiatives.

Some variables were measured using open-ended questions, such as the size of population served by the community, the percentage of funding that the local government has dedicated to smart city development, and the type of the local government. Some were measured using multiple-choice questions. For example, we were asking whether they have a smart city office that supports the smartness development in their community, and whether they have an official smart city strategy that guides their smartness development. Economic development and citizen educational attainment were variables measured using secondary data from the Census.[1] The dependent variable smart city and community development was measured by the total amount of types of smart city projects that the local government has invested in.

---

[1] Source: US Census Bureau 2015–2019 American Community Survey 5-Year Estimates.

3.2 Sample and Methods

For the 167 responses that we received, we used the multiple imputation technique to address missing data in scale-response and open-ended questions. In the end, 143 responses were used in our descriptive analysis and 98 responses were used in the regression analysis. Among the local governments that participated in our survey, about half of the local governments are cities. One third of them has an annual budget that is between 5 to 10 million dollars. About 20% of the respondents are town managers. About 40% of them have less than five year of experience in their current position. In this study, we first conducted descriptive analysis on the variables included in the model, then a multiple regression was conducted to test which factor has a significant impact on the development of smart cities and communities.

4 Results

Table 1 shows the descriptive analysis of the factors and dependent variable that we included in this study. We can see that among the samples in our study, the average number of the types of smart city projects that the local government has invested is still quite limited (less than 4). Less than 17% of the local governments have a smart city department that supports their smartness development, and less than 12% of them have an official smart city strategy to guide their smartness development. About the influential factors, protective regulations and policies on IT security and privacy exist in most of the local governments, and citizens' participating in designing and implementing smart city/community initiatives is the least mentioned by local governments.

Before hypothesis testing, all the assumptions were checked, including linear relationship between independent variables and the dependent variable, independence of errors, multicollinearity, normality, and homoscedasticity of the errors. Table 2 summarizes the results of the multiple regression.

We can see that in this model, 42.4% of the variance in the local governments' investment in smart city projects can be explained by all these factors included in the model, once adjusting for the number of variables included. Looking at the impact of each individual factor, the result shows that economic development ($\beta = .403, p = .005$), organization structure ($\beta = .186, p = .068$), staff skills ($\beta = .355, p = .023$), percentage of funding ($\beta = .204, p = .031$), collaboration ($\beta = .210, p = .081$) and citizen current IT skills ($\beta = .301, p = .017$) all have a significant positive impact on the extent that local governments invest in smart city projects. And compared to city governments, villages have significant less investment in smart city projects ($\beta = -260, p = .012$). Overall, hypotheses 2, 4, 5, 6, 7, 13 and 16 are supported by the data from this study.

5 Discussion

This quantitative study was conducted to investigate what factors have a significant impact on the development of smart cities and communities. Based on the results of multiple regression, the level of economic development, the existence of a smart city office, the availability of local government funding, the skill level of local government

Table 1. Descriptive statistic of independent and dependent variables

Variables	Mean/Percentage	Sd. dev.
DV: Smart city projects (0–10)	3.682	2.059
IV1: External forces	6.082	1.980
IV2: Economic development	61131.694	26592.384
IV3: Size of population served	43438.174	80712.729
IV4: Organization structure	Yes: 16.8% No: 83.2%	
IV5: Type of local government (Dummy variables)	County: 12.6% Township: 2.1% Town: 19.6% Borough: 3.5% Village: 13.3%	
IV6.1: Adequate funding	3.874	2.468
IV6.2: Percentage of funding (0–100)	4.481	6.413
IV7: Staff skill	4.907	2.418
IV8: Organizational culture	5.412	2.351
IV9: Legislation and Policy	3.535	2.041
IV10: Regulation on IT security and privacy	6.493	2.061
IV11: Official smart city strategy	Yes: 11.8% No: 88.2%	
IV12: Leadership	4.772	2.140
IV13: Collaboration	6.168	2.147
IV14: Existing IT infrastructure	6.036	2.527
IV15: Citizen educational attainment (0–1)	.880	.070
IV16: Citizen current IT skills	5.094	2.012
IV17: Training and education	4.767	2.259
IV18: Citizen engagement	3.482	2.268

staff, adopting a collaborative approach, and citizens' current IT skills all show significant positive impact on the extent that a local government invests in smart city projects. And there is a significant difference between city governments' investment in smart city projects and village governments' investment. Consistent with previous research [15], the level of the economic development, as one of the elements in the domain of external environment, is proven to have a significant positive impact on the development of smart cities and communities. Communities with high level of economic development usually have funding and resources, which help them develop the necessary infrastructure and capabilities, especially IT-related, to support the development of smart cities and communities.

Table 2. Results of the regression analysis: smart city development

	Unstandardized coefficients		Standardized coefficients	
	B	Std. error	Beta	Sig.
(Constant)	4.061	2.693		.136
IV1: External forces	.040	.094	.039	.669
IV2: Economic development	3.120E-5	.000	.403	.005***
IV3: Size of population served	5.126E-7	.000	.020	.857
IV4: Organization structure	1.005	.543	.186	.068*
County	.420	.557	.072	.453
Township	−1.951	1.304	−.135	.139
Town	−.364	.546	−.064	.507
Borough	−1.198	1.268	−.083	.348
Village	−1.519	.587	−.260	.012**
IV6.1: Adequate funding	−.205	.150	−.246	.175
IV6.2: Percentage of funding	.066	.030	.204	.031**
IV7: Staff skill	.303	.130	.355	.023**
IV8: Organizational culture	−.015	.128	−.017	.906
IV9: Legislation and Policy	−.181	.156	−.179	.251
IV10: Regulation on IT security and privacy	−.198	.125	−.198	.117
IV11: Official smart city strategy	−.551	.626	−.085	.382
IV12: Leadership	−.067	.219	−.070	.760
IV13: Collaboration	.201	.114	.210	.081*
IV14: Existing IT infrastructure	−.008	.086	−.010	.924
IV15: Citizen educational attainment	−5.658	3.491	−.192	.109
IV16: Citizen current IT skills	.308	.126	.301	.017**
IV17: Training and education	.051	.098	.056	.607
IV18: Citizen engagement	.266	.171	.294	.124
R^2: .560				
Adjusted R^2: .424				

Note: *$p < 0.10$, **$p < 0.05$, ***$p < 0.01$

Our results are also consistent with previous research that argue that the different capabilities and resources of local governments lead to different performance in terms of the development of smart cities and communities [14–17]. In our study of local governments, having a dedicated smart city office, more funding dedicated to smart city development. and staff with higher skills all prove to have a significant positive impact on the development of smart cities and communities. Villages seem to invest in significant fewer smart city projects than city governments, which may be due to a lack of financial and human resources or the fact that they have different needs in their communities. Collaboration among different stakeholders, as one of the most mentioned governance factors by previous research [10–13, 15, 16], has a significant (although at the 0.10

level) positive impact on the development of smart cities and communities. A holistic collaborative approach in developing smart cities and communities could help mobilize multidisciplinary resources to better address issues and make a community smarter.

Citizens are not only final users, but also participants in smart cities [19, 20]. Their IT skills show a significant positive impact on the development of smart cities and communities. This finding is consistent with previous research that emphasized the importance of citizens' IT skills which not only affect citizens' awareness of the smart city concept, but also their abilities to participate in developing smart cities and communities and to use smart city programs and services [14, 15, 18, 23]. It is somewhat unexpected that none of the variables related to the governance category, with the exception of collaboration, has a significant impact on the development of smart cities and communities in our study. For instance, several previous studies have stated that supportive legislation and regulation, the existence of an official smart city strategy, and supportive leadership are all factors that will benefit the development of smart cities and communities [10, 12, 14–17]. However, from these variables only collaboration was statistically significant in our study.

6 Conclusion

Local governments have adopted smart city strategies to face a variety of challenges in their communities. Previous research has identified factors related to external environment, organization, governance, technology and citizens as all having an impact on the development of smart cities and communities. This study shows that the level of economic development, the existence of a smart city office, the availability of local government funding, the skill level of local government staff, adopting a collaborative approach, and citizens' current IT skills all have a significant positive impact on the extent to which a local government invests in smart city projects. In addition, city governments invest in significantly more smart city projects than villages.

The findings are based on a national survey to local governments across the United States. However, at least in part due to the COVID-19 situation, we had a very low response rate. Therefore, the results should be further tested in different context and attempting to have a higher response rate. In addition, future studies should be conducted to refine the constructs in the model and re-test the influence of these factors with samples from different countries or different levels of government in the United States. Finally, in-depth case studies should be also conducted to better understand how and why these factors influence the implementation of smart city initiatives in different cities and communities around the world.

Acknowledgement. This project was supported by the Grant No. LG-96-17-0144-17 awarded by the Institute of Museum and Library Services (IMLS). The views and opinions expressed in this paper are those of the authors and do not necessarily reflect the views of IMLS.

References

1. Chourabi, H., et al.: Understanding smart cities: an integrative framework. In: 45th Hawaii International Conference on System Sciences, pp. 2289–2297. IEEE Press, New York (2012). https://doi.org/10.1109/HICSS.2012.615
2. Alawadhi, S., et al.: building understanding of smart city initiatives. In: Scholl, H.J., Janssen, M., Wimmer, M.A., Moe, C.E., Flak, L.S. (eds.) EGOV 2012. LNCS, vol. 7443, pp. 40–53. Springer, Heidelberg (2012). https://doi.org/10.1007/978-3-642-33489-4_4
3. Nam, T., Pardo, T.A.: Conceptualizing smart city with dimensions of technology, people, and institutions. In: 12th Annual International Digital Government Research Conference on Digital Government Innovation in Challenging Times - dg. o '11, p. 282. ACM Press, College Park (2011). https://doi.org/10.1145/2037556.2037602
4. Gasco, M.: What makes a city smart? Lessons from Barcelona. In: 49th Hawaii International Conference on System Sciences, pp. 2983–2989. IEEE Press, New York (2016). https://doi.org/10.1109/HICSS.2016.373
5. Giffinger, R., Fertner, C., Kramar, H., Kalasek, R., Pichler-Milanovic, N., Meijers, E.: Smart cities - ranking of European medium-sized cities. Vienna University of Technology (2007)
6. Gil-Garcia, J.R., Pardo, T.A., Nam, T.: What makes a city smart? Identifying core components and proposing an integrative and comprehensive conceptualization. IP. **20**, 61–87 (2015). https://doi.org/10.3233/IP-150354
7. Oktaria, D., Suhardi, Kurniawan, N.B.: Smart city services: a systematic literature review. In: 2017 International Conference on Information Technology Systems and Innovation, pp. 206–213. IEEE Press, New York (2017). https://doi.org/10.1109/ICITSI.2017.8267944
8. Mora, L., Deakin, M., Reid, A.: Combining co-citation clustering and text-based analysis to reveal the main development paths of smart cities. Technol. Forecast. Soc. Chang. **142**, 56–69 (2019). https://doi.org/10.1016/j.techfore.2018.07.019
9. Mora, L., Deakin, M., Reid, A.: Strategic principles for smart city development: a multiple case study analysis of European best practices. Technol. Forecast. Soc. Chang. **142**, 70–97 (2019). https://doi.org/10.1016/j.techfore.2018.07.035
10. Harms, J.: Critical success factors for a smart city strategy. In: 25th Twenty Student Conference on IT, pp. 1–8 (2016)
11. Joshi, S., Saxena, S., Godbole, T.: Shreya: developing smart cities: an integrated framework. Procedia Comput. Sci. **93**, 902–909 (2016). https://doi.org/10.1016/j.procs.2016.07.258
12. Myeong, S., Jung, Y., Lee, E.: A Study on determinant factors in smart city development: an analytic hierarchy process analysis. Sustainability **10**(8), 1–17 (2018). https://doi.org/10.3390/su10082606
13. Nurdin, N., Stockdale, R., Scheepers, H.: Understanding organizational barriers influencing local electronic government adoption and implementation: the electronic government implementation framework. J. Theor. Appl. Electron. Commer. Res. **6**(3), 5–6 (2011). https://doi.org/10.4067/S0718-18762011000300003
14. Haneem, F., Kama, N.: Recent progress of factors influencing information technology adoption in local government context. J. Theor. Appl. Inf. Technol. **96**, 5510–5521 (2018)
15. Müller, S.D., Skau, S.A.: Success factors influencing implementation of e-government at different stages of maturity: a literature review. IJEG. **7**(2), 136 (2015). https://doi.org/10.1504/IJEG.2015.069495
16. Manville, C., et al.: Mapping smart cities in the EU (2014)
17. Gil-García, J.R., Pardo, T.A.: E-government success factors: mapping practical tools to theoretical foundations. Gov. Inf. Q. **22**(2), 187–216 (2005). https://doi.org/10.1016/j.giq.2005.02.001

18. Mersand, S., Gasco-Hernandez, M., Udoh, E., Gil-Garcia, J.R.: Public libraries as anchor institutions in smart communities: current practices and future development. In: 52nd Hawaii International Conference on System Sciences, pp. 3305–3314. IEEE Press, New York (2016). https://doi.org/10.24251/HICSS.2019.399

19. Borghys, K., van der Graaf, S., Walravens, N., Van Compernolle, M.: Multi-stakeholder innovation in smart city discourse: quadruple helix thinking in the age of "platforms." Front. Sustain. Cities. **2**, 5 (2020). https://doi.org/10.3389/frsc.2020.00005

20. Cardullo, P., Kitchin, R.: Being a 'citizen' in the smart city: up and down the scaffold of smart citizen participation in Dublin, Ireland. Geo. J. **84**(1), 1–13 (2018). https://doi.org/10.1007/s10708-018-9845-8

21. Nilssen, M.: To the smart city and beyond? Developing a typology of smart urban innovation. Technol. Forecast. Soc. Chang. **142**, 98–104 (2019). https://doi.org/10.1016/j.techfore.2018.07.060

22. Nevado Gil, M.T., Carvalho, L., Paiva, I.: Determining factors in becoming a sustainable smart city: an empirical study in Europe. Econ. Sociol. **13**, 24–39 (2020). https://doi.org/10.14254/2071-789X.2020/13-1/2

23. Simonofski, A., Vallé, T., Serral, E., Wautelet, Y.: Investigating context factors in citizen participation strategies: a comparative analysis of Swedish and Belgian smart cities. Int. J. Inf. Manag. **56**, 102011 (2021). https://doi.org/10.1016/j.ijinfomgt.2019.09.007

The Social Representation of Smart Cities: A View from Brazil

Flavia Michelotto[✉] and Luiz Antonio Joia

Fundação Getulio Vargas, Rio de Janeiro, RJ 22231-010, Brazil
flavia.michelotto@fgv.edu.br, luiz.joia@fgv.br

Abstract. About 6,000 years after the emergence of the first cities, humanity faces the challenges and consequences of the development of cities, which threaten the quality of life of people and the world environment. To date, more than half of world's population live in urban areas and, by 2050, one estimates that almost 70% of them will live in cities. Thus, in order to avoid a total collapse, cities' urban planning must be rethought urgently by means of new planning and management models largely supported by robust digital technologies, innovations and a sustainable agenda. In this scenario, the concept of smart city emerges yet without a formal consensus. Smart city definitions have been derived from interdisciplinary concepts applied to cities most of them based on the management and heavy use of information and communication technology in cities. Thus, to allow a better comprehension of what is understood by smart city mainly under the perspective of emerging markets, this work seeks to identify what is the social representation of smart city amongst Brazilian citizens, comparing same to the extant literature on smart city definition.

Keywords: Smart city · Mobility · Sustainability · ICT · Social representation theory

1 Introduction

After many centuries of development and as the urban population have grown at an increasing rate, cities have become increasingly complex and important [1, 2]. This high-speed population growth tends to worsen more and more the urbanization process [3]. One estimates that, by 2050, almost 70% of the world's population will live in cities [4]. This growth has made the management of cities increasingly complex, creating great challenges for their sustainable development, such as respect for the environment, provision of adequate transport, energy, and health for the community, in addition to attention to citizens, among others. Thus, there is an urgent need to find smarter ways to overcome these new challenges faced by cities worldwide [5, 6].

In this context of concern with the risks arising from the accelerated growth of the urban population, associated with an urgency for the search for sustainability, the concept of smart city emerges associated with several definitions and encompassing, among others, the domains of technology, public policies, society, and politics [7]. Thus,

© IFIP International Federation for Information Processing 2021
Published by Springer Nature Switzerland AG 2021
H. J. Scholl et al. (Eds.): EGOV 2021, LNCS 12850, pp. 217–228, 2021.
https://doi.org/10.1007/978-3-030-84789-0_16

as there is still no single definition for the concept of smart city [1], a research gap opens up to refine its conceptualization.

Amid a scenario of challenges and possibilities, in addition to the lack of a consensual and comprehensive definition for the smart city construct, it is common to have questions about what leads a city to be considered smart or what are the main characteristics of a smart city.

As such, to improve the understanding of that social phenomenon and thus contribute to local development, this study aims to identify how Brazilian citizens perceive smart cities by using the Social Representation Theory [8].

The Social Representation Theory (SRT) is an efficient approach to better understand constructs in the Information Systems area [9], complying with the requirements to make clear the definition of a construct [10]. Thus, this paper aims to answer the following research question: what is the social representation of smart city for people in Brazil?

The focus in Brazil is supported by the very fact that the Brazilian context can be considered a proxy for other emerging economies in which concerns to smart cities. This statement can be backed by a double evidence. First, Brazil, like other emerging economies, has few smart city initiatives. Second, Brazil presents significant challenges for implementing smart cities, being the main one an inefficient connectivity infrastructure, besides a still large digital divide, which has limited the design and implementation of smart cities in the country, as well as in other emerging economies.

This article is divided into four sections after this introduction. The next section presents the theoretical background used in this work. Then, the methodological procedures adopted are described so that, in the next section, the results are presented. In the last section, the results are discussed, and the conclusions of the study are unveiled, including its implications for academia and public policy, as well as its limitations.

2 Theoretical Background

2.1 Smart City

The rapid growth of urban populations has led to several problems for the basic operation of a city, such as: poor waste management, scarcity of resources, pollution, deterioration of public health, traffic congestion, etc. [11]. To overcome these challenges, many cities in the world have sought to be better managed through the intensive use of new technologies, in order to guarantee adequate living conditions for their citizens in a context of rapid growth. In this context, the concept of smart city emerges [5].

However, there is so far no consensus on the definition of the "smart city" construct. In fact, the term smart city has been used around the world under different names and circumstances, which has generated several conceptual variants for same [1, 7].

In fact, smart city is an interdisciplinary concept, whose sub-construct "smart" is not easy to define since it can be associated with different areas and connotations [12]. The first attempts to define this concept focused on the intelligence provided by information and communication technology (ICT) to manage various operations in a city, revitalize its economic opportunities, and strengthen its global competitiveness. Subsequently, the studies expanded their scope to include other issues, such as sustainability, quality of life, and services for citizens [3, 7].

The concept was used, for the first time, to highlight the importance of ICT to overcome the challenges faced by modern cities [13, 14]. Thus, the use of ICT has been considered a key factor to provide intelligence to a city, as it allows to detect, monitor, and control most services in same [7].

Academics point out problems associated with the concept of smart city, such as the dissonance between the construct and its reality and the difference between a true smart city and one that simply has a marketing label [15]. However, although there are different definitions for a smart city, some points in common appear in most of them: (1) the use of ICT in the city; (2) the presence of physical and network infrastructure; (3) better provision of services to the population; (4) the integration of systems and infrastructures that allow social, cultural, economic, and environmental development; and (5) the vision of a better future [11]. Despite this, the lack of consensus on a single definition for smart city has led to the formulation of different concepts on the topic.

In this research, 21 articles were obtained from a literature review on the concept of smart city. Analyzing these articles, 16 categories were found with significant association with the subject, as shown below in decreasing order of the number of related articles, namely: Technology (21), Sustainability (21), Innovation (20), Services (20), Economy/Business (20), Infrastructure (20), Quality of Life (20), People (20), Mobility/Transport (19), Planning (19), Society (19), Integration (19), Efficiency (18), Culture (18), Connectivity (16), and Security (16).

To consolidate and summarize the theoretical framework on smart city, Table 1 was organized, showing the 16 categories that present a significant association with the subject. The table identifies, for each publication, whether the category in question was cited by it. In addition, Table 1 is ranked according to the categories most frequently present in the publications, whose count appears in the final line.

2.2   Social Representation Theory

Conceived in the 1960s by Serge Moscovici, the Social Representation Theory (SRT) has become one of the predominant approaches to understand the development of common sense in different human groups [8, 16, 17].

The emergence of any social representation always coincides with the emergence of an unprecedented situation, an unknown phenomenon, or an unusual event [8]. Actually, social representations are not the product of society, but of the social groups that comprise it [18].

Academics conceptualize social representations as images that bring together multiple meanings, so that people can interpret what is happening [19]. Thus, social representations consist of a set of information, beliefs, opinions, and attitudes obtained to conceptualize a specific object through the organization and structuring of this set of elements [19].

Central Nucleus Theory. A social representation comprises two subsystems: the central nucleus and the peripheral system [20]. All representations are organized around a central nucleus, being this a fundamental element as it determines the meaning and organization of the representation [21]. The central nucleus is, therefore, strongly linked to the collective memory and history of the social group considered [21]. The central nucleus comprises, therefore, the fundamental meanings of the representation, namely those that give it identity [20] - in this case, the smart city.

Table 1. Smart cities main categories from the literature review

Theoretical References	MAIN CATEGORIES - SMART CITIES															
	Technology	Sustainability	Innovation	Services	Economy/Business	Infrastructure	Quality of Life	People	Mobility/Transport	Planning	Society	Integration	Efficiency	Culture	Connectivity	Safety
[1]	o	o	o	o	o	o	o	o	o	o	o	o	o	o	o	o
[3]	o	o	o	o	o	o	o	o	o	o	o	o	o	o	o	o
[5]	o	o	o	o	o	o	o	o	o	o	o	o	o	o	o	o
[11]	o	o	o	o	o	o	o	o	o	o	o	o	o	o	o	o
[13]	o	o	o	o	o	o	o	o	o	o	o	o	o	o	o	o
[15]	o	o	o	o	o	o	o	o	o	o	o	o	o	o	o	o
[36]	o	o	o	o	o	o	o	o	o	o	o	o	o	o	o	o
[37]	o	o	o	o	o	o	o	o	o	o	o	o	o	o	o	o
[39]	o	o	o	o	o	o	o	o	o	o	o	o	o	o	o	o
[41]	o	o	o	o	o	o	o	o	o	o	o	o	o	o	o	o
[31]	o	o	o	o	o	o	o	o	o	o	o	o	o	o	o	
[34]	o	o	o	o	o	o	o	o	o	o	o			o	o	o
[30]	o	o	o	o	o	o	o	o			o	o	o	o	o	
[38]	o	o	o	o	o	o	o	o	o	o	o	o	o	o		
[35]	o	o	o	o	o	o	o	o	o	o	o	o	o			o
[7]	o	o	o	o	o	o	o	o	o	o	o		o	o		o
[29]	o	o	o	o	o	o	o	o	o	o		o		o	o	
[40]	o	o	o	o	o	o	o	o				o	o	o	o	
[33]	o	o	o		o	o		o	o	o	o	o				o
[14]	o	o	o	o			o		o	o	o	o	o			o
[32]	o	o		o	o	o	o	o	o	o	o	o	o	o	o	o
	21	21	20	20	20	20	20	20	19	19	19	19	18	18	16	16

On the other hand, the peripheral system addresses the differences in perception of the subjects involved in the research, thereby supporting the group's heterogeneity, and accommodating the contradictions brought by the immediate context [9, 22, 23]. It is composed of elements around the central nucleus that the individual may revise and negotiate. It constitutes a protection shield for the central nucleus, allowing exchanges with other groups. It therefore enables the evolution of the social representation without modifying same [9, 23].

3   Methodological Procedures

This study uses a quali-quantitative methodological approach, the data being collected via the words evocation technique and analyzed by means of the four-quadrant technique, namely Vergès' quadrants. Data collection took place between April and June 2020. Questionnaires were sent by email, in addition to direct messages via social networks.

The questionnaire had two parts, totaling 25 questions, namely: part 1 with 12 questions, including the word evocation test and other information about smart city; part 2 with 13 questions related to the sample profile. The questionnaire was validated by two specialists in SRT and word evocation technique.

3.1 Sample

The sample included participants with the following profile: over 18 years old, with higher education and who were not completely unaware of the term smart city. To compose the sample, 1,100 people were contacted, of which 348 accepted the invitation. Of this total, 284 fully answered the questionnaire and the remaining 64 left the questionnaire incomplete, being therefore eliminated. In addition, of the 284 respondents considered, 205 said they have heard about smart city (72%), against 79 respondents who said they did not know the term (28%). These latter were also discarded. Thus, the final sample comprised 205 respondents.

3.2 Word Evocation Technique

There are distinct techniques to identify social representations, such as the words evocation technique [24]. The words evocation technique herein adopted is based on collecting words expressed by the respondents when a specific suggestive word or expression is presented to them orally or in writing [25]. Thus, in this work, the participants were asked to list the five words or expressions that immediately came to their minds [9] when they were faced with the expression smart city. The words evoked were then analyzed using the four-quadrant technique developed by Pierre Vergès, by means of which the words evoked were divided up and grouped into categories or clusters associated with the social representation under study [22, 26]. The software EVOC was used to perform this operation. The four-quadrant technique cross-checks evocation frequency of the categories – of a quantitative nature – with the order of evocation of same – of a qualitative nature, as seen in Fig. 1 [27, 28].

The average frequency of evocation (AFE) is calculated by the total number of evocations over the total number of distinct evoked words [9]. Furthermore, the average order of evocation (AOE) of a category is obtained by considering the average order in which the words pertaining to this category were evoked by the respondents, namely first, second, third, fourth or fifth place. The average of the AOE is then obtained by dividing the sum of all AOEs calculated by the number of distinct categories.

3.3 Vergès' Four-Quadrant Technique

The following steps constitute the Vergès' four-quadrant technique: i) organization of the words evoked into categories; ii) calculation of the frequency of evocation of the words via EVOC; iii) calculation of the average order of evocation of the categories via EVOC; iv) deployment of the reference points (averages) such that the categories are placed

CENTRAL NUCLEUS	FIRST PERIPHERY
Categories with evocation frequency higher than or equal to the Average Frequency of Evocation (AFE) and evocation order lower than the mean figure for the Average Order of Evocation (AOE).	Categories with evocation frequency higher than or equal to the Average Frequency of Evocation (AFE) and evocation order higher than or equal to the mean figure for the Average Order of Evocation (AOE). Close link with the Central Nucleus.
CONTRAST ZONE	PERIPHERAL SYSTEM
Categories with evocation frequency lower than the Average Frequency of Evocation (AFE) and evocation order lower than the mean figure for the Average Order of Evocation (AOE). Close link with the Central Nucleus.	Categories with evocation frequency lower than the Average Frequency of Evocation (AFE) and evocation order higher than or equal to the mean figure for the Average Order of Evocation (AOE). Remote link with the Central Nucleus.

Fig. 1. Vergès' four-quadrants technique

correctly within Vergès' four-quadrant technique, i.e., calculation of the AFE and mean figure for the AOE via EVOC; and v) individual comparison of the values referring to the categories with the AFE value and the mean figure for the AOE, whereby the Vergès' framework of smart city is obtained [20, 24].

In this work, categories were sought to fulfil Vergès' quadrants, with special emphasis on same located in the upper left quadrant, referred to as the central nucleus, and in the lower right quadrant, referred to as the peripheral system [24, 27]. The lower left quadrant (contrast zone) and upper right quadrant (first periphery) merely permits an indirect interpretation of the social representation, as they represent cognitions that are not as close to the central nucleus [27].

4 Results

4.1 Central Nucleus and Peripheral System

To define the central nucleus and the peripheral system, the participants had to answer the following question: "When you think of smart city, what are the first five expressions that come to your mind?" From the 205 questionnaires considered, 1,025 evoked terms were obtained (five per questionnaire), being used the Excel and EVOC software to generate the results. Once the tabulation of the results was performed, 88 different terms were obtained, which were grouped into 12 categories or clusters.

Then, it was verified which categories would be placed in the four quadrants of Vergès, with emphasis on the central nucleus and the peripheral system. For this, the minimum value of the evocation frequency was calculated. Academics [45] point out that the frequency that represents the average of evocations is academically accepted as the minimum frequency for studies on social representation - in this research, this figure was 22.

Of the 162 different categories surveyed, 12 were evoked 22 or more times (7.4% of the total). Technology was the most cited category (8.6%), followed by Mobility (8.2%) and Sustainability (6.7%).

A final step for assembling the quadrants is the calculation of the AOE (Average Order of Evocation), which represents the weighted average of the average order of evocation of each category i evoked (AOEi). Thus, of the 1,025 words evoked, 162 distinct categories were created, of which 12 (74% of 162) reached an AFE (average frequency of evocation) of at least 22. That way, it was possible to build the Vergès' quadrant generated by EVOC, composing the social representation of smart city, as shown in Fig. 2.

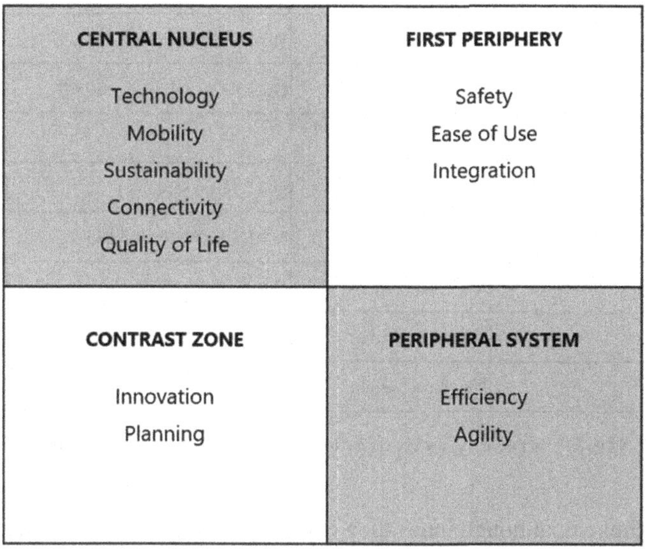

CENTRAL NUCLEUS	FIRST PERIPHERY
Technology	Safety
Mobility	Ease of Use
Sustainability	Integration
Connectivity	
Quality of Life	
CONTRAST ZONE	**PERIPHERAL SYSTEM**
Innovation	Efficiency
Planning	Agility

Fig. 2. Smart city social representation

5   Discussion and Conclusions

By means of the social representation of smart city, it is possible to identify the categories that are most strongly associated with this concept - that is, the categories that represent the collective thinking of the research sample carried out in Brazil. Academics then suggest a comparison between the social representation found and the theoretical references on the concept under analysis [20] – in this case, smart city.

As one can see in Fig. 3, all categories of the central nucleus of the social representation - technology, mobility, sustainability, connectivity, quality of life - are among the most cited by the theoretical references.

Innovation, Services, Economy, and Infrastructure are very common themes in the theoretical references, but they are not part of the central nucleus according to the words'

Smart City Categories	Category Status	Theoretical References	Quantity
Technology	Central Nucleus	[1,3,5,7,11,13-15,29-41]	21
Sustainability	Central Nucleus		21
Innovation	Contrast Zone	[1,3,5,7,11,13-15,29-31,33-41]	20
Services	Cited but not located in the Vergès' Quadrant		20
Economy/Business	Cited but not located in the Vergès' Quadrant	[1,3,5,7,11,13,15,29-41]	20
Infrastructure	Cited but not located in the Vergès' Quadrant		20
Quality of Life	Peripheral System	[1,3,5,7,11,13-15,29-32,34-41]	20
People	Cited but not located in the Vergès' Quadrant	[1,3,5,7,11,13,15,29-41]	20
Mobility/Transport	Central Nucleus	[1,3,5,7,11,13-15,29-32,34-39,41]	19
Planning	Contrast Zone	[1,3,5,7,11,13-15,29,31-39,41]	19
Society (Citizen Participation)	Very little cited but not located in the Vergès	[1,3,5,7,11,13,15,30-41]	19
Integration	First Periphery	[1,3,5,11,13-15,30-41]	19
Efficiency	Peripheral System	[1,3,5,7,11,13-15,30-32,35-41]	18
Culture	Not cited at all	[1,3,5,7,11,13,15,29-32,34,36-41]	18
Connectivity	Central Nucleus	[1,3,5,11,13,15,29-34,36,37,39,41]	16
Safety	Peripheral System	[1,3,5,7,11,13,15,29,30,33-37,39,41]	16

Fig. 3. Smart city social representation vs. theoretical references

evocation technique, although innovation is part of the contrast zone of the social representation. Besides, People, Society (also called Citizen Participation) and Culture do not appear in the social representation but are among the most cited subjects in the theoretical references. Security appears less prominently in the theoretical context, also remaining absent in the central nucleus.

However, a fact that draws attention in this study is the strong presence of the categories Culture and Citizen Participation in the theoretical framework on smart city and conversely their almost total absence in the respondents' evocations. The Culture category appears related to smart city in 18 of the 21 articles in the theoretical framework. For example, in the ontological framework proposed by Ruhlandt [44], Culture appears as one of the enablers of intelligence of a city. Although it does not reach the same weight as other categories such as Technology, Environment, and Infrastructure, it still has prominence. Culture also figures as an important component in the rankings of smart cities [45], which consider the number of museums, art galleries and theaters, as well as the spending on leisure and recreation, as a reflection of the city's commitment to the theme [45].

The importance given to cultural aspects by developed countries, therefore, is quite different from that of Brazil. Culture does not appear in any of the 1,025 words evoked. One explanation may be the low importance of this category in the lives of Brazilians when compared to the diverse and enormous basic difficulties faced locally. Therefore, amid so many categories related to smart city, the Culture dimension is still not seen by Brazilians as a priority need.

Citizen Participation is another category that presented very low representativeness among the citations. However, the participation of citizens in the management of cities appears as an essential issue when talking about smart cities in developed countries [46]. Academics point to an evolution from the concept of smart city to "smart human city", focusing on the human aspect of cities, where a new type of governance is needed to plan and develop cities that take care of their citizens' interests [47]. However, for this to happen, citizens must be involved in the planning and execution of smart city projects, assuming that cities are willing to open their databases. In Brazil, there is still a huge gap to be covered in terms of transparency and social participation. However, in recent years, with the advent of ICT, which allows greater access for citizens to public actions through websites and applications, it is already possible to see the emergence of citizens showing greater interest in government initiatives and seeking a more active participation in issues related to their cities [43].

5.1 Research Implications

In discussions and planning about smart cities, it is important to have prior knowledge of the common sense about this subject. While there are excellent foreign examples of successful smart city initiatives, their mere replications in the context of emerging economies can be a resounding failure. Thus, the use of social representation is quite relevant for a deeper understanding of the perceptions of society or groups of local decision makers on the concept of the smart city. That way, this research can be a catalyst for raising local issues that can be solved through smart city initiatives.

This study, therefore, aims to help academics and public policy makers alike to understand how smart city initiatives can be successful in cities located in emerging markets.

5.2 Research Limitations

This research has limitations as detailed below.

Initially, the sample of respondents was very concentrated (over 90%) in the wealthiest states of Brazil - Rio de Janeiro and São Paulo. These two states account for about 30% of the Brazilian population. Thus, this research is not fully representative of the Brazilian population, although these states have as their capitals the two largest Brazilian cities - São Paulo and Rio de Janeiro.

In addition, the identification of the categories of the central nucleus of social representation was carried out through the interpretation of the evoked expressions and their consequent consolidation into categories. Therefore, this process may have given rise to bias in the interpretation, although two invited scholars have helped in the quality control of this categorization.

Finally, as detailed in the introduction of this research, Brazil was considered a proxy for other emerging economies, regarding the implementation of smart city initiatives. However, although there are huge similarities of contexts in these countries, it cannot be guaranteed that the social representation of smart city in Brazil corresponds exactly to the same to be found in other emerging economies.

5.3 Final Remarks

As demonstrated in the scientific literature, smart city is a polysemic construct, encompassing and linking a wide range of concepts and areas. Therefore, to make sense of the potential of smart cities, it is necessary to understand the demographic, environmental, economic, and institutional context in which they are implemented [48].

There is no doubt that smart cities have brought many opportunities to everyday life through ICT - the main factor for the advent of this new paradigm. However, smart city is not just about ICT, since some other critical categories, such as Quality of Life and Sustainability, to name just a few, are becoming increasingly associated with smart cities.

In sum, it is imperative to have defined, in a univocal way, what is a smart city. It is hoped that this work has helped clarifying this important issue.

References

1. Nam, T., Pardo, T.A.: Conceptualizing smart city with dimensions of technology, people, and institutions. In: Proceedings of the 12th Annual International Digital Government Research Conference: Digital Government Innovation in Challenging Times, pp. 282–291 (2011)
2. Buhaug, H., Urdal, H.: An urbanization bomb? Population growth and social disorder in cities. Global Env. Change 23(1), 1–10 (2013)
3. Lee, J.H., Hancock, M.G., Hu, M.C.: Towards an effective framework for building smart cities: lessons from Seoul and San Francisco. Technol. Forecast. Soc. Chang. 89, 80–99 (2014)
4. United Nations: Department of Economic and Social Affairs. Population Division. World population prospects: the 2017 revision: key findings and advance tables (2017)
5. Neirotti, P., De Marco, A., Cagliano, A.C., Mangano, G., Scorrano, F.: Current trends in Smart City initiatives: Some stylised facts. Cities 38, 25–36 (2014)
6. Broere, W.: Urban underground space: solving the problems of today's cities. Tunn. Undergr. Space Technol. 55, 245–248 (2016)
7. Ramaprasad, A., Sánchez-Ortiz, A., Syn, T.: A unified definition of a smart city. In: Janssen, M., et al. (eds.) EGOV 2017. LNCS, vol. 10428, pp. 13–24. Springer, Cham (2017). https://doi.org/10.1007/978-3-319-64677-0_2
8. Moscovici, S.: La psychanalyse: son image et son public: étude sur la representation sociale de la psychanalyse. Presses Universitaires de France, Paris (1961)
9. Joia, L.A., Marchisotti, G.: It is so (if you think so): social representation theory and constructs definition in the MIS area in Brazil. In: Proceedings of the Americas Conference on Information Systems, New Orleans, USA (2018)
10. Audebrand, L.K., Iacobus, A.: Avoiding potential traps in fair trade marketing: a social representation perspective. J. Strat. Market. 16(1), 3–19 (2008)
11. Gil-Garcia, J.R., Pardo, T.A., Nam, T.: What makes a city smart? Identifying core components and proposing an integrative and comprehensive conceptualization. Inf. Polity 20(1), 61–87 (2015)

12. Albino, V., Berardi, U., Dangelico, R.M.: Smart cities: definitions, dimensions, performance, and initiatives. J. Urban Technol. **22**(1), 3–21 (2015)
13. Chourabi, H., et al.: Understanding smart cities: an integrative framework. In: 2012 45th Hawaii International Conference on System Sciences, pp. 2289–2297. IEEE (2012)
14. Murgante, B., Borruso, G.: Smart cities in a smart world. In: Rassia, S.Th., Pardalos, P.M. (eds.) Future city architecture for optimal living. SOIA, vol. 102, pp. 13–35. Springer, Cham (2015). https://doi.org/10.1007/978-3-319-15030-7_2
15. Hollands, R.G.: Will the real smart city please stand up? Intelligent, progressive or entrepreneurial? City **12**(3), 303–320 (2008)
16. Vergara, S.C., Ferreira, V.C.P.: A representação social de ONGs segundo formadores de opinião do município do Rio de Janeiro. Revista de Administração Pública **39**(5), 1137–1159 (2005)
17. Joia, L.A.: A teoria da representação social e a definição de constructos na área de administração da informação. VI EnADI (2017)
18. Rateau, P., Moliner, P., Guimelli, C., Abric, J.C.: Social representation theory. In: Handbook of Theories of Social Psychology, vol. 2, pp. 477–497 (2011)
19. Jodelet, D.: Madness and Social Representations. Harvester Wheatsheaf, Hemel Hempstead (1991)
20. Joia, L.A., Correia, J.C.P.: CIO competencies from the IT professional perspective: insights from Brazil. J. Global Inf. Manage. (JGIM) **26**(2), 74–103 (2018)
21. Abric, J.C.: A structural approach to social representations. In: Deaux, K., Philogène, G. (eds.) Representations of the Social, pp. 42–47. Blackwell, Oxford (2001)
22. Abric, J.C.: A abordagem estrutural das representações sociais. Estudos interdisciplinares de representação social **2**(1998), 27–38 (1998)
23. Sá, C.P.: Núcleo Central das representações sociais. 2nd edn. Vozes, Petrópolis (2002)
24. Vergara, S.C.: Projetos e relatórios de pesquisa em administração. Atlas, São Paulo (2013)
25. Piermatteo, A., Tavani, J.L., Monaco, G.L.: Improving the study of social representations through word associations: validation of semantic contextualization. Field Methods **30**(4), 329–344 (2018)
26. Ma, X.: Evocation: analyzing and propagating a semantic link based on free word association. Lang. Resour. Eval. **47**(3), 819–837 (2013)
27. Abric, J.C.: La recherche du noyau central et de la zone muette des représentations sociales. Méthodes d'étude des représentations sociales, 296 (2003)
28. Marchisotti, G.G., Joia, L.A., de Carvalho, R.B.: A representação social de cloud computing pela percepção dos profissionais brasileiros de tecnologia da informação. RAE-Revista de Administração de Empresas **59**(1), 16–28 (2019)
29. Giffinger, R., Fertner, C., Kramar, H., Meijers, E.: City-ranking of European medium-sized cities. Cent. Reg. Sci. Vienna UT, 1–12 (2007). http://www.smartcities.eu/download/smart_cities_final_report.pdf
30. Schaffers, H., Komninos, N., Pallot, M., Trousse, B., Nilsson, M., Oliveira, A.: Smart cities and the future internet: towards cooperation frameworks for open innovation. In: Domingue, J., et al. (eds.) FIA 2011. LNCS, vol. 6656, pp. 431–446. Springer, Heidelberg (2011). https://doi.org/10.1007/978-3-642-20898-0_31
31. Caragliu, A., Del Bo, C., Nijkamp, P.: Smart cities in Europe. J. Urban Technol. **18**(2), 65–82 (2011)
32. Batty, M., et al.: Smart cities of the future. Eur. Phys. J. Spec. Top. **214**(1), 481–518 (2012)
33. Komninos, N.: What makes cities intelligent. In: Smart Cities: Governing, Modelling and Analysing the Transition, pp. 77–87 (2013)
34. Harrison, C., Donnelly, I.A.: A Theory of Smart Cities, pp. 2–7. IBM Corporation (2011)
35. Angelidou, M.: Smart Cities: a conjuncture of four forces. Cities **47**, 95–106 (2015)

36. Letaifa, S.B.: How to strategize smart cities: revealing the SMART model. J. Bus. Res. **68**(7), 1414–1419 (2015)
37. Bouskela, M., Casseb, M., Bassi, S., Facchina, M.: The Road Toward Smart Cities: Migrating from Traditional City Management to the Smart City, pp. 1–128. Inter-American Development Bank, Washington DC (2016)
38. Brandão, M., Joia, L.A.: A influência do contexto na implantação de um projeto de cidade inteligente: o caso Cidade Inteligente Búzios. Revista de Administração Pública **52**(6), 1125–1154 (2018)
39. Silva, B.N., Khan, M., Han, K.: Towards sustainable smart cities: a review of trends, architectures, components, and open challenges in smart cities. Sustain. Cities Society **38**, 697–713 (2018)
40. Azevedo, A.L., et al.: Smart cities: the main drivers for increasing the intelligence of cities. Sustainability **10**(9), 3121 (2018)
41. Joia, L.A., Kuhl, A.: Smart city for development: a conceptual model for developing countries. In: Nielsen, P., Kimaro, H.C. (eds.) ICT4D. IAICT, vol. 552, pp. 203–214. Springer, Cham (2019). https://doi.org/10.1007/978-3-030-19115-3_17
42. Sarubbi, V.S., Jr.: Representações sociais das equipes técnicas acerca do cuidado à criança nas creches da Universidade de São Paulo. Doctoral Dissertation, Universidade de São Paulo, São Paulo, Brazil (2012)
43. Viale Pereira, G., Cunha, M.A., Lampoltshammer, T.J., Parycek, P., Testa, M.G.: Increasing collaboration and participation in smart city governance: a cross-case analysis of smart city initiatives. Inf. Technol. Dev. **23**(3), 526–553 (2017)
44. Ramaprasad, A., Sánchez-Ortiz, A., Syn, T.: Ontological review of smart city research. In: Proceedings of the Americas Conference on Information Systems, Boston, vol. 23 (2017b)
45. IESE: Cities in Motion Index 2019. IESE Business School, University of Navarra, Barcelona, Spain (2019). https://media.iese.edu/research/pdfs/ST-0509-E.pdf.
46. Ruhlandt, R.W.S.: The governance of smart cities: a systematic literature review. Cities **81**, 1–23 (2018)
47. Almeida, V.A., Doneda, D., da Costa, E.M.: Humane Smart Cities: the need for governance. IEEE Internet Comput. **22**(2), 91–95 (2018)
48. Davison, R.M., Martinsons, M.G.: Context is king! Considering particularism in research design and reporting. J. Inf. Technol. **31**(3), 241–249 (2016)

Trust Factors Affecting the Adoption of E-Government for Civic Engagement

Suha AlAwadhi[✉]

Department of Information Studies, College of Social Sciences, Kuwait University, Safat, P.O. Box 68168, 71962 Kuwait City, Kuwait
s.alawadhi@ku.edu.kw

Abstract. This study aims to investigate trust factors affecting the use and adoption of e-government services, which lead to civic engagement. The constructs identified in this study are related to the theories of technology adoption in addition to trust constructs: trust in government, trust in technology, and trust in e-government. The study adopted the quantitative approach and surveyed more than 500 individuals in Kuwait. The findings indicate positive correlations between research constructs. Moreover, trust factors and perceived usefulness are found to be critical factors in the adoption and use of e-government services which greatly contribute to the achievement of civic engagement.

Keywords: E-government · Trust · Trust in technology · Trust in government · Trust in e-government · Adoption · Perceived usefulness · Civic engagement

1 Introduction

The past decades have witnessed a decline in government trust to a great extent [48]. Trust in government, which encapsulates the interaction between government institutions and the public, has been investigated by a number of researchers as the decline of trust in government is considered one of the dilemmas of modern governance [48]. Craig [19], Hetherington [28] and Norris [40] in their research found a significant association between the declining trust in government and the decline in political participation. Moreover, citizens have been isolated from community life, and their ability to articulate demands for a good government that ensures quality of life has noticeably decreased [33, 35]. Norris [40, p. 113] reports: "There is widespread concern that the public has lost faith in the performance of the core institutions of representative government, and it is hoped that more open and transparent government and more efficient service delivery could help restore that trust". The use of Information and Communication Technology (ICT) in governments has introduced new forms of interaction that could enhance different types of relationships, including a government–public relationship [50, 56].

The proposals of e-government initiatives have served as solutions for meeting citizens' needs and expectations, improving public-government communication and

© IFIP International Federation for Information Processing 2021
Published by Springer Nature Switzerland AG 2021
H. J. Scholl et al. (Eds.): EGOV 2021, LNCS 12850, pp. 229–244, 2021.
https://doi.org/10.1007/978-3-030-84789-0_17

increasing trust in governments [47]. Therefore, many local, regional, and national governments around the world have adopted ICT solutions to offer effective government information and services, to achieve economic and social development, and to enable social inclusion [10]. West [57] and Lollar [37] projected that e-government and its use help bring about positive change in citizens' beliefs about government effectiveness and re-build citizens' trust in government. E-government projects have introduced several opportunities for online interactions, which subsequently empower citizens at various levels, such as: information accessibility, political participation, influencing government decisions, linking groups to the broader community, and making governments more accountable to their citizens [2, 8, 10].

There is a growing body of literature that investigates trust in e-government, for example: [29, 45, 47]. Other research focuses on e-government and user engagement [17, 27, 31], that has contributed greatly in developing an understanding of the impact of ICT on civic engagement [34]. Moreover, researchers have indicated that some political behaviours have linked trust and civic engagement [43, 50] that such linkage is complex, and trust is the "magic elixir for civic engagement" [50]. However, the literature has little explanation on the relationships between building trust in e-governments, the adoption and use to e-government and civic engagement. Moreover, to the best of the researcher's knowledge, studies on such relationships in developing countries, specifically in the Middle East, are either non-existent or insufficient. In previous research, we validated the research model of trust factors that are expected to have significant relationships with the adoption of e-government services and leading to civic engagement [4]. Therefore, this study is a continuation of previous research that aims to investigate trust factors (technology, government, and e-government) related to the use and adoption of e-government for civic engagement, using Kuwait as an example of a developing country.

The paper is organized as follows: Sect. 2 presents the literature review followed by the background of the study in Sect. 3. Then, Sect. 4 describes the research model and hypotheses. The methodology used is the study is explained in Sect. 5. The findings of the study are depicted in Sect. 6. Finally, the discussion and conclusions are presented in Sects. 7 and 8 respectively.

2   Literature Review

Many studies in the literature have provide evidence that trust is an important factor in the acceptance and adoption of e-government services [16]. Trust has been defined as "a psychological state comprising the intention to accept vulnerability based upon positive expectations of the intentions or behavior of another" [46, p. 395]. Several researchers found that the use of e-government services is correlated with the trust in government; for example: [15, 41, 55, 57]. Other researchers, conversely, found that trust in government is not necessary for using e-government services; for example: [29]. Scholars have also explored the relationship between the citizens' use of e-government services and their trust in technology. A study investigating the relation between trust and e-government [18] found that citizens with higher perceptions of technological and organizational trustworthiness, have higher trust in e-government. Users with positive experience of the technology and satisfactory use of the services are more likely to develop a positive attitude and thus adopt online services than those with a negative experience [52]. Horsburgh [29] confirms that users' trust in technology is more likely to increase as their personal information is not misused by authorities or released to third parties. Internet business is linked to Internet experience that novice users are less likely to conduct business online than experienced users [25]. Also, security and reliability of e-services are the most important dimensions that, if experienced, would incline customers to report a positive experience of e-services [52]. Similarly, Dutton and Shepherd [21] found that trust in the Internet would shape the future of online services. Such trust is undermined by negative experiences while using the Internet, such as computer viruses.

Once citizens' adoption of e-government services is achieved, it should have an impact on their engagement as it is associated with the successful e-government and its sustainability [17, 31]. Civic engagement which enhances social trust, norms, and values [26], could be a "bit of everything": political participation, volunteering, community services, and social networks and interpersonal trust to associational involvement [1, 11, 22, 44]. Not only civic engagement stems from trust, but also can lead to greater trust [22]. Putnam confirms [38] that there is a relationship between civic engagement and trust, however it is complex. Also, Brehm and Rahn [13] found a linkage between civic engagement and trust. Gil de Zúñiga et al. [27] found that individuals were more likely to display political behavior and engage in civic life in both online and offline conversations. Several researchers found that civic engagement is significantly related to the participation in the political process of government; for example: [9, 24, 51]. Moreover, the use of available e-government information and services and interaction platforms with government allow direct contact and interaction with governments, thereby promoting transparency, participation, and collaboration [12, 30]. However, Jaeger and Bertot [30] argued that the use of new technologies might marginalize disadvantaged people that did not have access to the Internet.

To sum up, the review of the literature identifies trust in government and technology as factors significant in the adoption of e-government. Moreover, the use of e-government positively impacts civic engagement which has a significant association with trust.

3   Study Background

E-government initiative has been adopted in Kuwait since 2000 as a tool to improve the government's performance, and services and to promote transparency [5, 36]. A lot of efforts are devoted to the improvement of e-government in Kuwait to present government information and services needed by the public [32]. Although many government organizations and ministries have produced government information and offered services online using ICT tools, such as websites and social media networks, the adoption of such e-government is still limited. According to the United Nations E-Government Survey 2020 [49] Kuwait has shown a substantial development in e-government as it is ranked 46 out of 193 countries in 2020 compared to its 63 rank in 2012. E-government in Kuwait has been investigated from different perspectives by a number of researchers, such as its benefits, challenges and adoption [5–7]; however, to the best of the researcher's knowledge, little is known about public trust in e-government that leads to civic engagement. This limitation in the literature has commended to conduct this study to fill the gap by investigating the trust factor and how it is associated with the adoption factors of e-government information and services that lead to achieving civic engagement.

4 Research Framework

Technology acceptance and adoption theories, such as theory of reasoned action (TRA) [23], technology acceptance model (TAM) [20], theory of planed behavior (TPB) [3], and unified theory of acceptance and use of technology (UTAUT) [53], have been extensively used in the literature to investigate and discuss the acceptance and adoption of e-government services. Such empirical studies have identified numerous factors related to e-government adoption, such as perceived usefulness, perceived ease of use, subjective norms, intention to use and attitude behavior. However, other important factors relating to trust and culture have little been considered with adoption theories, such as [45] and [54]. Thus, based on the literature review, this study focuses on trust as an important factor related to the adoption of e-government. Other factors that enhance trust in e-government services are also considered. The following factors are identified and expected to be significantly correlated with the adoption e-government services and have positive impact on civic engagement:

- Trust in government (TG) has been found to be associated with the trust in e-government services [15]. It refers to one's perceptions regarding the integrity and ability of the agency providing the services [15]. Therefore, the following hypothesis is developed:
  H1: Trust in government has significant relationship with trust in e-government.
- Trust in technology (TT) has also been found to be associated with the trust in e-government [29]. Users having positive experiences with the technology would trust e-government as they feel that their personal and financial information are secure. This leads to posit the following hypothesis:
  H2: Trust in technology leads to trust in e-government.
- Trust in e-government (TEG) is the outcome of citizens' trust in government and technology [14]. Such construct depends also on other personal characteristics, such as age, and gender. Once citizens have trust in e-government, they become more likely to increase their intention to use (IU) and adopt e-government services. Intentions to use (IU) e-government services is one of the main factors that measures the citizens' use of e-government services. The following hypothesis is suggested:
  H3: There is significant relationship between trust in e-government and intention to use.
- Perceived usefulness (PU) of e-government services is also an important factor for enhancing trust in e-government and increasing citizens' intention behavior. It is "the degree that users believe that a particular system facilitates their activity" [20]. If users perceive that e-government facilitates their interaction with government, they become more likely to trust e-government services and intend to use e-government services. The following hypothesis is suggested:
  H4: Perceived usefulness positively influences trust in e-government.
  H5: Perceived usefulness positively influences intentions to use e-government.

- Civic engagement (CE) as defined by the world bank [58] is the "participation of private actors in the public sphere, conducted through direct and indirect interactions of civil society organizations and citizens-at-large with government, multilateral institutions and business establishments to influence decision making or pursue common goals". As e-government services are adopted and used by citizens, this means that citizens become able to interact and engage with government, and thereby achieving civic engagement. The following hypothesis is developed:
  H6: There is significant relationship between trust in e-government and civic engagement.

Appendix 1 presents the constructs used in the study and the related statements which have been modified to reflect the context of the study.

5 Methodology

This study aims to investigate trust factors affecting the use and adoption of e-government services, which lead to civic engagement. The quantitative approach was adopted in this study for data-collection using a questionnaire survey method. The survey tool was designed in a clear and straightforward way, using simple language as it targets various groups in the community with different educational, cultural, and social backgrounds. The questionnaire is divided into two main sections: the first section gathers demographic information of respondents and their technology proficiency; the second section investigates the identified research constructs as respondents should give their opinions using a Likert scale ranging from 1 "strongly disagree" to 5 "strongly agree".

The questionnaire was designed in both English and Arabic. This gives everyone residing in Kuwait the opportunity to participate in the study. To ensure the validity and reliability of the questionnaire, a panel made up of two faculty members from the Information Studies Department and one statistician revised the survey for any errors or ambiguities. All corrections and changes suggested by the panel were taken into consideration. Moreover, a pilot study was undertaken using 50 participants to evaluate the feasibility of the questionnaire statements. The 50 questionnaire responses were statistically analysed and the suggested changes were made to ensure better clarity of statements. The questionnaire targeted individuals in Kuwait who are eligible to use e-government services, mainly those who are 18 years old and above. A non-probability, convenience sampling method was employed to target a large number of participants. The questionnaire was distributed by hand and online using email and social media networks to reach as many individuals as possible. Luckily, 524 responses were received. Data extracted from questionnaire responses were analyzed using SPSS and Minitab software.

6 Results

6.1 Demographic Characteristics

The demographic characteristics of the sample shows that the majority of respondents were 348 females (66.4%) and 176 males (33.6%). The most respondents (244) were aged between 18 and 25 (46.5%), and 323 of them (61.6%) hold undergraduate degree. The majority of questionnaire respondents 482 (92%) were Kuwaiti nationals and 377 of them (71.9%) had excellent technology skills, as shown in Table 1.

Table 1. Demographic characteristics of the research sample

Demographics		Frequency	Percent
Gender	Male	176	33.6%
	Female	348	66.4%
Age	18–25	244	46.5%
	26–35	161	30.7%
	36–45	51	9.7%
	46–above	68	13%
Education	High School	59	11.3%
	Diploma	55	10.5%
	University Degree	323	61.6%
	Graduate Degree	87	16.6%
Technology Skills	Poor	2	1.5%
	Good	145	27.7%
	Excellent	377	71.9%
Nationality	Kuwaiti	482	92%
	Non-Kuwaiti	42	8%

6.2 Validity and Reliability of Constructs

The factor analysis is used in the statistical data analysis of this study to reduce the dimensionality of data sets and to identify the validity and reliability of research construct items. The reliabilities of the constructs are greater than 80% of the Cronbach alpha coefficient, which proves high internal consistency between instruments for each construct. Also, the explained variance is larger than 70%, indicating excellent goodness of fit of the model and valid constructs. Factor loadings, which are greater than 50%, reflect the degree of association between instruments and the construct it measures. Once each construct and its instruments are identified, we express each construct as a weight average. These averages are used to model the relationship between Civic engagement (CE) as a dependent variable, and a set of predictors including: Trust in government (TG), Trust in technology (TT), Trust in e-government (TEG), Intention to use e-government (IU), and Perceived usefulness of e-government (PU).

6.3 Measurements of Construct

Table 2 indicates statistical analysis results of the sample data to show that respondents displayed positive attitudes towards trust in technology (Mean = 3.8, p-value = 0.000), trust in e-government (Mean = 3.8, p-value = 0.000), intension to use (Mean = 3.6, p-value 0.000), perceived usefulness (Mean = 3.6, p-value = 0.000). Respondents were neutral in their attitudes towards civic engagement (Mean = 3.0, p-value = 0.967). On the contrary, respondents expressed negative attitudes towards trust in government (Mean = 2.2, p-value 0.000).

Table 2. Description of constructs and their measurements

Construct	N	Mean	Std. deviation	Std. error mean	Sig. (2-tailed)
TG	524	2.20	.856	.037	.000
TT	524	3.81	.922	.040	.000
TEG	524	3.85	1.023	.044	.000
CE	524	3.00	1.240	.054	.967
IU	524	3.62	1.066	.046	.000
PU	524	3.63	1.112	.048	.000

6.4 Research Construct Correlations

The Correlation Coefficient test was conducted to show if there is a relationship between two variables (constructs) and indicates the direction of the relationship. The results indicate that all research constructs are positively correlated with each other and greater or equal to r = 0.22, p-value = 0.000. Trust in government has positive and significant correlations with Trust in technology (r = 0.25, p-value = 0.000), trust in e-government (r = 0.30, p-value = 0.000), civic engagement (r = 0.22, p-value = 0.000), intention to use e-government services (r = 0.30, p-value = 0.000), and perceived usefulness (r = 0.27, p-value = 0.000). Trust in technology has moderate positive and significant correlation with trust in e-government a moderate positive and significant correlation with trust in e-government (r = 0.44, p-value = 0.000), intention to use e-government services (r = 0.48, p-value = 0.000) and perceived usefulness (r = 0.45, p-value = 0.000); however a weak positive and significant correlation with civic engagement (r = 0.32, p-value = 0.000). Trust in e-government has strong positive and significant correlation with intention to use e-government services (r = 0.72, p-value = 0.000) and perceived usefulness (r = 0.72, p-value = 0.000), and a moderate positive and significant correlation with civic engagement (r = 0.52, p-value = 0.000). Civic engagement also has a strong positive and significant correlation with perceived usefulness (r = 0.65, p-value = 0.000) and intention to use e-government services (r = 0.57, p-value = 0.000). Finally, a strong positive and significant correlation was found between intention to use e-government services and perceived usefulness (r = 0.76, p-value = 0.000).

6.5 Effect of Respondents' Demographic Characteristics on Research Constructs

The study utilized several non-parametric tests to investigate the effects of demographic characteristics on research constructs. The results indicate that both male and female respondents expressed positive attitude towards their trust in e-government with a significant effect of (p-value = 0.000), trust in technology (p-value = 0.057), intention to use e-government (p-value = 0.041), and perceived usefulness (p-value = 0.031).

All age groups expressed positive perceptions towards trust in technology, however, significant relationships were found between age and trust in government (p-value = 0.014), civic engagement (p-value = 0.003), and trust in technology (p-value = 0.059).

With regards to the respondents' educational background, a significant relationship was found with only their trust in technology (p-value = 0.028). Nationality difference did not show any significant relationship with any construct except trust in government which indicates the respondents' negative attitude but significant relationship with the nationality (p-value = 0.002). Finally, the respondents' various levels of technological skills did not show any significant relationship with any constructs accept trust in technology (p-value = 0.000).

6.6 Testing Research Hypotheses

In order to prove or negate the study's hypotheses, the Two-sample T-test, using Minitab software, was performed to test various relationships between constructs. Constructs' means (M) and standard deviation (SD) were compared. Also, to determine whether the difference between the means was statistically significant, the p-value was compared to the significance level. The findings show that among respondents (N = 524), there was a statistically significant difference between trust in government (M = 2.20, SD = 0.85) and trust in e-government (M = 3.86, SD = 1.02), with the degree of freedom (DF = 1046), and obtained t-value = −28.36 and the P-Value = 0.000. Therefore, *H1* is supported; see Table 3.

Table 3. Two-sample T-test: the relationship between TG and TEG

Construct	N	Mean	StDev	SE mean
TG	524	2.20	0.85	0.03
TEG	524	3.86	1.02	0.04
T-value = −28.36 DF = 1046 P-value = 0.000				

The relationship between trust in technology and trust in e-government was also tested. As shown in Table 4, trust in technology (M = 3.81, SD = 0.92) and trust in e-government (M = 3.86, SD = 1.02), (DF = 1046), obtained t-value = −0.73 and P-Value = 0.466; thus, rejecting *H2*.

Table 4. Two-sample T-test: the relationship between TT and TEG

Construct	N	Mean	StDev	SE mean
TT	524	3.81	0.92	0.04
TEG	524	3.86	1.02	0.04
T-value = −0.73 DF = 1046 P-value = 0.466				

The results show a significant relationship between trust in e-government ($M = 3.86$, $SD = 1.02$) and the intention to use e-government services ($M = 3.63$, $SD = 1.07$), (DF = 1046), obtaining t-value $= -3.60$ and P-Value $= 0.000$, supporting $H3$; see Table 5.

Table 5. Two-sample T-test: the relationship between TEG and IU

Construct	N	Mean	StDev	SE mean
TEG	524	3.86	1.02	0.045
IU	524	3.63	1.07	0.047
T-value = −3.60 DF = 1046 P-value = 0.000				

Another significant relationship was also found between perceived usefulness ($M = 3.63$, $SD = 1.11$) and trust in e-government ($M = 3.86$, $SD = 1.02$), (DF = 1046), attaining t-value $= -3.43$ and P-Value $= 0.001$, therefore, supporting $H4$; see Table 6.

Table 6. Two-sample T-test: the relationship between PU and TEG

Construct	N	Mean	StDev	SE mean
PU	524	3.63	1.11	0.049
TEG	524	3.86	1.02	0.045
T-value = −3.43 DF = 1046 P-value = 0.001				

However, the relationship between perceived usefulness (M = 3.63, SD = 1.11) and intention to use (M = 3.63, SD = 1.07), (DF = 1046), was not statistically significant as it obtained t-value = 0.08 and P-Value = 0.932; thus, rejecting $H5$; see Table 7.

Table 7. Two-sample T-test: the relationship between PU and IU

Construct	N	Mean	StDev	SE mean
PU	524	3.63	1.11	0.049
IU	524	3.63	1.07	0.047
T-value = 0.08 DF = 1046 P-value = 0.932				

Finally, the results show a significant relationship between trust in e-government ($M = 3.86$, $SD = 1.02$) and civic engagement ($M = 3.00$, $SD = 1.24$), (DF = 1046), acquiring t-value = 12.20 and the P-Value = 0.000, consequently supporting $H6$; see Table 8.

Table 8. Two-sample T-test: the relationship between TEG and CE

Construct	N	Mean	StDev	SE mean
TEG	524	3.86	1.02	0.045
CE	524	3.00	1.24	0.054
T-value = 12.20 DF = 1046 P-value = 0.000				

7 Discussion

Researchers around the world explored the adoption of e-government services from various perspectives and identified factors that were critical in the acceptance and the adoption of the services, such as perceived usefulness, subjective norms, and attitude behavior. However, a few of such studies explored the trust factor and its relation to civic engagement, which is the main aim of implementing electronic government. This study, therefore, has investigated trust factors affecting the use and adoption of e-government services for civic engagement, using a questionnaire that targeted adult individuals in the Kuwaiti society. The results of constructs measurement and statistical analysis show that respondents displayed positive attitudes towards trust in technology and e-government. Moreover, they had high perceptions of the usefulness of e-government services and they intended to use them. This could be attributed to the fact that the majority of respondents had high skills in technology, and they were aware of the potential benefits when they conduct transactions online. However, respondents showed negative attitudes towards trust in government, confirming results in [19, 28, 39, 40, 47], and that the Kuwait government is not revealing adequate information to the public and not sufficiently engaging the public in the political process [48]. Therefore, respondents showed neutral attitudes towards civic engagement which is correlated with trust in government, as found by [43].

The relationships between constructs which are presented in the hypotheses are also explored in this study. The findings indicate that there was a significant relationship between trust in government and trust in e-government, confirming $H1$ and suggesting that trust in government is necessary for trusting and using e-government as confirmed by [14]. $H3$ was also confirmed as the findings show a significant relationship between trust in e-government and intentions to use e-services. This explains that trusting e-government has a positive impact on the respondents' intentions to use e-services and information offered by the government. Another association was found between respondents' perceptions of the usefulness offered by the use of online services and trust in e-government, supporting $H4$. This indicates that if e-government services and information are beneficial and helpful to respondents as they enhance their performance and facilitate government knowledge and information challenges, then this would lead to their trust in e-government, confirming results in many studies, for example [18, 52]. However, trust in technology did not show any significant relationship with the trust in e-government, rejecting *H2*. This could be justified by the fact that the majority of respondents were confident in their technological skills which might not be necessary for trusting e-government. *H5* was also negated as no significant relationship was found between perceived usefulness and intentions to use e-government services. Finally, a significant relationship was found between trust in e-government and civic engagement, confirming *H6*. These results indicate that public's trust in e-government is associated with their engagement in the society and that their views could be taken into consideration by government officials.

The study also explored the effect of respondents' demographic features on the research constructs. The results indicate that gender indicated significant relationship with trust in technology, trust in e-government, perceived usefulness and their intentions to use e-government services. This suggests that gender type could affect such factors leading to the adoption of e-government services. Also, age could affect e-government adoption when it is related to trust in government, trust in technology and their perceptions towards civic engagement. Educational background and technology skills of respondents only affected trust in technology factor. This could be attributed to the awareness levels regarding the privacy and security of the technology as well as the knowledge received through education about the benefits of technology, which could be employed to improve individuals' life. Interestingly, the nationality showed significant effect only on trust in government as residents showed higher trust in government than Kuwaitis. This could be explained by the better quality of life the residents have in Kuwait, compared with the living standard of their countries of origin.

8 Conclusion

In conclusion, this study has achieved its aim and investigated the trust factors that affect the use and adoption of e-government services for civic engagement. This study provides practical implications for government officials to devote efforts to re-build trust with the public and consider trust in technology, government and e-government as important factors associated with the acceptance, adoption and use of e-government services. This can be done through improving e-government services and making them useful, beneficial and easy to use to save the public's time and effort. Also, e-government programs, specifically in Kuwait, are expected to share and exchange government information, enable interaction with the public and offer them the tools through which they are able to express their views and specific needs and become part of the political process. This positively impacts the citizens' trust in government, thus achieving civic engagement.

The study used a relatively large number of individuals in Kuwait and the results could be generalized to all individuals in the society and specifically to countries in the Gulf region that share similar cultural, political and economic backgrounds; however, the characteristics of the sample could be biased to female and younger individuals with university degrees. Therefore, the findings are validated by establishing connections with relevant literature and by using statistical anlysis to report the results. This study is expected to add to the adoption literature on how trust is associated with the adoption of e-government services and how this association assists in the achievement of civic engagement. Further research is still required to investigate factors that increase the adoption and use of e-government services.

Acknowledgment. I hereby acknowledge the support of Kuwait University Research Administration in granting the Project (Grant No. OI02/18) and facilitating the research implementation.

Appendix 1: Research Constructs

Constructs	Statements	Sources
Trust in Government (TG)	I trust government agencies	Colesca [18]
	Government agencies keep my best interests in mind	
	In my opinion, government agencies are trustworthy	
	The trust in a governmental agency increase once with its reputation	
Trust in Technology (TT)	Technologies supporting the system (such as enquiring about traffic violations) are reliable all the time	Colesca [18]
	Technologies supporting the system are secure all the time	
	The technology used by government agencies is trustworthy	
	Overall, I have confidence in the technology used by government agencies to operate the e-government services	
Trust in e-Government (TEG)	E-government services are useful for me	Colesca [18]
	I believe that e-government services are trustworthy	
	I believe that e-government services will not act in a way that harms me	
	I trust e-government services	
Civic Engagement (CE)	The use of e-government information and services makes me willing to interact with government officials	Pavlou [42]
	The use of e-government information and services enables me to communicate my ideas to government	

(*continued*)

(*continued*)

Constructs	Statements	Sources
	The use of e-government information and services makes it easier for me to attend government public meeting to discuss government performance	
	The use of e-government information and services makes government officials accountable	
Intention to Use (IU)	I am intending to use e-government information to conduct my business with government	Kalu and Remkus [34]
	Most probably that I will continue to use the e-government information	
	I am planning to continue to use the e-government services in the future	
	I will use the e-government information if it is handy and available	
Perceived Usefulness (PU)	Using e-government helps me greatly in doing my work	Pavlou [42]
	Using e-government enhance my performance	
	Using e-government improves performance quality	
	Using e-government facilitates knowledge challenges	

References

1. Adler, R.P., Goggin, J.: What do we mean by "civic engagement"? J. Transform. Educ. **3**, 236–2533 (2005)
2. Adnan, H.M., Mavi, S.R.: Bridging social capital on Facebook as a platform: a case study of Malaysian college students. Asian Soc. Sci. **11**(15), 1–9 (2015)
3. Ajzen, I.: The theory of planned behavior. Organ. Behav. Hum. Decis. Process. **50**(2), 179–211 (1991)
4. AlAwadhi, S.: A proposed model of trust factors for e-government adoption and civic engagement. In: 52nd Hawaii International Conference on System Sciences, Hawaii, January 2019. IEEE (2019)
5. AlAwadhi, S., Morris, A.: Factors influencing the adoption of e-government services. J. Softw. **4**(6), 584–590 (2009)
6. Alenezi, H., Tarhini, A., Masa'deh, R., Alalwan, A., Al-Qirim, N.: Factors affecting the adoption of e-government in Kuwait: a qualitative study. Electron. J. e-Gov. **15**(2), 84–102 (2017)

7. Alotaibi, R.M., Ramachandran, M., Kor, A.L., Hosseinian-Far, A.: Factors affecting citizens' use of social media to communicate with the government: a proposed model. Electron. J. e-Gov. **14**(1), 60–72 (2016)

8. Amichai-Hamburger, Y., McKenna, K., Tal, S.: E-empowerment: empowerment by the internet. Comput. Hum. Behav. **24**(5), 1776–1789 (2008)

9. Andrews, R.: Civic engagement, ethnic heterogeneity, and social capital in urban areas: evidence from England. Urban Aff. Rev. **44**(3), 428–440 (2009)

10. Asgarkhani, M.: The reality of social inclusion through digital government. J. Technol. Hum. Serv. **25**(1), 127–146 (2007)

11. Berger, B.: Political theory, political science, and the end of civic engagement. Perspect. Polit. **7**(2), 335–350 (2009)

12. Bonsón, E., Torres, L., Royo, S., Flores, F.: Local e-government 2.0: social media and corporate transparency in municipalities. Gov. Inf. Q. **29**(2), 123–132 (2012)

13. Brehm, J., Rahn, W.: Individual level evidence for the causes and consequences of social capital. Am. J. Polit. Sci. **41**, 881–1023 (1997)

14. Carter, L., Belanger, F.: Citizen adoption of electronic government initiatives. In: 37th Annual Hawaii International Conference on System Sciences, Hawaii, (2004)

15. Carter, L., Belanger, F.: The utilization of e-government services: citizen trust, innovation and acceptance factors. Inf. Syst. J. **15**(1), 5–25 (2005)

16. Carter, L., Weerakkody, V.: E-government adoption: a cultural comparison. Inf. Syst. Front. **10**(4), 473–482 (2008). https://doi.org/10.1007/s10796-008-9103-6

17. Chan, C., Pan, S.: User engagement in e-government systems implementation: a comparative case study of two Singaporean e-government initiatives. J. Strat. Inf. Syst. **17**(2), 124–139 (2008)

18. Colesca, S.E.: Understanding trust in e-government. Eng. Econ. **63**(4), 7–15 (2009)

19. Craig, S.: The Malevolent Leaders: Popular Discontent in America, Boulder (1998)

20. Davis, F.D.: Perceived usefulness, perceived ease of use, and user acceptance of information technology. MIS Q. **13**(3), 319–339 (1989)

21. Dutton, W.H., Shepherd, A.: Trust in the internet as an experience technology. Inf. Commun. Soc. **9**(4), 433–451 (2006)

22. Ekman, J., Amnå, E.: Political participation and civic engagement: towards a new typology. Hum. Aff. **22**(3), 283–300 (2012). https://doi.org/10.2478/s13374-012-0024-1

23. Fishbein, M., Ajzen, I.: Belief, Attitude, Intention and Behavior: An Introduction to Theory and Research. Addison Wesley, Reading (1975)

24. Freeman, R., Loo, P.: Web 2.0 and E-government at the municipal level. In: 5th International Conference on e-Government, Boston, MA, 19–20 October 2009 (2009)

25. George, J.F.: Influences on the intent to make internet purchases. Internet Res. Electron. Netw. Appl. Policy **12**(2), 165–180 (2002)

26. Geys, B., Murdoch, Z.: Measuring the 'bridging' versus 'bonding' nature of social networks: a proposal for integrating existing measures. Sociology **44**(3), 523–540 (2010)

27. Gil de Zúñiga, H., Jung, N., Valenzuela, S.: Social media use for news and individuals' social capital, civic engagement and political participation. J. Comput. Mediat. Commun. **17**(3), 319–336 (2012)

28. Hetherington, M.J.: The political relevance of political trust. Am. Polit. Sci. Rev. **92**(4), 791–808 (1998)

29. Horsburgh, S., Goldfinch, S., Gauld, R.: Is public trust in government associated with trust in e-government? Soc. Sci. Comput. Rev. **29**(2), 232–241 (2011)

30. Jaeger, P., Bertot, J.: Transparency and technological change: ensuring equal and sustained public access to government information. Gov. Inf. Q. **27**(4), 371–376 (2010)

31. Jiang, J., Klein, G., Chen, H.: The effects of user partnering and user non-support on project performance. J. Assoc. Inf. Syst. **7**(2), 68–89 (2006)

32. Johannessen, M.R.: Social capital and the networked public sphere: implications for political social media sites. In: 45th of the Hawaii International Conference on System Sciences, Maui, Hawaii (2012)
33. Juris, J.S.: Networked social movements: global movements for global justice. In: Castells, M. (ed.) The Network Society: A Cross-Cultural Perspective. Edward Elgar, London (2004)
34. Kalu, K., Remkus, B.: The evolution of social capital and civic engagement between non-profit networks and country samples: a social constructivist approach. Soc. Sci. Comput. Rev. **28**(1), 135–150 (2010)
35. Kang, S., Gearhart, S.: E-government and civic engagement: how is citizens' use of city web sites related with civic involvement and political behaviors? J. Broadcast. Electron. Media **54**(3), 443–462 (2010)
36. Kuwait Government. https://www.e.gov.kw
37. Lollar, X.L.: Assessing China's E-government: information, service, transparency and citizen outreach of government websites. J. Contemp. China **15**(46), 31–41 (2006)
38. Mandarano, L., Meenar, M., Steins, C.: Building social capital in the digital age of civic engagement. J. Plan. Lit. **25**(2), 123–135 (2010)
39. Moon, J.M.: The evolution of e-government among municipalities: rhetoric or reality? Public Adm. Rev. **62**(4), 424–433 (2002)
40. Norris, P.: Digital Divide: Civic Engagement, Information Poverty, and the Internet World-wide. Cambridge University Press, Cambridge (2001)
41. Parent, M., Vandebeek, C.A., Gemino, A.C.: Building citizen trust through e-government. In: 37th Annual Hawaii International Conference on System Sciences, Hawaii (2004)
42. Pavlou, P.A.: Consumer acceptance of electronic commerce: integrating trust and risk with the technology acceptance model. Int. J. Electron. Commer. **7**(3), 69–103 (2003)
43. Putnam, R.D.: Bowling Alone. Simon and Schuster, New York (2000)
44. Putnam, R.D., Leonardi, R., Nanetti, R.: Making Democracy Work. Civic Traditions in Modern Italy. Princeton University Press, Princeton (1993)
45. Ranaweera, H.: Perspective of trust towards e-government initiatives in Sri Lanka. Springer-Plus **5** (2016). Article number: 22. https://doi.org/10.1186/s40064-015-1650-y
46. Rousseau, D., Sitkin, S., Burt, R., Camerer, C.: Not so different after all: a cross discipline view of trust. Acad. Manag. Rev. **23**(3), 393–404 (1998)
47. Tolbert, C.J., Mossberger, K.: The effects of e-government on trust and confidence in government. Public Adm. Rev. **66**(3), 354 (2006)
48. Transparency International. http://www.transparency.org
49. United Nations: United Nations E-Government Survey (2020). https://publicadministration.un.org/egovkb/Portals/egovkb/Documents/un/2020-Survey/2020%20UN%20E-Government%20Survey%20(Full%20Report).pdf
50. Uslaner, E.M., Brown, M.: Inequality, trust, and civic engagement. Am. Polit. Res. **33**(6), 868–894 (2005)
51. Valenzuela, S., Park, N., Kee, K.: Is there social capital in a social network site? Facebook use and college students' life satisfaction, trust, and participation. J. Comput.-Mediat. Commun. **14**(4), 875–901 (2009)
52. Van Riel, A.C.R., Semeijn, J., Janssen, W.: E-service quality expectations: a case study. Total Qual. Manag. **14**(4), 437–450 (2003)
53. Venkatesh, V., Morris, M.G., Davis, G.B., Davis, F.: User acceptance of information technology: toward a unified view. MIS Q. **27**(3), 425–478 (2003)
54. Voutinioti, A.: Determinants of user adoption of e-government services in greece and the role of citizen service centres. Procedia Technol. **8**, 238–244 (2013). 6th International Conference on ICT in Agriculture, Food and Environment
55. Warschauer, M.: Technology and social inclusion: rethinking the digital divide. Educ. Inf. **21**(2 & 3), 195–196 (2003)

56. Wellman, B., Anabel, H., Witte, J., Hampton, K.: Does the internet increase, decrease, or supplement social capital? Social networks, participation, and community commitment. Am. Behav. Sci. **45**(3), 436–455 (2001)

57. West, D.: E-government and the transformation of service delivery and citizen attitudes. Public Adm. Rev. **64**, 15–27 (2004)

58. World Bank: Enabling Environments for Civic Engagement in PRSP Countries. Social Development Notes, no. 82, Washington, DC (2003). License: CC BY 3.0 IGO. https://openknowl edge.worldbank.org/handle/10986/11319

Data Analytics, Decision Making, and Artificial Intelligence

Applying Explainable Artificial Intelligence Techniques on Linked Open Government Data

Evangelos Kalampokis[1,2(✉)] ⓘ, Areti Karamanou[1,2] ⓘ,
and Konstantinos Tarabanis[1,2] ⓘ

[1] Centre for Research and Technology Hellas (CERTH), Thessaloniki, Greece
{ekal,akarm,kat}@iti.gr
[2] University of Macedonia, Thessaloniki, Greece

Abstract. Machine learning and artificial intelligence models have the potential to streamline public services and policy making. Frequently, however, the patterns a model uncovers can be more important than the model's performance. Explainable Artificial Intelligence (XAI) have been recently introduced as a set of techniques that enable explaining individual decisions made by a model. Although XAI has been proved important in various domains, the need of using relevant techniques in public administration has only recently emerged. The objective of this paper is to explore the value and the feasibility of creating XAI models using high quality open government data that are provided in the form of linked open statistical data. Towards this end, a process for exploiting linked open statistical data in the creation of explainable models is presented. Moreover, a case study where linked data from the Scottish open statistics portal is exploited in order to predict and interpret the probability the mean house price of a data zone to be higher than the average price in Scotland is described. The XGBoost algorithm is used to create the predictive model and the SHAP framework to explain it.

Keywords: Linked data · Open Government Data · Machine learning · Artificial intelligence · XAI · SHAP · XGBoost

1 Introduction

Machine learning and artificial intelligence models have been recently employed to improve public services and policy making [25]. In many cases these models have been proven accurate to predict the outcome of relevant events and thus effective to support public administration and policy makers [12, 22]. It is common, however, the patterns a model uncovers to be more important than the model's prediction performance [3]. Explainable Artificial Intelligence (XAI) techniques have been recently introduced to explain individual decisions made by the model [1]. XAI aims at producing more explainable models while maintaining a high level of learning performance (e.g., prediction accuracy), and enabling humans to understand, appropriately trust, and effectively manage the emerging generation of artificially intelligent partners [7]. XAI has been already

© IFIP International Federation for Information Processing 2021
Published by Springer Nature Switzerland AG 2021
H. J. Scholl et al. (Eds.): EGOV 2021, LNCS 12850, pp. 247–258, 2021.
https://doi.org/10.1007/978-3-030-84789-0_18

proved particularly important in medical applications [13] and in transport [18]. However, the need for using relevant techniques in policy making and public administration only recently has emerged, and their value and feasibility are still not clear [8].

At the same time, Open Government Data (OGD) can play an important role in creating machine learning and artificial intelligence models [6]. Linked Data technologies can further contribute towards this direction because they enable the creation and dissemination of high-quality data that can be easily combined across disparate sources [10]. In particular, linked open statistical data provide statistics such as demographics (e.g., census data), economic, and social indicators (e.g., number of new businesses, unemployment). In statistics, linked data enable the application of analytics on top of disparate and previously isolated datasets.

The objective of this paper is to explore the value and the feasibility of creating XAI models using high quality OGD that are provided in the form of linked open statistical data. Towards this end, a process for exploiting linked open statistical data for the creation of explainable models is presented. Moreover, a case study where linked data from the Scottish open statistics portal are exploited in order to predict and interpret the probability the mean house price of a data zone to be higher than the average price in Scotland. eXtreme Gradient Boosting (XGBoost) is used to create the predictive model [2] and the SHapley Additive exPlanation (SHAP) framework to explain the predictive model [16].

The rest of this paper is structured as follows: In Sect. 2 the process for applying XAI techniques on Linked Open Government Data is presented. Section 3 presents the research approach that is followed to achieve the objective of the paper. Section 4 describes the case of creating an explainable predictive model using data from the Scottish open data portal. Finally, Sect. 5 summarizes the results and identifies open research issues.

2   Create Explainable Models Using LOGD

By adapting explainable machine learning processes in the literature [21], the four broad steps of our approach are defined:

Specifying the Problem: A supervised machine learning problem can be specified as either regression or classification. Government data and statistics typically include continuous variables and thus natively support regression analysis. However, classification problems can be addressed more easily and with higher accuracy. So, it is important in this step to transform a regression problem into a classification one. Moreover, the level of analysis should be decided in order to enable the use of a big number of data samples. For example, fine grained geographical areas (e.g., LAU levels in Europe) or time periods should be considered. Finally, the setting of the problem can be based either on time series analysis or on tabular analysis.

Collecting the Data: Today, a large volume of statistical data is disseminated using linked data technologies [9]. This linked open statistical data is provided on the Web through official open government data portals launched by organizations and public authorities. Examples include the data portals of the Scottish and Japan's (e-Stat) governments, the data portal of the environmental department of the Flemish government (VLO), DCLG in the UK, and the data portals that host the Italian (ISTAT) and Irish (Irish CSO) 2011 censuses. The connection of these data portals would create a Knowledge Graph of quality and fine-grained statistical data including demographical, social and business indicators across countries. This knowledge graph, that would facilitate data discovery and collection, can be created by identifying [9] and addressing [11] interoperability challenges for connecting statistical data from multiple trustworthy sources. All the official portals provide SPARQL endpoints and thus the data can be easily collected by specifying and submitting relevant queries.

Creating the Predictive Model: In this step the actual predictive model is created. This includes selecting the algorithm, tuning the model to the optimal hyper-parameter values, and selecting the evaluation score. The fact that the result of a SPARQL query is a tabular-style dataset should be taken into account. For example, tree-based models can be more accurate than neural networks in many applications. While deep learning models are more appropriate in fields like image recognition, speech recognition, and natural language processing, tree-based models consistently outperform standard deep models on tabular-style datasets [2].

Explaining the Predictive Model: An explanation is the collection of features in the interpretable domain that have contributed to produce a decision (e.g., classification or regression) [17] for a given example. Various approaches have been proposed for explaining model predictions varying in scope and flexibility [19]. The scope indicates whether the method generates global explanations or local explanations, whereas the flexibility indicates whether the approach is model-specific or model-agnostic. Local explanations reveal the impact of input features on individual predictions of a single sample. Two recently proposed model-agnostic methods are the linear interpretable model-agnostic explainer (LIME) [20] and Shapley additive explanations (SHAP) [14]. Although SHAP is a local explainability model, it introduces global interpretation methods based on aggregations of Shapley values. Due to their generality, these methods have been used to explain a number of classifiers, such as neural networks and complex ensemble models, and in various domains ranging from law, medicine, finance, and science [24].

3   Research Approach

In order to demonstrate the applicability and value of applying XAI techniques on open government data, the Scottish government data portal (http://statistics.gov.scot) providing statistical data for free reuse is employed.

Currently, the portal contains 250 datasets covering various societal and business aspects of Scotland at different granularity levels. Data Zones refer to the primary geography for the release of small areas statistics in Scotland, while Council Areas are the coarser geographical units in Scotland.

The portal utilizes linked data technologies in order to improve data quality and also to make available the data as a unified knowledge graph. The different datasets are connected through typed links (mainly using the RDF Data Cube vocabulary) enabling users to search in a uniform way across all the available datasets and to easily combine data from different datasets. The portal has released a SPARQL endpoint (https://statis tics.gov.scot/sparql), where users can submit queries to retrieve data.

In this case, eXtreme Gradient Boosting (XGBoost) is used to create the predictive model. XGBoost is an implementation of a generalized gradient boosting algorithm [2]. Boosting refers to the general problem of boosting the performance of weak learning algorithms by combining all the generated hypotheses into a single hypothesis [4]. This idea was further elaborated in gradient boosting [5]. In this case, one new weak learner is added at a time and existing weak learners in the model are frozen and left unchanged. The XGBoost algorithm has been applied to many domains, such as transportation, health, and energy, because of its high speed, high accuracy, and good robustness. It is indicative that during 2015, the 17 out of 29 winning solutions that were submitted to Kaggle competitions used XGBoost [2].

Moreover, the SHapley Additive exPlanation (SHAP) framework is employed for explaining the predictive model. SHAP, a local explainability model that is based on Shapley values, is employed [16]. The Shapley value method is a game theory method that assigns payouts to players depending on their contribution to the total payout where players cooperate in a coalition [23]. In machine learning the "game" is the prediction task for a single instance of the dataset. The "gain" is the prediction minus the average prediction of all instances and the "players" are the feature values of the instance that collaborate to receive the gain. The Shapley value is the average marginal contribution of a feature value across all possible coalitions.

The Shapley value method is computationally expensive because going over all coalitions scales exponentially with the increase in the number of features. SHAP solved this problem by enabling the exact computation of Shapley values in low order polynomial time instead of exponential by leveraging the internal structure of tree-based models [14, 15]. SHAP also proposed SHAP interaction values, which are an extension of Shapley values that directly capture pairwise interaction effects. Moreover, SHAP introduced global interpretation methods based on aggregations of Shapley values such as the SHAP feature importance, which is measured as the mean absolute Shapley values.

4   Predicting and Explaining House Prices in Scotland

In this section, the results of applying XAI techniques to linked open government data is presented according to the four broad steps defined in Sect. 2 and the detailed setting described in Sect. 3.

4.1   Specifying the Problem

In our case, the 2011 Data Zones are employed as the geographical units of analysis for the case study. Data zones are the core geography for dissemination of results from Scottish Neighborhood Statistics. They are designed to have roughly standard populations of 500 to 1,000 household residents. There are 6,976 2011 Data Zones.

The topic that will be explored is the mean house prices in the 2011 Data Zones in the year 2017. The average mean house price in 2017 across the 6,976 data zones is £168,285, while the median mean house price is £148,375. The problem that will be explored is the prediction of the probability the mean house price of a data zone is higher than the average price (£168,285). Moreover, what are the factors that contribute towards this prediction in each data zone.

4.2 Collecting Data from the Scottish LOGD Portal

In order to solve the specified problem, compatible datasets that can be exploited are collected from the Scottish open data portal. Towards this end, two criteria are specified: (a) the dataset includes data for 2017 as the year of reference, and (b) the dataset includes data at the granularity level of 2011 data zones. Because the available data have been shaped as Linked Data, a SPARQL query is structured in order to formally specify these criteria. In particular, the following query was submitted to the SPARQL endpoint of the Scottish portal to retrieve the compatible datasets.

```
PREFIX sdmx-dim:<http://purl.org/linked-
data/sdmx/2009/dimension#>
SELECT distinct ?b
WHERE {?a qb:dataSet   ?b;
       sdmx-dim:refPeriod <http://refer-
ence.data.gov.uk/id/year/2017>.
       ?a sdmx-dim:refArea   [?m <http://statis-
tics.gov.scot/def/foi/collection/data-zones-2011>].}
```

The query resulted in 17 datasets other than the "House Sales Prices" dataset. Each dataset includes one or more measures and thus the final list includes 23 variables that will be used in the creation of the predictive model. The final dataset containing the 23 variables was created by submitting a second query to the Scottish SPARQL endpoint. Table 1 presents the variables along with the results of an initial statistical analysis. Two Independent Sample t Test was used for the 23 continuous variables. Statistical analysis was performed using Python's SciPy library and values of $p < 0.05$ were considered statistically significant.

There are 2,340 data zones with mean house price above the average price. These areas are more likely to have dwellings with more rooms, dwellings that are not someone's main residence (second homes), healthier population, and to be more populated. In addition, they were less likely to have good accessibility to public transport, flats, families receiving child benefits, hospital stays related to alcohol misuse, people who are employment deprived, people being prescribed drugs for anxiety, and people living within 500 m of a derelict site.

4.3 Create a Predictive Model

In this paper, XGBoost is used to create the predictive model. The dataset created in the previous step was split in train and test sets in order to ensure that the evaluation of the model is unbiased. We tune the model using the train set and then we evaluate

Table 1. The data collected from the Scottish portal. Values are mean (±SD).

Variables	Overall (N = 5,841)	Above average (n = 2,340)	Below average (n = 3,501)	p value
Number of house sales	14.37 (11.36)	17.08 (15.39)	12.55 (6.99)	<0.001
Number of dwellings per hectare	19.91 (20.89)	15.99 (22.16)	22.53 (19.58)	<0.001
Number of flats	144.68 (168.62)	109.11 (162.31)	168.45 (168.59)	<0.001
Percentage of flats	33.43 (32.01)	25.02 (30.45)	39.05 (31.8)	<0.001
Median number of rooms in dwellings	3.99 (0.89)	4.52 (0.91)	3.63 (0.69)	<0.001
Number of dwellings	383.66 (117.88)	376.56 (126.75)	388.4 (111.32)	<0.001
Percentage of total dwellings that are long empty	1.37 (1.48)	1.41 (1.5)	1.34 (1.47)	0.08
Percentage of total dwellings that are occupied	96.12 (3.98)	95.81 (4.47)	96.33 (3.6	<0.001
Percentage of total dwellings that are second homes	0.93 (2.69)	1.43 (3.37)	0.59 (2.05)	<0.001
Percentage of population living proxime to derelict site	28.12 (39.05)	14.43 (28.62)	37.26 (42.28)	<0.001
Scottish access to bus indicator (weekday)	23.66 (36.73)	21.17 (40.97)	25.33 (33.5)	<0.001
Scottish access to bus indicator (weekend)	15.73 (25.22)	14.07 (27.6)	16.84 (23.44)	<0.001
Number of births	7.61 (5.3)	7.51 (6.56)	7.67 (4.25)	0.26
Number of deaths	8.51 (6.6)	7.56 (6.81)	9.15 (6.37)	<0.001
Mid-year population estimates	799.12 (221.37)	841.8 (267.66)	770.6 (178.49)	<0.001
Number of families receiving child benefit	80.15 (33.99)	72.77 (36.58)	85.08 (31.19)	<0.001
Number of children receiving child benefit	131.56 (58.55)	120.27 (61.9)	139.11 (54.93)	<0.001
Comparative illness factor	94.68 (50.64)	57.93 (28.25)	119.24 (47.32)	<0.001
Standardised mortality ratio	96.03 (42.38)	79.33 (39.34)	107.2 (40.64)	<0.001
Hospital stays related to alcohol misuse: standardized ratio	92.95 (88.95)	49.78 (48.9)	121.8 (97.61)	<0.001
Proportion of population being prescribed drugs for anxiety, depression or psychosis	18.56 (5.1)	15.2 (3.69)	20.81 (4.65)	<0.001

(*continued*)

Table 1. (*continued*)

Variables	Overall (N = 5,841)	Above average (n = 2,340)	Below average (n = 3,501)	p value
The number of people who are employment deprived	43.18 (33.98)	23.2 (19.37)	56.54 (35.07)	<0.001
The percentage of people who are employment deprived	8.58 (6.22)	4.35 (3.07)	11.41 (6.18)	<0.001

the final model in the test set. A total of 4,380 (75%) and 1,461 (25%) data zones were randomly assigned to the train and test sets, respectively. Repeated k-fold Cross-Validation was employed in order to ensure that our model will have low variance and bias. Part of data (the training sample) is used for training each algorithm, and the remaining part (the validation sample) is used for estimating the risk of the algorithm. Using Cross-Validation, several XGBoost parameters were selected to maximize model performance.

The performance of the models was assessed by measuring the total area under the receiver-operating curve (AUC). The model that was created and tuned is applied to the test set to get the AUC score in the holdout data.

The results of the machine learning model creation along with the optimal hyper-parameter values selected are depicted in Table 2. The holdout AUC score is 0.91.

Table 2. The AUC score to the created model along with the optimal hyper-parameter values

Train set AUC	Test set AUC	XGBoost parameter values
0.915	0.91	'colsample_bylevel': 0.8, 'colsample_bytree': 0.6, 'learning_rate': 0.1, 'max_depth': 3, 'n_estimators': 400, 'subsample': 0.8

4.4 Explain the Predictive Model

In this study the following types of visualizations are employed to explain the created predictive model:

- SHAP summary plots: beeswarm plots where the dot's position on the y-axis is determined by the feature and on the x-axis by the Shapley value. The color represents the value of the feature from low to high.
- SHAP Dependence Plots show how a feature's value (x-axis) impacts the prediction (y-axis) of every sample (each dot) in a dataset
- SHAP Interaction Value Dependence Plots: dependence plot on the SHAP interaction values, which allows to separately observe the main effects and the interaction effects.

SHAP Summary Plots. In Fig. 1 the SHAP summary plot is presented in the form of a set of beeswarm plots. The order of the features reflects their importance, i.e., the sum of the SHAP value magnitudes across all samples. Each point on the summary plot is a Shapley value for a feature and an instance. The position on the y-axis is determined by the feature and on the x-axis by the Shapley value. The color represents the value of the feature from low to high.

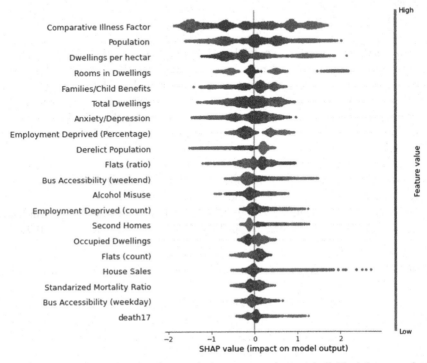

Fig. 1. A set of beeswarm plots, where each dot corresponds to an individual data zone in the study.

The plot reveals that the Comparative Illness Factor (CIF) is the most important feature globally. CIF is a measure of chronic health conditions that takes account of people from all ages. CIF greater than 100 indicates poorer health conditions relative to Scotland and vice-versa. The plot indicates the direction of the effects, meaning, for example, that low CIF data zones (blue) have higher probablity of having expensive houses than high CIF data zones (red). Moreover, the plot presents the distribution of effect sizes, such as the long tails of many variables. These long tails mean that features with a low global importance can be extremely important for specific data zones. For example, although the number of house sales normally do not imply the level of house prices, in some abnormal cases the high number of sales indicate areas with expensive houses.

SHAP Dependence Plot. The Impact of a feature's value to the prediction can be revealed by using the SHAP dependence plots. Figure 2-a clearly reveals the inflection point on the impact of the comparative illness factor (CIF) to the house prices. For low CIF values overall SHAP values are positive up to a point around 75. Then, SHAP values are negative, which means that by increasing CIF, the probability of high house prices decreases.

The vertical dispersion of SHAP values at a single feature value is driven by interaction effects. In Fig. 2-b, the number of people who are employment deprived is chosen for coloring to highlight possible interactions. The blue points mostly appear for lower values of CIF, meaning that areas of poorer health conditions tend to have more unemployed people.

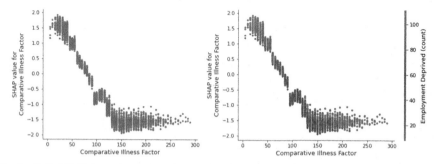

Fig. 2. (left) SHAP dependence plot of comparative illness factor vs. its SHAP value in the created predictive model, (right) SHAP dependence plot of comparative illness factor with interaction visualization with the number of people who are employment deprived.

SHAP Interaction Value Dependence Plot. SHAP interaction values can be interpreted as the difference between the SHAP values for feature i when feature j is present and the SHAP values for feature i when feature j is absent [18]. The interaction effect is the additional combined feature effect after accounting for the individual feature effects. In this sub-section SHAP interaction effects are explored. Towards this end, the plots of the SHAP interaction values of multiple pairs of variables are created and presented in Fig. 3.

The plot of the SHAP interaction value of 'Total Dwellings' with 'Population' (Fig. 3-a) shows how the effect of total number of dwellings on the probability of high house prices varies with population. The plot of the SHAP interaction value of 'Anxiety/Depression' (i.e., proportion of population being prescribed drugs for anxiety, depression or psychosis) with 'Population' (Fig. 3-b) shows that in data zones with depressed population of more than 23%, total population has a different effect on the probability of high house prices depending on the size of the total population. Small population size has negative effect, while large population size has positive effect. Moreover, the plot of SHAP interaction value of the percentage of flats with the comparative illness factor (CIF) (Fig. 3-c) shows that in data zones of poor health condition (CIF > 100) the effect of the percentage of flats reverses at a point around 25%. Similar patterns can be found in three more plots. Figure 3-d shows that the effect of 'dwellings per hectar' is different in data zones with small and large number of births. The same holds in Fig. 3-e and Fig. 3-f that depict the effect of house sales in data zones with high and low number of dwellings and dwellings per hectar respectively.

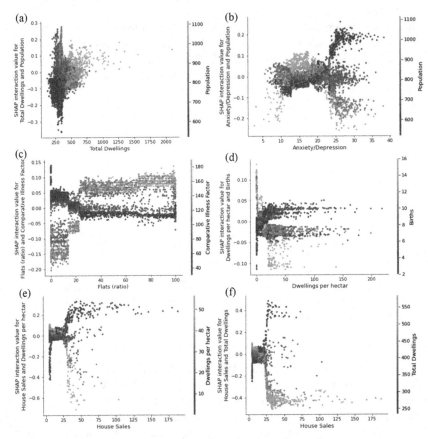

Fig. 3. SHAP interaction value dependence plots

5   Conclusion

Machine learning and artificial intelligence models promise to streamline public services and policy making. In many cases these models have been proven accurate to predict the outcome of relevant events and thus effective to support public administration and policy makers. However, there is growing emphasis on building tools and techniques for explaining these models in an interpretable manner. The objective of this paper is to illustrate the applicability and the value of applying eXplainable Artificial Intelligence (XAI) techniques on open government data that are formulated as linked open statistical data. Towards this end, a case study using data from the official open data portal of the

Scottish Government is presented. In this case, an XGBoost algorithm is used to create and SHAP framework to explain a model that predicts the probability the mean house price of a data zone to be above the average price across all 6,976 data zones. The AUC score of the created model was 0.91, while the analysis based on Shapley values revealed some interesting insights.

The analysis demonstrated that linked data facilitate the discovery and collection of high-quality data. The definition and submission of two SPARQL queries was sufficient to create the final dataset that was used for the creation of the predictive model. The first query identified 17 compatible and thus candidate datasets, while the second revealed 23 variables populated with data for the 2011 data zones. An important direction for future research in this area is to combine datasets that span across different data portals and countries. Interoperability challenges across data portals need to be further analyzed and addressed.

The creation of an accurate model using an advanced tree-based ensemble algorithm demonstrates that open government data can be used in machine learning scenarios. In this direction, the specification of an appropriate question to answer is of vital importance.

The local explanation analysis using Shapley values demonstrated the importance of such an analysis in policy making and/or public administration context. The computation of a feature's effect per individual case (e.g., in each data zone area in our case study) enables applying different policies or making different decisions based on the distinct characteristics of each case. For example, although in general the high proportion of population being prescribed drugs for anxiety, depression or psychosis indicates areas with low house prices, in few areas this high proportion abnormally contributes to predict an area of high prices. This significantly improves the ability of public administrations and policy makers to make more accurate data-driven decisions and apply more focused evidence-based policies.

Acknowledgements. This publication has been produced in the context of the EU H2020 Project inGOV which is co-funded by the European Commission under the Grant agreement ID: 962563.

References

1. Arrieta, A.B., et al.: Explainable Artificial Intelligence (XAI): concepts, taxonomies, opportunities and challenges toward responsible AI. Inf. Fusion **58**, 82–115 (2020)
2. Chen, T., Guestrin, C.: XGBoost: a scalable tree boosting system. In: Proceedings of the 22nd ACM SIGKDD International Conference on Knowledge Discovery and Data Mining (KDD 2016), pp. 785–794. Association for Computing Machinery, New York (2016)
3. Deeks, A.: The judicial demand for explainable artificial intelligence. Columbia Law Rev. **119**(7), 1829–1850 (2019)
4. Freund, Y., Schapire, R.E.: A decision-theoretic generalization of on-line learning and an application to boosting. J. Comput. Syst. Sci. **55**(1), 119–139 (1997)
5. Friedman, J.: Greedy function approximation: a gradient boosting machine. Ann. Stat. **29**(5), 1189–1232 (2001)
6. Gao, Y., Janssen, M.: Generating value from government data using AI: an exploratory study. In: Viale Pereira, G., et al. (eds.) EGOV 2020. LNCS, vol. 12219, pp. 319–331. Springer, Cham (2020). https://doi.org/10.1007/978-3-030-57599-1_24

7. Gunning, D.: Explainable artificial intelligence (XAI). Defense Advanced Research Projects Agency (DARPA), nd Web 2(2) (2017)

8. Janssen, M., Hartog, M., Matheus, R., Yi Ding, A., Kuk, G.: Will algorithms blind people? The effect of explainable AI and decision-makers' experience on AI-supported decision-making in government. Soc. Sci. Comput. Rev. (2021). https://doi.org/10.1177/0894439320980118

9. Kalampokis, E., Karamanou, A., Tarabanis, K.: Interoperability conflicts in linked open statistical data. Information 10(8), 249 (2019)

10. Kalampokis, E., Tambouris, E., Tarabanis, K.: Linked open cube analytics systems: potential and challenges. IEEE Intell. Syst. 31(5), 89–92 (2016)

11. Kalampokis, E., Zeginis, D., Tarabanis, K.: On modeling linked open statistical data. J. Web Semant. 55, 56–68 (2019)

12. Kouziokas, G.N.: The application of artificial intelligence in public administration for forecasting high crime risk transportation areas in urban environment. Transp. Res. Procedia 24, 467–473 (2017)

13. Lundberg, S.M., et al.: Explainable machine learning predictions to help anesthesiologists prevent hypoxemia during surgery. Nature Biomed. Eng. 2, 749–760 (2018)

14. Lundberg, SM., et al.: From local explanations to global understanding with explainable AI for trees. Nature Mach. Intell. 2(1), 2522–5839 (2020)

15. Lundberg, S.M., Erion, G.G., Lee, S.I.: Consistent individualized feature attribution for tree ensembles. arXiv preprint arXiv:1802.03888 (2018)

16. Lundberg, S., Lee, S.I.: A unified approach to interpreting model predictions (2017). arXiv preprint arXiv:1705.07874

17. Montavon, G., Samek, W., Müller, K.R.: Methods for interpreting and understanding deep neural networks. Digital Signal Process. 73, 1–15 (2018)

18. Parsa, A.B., Movahedi, A., Taghipour, H., Derrible, S., Mohammadian, A.K.: Toward safer highways, application of XGBoost and SHAP for real-time accident detection and feature analysis. Acc. Anal. Prev. 136, 105405 (2020)

19. Ramon, Y., Martens, D., Provost, F., Evgeniou, T.: A comparison of instance-level counterfactual explanation algorithms for behavioral and textual data: SEDC, LIME-C and SHAP-C. Adv. Data Anal. Classif. 14(4), 801–819 (2020). https://doi.org/10.1007/s11634-020-00418-3

20. Ribeiro, M.T., Singh, S., Guestrin, C.: Why should I trust you? Explaining the predictions of any classifier. In: Proceedings of the 22nd ACM SIGKDD International Conference on Knowledge Discovery and Data Mining, pp. 1135–1144 (2016)

21. Roscher, R., Bohn, B., Duarte, M.F., Garcke, J.: Explainable machine learning for scientific insights and discoveries. IEEE Access 8, 42200–42216 (2020)

22. Saltos, G., Cocea, M.: An exploration of crime prediction using data mining on open data. Int. J. Inf. Technol. Dec. Making 16(5), 1155–1181 (2017)

23. Shapley, L.S.: A value for n-person games. In: Contributions to the Theory of Games, pp. 307–317 (1953)

24. Slack, D., Hilgard, S., Jia, E., Singh, S., Lakkaraju, H.: Fooling LIME and SHAP: adversarial attacks on post hoc explanation methods. In: Proceedings of the AAAI/ACM Conference on AI, Ethics, and Society, pp. 180–186 (2020)

25. de Sousa, W.G., de Melo, E.R.P., Bermejo, P.H.D.S., Farias, R.A.S., Gomes, A.O.: How and where is artificial intelligence in the public sector going? A literature review and research agenda. Gov. Inf. Q. 36(4), 101392 (2019)

A Trustable and Interoperable Decentralized Solution for Citizen-Centric and Cross-Border eGovernance: A Conceptual Approach

George Domalis[1,3], Nikos Karacapilidis[2(✉)], Dimitris Tsakalidis[1], and Anastasios Giannaros[3]

[1] Novelcore, Patras, Greece
{domalis,tsakalidis}@novelcore.eu
[2] IMIS Lab, MEAD, University of Patras, Patras, Greece
karacap@upatras.gr
[3] Computer Engineering and Informatics Department, University of Patras, Patras, Greece
up1070374@upatras.gr

Abstract. Aiming to support a cross-sector and cross-border eGovernance paradigm for sharing common public services, this paper introduces an AI-enhanced solution that enables beneficiaries to participate in a decentralized network for effective big data exchange and service delivery that promotes the once-only priority and is by design digital, efficient, cost-effective, interoperable and secure. The solution comprises (i) a reliable and efficient decentralized mechanism for data sharing, capable of addressing the complexity of the processes and their high demand of resources; (ii) an ecosystem for delivering mobile services tailored to the needs of stakeholders; (iii) a single sign-on Wallet mechanism to manage transactions with multiple services; and (iv) an intercommunication layer, responsible for the secure exchange of information among existing eGovernment systems with newly developed ones. An indicative application scenario showcases the potential of our approach.

Keywords: Disruptive services in public sector · AI-enabled digital transformation · Distributed applications

1 Introduction

The rapid growth of Internet technologies, mobile communications, cloud infrastructures and distributed applications have brought an unprecedented impact to all spheres of the society and a great potential towards the establishment of novel eGovernance models [28]. These models should deploy core values such as improved public services and administrative efficiency, open government capabilities, improved ethical behavior and professionalism, improved trust and confidence in governmental transactions [25]. Towards the modernization of their

© IFIP International Federation for Information Processing 2021
Published by Springer Nature Switzerland AG 2021
H. J. Scholl et al. (Eds.): EGOV 2021, LNCS 12850, pp. 259–270, 2021.
https://doi.org/10.1007/978-3-030-84789-0_19

services and the reduction of the associated bureaucracy, public administrations need to transform their back-offices, upgrade their existing internal processes and services, and provide privacy-preserving and secure solutions. It is necessary to leverage key digital enablers, such as open services and technical building blocks (eID, eSignature, eProcurement, eDelivery and eInvoice), shared and reusable solutions based on agreed standards and specifications (Single Digital Gateway), as well as common interoperability practices (e.g. European Interoperability Framework). This leads to the upgrade of services that enable cross-border data sharing among public administrations, businesses and citizens. A vital part of delivering digital eGovernment services is related to the security principles, which demand the adequate identification of citizens and businesses that interact with these entities, while also assuring data protection and privacy.

Governance models, in general, do not adopt a citizen-centric paradigm [6]; they do not take into account citizens' needs and expectations of new services, often excluding them from operational and decision making processes. Moreover, documentation exchanges, processes and contact points do not function as a whole; they are rather dispersed and not sufficiently inter-connected among countries and organizations. Transparency and accountability are additional aspects of major importance towards building a good and fair governance model [2]. Admittedly, governments that employ models to make information sharing and decision-making processes transparent improve the principle of accountability and augment the participation of citizens and other stakeholders in related actions [7]. The corresponding digital transformation of public services can reduce administrative burdens, enhance productivity of governments, minimizing at the same time all the extra cost of traditional means to increase capacity, and ultimately improve the overall quality of interactions with and within public administrations [1].

Taking into account the above issues, this paper introduces a transparent, cross-border and citizen-centric eGovernance model for public administration services, which automates the processes and safeguards the integrity of interactions among citizens, businesses and public authorities. By taking advantage of emerging ICT technologies, such as Peer-to-Peer (P2P) networks, Distributed Ledger Technologies (DLTs) and smart data structures, we deploy a public distributed infrastructure, based on the InterPlanetary File System (IPFS) and a distributed ledger. This solution is based on a single sign-on Wallet mechanism that interconnects distinct decentralized applications (dApps) responsible for ID authentication, document sharing, information exchange and transactions validation, enabling a single point of access to information. The proposed solution is fully in line with the Government 3.0 paradigm, in that it meaningfully integrates a diverse set of disruptive and established ICTs [24].

The remainder of this paper is organized as follows: Sect. 2 is devoted to the presentation of the underlying technologies employed in our approach. The proposed digital transformation model, enabled through an architecture incorporating a series of prominent technologies, is presented in Sect. 3. Particular emphasis is given to the inclusion of data governance and knowledge management services to best facilitate and eventually reduce lengthy, cumbersome and repetitive bureaucratic eGovernment transactions. Section 4 validates the potential of our approach through a representative application scenario. Finally, Sect. 5 outlines concluding remarks and future research directions.

2   Underlying Technologies

Interplanetary File System. It is a P2P distributed file sharing system that seeks to connect all computing devices with the same file system by providing a high throughput content-addressing block storage model. IPFS distributes files across the network. Each file is addressed by its cryptographic hash based on its content, rather than its location as in traditional centralized systems where a single server hosts many files and information has to be fetched by accessing this server. This characteristic renders IPFS an ideal data storage solution for eGovernment services, where security and transparency are of utmost importance, since there is no single point of failure. One of the main content routing systems of the IPFS architecture is the Distributed Hash Table (DHT), which allows key-based lookup in a fully decentralized manner. IPFS leverages a DHT system, in that all IPFS nodes "advertise" content items stored in the DHT and this results in a distributed dictionary used for looking up content. Various applications integrating IPFS with ledger and blockchain technologies have already been reported in the literature for transactions recording [9] and secure file sharing with decentralized user authentication, access control and group key management mechanisms [16,21]. In the approach described in the next section, we leverage IPFS to provide increased capacity for managing large datasets in a decentralized manner and complement the throughput limitations of distributed ledger technologies.

Distributed Ledger. It is a distributed database architecture that records transactions on a P2P network and enables multiple members to maintain their own identical copy of a shared ledger without the need for validation from a central entity. Transaction data are scattered among multiple nodes using the P2P protocol principles, and are synchronized at the same time in all nodes. A public distributed ledger is characterized by an open unprotected environment with millions of participants, most of which have limited computational power and bandwidth, while most of the power is in the hands of a small fraction of the participating nodes. Thus, there is a significant risk of a "majority attack", in which a few nodes can dictate the choice of transactions. For eGovernance purposes, the design of a distributed ledger requires a comprehensive approach taking into account diverse aspects such as intermediate scale, high processing rate and low completion time with moderate energy consumption, unique attack model, and utilization of the underlying data structures.

Smart Contracts. They are decentralized, trusted computer programs stored on a blockchain that are automatically executed when predetermined terms and conditions are met. They facilitate, verify, or enforce documents and actions according to the terms of a contract or an agreement between two parties (i.e. agreements between eGovernance operators of two countries and end-users) that consist of a set of rules dictating a reaction when specific actions occur [27]. This set of rules is deployed on blockchain to ensure decentralized, transparent and secure characteristics. Upon meeting predefined conditions, a smart contract is executed automatically, making it independent of any central entity. Shields et al. [17] discuss the use of smart contracts for legal agreements and conclude that smart contracts will benefit from the legal precedent established in the electronic marketplace. In our approach, smart contracts are employed to manage the automatic execution of policies for the proposed services.

Decentralized Applications. They are composed of distributed entities that directly interact with each other and make local autonomous decisions in the absence of a centralized coordinating authority. According to Raval [20], a dApp is characterized by four features: (i) open source, (ii) internal currency, (iii) decentralized consensus, and (iv) no central point of failure. Bittorrent [3] was the initial dApp, enabling users to connect and exchange files. Soon afterwards, blockchain technology was introduced to manage the decentralization and enable the immutability of data. In the context of eGovernment 3.0, dApps can be leveraged to deliver diverse services such as ID authentication, document sharing, information exchange and transactions validation.

Smart Data Structures. The incorporation of Machine Learning techniques to explore causal relations among Big Data [22] in eGovernment systems is often deterred by interoperability inefficiencies [12]. *Smart data structures* [5] are a new class of parallel data structures that leverage online Machine Learning and self-aware computing principles to tune themselves automatically. They can replace existing index structures with other types of models, including deep learning models, referred to as learned indexes [4,15,23]. Recent works present preliminary outcomes of the conceptual and methodological aspects of semantic annotation of data and models, which enable a high standard of interoperability of information [26] and showcase how multi-input deep neural networks can detect semantic types [10]. We utilize smart data structures to identify and effectively transform data schemas and interconnect existing centralized systems with our decentralized solution.

Single Sign-On. It is an authentication mechanism that enables the use of a unitary security credential to access related, but independent, software systems or applications [14]. It enables simple username and password management, improved identity protection, increased speed and reduction of security risks. It also includes functionalities such as password grant (sign-in directly on the web), authorization code grant (user authorizes third-party), implicit grant (third-party web app sign-in), web services API that can effectively authenticate requests, and seamless user authorization experience on client-side technology. Various types of schemas exist based on (i) the type of infrastructure, (ii) the system architecture, (iii) the credential forms (token, certificate), and (iv) the protocols used. While single sign-on has been mainly used in mobile and Internet of Things applications, its integration with distributed file systems still remains a challenge.

3   The Proposed Solution

3.1   Research Methodology

For the development of the proposed open and cross-border eGovernance model, we have adopted the *design science paradigm* [8], which aims to extend the boundaries of human and organizational capabilities by creating new and innovative artifacts, especially for the information technologies domain. For our purposes, we have used the specific design science research methodology proposed by Peffers et al. [18] for the domain of Information Systems (IS) research, which includes the following stages: identify problem and motivation, define objectives of a solution, design and development, demonstration, evaluation and communication.

Furthermore, we have combined the above paradigm with that of *action research*, which aims to contribute both to the practical concerns of people in an immediate problematic situation and to the goals of social science by joint collaboration within a mutually acceptable ethical framework. It has been recognized that action research can be quite important in the IS domain, as it can contribute to improving its practical relevance [11]. In particular, it enables the design, implementation and evaluation of ICT-based actions/changes in organizations, which address specific problems and needs that are of high interest for practitioners, and at the same time create scientific knowledge that is of high interest for the researchers. The complementarity between these two research paradigms, as well as the great potential of integrating them, have been extensively discussed in the literature; both paradigms aim to directly intervene in real-world domains and introduce meaningful changes in them.

In particular, to address the issues elaborated in this work, we cooperated with two Greek government agencies (the Ministry of Digital Governance and a big local municipality) and two organisations with long experience in the development of novel software solutions for eGovernment. Involving their most experienced staff, we organized three workshops of 2 h duration each. In these workshops, we followed a qualitative approach (in-depth discussions) to collect relevant information and accordingly shape the foreseen services. Based on the information collected, we designed the solution presented below.

3.2   Our Approach

We propose a novel eGovernance model that creates new digital governance pathways through the integration of emerging technologies and breakthrough cross-sector services. We deploy decentralized applications (dApps) to deliver efficient, reliable and secure data sharing, auditing mechanisms and communication channels for the eGovernment sector. Our overall approach is digital by default, transparent and interoperable by design, and fully adheres to the once only priority. All the individual modules are designed to be built on top of the IPFS and a distributed ledger, as illustrated in Fig. 1. This extended combination of distributed technologies and infrastructures constitutes the backbone of our solution, which is capable of efficiently addressing the complexity of the processes, providing at the same time the security, trustworthiness, immutability and auditability required by contemporary public services.

By combining functionalities enabled by *DLTs* and *IPFS*, our approach allows users to control their data without compromising security or limiting third-parties to provide personalized services. IPFS has specific features that remedy the performance issues of dApps, improving their performance through an ad-hoc engagement of existing computational and storage resources. These features include: (i) content indexing, (ii) hash lookup, (iii) distributed naming system (IPNS, similar to DNS), (iv) persistence and clustering of data that reduce latency, (v) decentralized archiving, and (vi) compliance with privacy regulations. The public ledger stores the users' digital identities, access consent

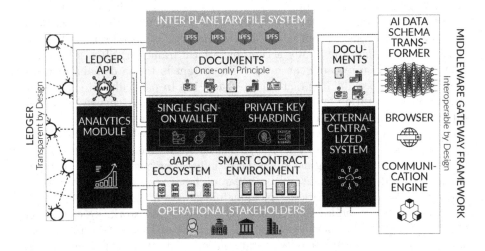

Fig. 1. The architecture of the proposed solution.

logs, and selected authentication transactions. It co-supports the public sharing resource infrastructure, providing the IPFS with advanced operational and technological capabilities, starting from security and privacy, up to immutability of transactions. It is located at the heart of the network to monitor and continuously record every approved interaction among the users' nodes. One of the major challenges is how to overcome the public nature of the ledger to ensure the security, privacy and anonymity of information. Towards this direction, we propose a combination of private and public keys to exchange information among end-users and services. In this way, a service does not observe raw data, but instead it runs its computations directly on the network and obtains the final results only after the consent of the user. We use DLTs since, from the data safety, authenticity and non-repudiation point of view, they provide an easily accessible and immutable history of all contract-related data, adequate for building applications with trust, accountability, and transparency.

The *dApps* are used to deliver dedicated services to users. They comprise smart contracts and are hosted in the nodes of the distributed network. The overall performance and storage capacity are increased through the participation of new nodes joining the network. Our approach renders legal and regulatory decisions simple, since law and regulations are programmed by smart contracts in the network and are enforced automatically, while the ledger acts as a legal evidence for storing such data.

A *single sign-on Wallet* is responsible for managing - with a common person registry - multiple services provided by various dApps, such as document sharing and information exchange, enabling a single sign-on user-centric document repository. This tool allows stakeholders to manage and share their personal and sensitive documents among different application environments in a single management kit, which can function in a fully distributed way, without a single point of failure. Hence, providing resilience and a continuum of service.

In addition, a middleware layer includes the following modules: (i) a *Secure Gateway Channel on-the-fly* to assure a secure intercommunication among systems, databases, apps, etc.; (ii) an *AI Data Schema Transformer*, which is based on well-defined libraries and AI models (i.e. GPT2 [19]) and encompasses the EU interoperability standards to effectively identify and transform data schemas, models and structures, and enable machine-to-machine communication among different types of systems across the EU. Synthetic data collections that map and simulate real data types (i.e. citizens ID, passport, birth certificate, criminal record, etc.) for different EU countries provide the backbone of this module's perception; (iii) a *Transactions-based Analytics Module* that runs as a back-end service on the network, gathering transaction histories and provide insights to users through a user interface developed and delivered as a dApp; and (iv) a *Browser Service Module* that acts as a search engine and facilitator of the network and other modules (i.e. the dApp ecosystem), providing users with diverse functionalities (locate files, documentation, services, entities, etc.) through user-friendly interfaces. This extended digital service availability enables any physical and/or legal entity (such as public administration, business and citizens) to integrate their own external centralized system in the network, enabling interoperability between users, cross-border and cross-sector organizations.

To effectively satisfy the desired interoperability by design principle, we deploy a machine learning based environment that automatically recognizes data structures in existing centralized systems. Specifically, we apply the notion of smart data structures by employing deep learning techniques to recognize and transform data schemas, data structures and data types. We apply data fusion techniques to meaningfully integrate heterogeneous information from multiple data sources that would otherwise remain uncorrelated and unexploited. To build a highly tuned system tailored to the specific needs of eGovernment services, we identify the data distributions and examine possible optimizations in the index structures to identify data patterns. The key idea is that a model can learn the sort order or structure of lookup keys and use this signal to effectively predict the position or existence of the associated records.

This holistic framework creates a novel eGovernance mechanism for communication, data sharing and information retrieval among centralized systems and decentralized/distributed applications. Stakeholders are able to use the single sign-on Wallet and the individual modules running on the network, while also having unrestricted access to the dApp ecosystem. This ecosystem hosts different dApps for each distinct service supported by the network, which are custom designed and deployed to meet the needs of the end users. The functionalities and the interdependencies of the dApps are formulated and defined with the use of dedicated smart contracts and user interfaces, hosted under the ecosystem. The dApp ecosystem includes libraries of common deployed smart contracts, enabling their reuse and activating users/developers to build and deploy their own applications. Finally, the distributed file storage architecture gives the opportunity to stakeholders to host their own custom applications in the network, thus contributing to its expansion and scalability.

4   An Application Scenario

According to the Treaty on European Union and Community law, EU citizens have the right to work and live in any EU Member State. However, the process of moving abroad to a foreign country is quite complex in terms of bureaucratic processes. For instance, a Social Security Number (SSN) is required in many EU countries before signing a rental contract. In most cases, the burden of such actions rests solely with the citizens, not in terms of legislation but in terms of complexity of the processes that need to be carried out, let alone the multiple visits people have to make to the relevant public authorities. The following scenario showcases the application of our user-centric solution, which simplifies the bureaucratic processes for citizens, businesses and public administrations.

Overview. Alice, a Greek citizen, finds a vacant job position in a private company in Portugal. She applies for the job and thankfully gets hired. In Portugal, she has to deal with a series of bureaucratic processes (issue an ID card and a SSN, open a bank account, provide evidence of her educational certificates etc.). To obtain a residence title, rent an apartment and open a bank account, she needs to present at least a validated ID documentation, a birth certificate, a nationality certification validated by a Greek Authority and a proof that she works in Portugal, along with the additional information that may be required by the employer. Adopting our solution, Alice is able to request from the Greek Authorities (Ministry of Digital Governance - MoDG) the proof of ID and the required data, validated. At the same time, Alice can remotely request from her formal educational institution (University of Patras - UoP) all the required certificates (diploma etc.).

In turn, MoDG issues the document and Alice gives permission (using a distributed application) to forward it to the respective public authorities in Portugal (Ministry of Justice - MoJ). As soon as this transaction is completed, Alice obtains, has access and is able to securely share her Portuguese SSN through her Wallet. Now, her employer in Portugal can directly get the validated SSN from the Portuguese MoJ, after her approval to register her credentials to their internal payroll system. Furthermore, the HR representative of the company needs a series of legal documents to proceed with the hiring process, including the permanent visa permit. Through her Wallet, Alice is able to provide and/or revise all the required personal documents.

Added Value. The contribution of this approach stands on the simplification of the processes and the significant reduction of bureaucracy. According to the current legislation and official procedures, the process to move to a foreign country for a new job is complex. Opening a bank account, renting an apartment or proving educational certification and achievements can be highly demanding in terms of paperwork, since in many cases there are requests that necessitate cross-border exchange of information and associated documents. Through the proposed eGovernance solution, inconsistencies in bureaucratic procedures will be avoided, such as requiring a local bank account before being able to rent an apartment, while at the same time requiring a local address before being able to open a bank account. Through a set of dApps from the distributed application ecosystem, which adopt a single sign-on Wallet approach and exploit the IPFS and distributed ledger infrastructure, Alice can use her validated digital identity to remotely request, obtain and share the required legal documents and certifications. Upon her permission, all these can be moved directly from the issuing authorities (MoDG, MoJ and UoP) to her new employer and any other potential entity (bank, utilities, etc.). These authorities digitally issue and validate the documentation and instantly push encrypted data into the distributed network, while the transactions among the users are being recorded. Any type of transactions, including requests, notifications and permissions, are monitored and safely

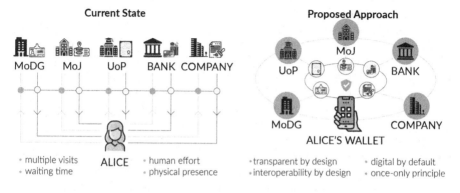

Fig. 2. Current practice compared to the proposed solution.

stored to protect Alice's privacy. All transactions are stored in a public ledger to enhance the security of information and eliminate any forgery attempts. Hence, enabling a secure-by-design eGovernment solution. This approach brings forward multiple advantages such as minimizing the chance of forged documentation, enhancing the transparency and security of information exchange in adherence with the relevant legislation, decreasing the overall effort of citizens and reducing significantly the waiting time to carry out the necessary transactions and issue the corresponding documents (Fig. 2).

5   Conclusions

This paper has described a novel eGovernance model that aims to make public administrations and public institutions open, efficient and inclusive, providing border-less, digital, personalised and citizen-driven public services. This solution offers citizens and businesses efficient and secure mobile public services and co-creation mechanisms, enabling governments to be extroverted and to preserve trust among public and private entities. The services delivered to citizens contribute to the digital by default principle for government and local authorities. In addition, our approach enables beneficiaries to participate and operate in a by design efficient, cost-effective, secure and cross-border distributed network for data exchange and service delivery.

The main contribution of this work is the meaningful integration and orchestration of a set of prominent tools and services, which build on state-of-the-art technologies from the areas of distributed computing and artificial intelligence, to address requirements concerning simplification of processes and reduction of bureaucracy in diverse eGovernment transactions. Our approach has been validated and elaborated in close co-operation with three government agencies (Portuguese Ministry of Justice, Greek Ministry of Digital Governance, and Istanbul Metropolitan Municipality), through which a series of rich application scenarios have been sketched and analyzed. While the feedback received from such a first-level validation was positive, and the proposed solution is open and inclusive by design, its application has to carefully consider the information capacity and available resources of each public sector organisation. Moreover, it has to be evaluated through diverse usefulness and ease-of-use indicators.

The proposed approach has interesting research and practical implications. With respect to research, it leverages the existing knowledge in the utilization of distributed computing and AI technologies in the public sector, and advances the digital transformation of eGovernment transactions. With respect to practice, our solution deploys a novel digital channel of communication and collaboration between citizens, businesses and governments. It addresses fundamental weaknesses of the existing eGovernment transactions in terms of bureaucracy, complexity, and unnecessary data entry, while also leveraging existing resources and infrastructures. As a last note, we mention that our approach can be applied in several real-life scenarios, such as the identification control in airports, where passengers need to be checked before departing and after reaching their destination. This application can also incorporate the management of the currently elaborated COVID-19 vaccination certificates [13]; the proposed decentralized blockchain ledger enable an immutable and transparent solution, according to which entries can be publicly audited and anonymity is protected.

Acknowledgements. This publication has been produced in the context of the EU H2020 Project "GLASS - SinGLe Sign-on eGovernAnce paradigm based on a distributed file exchange network for Security, transparency, cost effectiveness and truSt", which is co-funded by the European Commission under the Grant agreement ID: 959879. This publication reflects only the authors' views and the Community is not liable for any use that may be made of the information contained therein.

References

1. Androutsopoulou, A., Karacapilidis, N., Loukis, E., Charalabidis, Y.: Transforming the communication between citizens and government through AI-guided chatbots. Gov. Inf. Q. **36**, 358–367 (2018)
2. Bertot, J., Jaeger, P., Grimes, J.: Using ICTs to create a culture of transparency: E-government and social media as openness and anti-corruption tools for societies. Gov. Inf. Q. **27**, 264–271 (2010)
3. Cohen, B.: Incentives build robustness in BitTorrent. In: Workshop on Economics of PeertoPeer Systems, vol. 6, June 2003
4. Ding, J., et al.: ALEX: an updatable adaptive learned index. In: Proceedings of the 2020 ACM SIGMOD International Conference on Management of Data, SIGMOD 2020, p. 969–984. Association for Computing Machinery, New York (2020)
5. Eastep, J., Wingate, D., Agarwal, A.: Smart data structures: an online learning approach to multicore data structures. In: Proceedings of the 8th ACM International Conference on Autonomic Computing, ICAC 2011 and Co-Located Workshops, pp. 11–20, January 2011
6. Ghareeb, A., Ramadan, N., Hefny, H.: E-government adoption: a literature review and a proposed citizen-centric model. Electron. Gov. Int. J. **15**, 392–416 (2019)
7. Harrison, T.M., Sayogo, D.S.: Transparency, participation, and accountability practices in open government: a comparative study. Gov. Inf. Q. **31**(4), 513–525 (2014)
8. Hevner, A., Chatterjee, S.: Design Research in Information Systems: Theory and Practice, 1st edn. Springer, Boston (2010). https://doi.org/10.1007/978-1-4419-5653-8
9. Huang, H.S., Chang, T.S., Wu, J.Y.: A secure file sharing system based on IPFS and blockchain. In: Proceedings of the 2020 2nd International Electronics Communication Conference, IECC 2020, p. 96–100. Association for Computing Machinery, New York (2020)
10. Hulsebos, M., et al.: Sherlock: a deep learning approach to semantic data type detection. In: Proceedings of the 25th ACM SIGKDD International Conference on Knowledge Discovery and Data Mining, KDD 2019, pp. 1500–1508. Association for Computing Machinery, New York (2019)
11. Iivari, J., Venable, J.: Action research and design science research - seemingly similar but decisively dissimilar. In: ECIS (2009)
12. Kalogirou, V., Stasis, A., Charalabidis, Y.: Adapting national interoperability frameworks beyond EIF 3.0: the case of Greece. In: Proceedings of the 13th International Conference on Theory and Practice of Electronic Governance, ICEGOV 2020, pp. 234–243. Association for Computing Machinery, New York (2020)

13. Kofler, N., Baylis, F.: Ten reasons why immunity passports are a bad idea. Nature **581**(7809), 379–381 (2020)
14. Koundinya, V., Baliga, S.: A review on single sign on as an authentication technique. Int. Res. J. Eng. Technol. **7**(06), 409–414 (2020)
15. Kraska, T., Beutel, A., Chi, E.H., Dean, J., Polyzotis, N.: The case for learned index structures. In: Proceedings of the 2018 International Conference on Management of Data, SIGMOD 2018, pp. 489–504. Association for Computing Machinery, New York (2018)
16. Li, M., et al.: CrowdBC: a blockchain-based decentralized framework for crowdsourcing. IEEE Trans. Parallel Distrib. Syst. **30**(6), 1251–1266 (2019)
17. O'Shields, R.: Smart contracts: legal agreements for the blockchain. N. C. Bank. Inst. **21**, 177 (2017)
18. Peffers, K., Tuunanen, T., Rothenberger, M.A., Chatterjee, S.: A design science research methodology for information systems research. J. Manag. Inf. Syst. **24**(3), 45–77 (2008)
19. Radford, A., Wu, J., Child, R., Luan, D., Amodei, D., Sutskever, I.: Language Models are Unsupervised Multitask Learners (2019). https://openai.com/blog/better-language-models/
20. Raval, S.: Decentralized Applications: Harnessing Bitcoin's Blockchain Technology, 1st edn. O'Reilly Media Inc., Sebastopol (2016)
21. Sari, L., Sipos, M.: FileTribe: blockchain-based secure file sharing on IPFS. In: European Wireless 2019: 25th European Wireless Conference, pp. 1–6 (2019)
22. Somani, A., Deka, G.: Big Data Analytics: Tools and Technology for Effective Planning, 1st edn. Routledge (2017)
23. Tang, C., et al.: XIndex: a scalable learned index for multicore data storage. In: Proceedings of the 25th ACM SIGPLAN Symposium on Principles and Practice of Parallel Programming, PPoPP 2020, pp. 308–320. Association for Computing Machinery, New York (2020)
24. Terzi, S., Votis, K., Tzovaras, D., Stamelos, I., Cooper, K.: Blockchain 3.0 smart contracts in E-government 3.0 applications, October 2019
25. Twizeyimana, J.D., Andersson, A.: The public value of E-government - a literature review. Gov. Inf. Q. **36**(2), 167–178 (2019)
26. Villa, F., Balbi, S., Athanasiadis, I., Caracciolo, C.: Semantics for interoperability of distributed data and models: Foundations for better-connected information. F1000Research **6**, 686 (2017)
27. Wang, S., Yuan, Y., Wang, X., Li, J., Qin, R., Wang, F.: An overview of smart contract: architecture, applications, and future trends. In: 2018 IEEE Intelligent Vehicles Symposium (IV), pp. 108–113 (2018)
28. Wimmer, M.A., Viale Pereira, G., Ronzhyn, A., Spitzer, V.: Transforming government by leveraging disruptive technologies: identification of research and training needs. JeDEM - eJournal eDemocracy Open Gov. **12**(1), 87–113 (2020)

Using Business Data in Customs Risk Management: Data Quality and Data Value Perspective

Wout Hofman[1], Jonathan Migeotte[2], Mathieu Labare[2], Boriana Rukanova[3][(✉)], and Yao-Hua Tan[3]

[1] TNO, The Hague, The Netherlands
wout.hofman@tno.nl
[2] Belgian Customs, Brussels, Belgium
[3] Delft University of Technology, Jaffalaan 5, 2628 BX Delft, The Netherlands
{b.d.rukanova,y.tan}@tudelft.nl

Abstract. With the rise of data analytics use in government, government organizations are starting to explore the possibilities of using business data to create further public value. This process, however, is far from straightforward: key questions that governments need to address relate to the quality of this external data and the value it brings. In the domain of global trade, customs administrations are responsible on the one hand to control trade for safety and security and duty collection and on the other hand they need to facilitate trade and not hinder economic activities. With the increased trade volumes, also due to growth in eCommerce, customs administrations have turned their attention to the use of data analytics to support their risk management processes. Beyond the internal customs data sources, customs is starting to explore the value of business data provided by business infrastructures and platforms. While these external data sources seem to hold valuable information for customs, data quality of the external data sources, as well as the value they bring to customs need to be well understood. Building on a case study conducted in the context of the PROFILE research project, this contribution reports the findings on data quality and data linking of ENS customs data with external data (BigDataMari) and other customs (import declaration) data and we discuss specific lessons learned and recommendations for practice. In addition, we also develop a *data quality and data value evaluation framework applied to customs* as high-level framework to help data users to evaluate potential value of external data sources. From a theoretical perspective this paper further extends earlier research on value of data analytics for government supervision, by zooming on data quality.

Keywords: Data quality · Data analytics · Value · Government supervision · Customs · Risk analysis

1 Introduction

With the rise of data analytics use in government, government organizations are starting to explore the possibilities of using business data to create further public value [4].

Published by Springer Nature Switzerland AG 2021
H. J. Scholl et al. (Eds.): EGOV 2021, LNCS 12850, pp. 271–287, 2021.
https://doi.org/10.1007/978-3-030-84789-0_20

This process, however, is far from straightforward: key questions that governments need to address relate to the quality of this external data and the value it brings. In the domain of global trade, which is the domain of our investigation, with increased trade volumes due to for instance eCommerce, authorities like customs administrations rely more and more on IT-innovations to be able to perform their duties and deal with the large trade volumes. Customs administrations are responsible on the one hand to control the international trade for safety, security, and duty collection and on the other hand to facilitate fair trade and competition. Recently customs administrations around the world have turned their attention to the use of data analytics as part of their risk management framework.

Earlier research indicates that customs administrations face issues of low-quality data in customs declarations [7, 10, 18], which makes it hard to perform risk analysis and apply data analytics on such data [14]. Earlier e-government research has argued that government organizations can potentially create public value if they make use of business and other data beyond the data available in their government systems [4]. In the context of customs the goal is to improve its risk assessment processes and ensure public value such safety and security and revenue collection. More specifically, to improve the quality of data used in the customs risk assessment processes, customs starts exploring the value of business data provided by business infrastructures and platforms. But while external data sources hold a promise to enrich the customs data sets and provide better basis for analytics, the use of business data sources also raises issues and concerns such as: what is the quality of this data and is it of value [13, 14]? Other relevant aspects are data protection issues and use of the data in real-time risk assessment. While earlier eGovernment research has recognized the issues of data quality of customs data and the potential of using business data, so far the studies have remained on a high level and limited research has examined the issues of how business data can help to address data quality of customs data and how this business data can add value to customs. Especially as nowadays there is a large number of digital infrastructures and platforms for sharing business data that is potentially useful for customs, there is a need for a systematic approach for evaluating these data sources, their data quality, and how they contribute to improving data quality of customs data and generate value. The empirical basis for our study is the research performed in the EU-funded PROFILE project where variety of external data sources were acquired and evaluated for their potential for addressing deficiencies in customs data. Based on the case findings, detailed case-specific lessons learned for customs related to data linking and data quality of customs and business data are defined. Based on the insights form the literature and the case we also developed a high-level *data quality and data value evaluation framework applied to customs*. The remaining part of this paper is structured as followed. In Sect. 2 we provide a literature review on data quality, big data, value of data, and customs risk management. In Sect. 3 we present our case study method. The results of our case analysis are presented in Sect. 4. In Sect. 5 we present our *Data quality and data value evaluation framework applied to customs*. We end the paper with discussion and conclusions.

2 Related Research on Data Quality, Big Data, Value of Data, and Customs Risk Management

There are different definitions of data quality. Building on Vetrò et al. [20], we will focus on discussing two definitions of data quality First, looking at the inherent data quality characteristics rather than the technical characteristics, the ISO 25012 standard refers to the inherent data quality as "the degree to which quality characteristics of data have the intrinsic potential to satisfy stated and implied needs when data is used under specified conditions"[1]. Second, researchers have highlighted the "fitness for use" aspect when defining data quality [1, 17, 21], namely fit for use by a data consumer. For example, Strong et al. [17] argue that data quality research needs to look beyond the intrinsic properties related to data quality, and to focus also on the wider context and include data users. Strong et al. [17] distinguish between data producer or the party that produces the data, data custodian or parties that provide computing power to store and manage data and data consumers, or people who use the data. Strong et al. [17] define high-quality data as data that is fit for use by data consumers and they use four dimension categories and related dimensions to discuss high-quality data. The dimension categories and related dimensions are as follows: (1) Intrinsic data quality (accuracy, objectivity, believability, and reputation; (2) Accessibility data quality (accessibility, access security); (3) Contextual data quality (Relevancy, value-added, timeliness, completeness, amount of data); (4) Representational data quality (interpretability, ease of understanding, concise representation, consistent representation) [17]. Based on that they define data quality problem as "any difficulty encountered along one or more quality dimensions that renders data completely or largely unfit for use" [17, p. 104]. While this research dates back almost two decades ago, it is still used today [e.g. 9] and is very relevant for the context of our study. Especially linking data quality to use relates closely to the issue of value of data.

With the proliferation of platforms sharing large amount of business data, big data is becoming increasingly interesting for government organizations who may want to make use of this external data sources. Big data can be seen as "the information asset characterised by such a high volume, velocity and variety to require specific technology and analytical methods for its transformation into value" [3, p. 133]. Literature has identified various challenges related to big data. For example Sivarajah et al. [17] distinguish among (1) data challenges that are related to the data characteristics (i.e. volume, velocity, veracity, variability etc.); (2) process challenges (e.g. cleansing, data aggregation and integration etc.); (3) management challenges related to such topics as privacy, data ownership, security, data governance etc.

Cai et al. [2] specifically discuss the issue of data quality in the era of big data and identify several challenges, namely: (1) difficulty of data integration due to diversity of data sources and complex data structures; (2) the difficulty to judge data quality in a reasonable time due to the tremendous volumes; (3) fast changing time of data which adds requirements for processing time; and (4) lack of unified data quality standard. However, apart from these more technical aspects, research has argued that there is a need for understanding of value of big data and analytics performed on this data [5, 6, 15].

---

[1] https://iso25000.com/index.php/en/iso-25000-standards/iso-25012.

Looking at the eGovernment research specifically, the topics of data quality and big data are also of interest for the eGovernment research, where in the recent years these topics have gained attention in the area of open data research [8, 19, 20, 23]. Recent studies have also examined the use of big data and analytics for customs risk assessment [13, 14], where a value analysis framework was proposed. The value analysis framework [14] examines the value of big data and analytics from three views (interdependency view, process view and collective capability building view). The interdependency view examines value as an interdependency among the work practice level where the data and the related analytics are deployed in the customs risk assessment process, the organizational level where policies and priorities are set, as well as the supra-organizational level where interactions with external stakeholders are defined. Especially the supra-organizational view is very relevant for our study, as this is the interface with external data providers and it is at this interface where the engagement with the data providers will take place and the potential of the external data for customs will be examined. The process view from the value framework focusses on the processes of capability building and capability realization. The collective capability building view focussed on possible collaborative arrangements. While Rukanova et al. [14] explicitly include the external data providers and mention data quality issues, these are discussed on a very high-level and no in-depth understanding is provided on how customs can better understand what external data sources have to offer and how they add value in improving data quality of customs data for risk assessment purposes. This is the area which will further explore in this research.

3   Method

For this study we used interpretative case study approach [22], where in our study we were interested in exploring and gaining an in-depth understanding of the possibilities for customs to make use of external business data. The empirical context for our research was provided by the PROFILE project, more specifically the Belgian Living Lab, where research is focussed on examining the potential of external business data sources to improve the quality of customs declarations used for safety and security risk assessment (i.e. the Entry Summary Declarations (ENS)). It is important to notice that the intention is to improve data quality in the new customs regulation for incoming cargo, ICS2, but additional data can always be of value. Any changes will have to be implemented according to ICS2 from 2024 onwards, leading to different customs data sets. The external data source that is explored in the PROFILE project is BigDataMari (BDM). Customs declarations that are included in this paper are for outgoing cargo, the so-called Entry Summary Declaration (ENS), and import. We follow several steps in the case analysis, namely: (step 1) identification of data requirements for customs risk assessment where we took the focus on security and ENS declarations and (step 2) development of a domain model of data that is needed for customs risk analysis. We use this domain model as a basis of assessing data quality of the individual data sets:

customs data (in step 3^2) and the BigDataMari (in step 4). Based on the results of the previous step, in step 5 we made an analysis of the added value of customs and business data sets by linking those. In our assessment of data quality, we applied the approach of Strong et al. [17]: high-quality data as data that is fit for use by data consumers according to four categories with different dimensions:

1. *Intrinsic data quality* (accuracy, objectivity, believability, and reputation). We assume there are no challenges at this level, since we deal with known data sources.
2. *Accessibility* (accessibility, access security). This is not part of our study, since we received the data from their sources to study data linking.
3. *Contextual data quality* (relevancy, value-added, timeliness, completeness, amount of data). This is especially of interest from the perspective of data linking. The dimension 'value-added' will not be assessed, since it is assumed for each data set to be of value for particular processes like customs risk assessment or container shipment.
4. *Representational data quality* (interpretability, ease of understanding, concise representation, consistent representation). This category is also of relevance: are we able to interpret different data sets and create links. Concise representation will not be assessed for the same reason that 'value-added' is not assessed. Data sets are based on customs – and business standards for declarations and container shipping by sea respectively.

Based on these categories and dimensions Strong et al. [17] define data quality problem as "any difficulty encountered along one or more quality dimensions that renders data completely or largely unfit for use" [17, p. 104]. In our approach, we will focus on the last two categories: contextual and representational data quality. This refers to the aspects of Interpretation and Re-usability of data as explained by the FAIR principles[3] (FAIR – Findable, Accessible, Interpretable, and Re-usable). These principles can be expressed by the aforementioned data quality categories and dimensions.

4 Case Analysis

This section describes the case by first assessing customs data requirements, secondly map them to a domain model and thirdly relate the various data sets to this domain model. We will assess data quality by exploring links of BigDataMari data with Entry Summary Declarations (ENS) and ENS with import declarations.

---

[2] We first started with ENS customs data, then did the mapping of the BigDataMari data, based on gaps we examined BigDataMari, and subsequently added an additional customs data source, i.e. import declaration data.

[3] https://www.go-fair.org/fair-principles/.

4.1 Customs Data Requirements

Customs has developed a taxonomy of risks. The main groups of fiscal, economic, security, safety, drugs trafficking, and environmental risks are identified. These can be further decomposed, e.g. fiscal risks are decomposed into VAT, excise tax, anti-dumping, countervailing and customs duties.

Risks are perceived along two dimensions, namely the supply – and the logistics chain dimension. The supply chain dimension is on the movement of products and their components from a supplier to for instance an (eCommerce) buyer. These products flows can be triggered in different ways. Buy-sell is one approach, stock replenishment based on foreign production another, and Vendor Managed Inventory (VMI) yet another one. Stock replenishment can be based on internal production or purchasing orders, depending on the structure of a company. Stock replenishment can be supported by an third party or internal department providing purchasing services to for instance retail stores. On supply chain level, origin and destination, product composition, (invoice) value and product classification for customs purposes needs to be known, i.e. the Harmonised Systems code.

Logistics chains are on the movement of these products from an origin to a destination. Products become goods by packing them to facilitate transport. A variety of packaging types can be applied like boxes on pallets, that are put into containers. Each movement and unpacking or repacking can give a potential risk, e.g. fiscal risks like anti-dumping and economic risks lie IPR protection, quotas, and licenses of trade agreements.

This paper focusses on data requirements for customs risks assessment based on logistics chains. The following data is required:

- Transport flow – it concerns the flow of transport means with their various operations. It is decomposed into:

  o Itinerary - a timed sequence of transshipment locations or hubs (place of call) passed by a transport means for loading/discharging goods/containers (synonym: voyage, conveyance, trip)
  o Route - the use of the infrastructure taken by a transport means between any two places of call of its itinerary

- Cargo flow – it concerns the flow of package products, decomposed into:

  o Goods flow - timed sequence of transport legs and/or container tracks
  o Container track - timed sequence of transport legs for a container
  o Transport leg - transport of goods or containers between two adjacent (in time) locations with one transport means (e.g. POL, POD)

- Logistics chain structure - combination of physical flows (cargo/transport) and parties involved

These concepts will determine the data that has to be available from logistics chains.

4.2   Capturing the Domain of Interest

The domain of interest, the logistics domain, is characterized by the following concepts:

- Physical objects like packages, pallets, containers, and transport means like vessels and trucks.
- Locations where these physical objects can be transhipped, originate from, are destined for, or are stored under customs regime.
- Events representing associations in time between physical objects, like a container loaded on a vessel, or between a physical object and a location, like a container located on a terminal. The time can be in the past, present, or future, where a future time is represented from the expectation of a customer or the estimation of a service provider.
- Parties involved based on commercial transactions between these parties. For instance, a forwarder acting as service provider for shippers with the possibility to combine logistics flows for optimization.

These concepts construct so-called logistics chains in logistics systems. The system boundaries of our domain of interest are goods flows from outside into the European Union with containers via sea. This requires various transport modes, groupage and stripping, loading and discharge. The following Fig. 1 shows the physical flow from an origin, i.e. PLA – Place of Acceptance, to a destination, i.e. PLD – Place of Delivery.

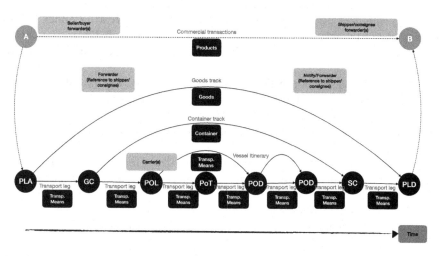

Fig. 1. Logistic chain.

Where the goods track is between PLA and PLD, container tracks are from a Groupage Centre (GC) to a Stripping Centre (SC) via a Port of Loading (POL; out-going) and a Port of Discharge (POD; incoming). In-between a POL-POD, containers might be transhipped in a Port of Transhipment (POT). The figure shows two Ports of

Discharge, where the first POD is the first port of call of a vessel in the EU and the second is where a container is discharged (these can be identical). The different transport legs visualize the movement of goods or containers from one location to another. At all locations, the relation between physical objects in time can be given. The goods – and container track information can be based on any reporting of a transport means of its load/unload operation of particular goods or containers. For instance, a container track is based on reporting by a carrier from a GC to POL, another carrier from POL to POD and a final one from POD to SC. This might be the same carrier, i.e. the shipping line, coordinating transport from GC-POL and POD-SC, in which case it is called carrier haulage.

The figure shows commercial transactions, e.g. purchasing orders and replenishment orders, trigger the processes. It also shows that location A can be a third party purchasing organization acting on behalf of buyers at location B, where location A differs from PLA and B differs from PLD.

4.3   Mapping and Analysing the Quality of the Different Data Sets

For maritime transport, the ENS, Entry Summary Declaration, has to be submitted 24 h prior to loading by a carrier in the port of loading, although there are exceptions. It provides data of containers that will be loaded and transported via sea to a European port. The Uniform Customs Code – Incoming Cargo System identifies two important European ports in this context, namely the first port of call of a vessel in an EU Member State (MS), the so-called Customs Office of Entry (COFE) and the actual port of unloading with the Customs Office of Unloading (COU). Figure a1 in Annex 1 shows the mapping of the relevant ENS concepts to the domain model. Table 1 presents the data quality of the ENS in relation to the data requirements expressed in the domain model.

The second data source is called 'BigDataMari' (BDM). The three data sets mentioned are linked, e.g. a shipping instruction refers to a booking and a container status message to a shipping instruction.

The functionality of these three data sets can be described as follows:

- Booking – an indication provide by a customer like a forwarder or a shipper to a carrier for the requirement of transport of a number of containers between two ports. Transport requirements are expressed by the number of Twenty feet Equivalent Units (TEU) to be transported from a POL to a POD with estimated dates/times.
- Shipping instruction – this data set contains details of containers and refers to a vessel for loading.
- Container Status Message – this data set has the actual status of container movements like loading in a POL onto a vessel and discharging in a POD, potentially from another vessel.

Table 1. Analysis of quality of individual data sets.

Data quality		ENS	BDM	Import
Contextual				
	Relevancy	The data set provides a part of a vessel itinerary or container track of containers shipped to the EU or transhipped in an EU country to a non-EU country	The data set provides a (part of) a container track. The data set contains sea containers shipped to a particular country	This data set refers to commercial transactions. It provides details of products imported in the EU like their value
	Timeliness	Time is not related to the physical activity, but to sharing the data set (creation – and issue date) In ICS2, the actual date of departure and estimated time of arrival will be included	The data set contains an expected container track and the actual one, given by Container Status Messages	Submission of an import declaration is completely independent of a container track. A declaration can be submitted before container arrival or many days later
	Completeness	The part of the data provided is not complete. It does not cover vessel itinerary (which can change) or container track	Data might be present in different data fields, e.g. a customs code (HS-code) might be in free text goods description The container track might change due to changes in a vessel itinerary and/or transhipment The data set does not cover all container flows to a particular country	The import declaration does not fully relate to commercial transactions, e.g. multiple invoices per declaration or multiple declarations per invoice With respect to the link to incoming containers, completeness is specified by the write-off process. This is an error prone (fuzzy) process, not always leading to complete links
Representational				
	Interpretability	A customs goods item is generated from a free text goods description, which does not make it reliable	Fits with the logistics perspective of the domain	The customs goods item will have an HS-code optimizing duty payment of an importer

(*continued*)

Table 1. (*continued*)

Data quality		ENS	BDM	Import
Contextual				
	Ease of understanding	Goods item is to be interpreted from a customs perspective – based on the Harmonised Systems Code. This differs from logistics	Fits with the logistics perspective of the domain	Same as for ENS. The write-off (error prone and fuzzy) relates an import declaration to container track and the HS-code should relate to a (commercial) product
	Consistent representation	Different use of free text fields like parties involved	Different use of data fields by different users, especially the free text fields, for instance goods description and parties involved	Different use of free text fields like parties involved. An importer can differ from a consignee or buyer

All relevant data elements in these three data sets can be mapped to the domain model, as shown in Figure a2 in Annex 1. The figure shows that a container can also be pickup at a GC, called place of receipt, and dropped off at an SC, called place of delivery. This relates to variants in logistics operations. The place of receipt can also be the PLA and the place of delivery can be identical to the PLD, in which case only container data is known and no data on goods is available. The latter case is known as carrier haulage with a Full Container Load (FCL).

The third data set is that of import, linked to incoming cargo movements. Import declarations are the basis for paying import duties. Undervaluation by an importer is one of the risks that needs to be assessed. Undervaluation can be a basis for unfair competition. Incoming cargo movements can refer to a container that might be present in an ENS and/or import declaration.

The following table lists the data quality of each of these three data sets on the relevant aspects (Sect. 2).

4.4 Linking Data Sets

Linking of data is based on (1) identifying data field similarities of and (2) finding data of those similar fields in two or more data sets.

Data field similarity relates to ontology alignment. An overview of ontology alignment approaches, algorithms, and indicators can be found in Mohammadi [11]. Data fields similarity is by mapping the data fields of different data sets to our domain model with data requirements and using data quality assessment. Figure a3 in Annex 1 shows potential similarities of BDM and ENS and Figure a4 in Annex 1 the ENS to the import via the write-off process. The links on containers of BDM to import has not yet been assessed (Table 2).

Table 2. Issues of linking.

Data quality		ENS – BDM	ENS – Import
Contextual			
	Relevancy	BDM – booking and shipping instructions are the basis for ENS declarations. These should map on container and potentially HS-code	Combination of ENS and import should provide more data on logistics – (ENS) and commercial flows (import). It might enable customs to configure data analytics for customs risk assessment using inspection results of both data sets. However, risk categories for both types of declarations might not completely overlap
	Timeliness	There is a fuzzy relation on date/time between ENS and BDM, since ENS does not contain a logistics time	Matching on 'time' cannot be done
	Completeness	BDM could complete the ENS data set with actual status date providing details of transhipment and itinerary deviations. However, BDM does not cover all incoming containers	The write-off of import data would complete the data requirements. However, fuzziness and error prone of write-off makes it difficult to construct this completeness
Representational			
	Interpretability	Linking is only feasible on containers	Linking only feasible via the write-off process
	Ease of understanding	Customs goods item can only be used if it is copied from BDM	The customs goods item (HS-codes) of ENS and Import will differ. Thus, they cannot be applied for linking, although they have the same definition
	Consistent representation	Different use of free text fields does not allow to use these for linking	Different use of free text fields does not allow to use these for linking

All data sets are of 2018. The ENS and import declaration data sets are of one EU Member State. The BDM data set contains container shipments to two EU Member States, including the one for which we have the ENS and import declaration data sets. Figures of the actual mapping cannot be given in this paper, since these are confidential. Our findings are as follows: the union of ENS and import consists of 20% of containers in ENS and 6% of the containers in import declarations, and the union of ENS and BDM consists of 20% of the containers in ENS and 11% of the containers in BDM.

The relative low percentage of linking data sets relates to issues on data quality and similarities. Other reasons are due to the fact that a customs administration links a declaration to a previous one, using a write-off process. A further issue on the low percentage of linking relates to different procedures on a data level. For instance, import can relate to products coming into the EU via sea, air, road, or rail, where ENS only refers to sea. Import can also be transit from another EU Member State, in which case there is not a link to ENS. Of the number of actual incoming sea container, a number will also be put into transit to other Member States or outside the EU countries, e.g. to Norway.

5 Discussion

5.1 Discussion on the Case Findings and Case-Specific Lessons Learned

In this contribution, we have explored data quality categories and dimensions for assessing the potential value of linking different customs data sets and linking a business data set to a customs data set. The value is expressed in terms of data requirements for customs risk assessment.

There is value in linking the business data set BDM to the ENS data set. It provides more information on vessel itinerary and container track required by customs authorities. In case the import data set can be properly linked to commercial transactions and incoming cargo, there could also be value in linking the import data set to ENS. This value could be realized by training data analytics based on inspection results, but only if risk assessment and targeting of import and ENS is identical, i.e. on identical risks in a risk taxonomy.

Due to data quality issues of the different data sets and differences in customs procedures like ENS and import, it is difficult to link different data sets as shown by our analysis on data level. Only structured data fields have been used to identify links. This is to do with dimensions 'time' and 'ease of understanding', where the latter refers to differences in HS-code for different customs procedures. The extension of 'time' with actual departure date and estimated arrival data in ICS2 is expected to improve linking.

Concluding, the value of linking data is based on data requirements. We have formulated these data requirements in terms of our domain and identified similarities in different data sets expressed in the domain. By increasing the similarities, data completeness and thus data quality will improve. However, it requires to address other dimensions like 'time', 'consistency', and 'ease of understanding'. These can be improved by for instance encapsulating logistics events like present in BDM in customs declarations, at least for outgoing (ENS) and incoming declarations. These logistics events can be generated by each transport leg, part of an itinerary. A second improvement would be to create a better link between import and cargo flows. It requires stuffing of containers, packing lists with reference to products and their (invoice) value, and an explicit relation between a customs goods item and (commercial) products in import declarations.

In fact, all types of links need to be created, resulting in complex data sets. A proposed approach is to create a semantic model reflecting all potential associations as a basis for analysing data from different perspectives. Such a model is under development in the CEF (Connecting European Facilities) funded FEDeRATED Action (www.federatedpla tforms.eu). Experiments for linking data sets to this model are performed by the H2020 PROFILE project.

5.2 Evaluation Framework for Data Value and Data Quality Applied to Customs

Beyond the case-specific findings, based on the insights from the theory and from the case we derived a general framework (Fig. 2) that can be used by customs for reasoning about the data quality and data value of external data that can be used for customs risk analysis.

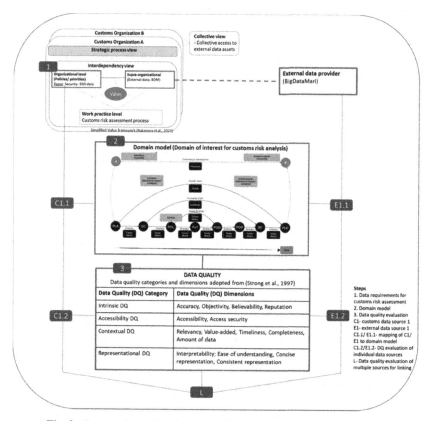

Fig. 2. Data quality and- value evaluation framework applied to customs.

Theoretically our framework combines the data value perspective (building on the value framework [14]), and the data quality categories and dimensions [17], and we explicitly added the domain model of the domain of interest for customs risk analysis derived from the case. In addition, our framework also captures the process steps that customs can follow when evaluating data quality and potential value of external data, as well as link to engagement with external data providers.

Starting form the value model and the organizational level, step 1 in our framework relates to data requirements for customs risk assessment. Step 2 in our framework focusses on the development of the domain model. In our framework we included the domain model of the domain of interest for customs risk analysis that we derived based on the case. We consider this model to be quite generic for different risk analysis purposes however in practice it may be limited for some situations and may need to be extended. Step 3 focusses on data quality evaluation using the domain model. Subsequently, our framework indicates that specific customs data sources (e.g. Customs data source 1 - C1 or external data source 1-E1) can be mapped to the domain model (step C1.1 and E1.1 respectively). Subsequently a data quality evaluation of each of the individual customs and externals data sources can be performed individually by using the categories of Strong et al. [17]. (see C1.2 and E1.2 in Fig. 2). Finally, data quality evaluation of multiple sources for linking can be also performed (marked with L in Fig. 2).

The detailed illustration of how the data quality assessment of the individual data sources and the linking is done was already discussed in the case analysis and these detailed illustrations can be used to guide such analysis on other data sources as well.

6   Conclusions

In this paper we provided a detailed case study on linking customs and business data and assessing their data quality and – value in the context of data requirements. Based on our analysis, we provide detailed lessons learned and recommendations for practice. In addition, we developed an evaluation framework for data quality and – value assessment of linked data sets based on data requirements and a domain model. This framework can be used as a support tool for customs experts (nationally and internationally) involved in data analytics for customs. The framework allows to go in-depth in order to provide detailed insights into what kind of data can be found in specific business data sources and how it adds/complements existing customs data. At the same time the framework allows for a level of abstraction from very technical details, which makes it also useful for people involved in data analytics projects at a managerial and policy level. The framework might, for instance, be useful to assess proposed changes of the ICS2 regulation. From a theoretical perspective this paper further extends earlier frameworks on value of data analytics for government supervision, by zooming in more specifically on data quality.

Our framework also has a number of limitations which open also possibilities for further research. First of all, our analysis and the resulting framework focus on specific aspects of the value framework of Rukanova et al. [15], mostly on the inter-dependency view and the organizational level. Further research can also examine what the effects of using the external data are at a work practice level, where data analytics based on combined customs and external data takes place. Furthermore, further research can also explore the effects taking the process view, as well as the collective view of the value model [15] into account.

Acknowledgement. This research was partially funded by the PROFILE Project (nr. 786748), which is funded by the European Union's Horizon 2020 research and innovation program. Ideas and opinions expressed by the authors do not necessarily represent those of all partners.

Annex 1. Using the Domain Model for Mapping of Data from ENS, BDM and Import Declarations

See Figs. a1, a2, a3, a4.

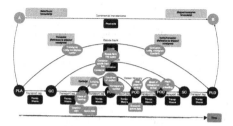

Fig. a1. Data in an ENS

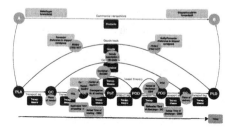

Fig. a2. Mapping BDM to the domain and linking data to ENS

Fig. a3. Linking BDM to ENS

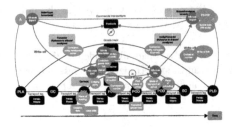

Fig. a4. ENS and import declarations

References

1. Batini, C., Cappiello, C., Francalanci, C., Maurino, A.: Methodologies for data quality assessment and improvement. ACM Comput. Surv. **41**(3), 52. Article 16 (2009). https://doi.org/10.1145/1541880.1541883
2. Cai, L., Zhu, Y.: The challenges of data quality and data quality assessment in the big data era. Data Sci. J. **14**, 2 (2015). https://doi.org/10.5334/dsj-2015-002
3. De Mauro, A., Greco, M., Grimaldi, M.: A formal definition of big data based on its essential features. Libr. Rev. **65**(3), 122–135 (2016)
4. Gil-Garcia, J.R.: Towards a smart State? Inter-agency collaboration, information integration, and beyond. Inf. Polity **17**(3, 4), 269–280 (2012)
5. Grover, V., Chiang, R.H., Liang, T.P., Zhang, D.: Creating strategic business value from big data analytics: a research framework. J. Manag. Inf. Syst. **35**(2), 388–423 (2018)
6. Günther, W.A., Mehrizi, M.H.R., Huysman, M., Feldberg, F.: Debating big data: a literature review on realizing value from big data. J. Strateg. Inf. Syst. **26**(3), 191–209 (2017). https://doi.org/10.1016/j.jsis.2017.07.003
7. Heijmann, F., Tan, Y.H., Rukanova, B., Veenstra, A.: The changing role of Customs: customs aligning with supply chain and information management. World Customs J. **14**(2) (2020)
8. Higgins, A., Klein, S.: Introduction to the living lab approach. In: Tan Y.H., Björn-Andersen N., Klein S., Rukanova B. (eds.) Accelerating Global Supply Chains with IT-Innovation, pp.37–54. Springer, Heidelberg (2011). https://doi.org/10.1007/978-3-642-15669-4_2
9. Janssen, M.F.W.H.A., van den Hoven, M.J.: Big and Open Linked Data (BOLD) in government: a challenge to transparency and privacy? Gov. Inf. Q. **32**(4), 363–369 (2015)
10. Juddoo, S., George, C., Duquenoy, P., Windridge, D.: Data governance in the health industry: investigating data quality dimensions within a big data context. Appl. Syst. Innov. **1**(4), 43. MDPI AG (2018). https://doi.org/10.3390/asi1040043
11. Klievink, B., et al.: Enhancing visibility in international supply chains: the data pipeline concept. Int. J. Electron. Gov. Res. **8**(4), 14–33 (2012)
12. Mohammadi, M.: Ontology alignment: Simulated annealing-based system, statistical evaluation, and application to logistics interoperability (2020). https://doi.org/10.4233/uuid:7d8ac519-f3f7-425f-82ce-1df481bc1c34
13. Pipino, L., Yang, L., Wang, R.: Data quality assessment. Commun. ACM **45**, 211–218 (2002)
14. Rukanova, B., Henningsson, S., Henriksen, H. Z., Tan, Y.-H.: Digital trade infrastructures: a framework for analysis. Complex Syst. Inform. Model. Q. **14**, 1–21 (2018). https://doi.org/10.7250/csimq.2018-14.01.
15. Rukanova, B., et al.: Identifying the value of data analytics in the context of government supervision: insights from the customs domain. Gov. Inf. Q. (2021). https://doi.org/10.1016/j.giq.2020.101496

16. Seddon, P.B., Constantinidis, D., Tamm, T., Dod, H.: How does business analytics contribute to business value? Inf. Syst. J. **27**(3), 237–269 (2017)
17. Sivarajah, U., Kamal, M.M., Irani, Z., Weerakkody, V.: Critical analysis of Big Data challenges and analytical methods. J. Bus. Res. **17**, 263–286 (2017)
18. Strong, D.M., Lee, Y., Wang, R.: Data quality in context. Commun. ACM **40**(5), 103–110 (1997)
19. Tan, Y.-H., Bjørn-Andersen, N., Klein, S., Rukanova, B.: Accelerating Global Supply Chains with IT-Innovation: ITAIDE Tools and Methods. Springer Science & Business Media, Heidelberg (2011). https://doi.org/10.1007/978-3-642-15669-4
20. Umbrich, J., Neumaier, S., Polleres, A.: Towards assessing the quality evolution of Open Data portals. In: ODQ2015: Open Data Quality: From Theory to Practice Workshop, Munich, Germany (2015)
21. Vetrò, A., Canova, L., Torchiano, M., Minotas, C.O., Iemma, R., Morando, F.: Open data quality measurement framework: definition and application to open government data. Gov. Inf. Q. **33**(2), 325–337 (2016)
22. Wang, R., Strong, D.: Beyond accuracy: what data quality means to data consumers. J. Manag. Inf. Syst. **12**, 5–33 (1996)
23. Yin, R.K.: Case Study Research: Design and Methods. Sage, Beverly Hills (1984)
24. Zuiderwijk, A., Janssen, M.: Participation and data quality in open data use: open data infrastructures evaluated. In: Proceedings of the 15th European Conference on eGovernment 2015. ECEG 2015 (2015)

Process Automation as Enabler of Prioritized Values in Local Government – A Stakeholder Analysis

Daniel Toll[✉] 🆔, Ida Lindgren 🆔, and Ulf Melin 🆔

Department of Management and Engineering, Information Systems and Digitalization,
Linköping University, 581 83 Linköping, Sweden
{daniel.toll,ida.lindgren,ulf.melin}@liu.se

Abstract. Local government organizations (municipalities) in Sweden are encouraged to pursue process automation to face upcoming challenges. In this paper we focus on a case where these recommendations are put into practice and explore the views on process automation held by different stakeholder groups, related to which values they prioritize in their respective area of work. We do this by applying stakeholder theory and the model of value ideals by [1] as a combined theoretical lens. Our results show that different stakeholder groups prioritize different value ideals in their areas of work and that their views on process automation as able to enable these value ideals vary from optimistic, to hesitant to pessimistic. In the studied case, the achievement of process automation is in part reliant on workers themselves seeking it out, meaning that the pessimistic view on process automation poses a problem in that it becomes an obstacle for this to function. We discuss the possible reasons for the differently held prioritized value ideals as well as the differently held views on process automation. We conclude that the studied case shows that implementing process automation includes establishing new structures, roles and responsibilities and comes with certain issues, as those highlighted by our analysis. We found the combination of value ideals and stakeholder theory useful in studying e-government initiatives and make some further recommendations on possible future, related, streams of research.

Keywords: Automation · Public sector · Municipality · Stakeholder theory · Public values

1 Introduction

Process automation has become a topic of attention within the e-government research, policies, and practice sphere in Sweden during the last few years. There are several reasons behind this, the most frequently stated one being that process automation is *needed* to face an ageing population and related demographic and economic challenges in local and regional government [2]. Process automation is expected to bring efficiency gains that are required to keep the welfare system operational when faced with insufficient

© IFIP International Federation for Information Processing 2021
Published by Springer Nature Switzerland AG 2021
H. J. Scholl et al. (Eds.): EGOV 2021, LNCS 12850, pp. 288–300, 2021.
https://doi.org/10.1007/978-3-030-84789-0_21

budgets for the increasing workload (ibid.). The advancement and availability of process automation technologies has also been crucial in enabling the possibility to pursue process automation. For Swedish local government organizations (municipalities), process automation of case handling processes and administrative processes is presented as a new era of digitalization, reflected in the many publications and inquiries published by SALAR and the Swedish Government Offices [2–10].

Much of the current focus on process automation stems from a success story of a particular Swedish municipality automating a case handling process, cutting down lead times and efforts required, as well as increasing the availability and service quality for the citizen [3]. This success story has been highlighted and heavily promoted in policies by the Swedish Association for Local Government and Regions (SALAR). SALAR coordinates, inspires, and guides local governments and regions in Sweden on multiple topics, e.g., digitalization. Despite the encouragements by SALAR and the Swedish government to pursue process automation, neither SALAR, nor any other public authority, has offered more detailed guidance on how to implement process automation, nor provided any indications as to what processes should be automated. This has left the 290 municipalities to find their own way, and many municipalities are struggling to do so. A report published in 2019 found that only 2.5% of Swedish municipalities had, at that time, implemented a process automation solution. However, the report also noted that several municipalities had planned to implement such a solution, meaning that by the end of the same year this figure was expected to rise to 4.5% [11]; this is still a low number. The report highlights that process automation require much more effort than simply installing a new software, and that the development is hindered by lack of knowledge and experience [11, 12], as well as by technological, organizational and legal obstacles typically seen in digital government initiatives (cf., [13]).

As stated above there is a gap between how process automation is presented in influential policy documents, and how local government organizations proceed and succeed in implementing this type of technology. Implementing process automation in local government is not only challenging in practice; the very idea of process automation being the savior of the welfare system should also be considered with some caution. Previous research illustrate that process automation technologies may be associated with overly optimistic expectations [14, 15], and thus be driven by techno-optimism [16]. This can lead to unexpected or even unwanted consequences in practice [17]. For instance, process automation holds great potential to increase efficiency [18, 19], but can at the same time bring unrealistic expectations of its promised business value. It is also likely that different stakeholders in local government perceive process automation differently, and that conflicting interests can impede the development and implementation of process automation.

Against this background, the aim of this paper is: (1) to explore stakeholder views on process automation in local government and (2) relate these views to prioritized values linked to the different stakeholders' area of work. There is typically a large number of stakeholders involved in e-government initiatives (e.g. [20]), and process automation in municipalities is no exception. Process automation involves a large number of stakeholders which contribute and interact in different ways, e.g., policy makers, promotors, managers, developers, and end users. How different stakeholders affect and are affected by e-government initiatives is central to our understanding of e-government [20, 21], and is important to explore also in the context of process automation. The academic community plays an important role in educating and extracting lessons from empirical cases on process automation [22]. There are some examples of e-government studies on the consequences of increased process automation in the public sector (e.g. [23–26], but much remains to be done in order to gain a better understanding of how process automation affects these organizations in particular and society at large in general [27]. We wish to contribute to this stream of research.

The paper is organized as follows: first we present the case along with details about our method for data collection, we then proceed to present the theoretical framework, our motivations for our choices and our approach during analysis. We then present our findings and describe the identified stakeholders, their roles, and their respective views on process automation. This is followed by a discussion of insights gained from our findings. We end by concluding our findings and provide some thoughts for future research.

2 Case Introduction and Data Collection

Our paper is based on a qualitative and interpretative case study [28], conducted as part of a larger research project where one of the goals is to map current developments of how digital technologies are implemented and used to automate case handling in local government of case handling processes [39]. The case is centered around an initiative to implement process automation in case handling and administration in a Swedish municipality; hereafter referred to as the Municipality. The Municipality is one of the larger municipalities in Sweden with approximately 160 000 citizens. The Municipality is organized into seven departments, each focused on a certain subset of services, e.g., education and labor market, environment and city planning or elderly- and childcare. There is also a city council department that includes internal support functions such as HRM and IT. In order to effectively strategize and coordinate its digitalization efforts, the Municipality has recently (2019–2020) formed a Digitalization Group under the City Council Committee. This Digitalization Group consists of five roles: A Director of Digital Transformation, an Automation Leader, a Project Management Office Leader, an Innovation Leader, and an IT-governance and IT-architect Leader. Concerning process automation, the Automation Leader is tasked with establishing what they themselves refer to as *automation capacity,* here understood as the name of a structure of processes that aim to enable co-workers within the Municipality to identify *automation ideas*, which then can be developed into *automation solutions*. The automation solution could be a simple script or a more advanced robotic case handling solution that executes a process instead of a caser worker. An important aspect of this automation capacity structure is that it is planned to function bottom-up, stemming from individual employee's ideas and wishes.

Between February 2020 and January 2021, we conducted 21 interviews with 18 different informants. The first of these interviews was conducted in person and the subsequent ones through video calls (Zoom and Microsoft Teams) due to the covid-19 pandemic. We used the Automation Leader as our point of departure, who recommended a first set of people to be interviewed, after which additional informants were identified through snowball sampling [29]. The Automation Leader was interviewed on three occasions, and one other informant was interviewed on two occasions. The informants are predominantly business developers or managers working in six of the seven departments. The interviews were semi-structured and focused on discussing the informant's role in general as well as their view on process automation and the initiative to establish automation capacity. Each interview had a duration of approximately 90 min and was recorded. The interviews were transcribed prior to analysis. In this paper, we focused on questions from the interviews concerning the role of process automation in the informants' current and future work situation.

3   Analytical Framework

In the analysis we focus on process automation of administrative processes, typically related to case work. Automation is understood as *"the execution by a machine agent (usually a computer) of a function that was previously carried out by a human"* (Parasuraman and Riley, 1997, p. 231). The focus on *process* automation specifies this definition somewhat, in that it focuses on processes as the things to be automated, but this definition is still very general. This general and inclusive definition means that process automation in practice can refer to the application of technologies that are contemporarily associated with process automation, such as robotic process automation (RPA) or different kinds of artificial intelligence (AI). Process automation however can also include older, more traditional methods, such as systems integration and application programming interfaces (API). As such, process automation as a concept and possibility is nothing new per say, but the more recent hype surrounding RPA and AI, combined with success stories of process automation in local government, has resulted in not-seen-before *explicit* initiatives focused to automate processes in the public sector. The scope of what is possible to automate has also widened [31], and AI now brings promises of being able to automate cognitive tasks, that before now have been impossible to automate due to their need of human discretion [32]. Throughout this paper we use this general and inclusive definition of process automation that includes several technologies, as it mirrors our empirical material, where no finer distinctions are made as to what process automation entails.

3.1   Stakeholder Theory

Stakeholder theory supplies concrete tools for how to identify and manage important actors; several of these ideas have been successfully transferred to the public sector [21]. As an entity, a stakeholder is *"[...] any group or individual who can affect or is affected by the achievement of the organization's objectives"* ([33], p. 46), and can refer to individuals, groups, organizations, or even the environment [34]. The core of stakeholder theory is the idea of identifying and managing stakeholders in various ways; managing the organization's stakeholders is seen as a way to ensure effective and efficient management. Stakeholder theory is highly useful for discussing the large variety of actors involved in e-government projects; visible in the successful transfers of stakeholder theory to the public sector and the e-government context (e.g., [20]).

3.2 Value Ideals

Government organizations are supposed to uphold public values [35], and digital technologies have the power to transform such public values [36]. There have been several contributions over the years to create inventories and models of public values to be used to study the transforming power of digital technologies, e.g. [37, 38]. In this paper we apply a theoretically grounded model that synthesizes previous research on value ideals [1]. This model has been applied in previous studies on automation technologies in a Swedish municipal context where it showed promise as an analytical tool [24]. The model categorizes public values into four value ideals. In Table 1 these four value ideals are presented, along with their definition and key values.

Table 1. Model of value ideals, adapted from [1].

Value ideal	Definition and key values
Professionalism	*"The professionalism ideal is focused on providing an independent, robust and consistent ad- ministration, governed by a rule system based on law, resulting in the public record that is the basis of accountability. Key representative values are durability, equity, legality and accountability"* (pp. 539–540)
Service	*"The service ideal involves maximising the utility of government to civil society by providing ser- vices directed towards the public good. Key representative values are public service, citizen orientation and service level and quality"* (p.540)
Efficiency	*"The efficiency ideal concerns providing lean and efficient administration that minimises waste of public resources gathered from taxpayers. Key representative values are value for money, cost reduction, productivity and performance"* (p. 540)
Engagement	*"This ideal focuses on engaging with civil society to facilitate policy development in accordance with liberal democratic principles, thus articulating the public good. Key representative values are democracy, deliberation and participation"* (p. 541)

3.3 Applying the Analytical Framework

When applying a stakeholder lens to our empirical material, four stakeholder groups became salient in the material: *The Digitalization Group, IT Department, Support Functions,* and *Operational Staff.* These groups are based on the informants' roles in the organization, and their interests in the ongoing automation initiative in the Municipality. These four categories of stakeholders largely mirror the already existing organizational structure of the Municipality in its division of different functions, although somewhat generalized.

We then applied Rose et al.'s (2015) model of value ideals on the empirical material. This was done in order to explore and illustrate which value ideals the informants view as important within their own area of work, and whether they view process automation as an enabler of these values. In our analysis we determined which value ideals they prioritize in their own area of work based on answers to questions about their role, their work content, what they see as important in their work, and what further developments they would like to see in their immediate work context. Which value ideals that are associated to process automation were determined by analyzing answers to questions regarding how they perceive process automation, how they define it, what potentials they see in process automation and their thoughts on the Municipality's move to develop process automation for administrative work. In order to convey the informants' dominant views on process automation as an enabler of the values they prioritize in their work, the following three views were created inductively:

- **Optimist**: Views process automation as able to enable the value ideals prioritized in the own area of work.
- **Hesitant**: Is unsure, or hesitant, about whether or not process automation is able to enable the value ideals prioritized in the own area of work.
- **Pessimist**: Does not view process automation as able to enable the value ideals prioritized in the own area of work.

We have incorporated these three views into our analytical framework, and these are presented together with the rest of our findings in Fig. 1 in the Findings section.

4   Findings

In Fig. 1 we present an overview of our findings. The middle column shows the categorization of informants into stakeholder groups. The left column shows which value ideals that are prioritized in the stakeholder groups' respective areas of work. The right column shows the stakeholder group's dominant view on process automation as enabler of their prioritized value ideals.

Our analysis covers which of the value ideals that are *prioritized* and visible in the empirical data. These findings should not be interpreted as an indication that certain stakeholder groups do not care about the value ideals that are not presented as prioritized. Following Fig. 1 we describe each row of the figure in turn according to stakeholder group and then summarize the Findings section.

The Digitalization Group consists of five informants that are explicitly working to further digitalization in the Municipality. The following quote illustrates this group's aims: *"We have two general main objectives: one is to increase efficiency, or free up resources, by the aid of digitalization, and the other is to increase the digital maturity [in the organization]."* These are proponents of automation capacity, as they are the ones creating and promoting it. They are also the ones funding its development. The Digitalization Group is building the automation capacity upon the notion of co-workers seeking out process automation voluntarily, with the automation capacity structure and its processes being readily available for them to utilize when doing so. They motivate this approach by stating that the individual co-worker is the most qualified to assess what is suitable to automate within their area of work, as they are the foremost experts on their

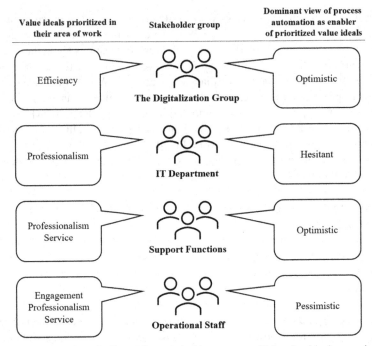

Fig. 1. An overview of our findings. The stakeholder groups, which value ideals are prioritized in their respective areas of work, and their view on process automation as enabler of their prioritized value ideals.

own processes. While noting that different kinds of values are of importance, they mainly prioritize *efficiency* in their work, also evident as part of their objective as seen in the quote above. They see efficiency gains as key to pursue other values, as efficiency means freeing up resources; meaning that process automation is seen as an indirect enabler of *all* value ideals. As this group consists of strategists that strategize not for their own sake but for the Municipality as a whole, this also indicates that they see efficiency as the most important value ideal to be enabled by the strategies and policies they create, one of which is the automation capacity structure itself. The following quote illustrates this stance: "*I am convinced that there is much we can automate and increase efficiency for in the organization*". As the automation capacity structure is initiated, developed, funded, and encouraged by this group it follows that this group are *optimists* in their attitude towards process automation as able to enable the value ideal they prioritize.

The IT department stakeholder group includes four informants from the IT department of the Municipality, whose daily work involve supporting and servicing the Municipality in matters involving IT. Concerning process automation, the IT department is the main supplier both of the different kinds of automation solutions as well as the underlying IT infrastructure. Representatives of this group also function as IT project managers for developing automation solutions within the automation capacity structure. The value ideal most prioritized for this group is professionalism, which is concerned with durability, robustness, legality, and security. Considering the role of the IT department as the governor of the infrastructure on which much of the daily operation of the municipality is built, this prioritization is understandable. They view process automation as something that is mostly concerned with efficiency gains and are *hesitant* towards process automation as an enabler of the value ideal they prioritize. While acknowledging that technologies such as RPA and AI have promising capabilities, they view them as volatile and unreliable, which is in direct conflict with the stability the professionalism ideal embodies. The following quote shows the view of RPA as a last-resort technology for process automation: *"There are some use cases where I don't really see any other alternative, and in those cases, it is an exceptionally good solution. It is good that the alternative exists, but often there are, in my opinion, better solutions, and in those cases I think those should be used."* As such, this group is in favor of traditional process automation technologies, e.g., systems integration using API, but are hesitant towards process automation technologies such as RPA and AI that are now becoming a part of the arsenal of process automation technologies. The following quote expresses one of the informant's overall thoughts of RPA, based on experiences from using it: *"I am doubtful. There are many complications, and it is very sensitive as well. Suddenly... well, if you change something in one end then you might have to go and make alterations and changes for both the robot and the process.".* This quote shows how they view RPA as unstable, thus conflicting with the stability of the professionalism value ideal.

The Support Functions stakeholder group includes four informants from departments that provide internal services to the Municipality; HRM and the City Contact Center. The Support Functions are potential users of the automation capacity, as they are performers of processes that potentially can be automated by utilizing the automation capacity structure. This group is also very positive towards process automation and is therefore also seen as proponents of process automation. The following quote shows their optimistic view, within the context of discussing digitalization and process automation in general: *"My objective is to ensure the resources needed to deliver welfare services, and digitalization is one of the strategies we use to be able to do that, as our personnel-resources will not be enough."* Like the IT Department, this groups' daily work consists of supporting other parts of the Municipality. In doing so, they prioritize providing services that are useful and of high quality, hence they prioritize the *service* value ideal. They are also concerned with *professionalism* as the robustness and legality of the services they provide are important. This group is optimistic in its attitude towards process automation as an enabler of the service and professionalism value ideals. They view process automation as both a direct and indirect enabler of these value ideals. Direct in that process automation does not suffer from human factor error, meaning that process automation can possibly lead to better and more correct service and record keeping, as well as faster service and increased availability. Indirect in that they acknowledge that the efficiency gains process automation provides would free up resources that can be reallocated to further pursue the professionalism and service value ideals in new ways, echoing the discourse of the Digitalization Group. The following quote shows how they view process automation as able to increase quality assurance: *"For us the purpose is, well part of it is to make it easier for our co-workers. We want the increased quality that*

*comes with a well-executed process, which is in large part performed manually today...-
...and automating [the process] so that it is performed the same every time becomes
something that is quality-assuring."*

The Operational Staff stakeholder group includes six informants from departments
within the Municipality that for the most part are concerned with providing external services to citizens. The informants span several different committees; the social and welfare
committee, the environment and city planning committee, the education and labor market committee and operational services. This stakeholder group therefore represents the
main bulk of the Municipality as well as being the group that most frequently interacts
with citizens. These are potential users of automation capacity in a similar manner to the
Support Functions group, as this group too are the performers of many processes that
potentially can be automated by the automation capacity. This group prioritizes three
value ideals: *service, professionalism,* and *engagement.* The reasons for prioritizing the
service and professionalism value ideals are much the same as for the Support Functions group, i.e., providing useful and high-quality services and in doing so ensuring the
robustness and legality of the municipality. This group is also particularly concerned
with professionalism in regard to record keeping and accountability, as many interactions with citizens can involve legal appeals. This incentivizes the individual co-worker
to keep extensive records for the sake of transparency and traceability in the event of
such appeals. This group also prioritizes the *engagement* value ideal, as interacting with
citizens is a large part of their area of work. They view the possibility to interact with
citizens as important in order to be able to offer quality services and take into consideration individual cases and circumstances; something they view as especially important
in areas of work that involves interacting with vulnerable groups of society. This group
are *pessimists* in their attitude towards process automation as enabler of the value ideals they prioritize. They view process automation as something that purely increases
efficiency of administrative processes, and while their area of work does include such
processes, these are not something this group focuses on. The following quote illustrates
this group's stance, from the context of talking about the push within the Municipality
to further digitalization and process automation: *"I almost feel that we focus too much
on achieving digitalization, when I think about my [business developer] purpose, it concerns improving our work, work smarter, have better meetings and create more value
for our citizens, and it should be easier for our co-workers to do so. So, I can sometimes
feel that digitalization becomes an aim in itself."* As such, this group is critical towards
digitalization in general and are pessimistic in their view of process automation as able
to enable the value ideals they prioritize.

To summarize, the initiative covered above is the Municipality's operationalization
of SALAR's encouragements to pursue process automation (as described in the introduction section). The analysis illustrates how one stakeholder group, the Digitalization
Group, with a clear focus on *efficiency* is guiding the work to establish structures for
promoting and realizing process automation in the organization. This work is founded
on an *optimistic* stance towards both process automation as an enabler of efficiency, and
an optimistic view on the organization's ability to identify and realize automation ideas
and implementation bottom-up. The effort of establishing 'automation capacity' in the

organization is further fueled by the Support Functions stakeholder group. Although prioritizing different value ideals, they too hold an optimistic view on process automation as an enabler of prioritized values. In contrast, the two stakeholder groups on which much of the realization of process automation relies – the IT Department and Operational Staff – hold hesitant and pessimistic views on process automation as an enabler of the values ideals which they prioritize.

5 Discussion

In this paper we applied stakeholder theory and the model of value ideals by [1] as a combined theoretical lens, which was combined with a set of inductively created views. We find value ideals useful to study process automation, in agreement with previous studies that have done so [24]. In addition, we find the combination of stakeholder theory and value ideals fruitful as it allowed to identify value ideals held by different groups to contrast and compare between them.

The case presented in this paper is an example of how the encouragements of SALAR (as described in the Introduction section) are put into action. This involves the creation of new structures, roles and responsibilities, and illustrates how process automation is a complex venture, as discussed by [11]. Our findings also show that the related issues are far from purely technological in nature, but instead shows that differentiating views becomes an important aspect to consider and manage, similar to those organizational obstacles discussed by e.g., [13].

The different stakeholder groups prioritize different value ideals in their different areas of work, which is a consequence of the type of work included in those different areas of work, as well as adhering to the objectives these different groups are responsible for. Concerning their views on process automation, the different groups hold different views, where The Digitalization Group and The Support Functions are optimistic, but the IT Department is hesitant, and the Operational Staff are pessimistic. Considering how process automation is being established in this particular case, reliant on co-workers themselves initiating automation ideas, this becomes a problematic paradox for the automation capacity structure to function as planned. As [31] points out, the scope of what is automatable has widened, but as can be seen in the view expressed by the Operational Staff group, this is not inherently clear to them, as they do not see process automation as applicable for their processes. This group values the *engagement* value ideal and the ability to consider individual circumstances when interacting with citizens, indicating that discretion [32] is important to this group and might be a reason for their pessimistic view, not believing technology capable of replacing how humans apply discretion.

All of the stakeholder groups we have identified are needed to play their part for the automation capacity to bear fruit, however the IT Department in particular holds a vital role in this, as they both supply the underlying infrastructure and act as project managers in the development of automation solutions. This means that the IT Department holds a position of great influence in the chain of events of achieving automation solutions. If they allow their hesitant view to affect what is automated and in what way, it may influence the effectiveness of the automation solutions. This shows that defining clear roles and responsibilities as well as creating alignment between the IT function and the goals of process automation is important, as discussed by [22].

The optimistic groups expresses that increases in efficiency frees up resources, which is a motivation for process automation that can be seen both in the marketing of e.g. RPA [15] as well as in the discourse of SALAR [2, 5]. As noted in the Introduction, not much detailed guidance has been given by SALAR or any other public authority on how to implement process automation. It is clear from the studied case that the encouragements of SALAR have been taken to heart and that the implementation of process automation is not without its related issues. In light of this, there is a gap between the policy and practice of process automation where both scholars and public authorities can play a role in providing insight and guidance on how to approach this type of e-government initiatives.

6 Conclusions, Limitations, and Future Research

In this paper we have presented a study focused on a case of a Swedish municipality establishing process automation ('automation capacity') as a way to face upcoming challenges. Our aim was to explore how different stakeholder groups view process automation as able to enable the value ideals the prioritize in their respective area of work. We have achieved this aim by illustrating a contemporary case study as one example of how policy and encouragements of pursuing process automation is put into practice within a municipality. In this case we have identified that the pursuit of process automation entails the creation of new structures, roles, and responsibilities. The study also illustrates that different stakeholder groups within local government prioritize different values depending on their area of work. This prioritization affects their views on process automation, and they hold different dominant views on process automation. These conclusions were made possible applying the model of value ideals [1], which we found useful in agreement with previous studies [24]. The empirical illustrations together with the theoretical lens applied in this paper can serve as inspirations for further research in the e-government domain focusing process automation and beyond. The results also present practical implications: within the particular case studied, but also for other local government organizations, policy making organizations (like SALAR) and national governance of process automation. In a decentralized governance model, like the Swedish one, we have identified that many municipalities are on separate, often non-coordinated, journeys to establish process automation. Here organizations like SALAR could play a larger, and more evident, role in providing more detailed guidance on how to approach such ventures, and still be sensitive towards local contexts and needs.

Doing a single case study, on one hand, makes a deep analysis possible, but on the other hand one limitation of this research is that case studied is one of 290 municipalities in Sweden, and more studies on process automation in other municipalities are needed in order to contrast and compare the findings. International comparisons could also be beneficial in order to contextualize the case-based results, and to explore other governance models (e.g., more centralized models) and other levels of government beyond the local. Comparisons to private organizations could also be made to further shed light on similarities and differences between these types of organizations. The stakeholder analysis in this paper categorizes the informants into stakeholder groups. Stakeholder theory can however be applied to make deeper, more detailed analyses in order to explore more fine-grained nuances and how this affects their views on process automation, as more conditions than area of work are likely to play a role. Studies that use more specific definitions of process automation, e.g., focused on specific technologies, could also be fruitful in exploring differences between different types of technologies. We also identify further research avenues exploring how the inductively generated views (optimist, hesitant, and pessimist) can be mirrored in previous research on organizational change in general and e.g., change management in particular.

Acknowledgement. This research is funded by AFA Insurance.

References

1. Rose, J., Persson, J.S., Heeager, L.T., Irani, Z.: Managing e-Government: value positions and relationships. Inf. Syst. J. **25**, 531–571 (2015). https://doi.org/10.1111/isj.12052
2. SALAR: Automatiserad ärendehantering: Att frigöra tid för värdeskapande arbete (2018)
3. SALAR: Beslut inom 24 timmar! (2017). https://moten.trelleborg.se/welcome-sv/namnder-styrelser/arbetsmarknadsnamnden/arbetsmarknadsnamnden-2017-09-18/agenda/artikel-tre lleborgskommun-170614pdf-1?downloadMode=open
4. SALAR: Automatisering i välfärden - möjligheter och utmaningar för kommuner och regioner (2019)
5. SALAR: Automatisering av arbete (2018)
6. SALAR: Digitalisering av ansökningsprocess för ekonomiskt bistånd (2020). https://skr.se/ tjanster/merfranskl/larandeexempel/larandeexempel/digitaliseringavansokningsprocessfor ekonomisktbistand.27482.html
7. Digitaliseringskommissionen: För digitalisering i tiden. Statens Offentliga Utredningar (SOU), Stockholm (2016)
8. E-delegationen: Automatiserade beslut - färre regler ger tydligare reglering. Statens Offentliga Utredningar (SOU), Stockholm (2014)
9. SALAR: Artificiell intelligens – möjligheter för välfärden (2017)
10. The Swedish Government Offices: Nationell inritkning för artificiell intelligens (2018)
11. Svensson, L.: Tekniken är den enkla biten. Om att implementera digital automatisering i handläggningen av försörjningsstöd, Lund (2019)
12. Svensson, L.: Automatisering-till nytta eller fördärv? Soc. Tidskr. **3**, 341–362 (2019)
13. Goldkuhl, G., Eriksson, O., Persson, A., Röstlinger, A.: Offentliggemensamma digitala resurser : Utmaningar i samstyrning och samanvändning inom svensk e-förvaltning (2014)
14. Toll, D., Lindgren, I., Melin, U., Madsen, C.: Values, benefits, considerations and risks of AI in government: a study of AI policy documents in sweden. eJournal eDemocracy Open Gov. **12**, 40–60 (2020). https://doi.org/10.29379/jedem.v12i1.593
15. Toll, D., Söderström, F.: What is this "RPA" they are selling? In: Virkar, S., et al. (eds.) EGOV-CeDEM-ePart 2020, pp. 365–370. Linköping, Sweden (2020)
16. Hood, C., Dixon, R.: A government that worked better and cost less?: Evaluating three decades of reform and change in UK central Government. Oxford University Press (2015)
17. Margetts, H., Hood, C. (eds.): Paradoxes of Modernization: Unintended Consequences of Public Policy Reform. Oxford University Press (2012)
18. Willcocks, L., Lacity, M.: A new approach to automating services. MIT Sloan Manag. Rev. **58**, 40–49 (2016)

19. Madakam, S., Holmukhe, R.M., Kumar Jaiswal, D.: The future digital work force: Robotic Process Automation (RPA). J. Inf. Syst. Technol. Manag. **16**, 1–17 (2019). https://doi.org/10.4301/s1807-1775201916001

20. Axelsson, K., Melin, U., Lindgren, I.: Public e-services for agency efficiency and citizen benefit - Findings from a stakeholder centered analysis. Gov. Inf. Q. **30**, 10–22 (2013). https://doi.org/10.1016/j.giq.2012.08.002

21. Rose, J., Flak, L.S., Sæbø, Ø.: Stakeholder theory for the E-government context: framing a value-oriented normative core. Gov. Inf. Q. **35**, 362–374 (2018). https://doi.org/10.1016/j.giq.2018.06.005

22. Willcocks, L., Lacity, M.: The IT Function and Robotic Process Automation (2015)

23. Ranerup, A., Henriksen, H.Z.: Digital discretion: unpacking human and technological agency in automated decision making in Sweden's social services. Soc. Sci. Comput. Rev. **47**, 1–17 (2020). https://doi.org/10.1177/0894439320980434

24. Ranerup, A., Henriksen, H.Z.: Value positions viewed through the lens of automated decision-making: the case of social services. Gov. Inf. Q. **36**, 101377 (2019). https://doi.org/10.1016/j.giq.2019.05.004

25. Wihlborg, E., Larsson, H., Hedström, K.: "The computer says no!" - a case study on automated decision-making in public authorities. In: Proceedings of the Annual Hawaii International Conference on System Sciences, pp. 2903–2912. IEEE (2016)

26. Denk, T., Hedström, K., Karlsson, F.: Medborgarna och automatiserat beslutsfattande. In: Andersson, U., Rönnerstrand, B., Öhberg, P., Bergström, A. (eds.) Storm och Stiltje: SOM-institutets 74: e forskarantologi, pp. 183–196. SOM-institutet, Göteborg (2019)

27. Lindgren, I., Madsen, C.Ø., Hofmann, S., Melin, U.: Close encounters of the digital kind: a research agenda for the digitalization of public services. Gov. Inf. Q. **36**, 427–436 (2019). https://doi.org/10.1016/j.giq.2019.03.002

28. Walsham, G.: Interpretive case studies in IS research: nature and method. Eur. J. Inf. Syst. **4**, 74–81 (1995). https://doi.org/10.1057/ejis.1995.9

29. Patton, M.Q.: Qualitative Evaluation Methods. Sage Publications, Beverly Hills (1980)

30. Parasuraman, R., Riley, V.: Humans and automation: use, misuse, disuse, abuse. Hum. Factors. **39**, 230–253 (1997). https://doi.org/10.1518/001872097778543886

31. Wajcman, J.: Automation: is it really different this time? Br. J. Sociol. **68**, 119–127 (2017). https://doi.org/10.1111/1468-4446.12239

32. Lipsky, M.: Street-level bureaucracy: Dilemmas of the individual in public service. Russell Sage Foundation (2010)

33. Freeman, E.: Strategic Management: A Stakeholder Approach. Pitman, Boston (1984)

34. Mitchell, R.K., Agle, B.R., Wood, D.J.: Toward a theory of stakeholder identification and salience: defining the principle of who and what really counts. Acad. Manag. Rev. **22**, 853–886 (1997). https://doi.org/10.5465/AMR.1997.9711022105

35. Almarabeh, T., AbuAli, A.: A general framework for E-government: definition maturity challenges, opportunities, and success. Eur. J. Sci. Res. **39**, 29–42 (2010)

36. Bannister, F., Connolly, R.: ICT, public values and transformative government: a framework and programme for research. Gov. Inf. Q. **31**, 119–128 (2014). https://doi.org/10.1016/j.giq.2013.06.002

37. Beck Jørgensen, T., Bozeman, B.: Public values inventory.pdf. Adm. Soc. **39**, 354–381 (2007)

38. Rutgers, M.R.: Sorting out public values? On the contingency of value classification in public administration. Adm. Theory Prax. **30**, 92–113 (2008). https://doi.org/10.1080/10841806.2008.11029617

39. Lindgren, I.: Exploring robotic process automation in local government. In: Virkar, S., et al. (eds.) EGOV-CeDEM-ePart 2020, pp. 249–258. Linköping, Sweden (2020)

$TLV\text{-}diss_\gamma$: A Dissimilarity Measure for Public Administration Process Logs

Flavio Corradini, Caterina Luciani[✉], Andrea Morichetta, Marco Piangerelli, and Andrea Polini

University of Camerino, 62030 Camerino, MC, Italy
{flavio.corradini,caterina.luciani,andrea.morichetta,
marco.piangerelli,andrea.polini}@unicam.it

Abstract. Every day Public Administrations (PA) provide citizens with plenty of services. Due to different factors, such as the involvement of different human resources or the will to deliver lean and versatile services, the same service can show some variability across different organizations. Log files contain the proof of PA process' variability thus, being able to analyze logs, can be very helpful both for the PA, in order to establish good practices or contextual rules, as well as for the software house companies that need to analyse and to better customize the software they provide. In this paper, we present a methodology that, using log files as inputs, and based on the so-called TLV-diss$_\gamma$, a parametric dissimilarity measure, allows a data analyst to perform a cluster analysis. This methodology helps both PA and software producers to better understand how services are delivered through informative systems and then to better customize them. We show that our methodology can be used to capture the differences in control flow and components resulting from the log files, and then to better reason on the delivery of public services.

Keywords: Log clustering · Similarity measure · Variance analysis

1 Introduction

Every day PA provide citizens with plenty of services that are very similar in scope, but that may vary in their internal management and organisation. Such divergence in the processes is called variability and can be due to many possible factors, such as differences in the human resources involved to carry out specific tasks, altered control flow necessary to deal with specific locally-applicable laws or requirements, specific aspects of external informative systems with which the supporting software has to interact, and to many other factors that could require specific customization on the delivery of public service.

Inevitably, this variability increases the complexity of data analysis in discovering possible deviations from expected procedures in which the PA analyst could be interested. In parallel, a software company, distributing services and applications for PA, could improve and optimize software, reducing the investment in the

© IFIP International Federation for Information Processing 2021
Published by Springer Nature Switzerland AG 2021
H. J. Scholl et al. (Eds.): EGOV 2021, LNCS 12850, pp. 301–314, 2021.
https://doi.org/10.1007/978-3-030-84789-0_22

development for uncommon behaviors and, at the same time, tuning the software for including non-standard procedures that are, instead, very common among PA employees. Moreover, given different installations of heterogeneous organisation, identifying regularities in activities or control flow, that may reveal good practices or contextual rules in the execution of a standard procedure, is very important for predictive installation configurations. In such a context, the data analyst has a unique source for discovering possible anomalies and elaborate possible statistics: the big amount of raw data collected in log files, generated from the execution of the software, supporting the delivery of the public service. Process mining is a recently developed discipline that aims at discovering business process models from log files in order to enable more abstract reasoning on the behaviour subsumed by a service and to possibly compare different service instances in relation to the behavioural characteristics associated to the derived business process models. Notwithstanding its numerous merit, the main limitation of this approach concerns the limited number of logs that can be analyzed concurrently, when, instead, thousands of comparisons would be needed. In particular, if we would like to carry on extensive analysis of the logs related to the delivery of a specific service by the municipalities of an average size European country, we would need to compare several thousand models. At the same time, the result could be strongly influenced by the adopted mining algorithm.

The methodology we propose is propaedeutic to Process Mining and it tries to solve some well-known problems when carrying on extensive log files comparison and clustering. Our aim is to satisfy the needs of PA data analysts, for instance, employed within a large PA software provider, equipping them with an instrument able to help them in collecting and comparing information derived from a huge amount of logs, generated by different municipalities. The methodology is based on a new (dis)similarity measure, named TLV-diss$_\gamma$, that is able to quantify on a numerical scale the pairwise (dis)similarity between logs, starting from their XES files. This measure will be used successively in a clustering procedure in order to group together comparable logs thus enabling a faster and cluster-based analysis. For such a reason, the proposed methodology is parametric and can be configured directly by the data analyst. According to the parameters' value, the similarity measure will give relevance to different characteristics of a log. In particular, the analyst will be able to focus more on the activity perspective (i.e. on how much logs are different in terms of reported performed activities) than on a control perspective instead (i.e. on how much logs report different ordering relations among the activities). Moreover, it is possible to have a trade-off between the two. Our methodology has been implemented in a tool and validated in relation to its effectiveness on 37 logs related to the same service and delivered by different Italian municipalities.

The rest of the paper is organized as follows: Sect. 2 presents the background, in Sect. 3 we provide the theoretical and technical details about the methodology that was applied to a real case study, and whose results are presented in Sect. 4. In Sect. 5 we have the related works and finally, in Sect. 6 we conclude and discuss possible future works.

2   Background

2.1   Information Systems and Event Logs

Public Administrations deliver complex services to citizens through the usage of dedicated Information Systems (IS). In the last years, the development of such systems have been more and more driven by the definition of business processes that are then embedded in the software [3], so that the activities to be performed in the delivery of a service and their ordering, are clearly specified and checked with respect to the norm. In such a context the term Process Aware Information System (PAIS) has been defined to refer to such kind of IS.

Among the various functionality made available, a PAIS generally includes diagnostic mechanisms in the form of events log. An event log is a collection of data connected to the execution of the embedded process, and each event in the log is associated with a specific process instance, which is usually referred to as a "case" [18]. A "case" is then constituted by an ordered sequence of events that are related to the delivery of a service in relation to a specific request by a citizen. There can be additional attributes for each event, such as the timestamp or the resource executing the activity. Each attribute may be considered as a classifier. If two events have the same value for a classifier they are considered equal. The default classifier is the name of the activity. Since 2010, the XES format has been the most widely used format in process mining to analyse event logs [18]. An XES document depicts a single log and an arbitrary number of traces. Each trace describes a sequence of events attributable to a single case. The log can have as many attributes as needed, which are mainly of type String, Date, Int, Float, and Boolean.

2.2   Clustering and K-Medoids Algorithm

Clustering analysis is a set of techniques for grouping (clustering) similar objects together, so that the dissimilarity among objects belonging to the same cluster is lower than the one among objects belonging to different clusters [6].

Among partitional clustering algorithms, K-means and K-medoids are very popular. They are based on a simple concept: be K, the number of clusters, the algorithms look for the K-most-representative elements, called centroids or medoids, and assign each object to its closest representative. One of the most relevant differences between the two algorithms is given by the selection of the medoids that are chosen among the collected data samples, while the centroids can be any point in the considered space [9]. It is for this reason that k-means is not suitable for non-Euclidean spaces (as in our case), and k-medoids has been used instead [17]. For optimizing the number of clusters K, some performance indexes, such as the silhouette index, have been defined [15]. Basically, varying K we look for the partition that ensures the maximum silhouette index. The method consists of three steps: calculate the average distance of a point from points in the same cluster $a(i)$, count the average distance of the same point from points in the nearest cluster $b(i)$, calculate $\frac{b(i)-a(i)}{max(b(i),a(i))}$.

3   TLV-diss$_\gamma$ Methodology

In this section, we present the TLV-diss$_\gamma$ methodology. It starts with the elaboration of the XES logs to successively make possible the application of the K-medoid algorithm on a generated distance matrix.

The proposed methodology consists of five phases executed in sequence:

- Definition of the Trace Matrices for each XES log
- Definition of the Log Matrix combining together the Trace Matrices
- Definition of the Variance Matrix for each possible combination of logs
- Definition of the Distance Matrix summarizing the results of the Variance Matrices
- Use of K-medoid algorithm on logs according to the Distance Matrix

In such a context, the term trace can be considered as the formal representation of a case, and it will permit to formally represent the sequence of activities performed to satisfy a request by a citizen.

3.1   Trace Matrix

A Trace Matrix defines the ordering relationship between activities in a trace extracted from a XES Log. In particular, a Trace Matrix is generated for each distinct trace existing in the Log. In this definition, we aim to extend the concept of order matrix already introduced by Reichert et al. [11].

Definition 1. *Let $\mathcal{A}$ a generic set of labels, denoting activities, being $a \in \mathcal{A}$ a generic activity. A **trace** σ is represented as an ordered sequence of activities, so that $\sigma = \langle a_1, a_2, ..., a_r \rangle$. We indicate with $\mathcal{A}^\sigma$ the set of labels appearing in the trace σ. A **log** $\mathcal{L}$ is constituted by a set of traces, so that $\sigma \in \mathcal{L}$. The set of all labels appearing in any trace of a log is then represented by $\mathcal{A}^\mathcal{L}$ (i.e. $\mathcal{A}^\mathcal{L} = \bigcup_{i=1}^n \mathcal{A}^{\sigma_i}$ where $\mathcal{L} = \{\sigma_i | i \in [1 \ldots n]\}$). We indicate with $|\mathcal{A}^\mathcal{L}|$ the cardinality of a set.*

Definition 2. *Given a trace σ the associated **trace matrix** T^σ will report the relations among the activities in the trace σ itself. T^σ is a squared matrix that has a number of rows, and columns, equal to $|\mathcal{A}^\mathcal{L}|$. Each row is associated to a label in $\mathcal{A}^\mathcal{L}$, and the same label is associated to the column with the same index. Therefore, the elements of T^σ are defined as follows:*

- $t_{ij}^\sigma := \triangleright$ *if a_i precedes, directly, a_j in σ*
- $t_{ij}^\sigma := \not\triangleright$ *if a_i precedes, but not directly, a_j in σ*
- $t_{ij}^\sigma := \triangleleft$ *if a_i follows, directly, a_j in σ*
- $t_{ij}^\sigma := \not\triangleleft$ *if a_i follows, but not directly, a_j in σ*
- $t_{ij}^\sigma := \emptyset$ *if a_i and a_j do not both appear in σ*

Given a log $\mathcal{L}$ the set of all trace matrices corresponding to the traces in $\mathcal{L}$ will be denoted as $T^\mathcal{L}$.

It is worth clarifying that an activity a_i precedes/follows directly a_j if it is in its immediate adjacency, so respectively it holds that $j = i + 1$ or $i = j + 1$; not directly means that one activity can precede/succeed the other in more than one step. For each log, the activities considered in the trace matrix corresponds to the activities existing in that specific log and not only the trace. This is necessary to have a more direct generation of the log matrix in the next step. Moreover, it is worth noticing that the expressed relations do not hold on to the same activity ($i = j$, $\forall i, j$). For this reason the diagonal is empty, and T^σ is "specular" with respect to its diagonal. Finally, in the proposed definition we treat equally activities that are reachable in more than two steps, differently from [8]. A more detailed distinction is possible, but it could affect the computational performance in dealing with a huge amount of data.

Running Example (1/4). To better illustrate the technicalities of our methodology we present here a running example. Let $\mathcal{L}_1$ be the log represented in Table 1a and $|\mathcal{L}_1| = n$ (i.e. $\mathcal{L}_1$ includes n traces). Then let the $\mathcal{L}_2$ be the log depicted in Table 1b.
The resulting trace matrices for $\mathcal{L}_1$ are Table 2a for the ABD trace and Table 2b for the ACD trace. Similarly, for $\mathcal{L}_2$ we have Table 2c and Table 2d for the traces ABCE and ACBE respectively.

Table 1. Running example logs

(a) $\mathcal{L}_1$

Case ID	Activity name
1	A
1	B
1	D
2	A
2	C
2	D
...	...

(b) $\mathcal{L}_2$

Case ID	Activity name
1	A
1	B
1	C
1	E
2	A
2	C
2	B
2	E
...	...

Table 2. Trace matrices

(a) ABD $\mathcal{L}_1$

	A	B	C	D
A		▷	0	⋫
B	◁		0	▷
C	0	0		0
D	⋪	◁	0	

(b) ACD $\mathcal{L}_1$

	A	B	C	D
A		0	▷	⋫
B	0		0	0
C	◁	0		▷
D	⋪	0	◁	

(c) ABCE $\mathcal{L}_2$

	A	B	C	E
A		▷	⋫	⋫
B	◁		▷	⋫
C	⋪	◁		▷
E	⋪	⋪	◁	

(d) ACBE $\mathcal{L}_2$

	A	B	C	E
A		⋫	▷	⋫
B	⋪		◁	▷
C	◁	▷		⋫
E	⋪	◁	⋪	

3.2 Log Matrix

A log matrix summarizes the behavior reported in the log and is obtained by the trace matrices previously generated. In addition to the relationships already described in the trace matrices, here we can express the relation of XOR or AND between activities.

In particular we use:

- ×, if the two activities never appear on the same trace (XOR);
- +, if there is at least one trace in which the activity t_i appears before the activity t_j and another trace with the same activities but with the inverse order (AND).

A log matrix is obtained by comparing all trace matrices of the Log.

Definition 3. *Let $\mathcal{LM}$ be the **Log Matrix** corresponding to a log $\mathcal{L}$, then a generic entry in $\mathcal{LM}$ is indicated as l_{ij} and is defined as follows (taking into account the trace matrices corresponding to the traces in log $\mathcal{L}$):*

- $l_{ij} := \triangleright$ *if $\exists \sigma \in \mathcal{L} : t_{ij}^{\sigma} = \triangleright$ and $\forall \sigma' \in (\mathcal{L}\backslash\sigma): t_{ij}^{\sigma'} = (\triangleright$ or $\emptyset)$*
- $l_{ij} := \triangleleft$ *if $\exists \sigma \in \mathcal{L} : t_{ij}^{\sigma} = \triangleleft$ and $\forall \sigma' \in (\mathcal{L}\backslash\sigma) : t_{ij}^{\sigma'} = (\triangleleft$ or $\emptyset)$*
- $l_{ij} := \not\triangleright$ *if $\exists \sigma \in \mathcal{L} : t_{ij}^{\sigma} = \not\triangleright$ and $\forall \sigma' \in (\mathcal{L}\backslash\sigma) : t_{ij}^{\sigma'} = (\triangleright$ or $\emptyset)$*
- $l_{ij} := \not\triangleleft$ *if $\exists \sigma \in \mathcal{L} : t_{ij}^{\sigma} = \not\triangleleft$ and $\forall \sigma' \in (\mathcal{L}\backslash\sigma) : t_{ij}^{\sigma'} = (\triangleright$ or $\emptyset)$*
- $l_{ij} := \times$ *if $\forall \sigma \in \mathcal{L} : t_{ij}^{\sigma} = \emptyset$;*
- $l_{ij} := +$ *if $\exists \sigma \in \mathcal{L} : t_{ij}^{\sigma} = (\not\triangleright$ or $\triangleright)$ and $\exists \sigma' \in (\mathcal{L}\backslash\sigma) : t_{ij}^{\sigma'} = (\not\triangleleft$ or $\triangleleft)$*

Running Example (2/4). Considering the Trace Matrices presented in Table 2, here below we define the corresponding Log Matrices following the rules defined above. In particular Table 3a shows the log matrix for $\mathcal{L}_1$ merging together the trace matrices defined in Table 2a and 2b. Table 3b represents the log matrix for $\mathcal{L}_2$ regarding the trace matrices defined in Table 2c and Table 2d.

Table 3. Log matrices

	A	B	C	D
A		$\triangleright$	$\triangleright$	$\not\triangleright$
B	$\triangleleft$		$\times$	$\triangleright$
C	$\triangleleft$	$\times$		$\triangleright$
D	$\not\triangleleft$	$\triangleleft$	$\triangleleft$	

(a) $\mathcal{L}_1$

	A	B	C	E
A		$\not\triangleright$	$\not\triangleright$	$\not\triangleright$
B	$\not\triangleleft$		$+$	$\not\triangleright$
C	$\not\triangleleft$	$+$		$\not\triangleright$
E	$\not\triangleleft$	$\not\triangleleft$	$\not\triangleleft$	

(b) $\mathcal{L}_2$

3.3 Variance Matrix

A Variance Matrix defines the distance between two log files. Each entry of the Variance Matrix is obtained by comparing the corresponding element of two Log Matrices and by weighting the result using parameters γ and β.

Definition 4. *Let $\mathcal{V}$ be a **Variance Matrix** corresponding to the logs $\mathcal{L}$ and $\mathcal{L}'$ then the elements of such a matrix are defined as follows:*

$$v_{ii} = \begin{cases} \gamma, & \text{if } a_i \in \mathcal{A}^{\mathcal{L}} \cap \mathcal{A}^{\mathcal{L}'} \\ 0, & \text{otherwise} \end{cases}$$

$$v_{ij} = \begin{cases} (1-\gamma), & \text{if } l_{ij} \text{ matches } l'_{ij} \\ \beta \cdot (1-\gamma), & \text{if } l_{ij} \text{ and } l'_{ij} \text{ have same order, with } \beta < (1-\gamma) \\ 0, & \text{otherwise} \end{cases}$$

where l_{ij} and l'_{ij} are the elements of the Log Matrices corresponding to logs $\mathcal{L}$ and $\mathcal{L}'$, respectively.

In particular, the entries corresponding to the diagonal of the matrix are used to keep track of the presence of the activities in the logs, while the remaining part of the matrix is used to annotate the relationship between them. If the activity a_i is present in the intersection of $\mathcal{A}^{\mathcal{L}}$ and $\mathcal{A}^{\mathcal{L}'}$ then the corresponding entries in the diagonal are filled with γ, 0 otherwise.

Considering instead the entries v_{ij} they are filled with $(1-\gamma)$ if the entries of the Log Matrices for $\mathcal{L}$ and $\mathcal{L}'$ are identical; $\beta \cdot (1-\gamma)$ if they respect the same order ($\triangleleft, \ntriangleleft$) or ($\triangleright, \ntriangleright$), 0 otherwise.

The parameter γ is used to control the impact of activities with respect to the relationship between them. Thus, it can be understood that it is possible to give more weight to the common existence of the activities giving more weight to the elements on the diagonal (γ close to 1) or more weight to the relationships between activities (flow) giving more weight to the elements that are not on the diagonal (γ close to 0). The parameter β is useful for discriminating that cases where the entries l_{ij} and l'_{ij} are not identical but still respect the same order of precedence. The usage of these parameters permits the final user to customize the measure according to his/her necessity and interest.

To notice, in order to compare matrices with different activities we use in the Variance Matrix the super-set of the activities between the two Log Matrices ($\mathcal{A}^{\mathcal{L}} \cup \mathcal{A}^{\mathcal{L}'}$) and we insert 0 on the entries that refer to the absent activity.

Running Example 3/5. Considering the two Log Matrices defined in Table 3a and 3b the resulting Variance matrix considering the parameter γ=0.6 and the parameter β=0.25 is defined in Table 4.

Table 4. Variance matrix $\mathcal{V}$ corresponding to logs $\mathcal{L}_1$ and $\mathcal{L}_2$

	A	B	C	D	E
A	0.6	0.1	0.1	0	0
B	0.1	0.6	0	0	0
C	0.1	0	0.6	0	0
D	0	0	0	0	0
E	0	0	0	0	0

3.4 Distance Matrix

The Distance Matrix summarizes the similarity between Logs using a range between 0 and 100. In particular, the closer the value is to zero, the more similar the two models are.

Definition 5. *Given a set of logs let $\hat{V}$ be the set of all Variance Matrices. Then $\mathcal{D}$ is the **Distance Matrix** among Variance Matrices, where each element of the matrix $d_{ij} = diss(\mathcal{L}_i, \mathcal{L}_j)$, is computed using Eq. (3)*

Given $|\hat{V}| = N$, $\mathcal{D}$ is a matrix of order N.

It is worth clarifying that a Variance Matrix $\mathcal{V}$ contains the similarity among the two Log Matrices associated with the logs $\mathcal{L}$ and $\mathcal{L}'$. In order to derive a value (real number), for quantifying the similarity between two Logs, we used the following relationships:

$$\text{sim}(\mathcal{L}_i, \mathcal{L}_j) = \frac{1}{\alpha}||\mathcal{V}||_1 = \frac{1}{\alpha}\sum_i^N \sum_j^N |v_{ij}| \tag{1}$$

$$\alpha = \begin{cases} n, & \text{if } \gamma = 1 \\ n(n-1), & \text{if } \gamma = 0 \\ n^2, & \text{otherwise} \end{cases} \tag{2}$$

$$\text{diss}(\mathcal{L}_i, \mathcal{L}_j) = (1 - \text{sim}(\mathcal{L}_i, \mathcal{L}_j)) * 100 \tag{3}$$

The similarity $\text{sim}(\mathcal{L}_i, \mathcal{L}_j)$ is calculated by dividing per α the 1-norm of the corresponding Variance Matrix $\mathcal{V}$, where α assumes a different value according to the definition (2). In other words, α should assume a value equal to the number of cells possibly different from 0 according to the definition of the parameter γ. Finally, the dissimilarity of two logs, $\text{diss}(\mathcal{L}_i, \mathcal{L}_j)$, is defined as one minus the similarity, expressed in hundredths.

Running Example (4/4). The distance matrix (Table 5) of the considered running example is defined on the dissimilarity of logs calculated in Table 4. In particular, for logs $\mathcal{L}_1$ and $\mathcal{L}_2$, we have the following distance:

$$\mathrm{diss}(\mathcal{L}_1, \mathcal{L}_2) = (1 - \mathrm{sim}(\mathcal{L}_1, \mathcal{L}_2)) * 100 = (1 - (\frac{(0.6 * 3) + (0.1 * 4)}{25})) * 100 = 91.2$$

Table 5. Distance matrix

	Log_1	Log_2
Log_1		91.2
Log_2		

3.5 Logs Clustering

The last step of our methodology consists in defining the Log clusters according to the generated Distance Matrix. The clustering algorithm that we take into consideration is the K-medoids for its characteristic to select the medoids among the collected Logs. The number of partitions K is selected automatically by the algorithm ensuring the maximum silhouette index.

4 Empirical Results/Case Study

To study and evaluate the performances of our (dis)similarity measure, we analyzed data provided by a company that sells information systems to the PA. We selected a single service offered by municipalities and we derived a set of logs that have been successively pre-processed by a semi-automatic procedure in order to anonymize and unify activities so to run our algorithm. The pre-processing phase permitted us to select 37 logs describing the same process. The first four phases of the proposed methodology were implemented in a Java tool[1]. In particular, after the selection of a folder containing the XES Logs to analyze the tool is able to derive a csv file containing the Distance Matrix between all Logs. Successively, the generated csv file has been imported in R, for performing the K-medoids algorithm thanks to the *cluster* library[2]. To evaluate and test the performance of the defined (dis)similarity measure and the corresponding cluster results, three configurations were studied. In particular, we set the parameter $\beta=0.1$ and the γ varying as follows:

---

[1] https://bitbucket.org/proslabteam/tlv-diss/downloads/.
[2] https://cran.r-project.org/web/packages/cluster/cluster.pdf.

- $\gamma = 0$ to reward control flow similarity (C_{Flow})
- $\gamma = 1$ to reward activities similarity (C_{Act})
- $\gamma = 0.5$ to equally reward control flow and activities ($C_{Fl/Act}$)

The optimal number of clusters K is found by calculating the Average Silhouette Value, $S_{average}$, for several K. The K-medoids algorithm then will select the K at which $S_{average}$ is maximum. This guarantee the best results of the algorithm. We obtained that K = 14 for configuration C_{Flow}, K = 15 for configuration C_{Act} and K = 12 for configuration $C_{Fl/Act}$.

Figure 1 shows the clusters obtained for each configuration. By observing Fig. 1a and 1b, we see that Log_{42} and Log_{43} appear in different clusters if $\gamma = 0$, while they belong to the same cluster if $\gamma = 1$. This fact is somehow expected, in fact $Log_{42} = \{\langle H, G\rangle, \langle T,Q\rangle\}$, while $Log_{43} = \{\langle T, G, Q, H\rangle, \langle G,T,H,Q\rangle\}$. This shows how our methodology allows the analyst to choose whether to give more weight to the similarity of activities or of control flows.

Log_6 and Log_{14} show a very interesting behavior, too. $Log_6 = \{\langle C, A\rangle\}$, while $Log_{14} = \{\langle A, C\rangle\}$. On the one hand, choosing $\gamma = 0$, Log_6 is a cluster of its own and Log_{14} is clustered with $Log_2 = \{\langle A, B, C, E\rangle, \langle A, C, B, E\rangle\}$, $Log_{34} = \{\langle A, C\rangle, \langle A, B\rangle\}$ and $Log_{37} = \{\langle B, A, C\rangle\}$. This is not surprising, in fact in this cluster the existence of the same $\langle A, C\rangle$ sub-sequence is identified. On the other hand, as can be seen in Fig. 1a and 1c, fixing $\gamma = 1$ and $\gamma = 0.5$, Log_6 and Log_{14} are in the same cluster: this behavior is consistent because the Logs share both activities.

Finally, $Log_4 = \{\langle A, B, C\rangle\}$ and $LOG_{35} = \{\langle A, B\rangle\}$ are clustered together when $\gamma = 0$ while if $\gamma = 1$, Log_{35} is cluster with $Log_7 = \{\langle B, A\rangle\}$ and if $\gamma = 0.5$ the three Logs above belong to the same cluster as shown in Fig. 1c.

While a thoughtful assessment of the approach is certainly needed, so far the results we got in terms of performance seem to support its applicability to the comparison of many logs. In particular, ten runs on our data-set composed of 37 logs the final Distance Matrix was generated with an average time of 4.3 s, using a consumer PC.

5   Related Works

There is a large literature on similarity measures between business models or logs. In [16] the authors identify four dimensions to quantify the similarity between models and between their elements.

The natural language dimension provides a syntactic comparison of labels in the model to determine the equality between two labels, or the semantic one, to identify the synonyms of the labels. The graph structure is the dimension that allows comparison of e.g. the largest sub-pattern in common between the two graphs or the position and type of the various control flow connectors. The human estimation dimension allows human opinion to be included in the judgment of how similar two processes are. Finally, behaviour dimension compares trace executions. Gerke et al. [7] and Zhou et al. [19] use the longest sub-traces

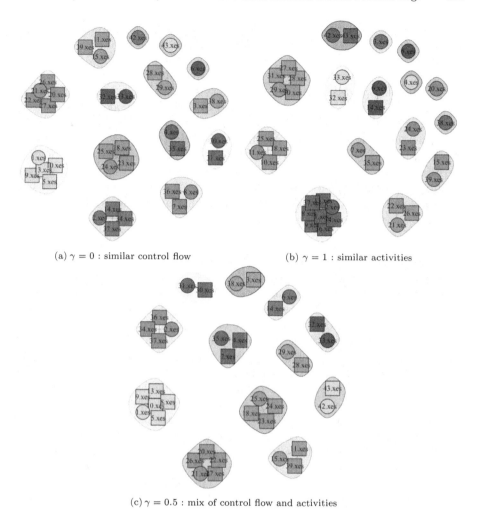

(a) $\gamma = 0$: similar control flow   (b) $\gamma = 1$: similar activities

(c) $\gamma = 0.5$: mix of control flow and activities

Fig. 1. Clustering. Each log file is indicated using the XES extension; the circles represents the medoids, i.e. the cluster's most representative object

to express Log similarity. In [4] van Dongen et al. use causal footprints to define relationships between activities. The similarity is then calculated by using the cosine distance. Kunze et al. [10] define a metric from order relationships between trace elements, i.e. strict order, exclusiveness, interleaving, and co-occurrence. The metric provides a weighted contribution of the similarity between the two models according to each of the order relationships. Our similarity measure differs from the mentioned works because it takes all traces into account, has the ability to consider AND and XOR, and thanks to the concept of follows (precedes) strictly, it is possible to express notions about the context. The effectiveness of our similarity measure is also tested through a clustering technique making our methodology suitable for large amounts of data.

Model clustering has already been explored in the literature, although existing works take business models as input. Our work instead involves the analysis of execution logs and this methodology is very suitable in case of a large number of logs, as using process mining techniques to derive the model would be very expensive. In [8] the authors use a metric that equally weighs the contribution of activities and transitions. They use hierarchical clustering to group the models. Again, using models, Bergmann et al. [1] tested the effectiveness of k-medoid for partitioning a recipe repository, in [5] the authors use clustering to identify fragments of patterns present in several processes that can be refactored as shared processes and in [13] the authors adopt a similarity function based on fuzzy logic, which is then used to cluster the models.

6   Conclusions and Future Works

In this paper, we derived a parametric dis(similarity) measure working on log files produced by PAs. Our approach, starting from the traces describing the executions of services, derives a distance matrix representing the (dis)similarity among logs, so to permit a deeper understanding of variability in the delivery of services to citizens by different organizations. The proposed methodology is particularly suited for comparing and analyzing large amounts of data, where standard techniques (e.g. process mining) are not indicated due to scalability issues. Furthermore, our approach is able to deal with the real behavior of systems, since it is completely data-driven, and does not rely on the knowledge of any model, which in general could not precisely reflect real IS executions.

The integration of a clustering procedure in the proposed methodology is twofold: first of all, it allows to evaluate the discriminating power of the TLV-diss$_\gamma$ measure, secondly, it permits to aggregate and analyze similar logs in order to provide the analyst with a more focused and complete view on the global behavior of the group.

As shown in Sect. 4, we obtained promising results on the analyzed logs. Indeed, the proposed parametric measure was able to discriminate logs according to the selected parameters, showing the efficacy and effectiveness of the approach. This confirms the goodness of the used parameters. Anyway, larger and deeper investigations on such field are needed, such as the possibility to introduce other perspectives in addition to control flow and activities or the possibility to test the application in other scenarios [2]; as well as using Topological Data Analysis-based clustering [12,14]. Furthermore, possible improvements of the dis(similarity) measure are under study.

Acknowledgements. Caterina Luciani's work has been funded by Maggioli Spa.

References

1. Bergmann, R., Müller, G., Wittkowsky, D.: Workflow clustering using semantic similarity measures. In: Timm, I.J., Thimm, M. (eds.) KI 2013. LNCS (LNAI), vol. 8077, pp. 13–24. Springer, Heidelberg (2013). https://doi.org/10.1007/978-3-642-40942-4_2
2. Corradini, F., Marcantoni, F., Morichetta, A., Polini, A., Re, B., Sampaolo, M.: Enabling auditing of smart contracts through process mining. In: ter Beek, M.H., Fantechi, A., Semini, L. (eds.) From Software Engineering to Formal Methods and Tools, and Back. LNCS, vol. 11865, pp. 467–480. Springer, Cham (2019). https://doi.org/10.1007/978-3-030-30985-5_27
3. Corradini, F., Marcelletti, A., Morichetta, A., Polini, A., Re, B., Tiezzi, F.: Engineering trustable choreography-based systems using blockchain. In: Symposium on Applied Computing, SAC 2020, pp. 1470–1479. Association for Computing Machinery (2020)
4. van Dongen, B., Dijkman, R., Mendling, J.: Measuring similarity between business process models. In: Advanced IS Engineering, pp. 450–464 (2008)
5. Ekanayake, C.C., Dumas, M., García-Bañuelos, L., La Rosa, M., ter Hofstede, A.H.M.: Approximate clone detection in repositories of business process models. In: Barros, A., Gal, A., Kindler, E. (eds.) BPM 2012. LNCS, vol. 7481, pp. 302–318. Springer, Heidelberg (2012). https://doi.org/10.1007/978-3-642-32885-5_24
6. Friedman, J., Hastie, T., Tibshirani, R., et al.: The Elements of Statistical Learning. Springer Series in Statistics, vol. 1. Springer, New York (2001). https://doi.org/10.1007/978-0-387-21606-5
7. Gerke, K., Cardoso, J., Claus, A.: Measuring the compliance of processes with reference models. In: Meersman, R., Dillon, T., Herrero, P. (eds.) OTM 2009. LNCS, vol. 5870, pp. 76–93. Springer, Heidelberg (2009). https://doi.org/10.1007/978-3-642-05148-7_8
8. Jung, J.Y., Bae, J., Liu, L.: Hierarchical clustering of business process models. Int. J. Innov. Comput. Inf. Control 5(12), 1349–4198 (2009)
9. Kaufman, L., Rousseeuw, P.J.: Finding Groups in Data: An Introduction to Cluster Analysis, vol. 344. Wiley, Hoboken (2009)
10. Kunze, M., Weidlich, M., Weske, M.: Behavioral similarity – a proper metric. In: Rinderle-Ma, S., Toumani, F., Wolf, K. (eds.) BPM 2011. LNCS, vol. 6896, pp. 166–181. Springer, Heidelberg (2011). https://doi.org/10.1007/978-3-642-23059-2_15
11. Li, C., Reichert, M., Wombacher, A.: On measuring process model similarity based on high-level change operations. In: Li, Q., Spaccapietra, S., Yu, E., Olivé, A. (eds.) ER 2008. LNCS, vol. 5231, pp. 248–264. Springer, Heidelberg (2008). https://doi.org/10.1007/978-3-540-87877-3_19
12. Merelli, E., Rucco, M., Tesei, L., Piangerelli, M., Mamuye, A.L., Quadrini, M.: Survey of TOPDRIM applications of topological data analysis. In: Armano, G., Bozzon, A., Cristani, M., Giuliani, A. (eds.) KDWeb Workshop. CEUR Workshop Proceedings, vol. 1748. CEUR-WS.org (2016)
13. Ordoñez, A., Ordoñez, H., Corrales, J.C., Cobos, C., Wives, L.K., Thom, L.H.: Grouping of business processes models based on an incremental clustering algorithm using fuzzy similarity and multimodal search. Expert Syst. Appl. **67**, 163–177 (2017)
14. Piangerelli, M., Maestri, S., Merelli, E.: Visualising 2-simplex formation in metabolic reactions. J. Mol. Graph. Model. **97**, 107576 (2020)

15. Rousseeuw, P.J.: Silhouettes: a graphical aid to the interpretation and validation of cluster analysis. J. Comput. Appl. Math. **20**, 53–65 (1987)
16. Schoknecht, A., Thaler, T., Fettke, P., Oberweis, A., Laue, R.: Similarity of business process models–a state-of-the-art analysis. ACM Comput. Surv. (CSUR) **50**(4), 1–33 (2017)
17. Schubert, E., Rousseeuw, P.J.: Faster k-medoids clustering: improving the PAM, CLARA, and CLARANS algorithms. In: Amato, G., Gennaro, C., Oria, V., Radovanović, M. (eds.) SISAP 2019. LNCS, vol. 11807, pp. 171–187. Springer, Cham (2019). https://doi.org/10.1007/978-3-030-32047-8_16
18. Aalst, W.: Data science in action. In: Process Mining, pp. 3–23. Springer, Heidelberg (2016). https://doi.org/10.1007/978-3-662-49851-4_1
19. Zhou, C., Liu, C., Zeng, Q., Lin, Z., Duan, H.: A comprehensive process similarity measure based on models and logs. IEEE Access **7**, 69257–69273 (2019)

Towards a Framework for the Adaptation of the Internet of Things in International Border Control Organizations

Paul Brous[1]([✉])([iD]), Monica den Boer[2], and Pascal Wolf[2]

[1] Legend Data Management, 3053WX Rotterdam, Netherlands
[2] Nederlandse Defensie Academie, Kraanstraat 4, 4811XC Breda, Netherlands
{mgw.d.boer,pr.wolf.01}@mindef.nl

Abstract. COVID-19, BREXIT, global terrorism, and political ideologies such as "America First" have increasingly laid bare ethical, political and operational stresses attached to international border crossings. Organizations tasked with the management of international borders are having to cope with new threats to border management and more and more are choosing to incorporate the Internet of Things (IoT) technologies within their border management processes as a means of governing mobility. However, whilst the introduction of IoT can introduce a number of benefits, the adaptation of new technologies presents substantial challenges to border management organizations and can introduce a number of unforeseen risks such as encroachment on the rights of the individual, lack of transparent governance, absence of legal legitimacy, opaque delegation of responsibilities between communitarian organizations and unethical decision-making or behavior. This article proposes a framework for the adaptation of IoT by border management organizations which aims at helping border management organizations overcome the challenges presented by the implementation of IoT. The implementation of this framework includes wide-ranging changes to the structure of the organization, changes to processes and systems, and changes to the continuous training and development of staff members.

Keywords: IoT · Internet of Things · Border management · Risks · Benefits

1 Introduction

COVID-19, global terrorism, BREXIT and political movements such as "America First" have increasingly laid bare ethical, political and operational stresses facing the government of international border crossings. In the face of heightened political pressure, organizations tasked with the management of international borders are having to cope with new threats to border management, despite traditional constraints such as limited budgets and reduced staff. As such, countries are increasingly choosing to digitalize the government of international borders by incorporating Internet of Things (IoT) technologies within their border management processes [1] as a means of improving the

H. J. Scholl et al. (Eds.): EGOV 2021, LNCS 12850, pp. 315–327, 2021.
https://doi.org/10.1007/978-3-030-84789-0_23

governance of mobilities [2] and improving the policing and security of international borders [3].

The IoT is a network of objects that communicate between themselves and other internet-enabled devices over the Internet allowing organizations to monitor and control the physical world remotely [4, 5]. However, border management organizations face unique challenges to IoT implementation, such as the large numbers of people and goods which cross international borders, the large areas which need to monitored and secured [6], and the need for international cooperation [7]. Furthermore, border management organizations are choosing more often for a pre-liminal and post-liminal approach to border security as opposed to a liminal approach. Whilst the introduction of IoT can introduce a number of benefits for border management purposes, the delegation of control to technology and the increasing lack of physical presence presents substantial challenges and can introduce a number of unforeseen risks such as encroachment on the rights of the individual, lack of transparent governance, lack of legal legitimacy, opaque delegation of responsibilities between organizations, unethical decision-making or behavior [8] and a mutual lack of trust.

Despite the popularity of IoT technology for border management, particularly with regards to biometrics such as fingerprint scanners, facial recognition or iris scanners, the adoption of such technologies has proved in the past to be challenging for border management organizations [9, 10]. The reasons for these failures are often due not to technological deficiencies but are often more rooted in social aspects. For example, because maritime rescue services are not part of EUROSUR, border guards do not necessarily share information with them due to ill-defined responsibilities within Europe [9]. Furthermore, despite the growing number of investigations into the technological possibilities of smart borders, little research has been done on the social impact of IoT implementation, in particular as to its impact on border management organizations as well as their inter-organizational relationships. This article addresses this knowledge gap by discussing a review of background literature and proposing a framework for the adaptation of IoT by border management organizations.

This research investigates the impact of IoT implementation on border management organizations using Duality of Technology theory [11] as underlying logic. The central question asks what conditions border management organizations should take into account when adapting IoT for the digitalization of border government? This article proposes a framework for the adaptation of IoT by border management organizations and concludes that implementing this framework requires organizations to develop capabilities which ensure that the introduction of IoT fits the purposes of border control whilst also mitigating the accompanying risks to the border management organization. The development of these capabilities may include wide-ranging changes to the structure of the organization, changes to processes and systems, and changes to the continuous training and development of staff members.

This article reads as follows, in Sect. 2 of this article the methodology followed to develop the framework for adaptation of IoT for border management on the basis of propositions developed in a systematic review of literature is described. In Sect. 3 the systematic review of literature is described and propositions for a framework of IoT adaptation for border management are synthesized. In Sect. 4 a framework for the adaptation of the IoT for border management organizations is described and discussed. In Sect. 5, conclusions are drawn and proposals are made for further research.

2 Methodology

The proposed framework for IoT adaptation for border management organizations was developed on the basis of a systematic review of background literature. This literature review follows the method proposed by Webster & Watson [12] and synthesizes literature with regards to the adaptation of IoT by border management organizations. Our research objective is to understand under what conditions IoT can best be adapted by border management organizations. However, there is only limited research on IoT adaptation for border management and models for the adaptation of IoT in border management organizations are missing This article fills this gap by describing a framework for IoT adaptation by border management organizations. The framework can be used by border management organizations to coordinate the successful adaptation of IoT and mitigate the negative impact of IoT implementations. Duality of technology theory [11] was used as underlying logic to order and analyze relevant literature in order to ensure sufficient coverage of essential topics. Based on Giddens' [13] theory of structuration, duality of technology [11] describes technology as assuming structural properties whilst being the product of human action. Orlikowski identifies four main relationships, namely: 1) technology as a product of human agency, 2) technology as a medium of human agency, 3) organizational conditions of interaction with technology and, 4) organizational consequences of interaction with technology. Using duality of technology theory as basis for the literature review serves to help us understand what adaptation of IoT for border management entails by providing a multi-perspective analysis of the phenomenon.

As suggested by Webster & Watson [12], the review of literature is limited to the adaptation of IoT by border management organizations, although due to the importance of interactions between cross-border organizations, these relationships have also been taken into consideration. Furthermore, because the adaptation of IoT for border management is a relatively new phenomenon, the literature review is restricted to literature published after 1999. The literature review was also limited to the databases Scopus, Web of Science and Google Scholar. On the 27th of February 2021, the search string ("Internet of Things" AND ("border management" OR "border control" OR "mobility governance" OR "border policing") AND "organizations") returned 684 hits. Forward and backward searches were conducted until saturation of information was achieved. Based on this consideration, a selection of 31 relevant articles was made based on the criteria that they specifically address the influence or impact of IoT applications on border management organizations and digital border government. When articles dealt with similar technologies or had similar conclusions, the most recently published article was selected for inclusion. The articles were then organized according to the logic provided by duality of technology theory in order to generate the requirements for the framework of IoT adaptation for border management organizations, and propositions which form the basis of the framework were synthesized out of the grouped literature.

3 Literature Review

According to Scholl [14, p. 1], digital government includes, "the use of information technology to support government operations, engage citizens, and provide government services". Border management organizations across the world are increasingly adapting digital technologies to support the interaction between travelers and border officials. According to Lindgren et al. [15] the adaptation of emerging technologies such as IoT helps fulfill the primary goals of digital government such as improving efficiency and service quality as well as increasing government transparency concerning, for instance, the search criteria that are being applied. The situation whereby a form of ubiquitous artificial intelligence is created by networking physical objects over the internet is commonly referred to as the IoT [16]. The automated generation and analysis of data provided by the IoT is often of better quality than traditional data generated by traditional means, is often more timely and has substantially larger volumes [17]. As such, much of the value of IoT is derived from the data the IoT produces [1]. As the concept of smart borders is data intensive [8], IoT has a large potential to improve the digital government of international borders [18] through the policing of international borders [19] such as using artificial intelligence to detect patterns in smuggling routes, improving mobility management [20] through the use of wifi-based pax tracking or check-in touchpoints for example the management of migration [21] through the use of entry decision-making engines, and improving support processes through data driven border management.

However, the development and use of IoT data and applications carries risk and is reliant on a number of conditions which are often more social in nature such as the need to ensure privacy [22] and security [19] and the need to maintain public trust and transparency [21], but also are related to organizational change such as the need for new skills and business processes [23]. This means that a mix of variant conditions are to be met prior to the border management adaptation process.

3.1 IoT as a Medium of Human Agency in Border Management Applications

IoT as a medium of human agency [11] takes the perspective that IoT is used by border management organizations in particular use cases to improve the efficiency or effectiveness of their processes or, for example, to reduce overhead, arbitrary decision-making, and lower costs. Due to the particular challenges facing border management organizations such as the need to monitor and control vast and sometimes sparsely populated border areas in a wide variety of conditions, as well as the need to protect the security of the many whilst ensuring the privacy and dignity of the individual, border management organizations are more frequently turning to automated IoT solutions to find solutions to these challenges. Table 1 below presents the popular uses for IoT in border management organizations. As such the framework for IoT adaptation for border management organizations should include these use domains.

Table 1. Uses of IoT for border management organizations

Business domain	IoT use domain	Literature
Border policing	• Predictive and prescriptive border policing (e.g. with regards to trafficking)	[10, 24, 25]
	• Non-invasive inspection	[6, 21]
	• Monitoring and surveillance	[9, 10, 19, 25]
	• Corruption prevention	[19, 26]
	• Fraud detection	[21, 26]
Mobility governance	• Migrant tracking and control	[2, 9, 10, 21, 27]
	• Health inspection	[21, 27]
	• Identification and authentication management	[2, 21, 28–30]
	• Seamless flow	[21, 27]
	• Asylum management	[6, 31]
	• Irregular immigration	[6, 7, 9, 25]
	• Identifying criminals and fugitives	[20, 27, 32]
Border security	• Crowd detection and management	[1]
	• Individual/personal security	[21]
	• Calamity prevention and control	[1]
	• Asset security	[6]
	• Cyber security	[19]
	• Weapons guidance	[1]
	• Anti-terrorism intelligence	[2]
	• Situational awareness	[1]
Support	• Logistics	[1]
	• Predictive maintenance	[1]
	• Fleet monitoring and management	[1]
	• Individual supplies	[1]
	• Workforce training and healthcare	[1]

More and more, border management organizations tend to focus their management processes on the generation of intelligence which allows them to predict and prescribe actions with regards to border policing [10], mobility governance [27], and border security [1], as well as improving necessary support processes such as logistics. This suggests that the digitalization of the border government process through IoT adaptation may improve the efficiency of operational and tactical processes. As such, proposition 1 reads as follows: *border management organizations which adapt IoT for border management purposes are more likely to have improved operational and tactical border management processes.*

3.2 IoT as a Product of Human Agency in Border Management Applications

IoT implementation projects in the past have not always been successful [9] as border management organizations have technological requirements which are specific to the border management domain. In addition to physical, economic and geographic requirements border management organizations also have to take complex issues into consideration such as national security and political pressures. This often requires border management organizations to develop and manage bespoke solutions in-house. Adaptation of IoT technology for border management is therefore often a complex undertaking. Table 2 below presents necessary adaptation issues of IoT for border management organizations. As such the framework for IoT adaptation for border management organizations should include these product development domains.

Table 2. Development of IoT for border management

Business domain	IoT product domain	Literature
IT management	• Redesign of Information Technology (IT) infrastructure	[1, 32–35]
	• Scalability	[32, 33]
	• Energy efficiency	[1]
	• Sensor development	[1, 33, 34]
	• Interoperability	[1, 10, 28, 33]
	• Rapid deployment	[1, 33]
	• Accessibility	[34]
	• Connectivity	[1, 32, 33]
Data management	• Redesign of data infrastructure	[29, 30]
	• Digital security	[32, 33]
	• International cyber security	[7, 36, 37]
	• Sensor calibration	[1, 33, 34]
	• Bias detection	[29, 30]

Many of the challenges associated with IoT adaptation are considered to be of a technical nature, particularly with regards to digital security [32], but it is often in the (mis)use or analysis of the data in which the failures of IoT implementations in border management settings occur [30]. This suggests that achieving the efficiency goals of digital border government may require that border management organizations address data and IT management considerations. As such, proposition 2 reads as follows: *border management organizations with mature IT and data management processes are more likely be able to successfully adapt IoT for border management purposes.*

3.3 Organizational Conditions of Interaction with IoT in a Border Management Context

Due to the complexity of IoT adaptation for border management successful IoT implementations require a number of organizational conditions to be met before implementation can occur in an operational setting. Modern border management is no longer a question of simply monitoring travelers at a single point of entry. The traveler's journey often begins before they have left home as many border crossings worldwide require such things as passports and visas. Contemporary border management is a combination of off-shore migration management, border crossing management and in-country mobility management and this requires not only interdepartmental coordination, but also international and inter-organizational cooperation. Table 3 below presents necessary organizational conditions for adaptation of IoT for border management organizations. As such the framework for IoT adaptation for border management organizations should include the fulfilment of these organizational conditions.

Table 3. Organizational conditions for IoT adaptation in border management organizations

Business domain	Organizational condition	Literature
IT governance	• Security framework (including budget, staff, processes, standards, policies, technology)	[19, 22, 34]
	• Technical framework (including budget, staff, processes, international standards, policies)	[26, 33–36]
	• Systemization of administrative policies	[10, 20, 33]
Data governance	• Legal frameworks for data collection, storage and analysis	[20, 21, 32, 34, 37]
	• Data quality management	[16, 19, 37]
	• Data protection (privacy) framework (including budget, staff, processes, standards, policies, technology)	[19, 22, 26, 28, 34]
	• Data access management	[19, 32, 38]
	• Data sharing framework (including budget, staff, processes, standards, policies, technology)	[19, 26, 32, 38, 39]
	• International cooperation frameworks	[32, 33, 36, 39]
	• Interorganizational cooperation frameworks	[10, 33, 38]
	• Interdepartmental cooperation	[10, 26, 33]
	• Data ethics framework	[10, 21, 34, 37]

Although the technical challenges of IoT adaptation are myriad, the importance of the data governance domain is often overlooked in implementation projects [22]. Data governance has been shown to be a vital component of successful artificial intelligence initiatives [40]. This suggests that IT governance and data governance may be essential processes for achieving the objectives of digital border government. As such proposition

3 reads as follows: *border management organizations with mature IT and data governance processes are more likely able to successfully adapt IoT for border management purposes.*

3.4 Organizational Consequences of Interaction with IoT in a Border Management Context

Once IoT has been adapted and implemented in a border management setting, many border management organizations are in turn faced with consequences which are often unanticipated and which, in turn, need to be managed. For example, the simple act of creating a new border entry point can create large changes in migration patterns. Table 4 below presents necessary potentially unforeseen organizational consequences of adaptation of IoT for border management organizations. As such the framework for IoT adaptation for border management organizations should include the taking into account of these consequences.

Table 4. Organizational consequences of IoT adaptation for border management organizations

Business domain	Organizational consequence	Literature
Direct organizational consequences	• New skills required, some skills become obsolete	[40, 41]
	• New departments required, some departments become obsolete	[40, 41]
	• New business processes required, some processes become obsolete	[40, 41]
	• Higher support costs	[21, 26, 34, 35, 42]
Indirect organizational consequences	• Lack of public trust	[8, 19, 26, 36]
	• Reduced transparency	[8, 19, 36]
	• Incorrect digital profiling/ chances of bias	[21, 29, 31]
	• Changing mobility patterns	[10, 32]
	• Heightened biopolitics	[21, 31]
	• Heightened chance of discrimination	[21, 31]

Implementation projects often necessarily focus on short-term goals and gains due to time and budgetary constraints [21]. However, many of the changes wrought by the implementation of IoT in border management settings can have long-term consequences for the public and for the border management organization itself. This suggests that border management organizations may need to be aware of these potential long-term consequences before IoT implementation occurs in order to be able to mitigate these consequences and achieve their digital border government goals. Proposition 4 therefore reads as follows: *border management organizations which are aware of the direct and indirect consequences of IoT are more likely to be able to adapt IoT for border management purposes in a sustainable fashion.*

4 A Proposed Framework for IoT Adaptation for Border Management Organizations

The review of background literature synthesized four propositions for the adaptation of IoT for border management organizations. Proposition 1 proposes that IoT may be adapted for use in border management operations. The literature review provides a plethora of potential use cases such as the use of IoT for border policing, border security, mobility governance and support. In order for these use cases to be implemented, IoT technology needs to be adapted for use in a border management setting. Proposition 2 proposes that IoT needs to be specifically developed for border management as border management organizations have specific requirements such as the need for international cooperation. The use of IoT in border management is also only possible if certain organizational conditions are met. As such, proposition 3 proposes that IoT initiatives in border management settings are more likely to be successful if these organizational conditions are met. As a result of meeting these requirements and implementing IoT applications, proposition 4 proposes that many border management organizations are faced with consequences which are often unanticipated and which, in turn, need to be managed. These propositions follow the underlying logic of duality of technology theory [11] and are included in the framework as depicted by Fig. 1 below.

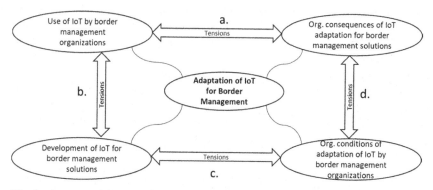

Fig. 1. A proposed framework for IoT adaptation for border management organizations

The framework of IoT adaptation for border management organizations as depicted in Fig. 1 above shows that tensions arise between each of the four focus domains. These tensions have been lettered 'a' through to 'd' and are explained as follows:

a) Effective use of IoT in border management situations requires legal and ethical frameworks, skilled staff, well-managed technology and new business processes, however, consequences such as privacy and security considerations can also constrain the use of IoT in border management.

b) IoT can only be used once it has been implemented, but IoT is generally only implemented once specific application to cases has been identified.

c) Adaptation of IoT for border management solutions requires innovative knowledge, new departments, additional staffing and greater investments in IT in border management organizations on the short term, however, on the long term the results may contribute to efficiency gains and cost reductions in operations.

d) Adaptation of IoT requires new legal frameworks, skills, processes and technology, but once implemented may cause other skills, staff and processes to become obsolete.

Many IoT applications in border management settings have not achieved the effect initially desired by the organization or have introduced unforeseen complexities for the organization. Moreover, costs of IoT implementations are often deemed exorbitant. The proposed framework as depicted above in Fig. 1 allows border management organizations to become aware of the conditions as well as tensions in the development of IoT as well as its implementation in an operational setting. A smart anticipation to these tensions allows border management organizations to decide on ways to mitigate accompanying risks and ensure that necessary organizational conditions have been met before being confronted by these risks in a post-pilot setting.

5 Conclusion

Border management organizations need to adapt IoT before use in border management situations. This adaptation of IoT introduces changes into the border management organization. In this article we applied the duality of technology theory [11] to the adaptation of IoT for border management and confirmed the dual nature of IoT in border management settings. The majority of studies on IoT in border management tend to focus on a single dimension such as the use of IoT for border management purposes, however, confirmation of the duality of IoT in border management shows that adaptation of IoT for border management is multi-dimensional. This means that when border management organizations choose to adapt IoT for their purposes, they need to understand how IoT adaptation will in turn structure the organization or introduce potentially unexpected risks before, during and after a border management pilot programme.

Based on a review of background literature, this article synthesized four propositions which were used to form the basis of the proposed framework. While this article is limited to a literature review, further research is recommended in order to test the propositions and the framework in a real-life setting. This direction can hardly be regarded as a luxury, given the high speed of developments in the arena of border management, where border control starts at home and only stops when one has reached his or her destination.

References

1. Fraga-Lamas, P., Fernández-Caramés, T., Suárez-Albela, M., Castedo, L., González-López, M.: A review on internet of things for defense and public safety. Sensors 16(10), 1644 (2016). https://doi.org/10.3390/s16101644

2. Amoore, L.: Biometric borders: governing mobilities in the war on terror. Polit. Geogr. **25**(3), 336–351 (2006)
3. Lehtonen, P., Aalto, P.: Smart and secure borders through automated border control systems in the EU? The views of political stakeholders in the Member States. Eur. Secur. **26**(2), 207–225 (2017)
4. van Kranenburg, R., et al.: Co-creation as the key to a public, thriving, inclusive and meaningful EU IoT. In: Hervás, R., Lee, S., Nugent, C., Bravo, J. (eds.) UCAmI 2014. LNCS, vol. 8867, pp. 396–403. Springer, Cham (2014). https://doi.org/10.1007/978-3-319-13102-3_65
5. Ramos, C., Augusto, J.C., Shapiro, D.: Ambient intelligence-the next step for artificial intelligence. IEEE Intell. Syst. **23**(2), 15–18 (2008). https://doi.org/10.1109/MIS.2008.19
6. Sharif, M.H.U., et al.: Physical security practices on international border management. Sci. Int. **31**(3), 525–528 (2019)
7. Koslowski, R.: International cooperation to create smart borders. In: Conference on North American Integration: Migration, Trade and Security, Ottawa, Canada, vol. 1, no. 2 (2004)
8. Den Boer, M.: Trusted travellers: managing mobility in challenging times. In: Hufnagel, S., McCartney, C. (eds.) Trust in International Police and Justice Cooperation, 1st edn., pp. 77–96. Hart Publishing, Oxford (2017)
9. Hayes, B., Vermeulen, M.: The EU's New Border Surveillance Initiatives, Brussels, Belgium (2012)
10. Topak, Ö.E., Bracken-Roche, C., Saulnier, A., Lyon, D.: From smart borders to perimeter security: The expansion of digital surveillance at the Canadian borders. Geopolitics **20**(4), 880–899 (2015)
11. Orlikowski, W.J.: The duality of technology: rethinking the concept of technology in organizations. Organ. Sci. **3**(3), 398–427 (1992). https://doi.org/10.1287/orsc.3.3.398
12. Webster, J., Watson, R.T.: Analyzing the past to prepare for the future: writing a literature review. MIS Q. **26**(2), 13–23 (2002)
13. Giddens, A.: New Rules of Sociological Method: A Positive Critique of Interpretative Sociology. Hutchinson, London (1976)
14. Scholl, H.J.: Digital government: looking back and ahead on a fascinating domain of research and practice. Digit. Gov.: Res. Pract. **1**(1), 7:1–7:12 (2020). https://doi.org/10.1145/3352682
15. Lindgren, I., Madsen, C.Ø., Hofmann, S., Melin, U.: Close encounters of the digital kind: a research agenda for the digitalization of public services. Gov. Inf. Q. **36**(3), 427–436 (2019). https://doi.org/10.1016/j.giq.2019.03.002
16. Brous, P., Janssen, M.: Advancing e-government using the internet of things: a systematic review of benefits. In: Tambouris, E., et al. (eds.) EGOV 2015. LNCS, vol. 9248, pp. 156–169. Springer, Cham (2015). https://doi.org/10.1007/978-3-319-22479-4_12
17. Brous, P., Janssen, M., Herder, P.: The dual effects of the Internet of Things (IoT): a systematic review of the benefits and risks of IoT adoption by organizations. Int. J. Inf. Manage. **51**, 101952 (2020). https://doi.org/10.1016/j.ijinfomgt.2019.05.008
18. Liutkevičius, M., Pappel, K.I., Butt, S.A., Pappel, I.: Automatization of cross-border customs declaration: potential and challenges. In: Viale Pereira, G., et al. (eds.) EGOV 2020. LNCS, vol. 12219, pp. 96–109. Springer, Cham (2020). https://doi.org/10.1007/978-3-030-57599-1_8
19. Cooke, P.: 'Digital tech' and the public sector: what new role after public funding? Eur. Plan. Stud. **25**(5), 739–754 (2017). https://doi.org/10.1080/09654313.2017.1282067
20. Vrăbiescu, I.: Deportation, smart borders and mobile citizens: using digital methods and traditional police activities to deport EU citizens. J. Ethnic Migration Stud. **56**, 1–18 (2020)
21. Abomhara, M., Yayilgan, S.Y., Nweke, L.O., Székely, Z.: A comparison of primary stakeholders' views on the deployment of biometric technologies in border management: Case study of Smart Mobility at the European land borders. Technol. Soc. **64**, 101484 (2021)

22. Martí, P., Morales, X., Mantzagriotis, S., Tadesse, L.: Awareness of the Internet of Things research regarding security and privacy risks. Meta Res. **45**, 74 (2018)

23. Brous, P., Janssen, M., Herder, P.: Internet of Things adoption for reconfiguring decision-making processes in asset management. Bus. Process Manage. J. **25**, 495 (2018)

24. Kim, S.-B., Kim, D.: ICT Implementation and its effect on public organizations: the case of digital customs and risk management in Korea. Sustainability **12**(8), 3421 (2020)

25. Bhattacharya, M., Roy, A.: Smart border security system using internet of things. In: Kar, N., Saha, A., Deb, S. (eds.) ICCISIoT 2020. CCIS, vol. 1358, pp. 268–279. Springer, Cham (2020). https://doi.org/10.1007/978-3-030-66763-4_23

26. Vos, M., Cullen, R., Cranefield, J.: RFID in the public and private sector: Key implementation considerations (2012)

27. Amoore, L., Marmura, S., Salter, M.B.: Smart borders and mobilities: spaces, zones, enclosures. Surveillance Soc. **5**(2), 3429 (2008)

28. Casiraghi, S., Calvi, A.: Biometric Data in the EU (Reformed) data protection framework and border management: a step forward or an unsatisfactory move? In: Personal Data Protection and Legal Developments in the European Union, pp. 202–223. IGI Global (2020)

29. Kloppenburg, S., Van der Ploeg, I.: Securing identities: biometric technologies and the enactment of human bodily differences. Sci. Culture **29**(1), 57–76 (2020)

30. Olwig, K.F., Grünenberg, K., Møhl, P., Simonsen, A.: The Biometric Border World: Technology, Bodies and Identities on the Move. Routledge (2019)

31. Ajana, B.: Asylum, identity management and biometric control. J. Refug. Stud. **26**(4), 576–595 (2013)

32. Koslowski, R.: Smart borders, virtual borders or no borders: homeland security choices for the United States and Canada. Law Bus. REv. Am. **11**, 527 (2005)

33. Coardoş, D., Tîrziu, E., Gheorghe-Moisii, M.: A general framework based on IoT technology for smart governance. In: Presented at the 18th International Conference on Informatics in Economy, Bucharest, Romania (2019). https://doi.org/10.12948/ie2019.06.03

34. Bigo, D., Carrera, S., Hayes, B., Hernanz, N., Jeandesboz, J.: Justice and home affairs databases and a smart borders system at EU external borders: an evaluation of current and forthcoming proposals. In: CEPS Papers in Liberty and Security in Europe, no. 52 (2012)

35. Jeandesboz, J., Bigo, D., Hayes, B., Simon, S.: The Commission's legislative proposals on smart borders: their feasibility and costs, vol. 493. European Parliament, PE, Brussels (2013)

36. Neisse, R., Baldini, G., Steri, G., Mahieu, V.: Informed consent in Internet of Things: the case study of cooperative intelligent transport systems. In: Presented at the 2016 23rd International Conference on Telecommunications (ICT) (2016)

37. Rudskoy, A., Borovkov, A., Romanov, P., Kolosova, O.: Reducing global risks in the process of transition to the digital economy. In: IOP Conference Series: Materials Science and Engineering, vol. 497, no. 1, p. 012088 (2019)

38. Anouche, M., Boumaaz, Y.: The potential of the blockchain for coordinated border management in developing countries. In: 2020 IEEE 13th International Colloquium of Logistics and Supply Chain Management (LOGISTIQUA), pp. 1–7 (2020)

39. Yang, T., Pardo, T.A.: How is information shared across boundaries? In: 2011 44th Hawaii International Conference on System Sciences, pp. 1–10, January 2011. https://doi.org/10.1109/HICSS.2011.226.

40. Janssen, M., Brous, P., Estevez, E., Barbosa, L.S., Janowski, T.: Data governance: organizing data for trustworthy artificial intelligence. Gov. Inf. Q. **67**, 101493 (2020)

41. Brous, P., Janssen, M., Vilminko-Heikkinen, R.: Coordinating decision-making in data management activities: a systematic review of data governance principles. In: Scholl, H.J., et al. (eds.) EGOVIS 2016. LNCS, vol. 9820, pp. 115–125. Springer, Cham (2016). https://doi.org/10.1007/978-3-319-44421-5_9

42. Neuby, B.L., Rudin, E.: Radio frequency identification: a panacea for governments? Public Organ. Rev. **8**(4), 329–345 (2008). https://doi.org/10.1007/s11115-008-0065-4

Author Index

Printed in the United States
by Baker & Taylor Publisher Services